All Creation Is Groaning

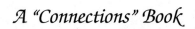

A "Connections" Book

All Creation Is Groaning

An Interdisciplinary Vision for Life in a Sacred Universe

Carol J. Dempsey and Russell A. Butkus

Editors and Weavers

A Michael Glazier Book
THE LITURGICAL PRESS
Collegeville, Minnesota

Cover design by Ann Blattner. Watercolor by Ethel Boyle.

A Michael Glazier Book published by The Liturgical Press.

	2	3	4	5	6	7	8

Library of Congress Cataloging-in-Publication Data

All Creation is groaning : an interdisciplinary vision for life in a
   sacred universe / Carol J. Dempsey and Russell A. Butkus, editors
   and weavers.
         p.   cm.
   "A Michael Glazier book."
   "A 'Connections' book"—T.p. verso.
   Includes bibliographical references (p.   ) and index.
   ISBN 0-8146-5932-2 (alk. paper)
   1. Human ecology—Religious aspects.   2. Human ecology—Moral and
ethical aspects.   3. Environmental ethics.   I. Dempsey, Carol J.
II. Butkus, Russell A.
GF80.A38   1999
261.8'362—dc21   99-29113
                                                                    CIP

Contents

Foreword

No discussion of the current and emerging environmental crisis can fail to refer to the now classic article of Lynn White, "The Historical Roots of Our Ecological Crisis." In that article White argued that the tap root of the crisis is found in the biblical mandate that human persons should "have dominion" over creation. Thus White laid at the door of the Bible and its interpretative communities the charge of generating the ideological framework for abuse of the earth. It is now accepted by most that White's argument is a deep distortion of the true facts of the case and all but wrong.

A second reading of the crisis, after White, makes a much more cogent case that it is the crisis of the modern period—rooted in the masculine rhetoric of conquest, control, and utility in Francis Bacon and René Descartes—that has legitimated and powered the modern turn to exploitation that seems almost without limit. That rhetoric of control that sets human agents as the key actors *upon* "nature" and celebrates human persons as the goal and end of "nature" has been joined to a certain kind of "scientific method," epistemology, and perspective of autonomy. That convergence has, not surprisingly in retrospect, set loose the huge technological enterprise of control that is in large part funded by state ideology in the use of military adventurism for "reasons of state."

The present, remarkable volume wades into the thick of this deep dilemma and sets itself—with powerful, knowing, and sensitive appeal to biblical imagination—to think alternatively about creation, as much as possible outside the assumptions of the political-economic-military interests that are the hallmarks of modernity.

The book is remarkable in its conceptualization. The contributors, all members of the faculty of the University of Portland, have generated a genuinely "multi-disciplined" academic discussion in which each of the colleagues operates fully and effectively in his or her own academic discipline, but all together share a common conviction that social power could be framed and enacted differently. This book is the best evidence I know that "faith seeking understanding" is a legitimate and powerful academic perspective whereby faith does not curb, limit, or flinch from serious intellectual pursuit but offers an important critical perspective against the illusions of Lockean neutrality.

It is important that this book should occur in the new series of The Liturgical Press, "Connections," for both the argument of the book and the colleagues who have produced it bear powerful witness to connectedness. Concerning the collegium that authored the book, such a work, with its rich, multifaceted perspective, would not be possible except for academics who are indeed connected to each other in a common vision that defines and situates specific disciplines of study. Indeed the modernist organization of higher education into discrete disciplines is increasingly inadequate for the real issues we face. Connectedness is a requirement for higher education if our academic work is not to be merely the technological equivalent of counting angels on pinheads. That the book itself has come into being is a powerful statement of the character of responsible higher education, an enactment of what Clifford Geertz has called "blurred genres," for the colleagues are clearly able to listen to each other and to learn from each other.

This collegial connectedness is matched by the core argument of the book, that creation is a series of delicately calibrated interrelations and interactions in which the abuse or destruction of any single element in the "system" will disrupt and impede each of its parts. This notion of creation is attested in the too-familiar phrase from Romans 8, the title of the book, "all creation is groaning." Without for a moment commenting on "groaning," simply the notion of "all creation" is itself a massively visionary statement, for it claims that each part and all parts of creation are doing the same thing, all interlinked to be generative, and now, in the present time, all interlinked in grief and hurt at the abuse creation has suffered.

Such a vision is not soft-headed religiosity but a genuine alternative, a deep and essential challenge to the atomization of "nature" enacted in mindless practices of consumerism propelled by self-justification and self-sufficiency. It is easily and thoughtlessly assumed, in a long established positivism, that impact on one part of "nature" can be continued without affecting anything else. Thus the atomization of "nature" is matched by the atomization of the academy. It is increasingly clear, however, that this well established assumption, here so vigorously challenged, is not a given around which soft-headed religionists tread in their innocence, but is an unexamined advocacy that has prevailed in the modern world. The argument of connectedness need not and dare not grant any privileged position or priority to the advocacy of atomization, but must proceed in the awareness that modernist atomization is one possible hypothesis in the face of which other advocacies—here the advocacy of connectedness—can indeed make serious intellectual headway. Thus the appeal to William Ruckert's dictum, "everything is united to everything else," is a major premise of the book, a major assumption of environmental advocacy, and a major critique of modernist technological assumptions.

The several chapters in the book that stretch across the curriculum of the university are themselves a statement of connectedness. The book is genuinely ecumenical. While it operates from a broad Jewish-Christian perspective—with special reference to the Benedictine tradition of spirituality—it includes a forceful statement of an Islamic vision of the integrity of creation. The religious formulation of the book is evident in the frequent citation of great biblical texts on creation and in reference to the teachings of the Vatican that effectively give the lie to White's thesis.

While well grounded theologically, this is not a book of religion. The middle chapters are a helpful discussion from other disciplines, notably an analysis of the food crisis and the question of restorable agriculture, an inventory of the modern pathologies that produce the crises of the ozone, pesticides, pollutants, acid rain, deforestation, overpopulation, and overconsumption. The book wisely knows that these are not simply technological "mistakes" but are the inevitable product of an ideology of fragmentation in which each on its own is free for what it wants without noticing human and non-human neighbors. The analysis of technological outcomes is matched by a formidable discussion of "global politics," including the group of G-Seven nations, itself the economic articulation of Baconian control, the role of Non-Governmental Organizations, and the peculiar role of the United States in keeping the pot stirring for environmental destructiveness. As a subset to this last, a discussion is offered of labor policy and employment systems that again reflect a deep and skewed ideological commitment.

Perhaps the most surprising element in a book on connections is the late chapters that take up what might be termed a "humanistic agenda." This includes such matters as childhood nurture and development in order that new generations be ecologically alert and responsible, care for the elderly with particular reference to health care and the cruciality of community connections of health, and the powerful world of stories of place in situating persons in life-generating contexts. These essays indicate, in each of these areas, how differently we may proceed in a vision of connectedness rather than in a vision of fragmentation:

- Children are nurtured to care and not simply to succeed;

- Older people are kept in a valuing social environment and not warehoused to wait for death;

- Stories give people belonging, as distinct from the sound-byte culture that has no time for narrative and no appreciation of place.

To my mind, however, the most suggestive of these latter chapters is a discussion of music with particular reference to Beethoven, Mahler, and Sibelius. This remarkable discussion shows how "audible aspects of nature" have been kept available in a musicology that sought to move beyond both rationalism and romanticism, though perhaps something of the romantic may itself be valued as a lyrical protest against "hard technology."

The University of Portland must be a remarkable place in which to study. It evidently is a remarkable place in which to teach, think, and write. The logistical problems of producing such a volume are immense, and one can only assume that the colleagues are as connected to each other at the end of the project as at the beginning. Across these essays there is a largeness of spirit, an openness to new learning that does not pretend to be the ultimate insight, a humility that recognizes that "my discipline" can contribute but is not the last word. The book is accessible and pedagogically friendly. We are deeply in the debt of this impressive collegium. The book is of value for its parts, and more so in the clarity with which its sum is more than its parts. The very tradition that stands accused by Lynn White is here shown to be the ground from which a serious, critical, viable alternative vision of creation may be articulated in the face of the inadequacy of modernity, its inherent violence, its easy control, and its ill-grounded self-confidence. For sure, newness every time begins in groaning.

Walter Brueggemann
Columbia Theological Seminary
January 12, 1999

Contributors

*A*ll of the authors, with the exception of Walter Brueggemann, are members of the faculty at the University of Portland, Portland, Oregon.

Walter Brueggemann, William Marcellus McPheeters Professor of Old Testament, teaches at Columbia Theological Seminary in Decatur, Georgia. A distinguished biblical scholar of international renown, he is a prolific writer and a most engaging public speaker. His two latest works include the foundational volume *Theology of the Old Testament: Testimony, Dispute, Advocacy* (Minneapolis: Fortress, 1997) and *A Commentary on Jeremiah: Exile and Homecoming* (Grand Rapids: Eerdmans, 1998).

Carol J. Dempsey, Assistant Professor of Theology, co-edited the book, wrote the Introduction and Chapter Fourteen, co-authored the Epilogue, and wove the various biblical texts and reflections into the volume. Named a 1997–98 National Regional Scholar by the Society of Biblical Literature, she has most recently published *The Prophets: A Liberation-Critical Perspective* (Minneapolis: Fortress, 2000). Her areas of interest, research, and writing include the Prophets, Biblical Ethics, Biblical Theology, and Hermeneutics. A member of the Dominican Sisters of Caldwell, N.J., she has taught on all levels, and is currently working on a manuscript on prophetic ethics to be published in 2001, in addition to editing the 2001 College Theology Society Annual Volume on Scripture and Theology.

Karen Vaught-Alexander, author of Chapter One and Associate Professor of English, directs a cross-disciplinary writing program and center at the University. She has published widely and has also contributed scholarship to engineering writing programs, writing programs for nursing, and various other interdisciplinary projects.

Norah Martin, Assistant Professor of Philosophy, wrote Chapter Two. She specializes in philosophy of science, philosophy of mind, and philosophy of psychiatry. She has presented papers in the area of feminist epistemology and psychiatric ethics, and is co-editor of *Externalism and Self-Knowledge* (Stanford: CSLI). Her most recent article, "Peterman and the Ideological Mind: Paradoxes of Subjectivity," is forthcoming in a volume entitled *Philosophical Reflections on Seinfeld: A Book about Everything and Nothing.*

Khalid H. Khan, author of Chapter Three, is Associate Dean of Engineering and Professor of Mechanical Engineering. Involved in teaching, research, and administration of educational activities for the past two decades in the Portland metropolitan area, he has developed courses and laboratories in material, manufacturing, and experimental mechanics. His current research project is entitled "Coupled Electro-Mechanical Effects in Materials."

Matthew Baasten, Associate Professor of Theology and writer of Chapter Four, teaches in the area of theological ethics. A recipient of the University's award for outstanding teaching, he is currently engaged in research and writing on the impact of Christian values on everyday ethical dilemmas.

David Alexander, author of Chapter Five, is Assistant Professor of Biology. He teaches Microbiology and Methods of Biological Research, Microbiology for Health Sciences, and Environmental Microbiology. His research focuses on symbiotic interactions of soil microbes with plants and plant pests.

Steven A. Kolmes occupies the Rev. John Molter, c.s.c., Chair in Science and is Director of the Environmental Studies Program at the University of Portland. He is author of Chapter Six. His special interests include the conversation between theology, science, engineering, business administration, and other disciplines in terms of the present environmental crisis, and the development of rational methods for the control of agricultural pest species. His research has involved twospotted spider mites and whiteflies, and he is currently exploring ways that environmental studies as a way of understanding can be brought into partnership with both engineers and business people to help find a path toward a sustainable society.

Claude Pomerleau is a member of the Congregation of the Holy Cross and Associate Professor of Political Science. The author of Chapter Seven, he teaches courses in European and Latin American politics and International Relations. He is a Visiting Professor at the University of Chile and enjoys playing the clarinet with the Rivercity Consort and Camerata Santiago.

Russell A. Butkus is Associate Professor and Chair of Theology. He co-edited the book, wrote Chapter Eight, co-authored the Epilogue, and wove various theological reflections into the volume. The Director of the University's BA Track in Environmental Ethics and Policy, he is currently engaged in research on the relationship between the science of ecology and its theological ramifications as well as research in the area of theological environmental ethics.

Joyce S. Osland, Associate Professor in the School of Business Administration, is the co-author of Chapter Nine. She has written and published textbooks as well as articles on comparative management. Her most recent book is *The Adventure of Working Abroad: Hero Tales from the Global Frontier* (San Francisco: Jossey-Bass, 1995), which describes the subjective experience of expatriates.

Howard Feldman, co-author of Chapter Nine, is Associate Professor of Business and teaches courses in corporate strategy, strategic planning, and entrepreneurship. His research interests have included minority entrepreneurship, venture capital, and entrepreneurship education, as well as strategic management.

Bruce H. Drake, Professor of Business, is the third co-author of Chapter Nine. He teaches in the areas of organizational behavior, design, and change. His research interests and publications concern leadership, ethics, and communication. He is past president of the Western Academy of Management.

Ardys Dunn is the author of Chapter Ten and Associate Professor of Nursing. A pediatric nurse practitioner with an emphasis on community health nursing and an interest in cultural health issues, she teaches pediatrics to graduate students in the Family Nurse

Practitioner program at the University and pediatrics and community health nursing to undergraduates. She is the co-author/editor of *Pediatric Primary Care: A Handbook for Nurse Practitioners* (Philadelphia: W. B. Saunders, 1996) and past president of the National Association of Pediatric Nurse Associates and Practitioners.

Joanna Rowe Kaakinen, Associate Professor of Nursing, wrote Chapter Eleven. Her area of expertise and research is in aging, and family and human communication. She has received two grants from the Western Region Campus Compact Consortium to develop service learning in gerontological nursing. She has written extensively in the area of family nursing theory development. Her current research project is a community needs assessment project that involves determining the health care needs of a specific elderly residential area.

Kenneth Kleszynski is the author of Chapter Twelve. He is an Associate Professor of Music and teaches in the areas of fine arts, music education, and music theory, and conducts the University Orchestra. His area of research and publication is in contemporary British music, particularly that of composers George Lloyd and Peter Maxwell Davies.

Frank Fromherz, Adjunct Assistant Professor of Theology, wrote Chapter Thirteen. Having a special interest in religion and society and social ethics, he is co-author of "Changing the Culture and Practice of Development: The Southern Oregon Economic Development Coalition," in *Sustainable Community Development: Studies in Economic, Environmental, and Cultural Revitalization* (Boca Raton, Fla.: Lewis, 1998). He serves as Director of the Office of Justice and Peace and the Catholic Campaign for Human Development for the Archdiocese of Portland.

Introduction

*F*illed with wonder and awe-struck by the mysteries of the universe, the poet William Blake once wrote:

> To see a world in a grain of sand
>   and Heaven in a wild flower,
> hold infinity in the palm of your hand
>   and eternity in an hour.

The vision of this poet is ever ancient, ever new, inspired by the same Divine Spirit who caused another poet from another time and another place to proclaim a vision that is just as extraordinary and just as compelling as Blake's:

> Behold, I am about to create new heavens
>   and a new earth;
> the former things shall not be remembered
>   or come to mind.
> But be glad and rejoice forever
>   in what I am creating. . . . (Isa 65:17-18)

The vision of Blake and Isaiah continues to burn deeply in the hearts of one small community of scholars on the Bluff at the University of Portland, Oregon, who gathered together early one morning and late one afternoon to say "yes" to a project that they hope will be received as a gift for all creation as it groans, waiting to be liberated from bondage while pushing to give birth to new heavens and a new earth where all people are able to see a world in a grain of sand, and heaven in a wild flower.

Distinctive in its nature, this volume is part of a new series entitled "Connections," the dream of Liturgical Press Senior Academic Editor Linda Maloney, whose own vision of creative scholarship inspired the editors and contributors of this volume. We, the book's editors and contributors, are indebted to Linda and to all the members of The Liturgical Press who risked with us to create something new, and whose constant words of encouragement and patience have helped us bring this project to life.

This volume is a work that presents multi-academic perspectives on contemporary environmental issues that have ethical implications for both humankind and the natural world. Fashioned as a series of stories and essays, these seemingly multivalent voices and perspectives are joined together with biblical stories and references and theological reflection to create a seamless story that is both provocative and revelatory. Truth is heard in the hearing of all stories from these dissonant yet symphonic voices and truths.

The book's aim is to provide a new vision for living life in a sacred universe. This vision is linked to the biblical vision of justice and righteousness for all of creation and humankind's responsibility to hasten the vision through a call to ethical practice. The book will be both critical and hermeneutical and will reflect an interdisciplinary approach so as to build bridges of understanding between the Bible and contemporary disciplines.

In keeping with the vision of the "Connections" series, this project is not only interdisciplinary but also the work of colleagues at various stages in their professional careers and in academe. Hence the format of the book shows an integrated, cooperative effort rather than a series of individually collected essays. The project represents not only thought from a Christian perspective but also thought from an Islamic perspective. Thus it presents two major religious traditions "in dialogue" on a common topic of world concern and interest. As scholars and teachers we have identified the fact that there is little material available on the environment from perspectives other than Christian, and so we welcome the interreligious dialogue and exchange that a volume such as this could engender.

The book is composed of fourteen chapters held together by an Introduction and Epilogue, with common strands of thought woven among the chapters. The first, "Stories from the Heart," is a tapestry of stories that author Karen Vaught-Alexander weaves together from literature and life experiences. The stories have the potential to connect us once again to the gift of land and the need for values to preserve and ensure quality of life for all creation. Highlights of this chapter include works by Pattiann Rogers, Robert Michael Pyle, Terry Tempest Williams, and Vaught-Alexander's original reflections that she blends with student meditations on literary themes and ideas gathered from various class assignments that dealt with the ideas presented by Rogers, Pyle, and Williams. Deeply personal, these stories call readers to return to a more compassionate and spiritual connection to all of life.

Attempting to move from objective to subjective ways of knowing, Norah Martin in Chapter 2, "New Ways of Knowing and Being Known," focuses on what it means "to know," "to be known," and to have knowledge and the responsibility that is part of knowing and being known. Drawn from a philosophical perspective, the chapter looks at the history of "the way of knowing" and the theory of knowledge (epistemology) that characterizes our present time. The chapter explores the way a conception of self that once was "relational" and "community-based" has evolved into one that is autonomous and rational. The consequences of this conception of self, on the one hand, are related to the violence done to and the exploitation of the natural world and people, and on the other hand have made possible unprecedented knowledge of the world and an understanding of how some people abuse it. The contribution suggests a way of revisioning humankind's theory of knowing and a way of knowing that retains the positive aspects of modern "scientism" while overcoming the violent elements. Such a revisioning of knowledge would involve reconceptualizing the self as a "community being" with responsibility for the common good rather than an isolated autonomous individual.

Since the beginning, the biblical vision has continually called us to be tillers and keepers of the land. Chapter 3, "An Islamic Perspective on the Environment" by Khalid Khan, recalls this ancient vision and stresses the following points: (1) God (Allah) has created humankind along with other creatures of the earth with a purpose. God (Allah) has put the human being as God's (Allah's) "vicegerent" on the planet, which means that human beings are supposed to be the caretakers and not the plunderers of the planet; (2) the human community has to live and act in ways that do not upset the balance of nature inherent in the process of creation since, as the Qur'an states, "Allah has created this Earth and things on it in due balance;" (3) if the human community acts and lives in a way that throws this "due balance" off it will bring disaster on all people as well as other creatures on this planet. In the main body of the chapter these points are elucidated from a Quranic perspective.

Chapter 4, "Christian Values, Technology, and the Environmental Crisis," is the work of Matthew Baasten, who investigates the impact of the technological and scientific revolutions on the ethical questions associated with the environmental crisis. The contribution outlines the challenges of technology as well as its problems, and beckons the human community to embrace the values of simplicity, moderation, frugality, and gratitude. The last section of the work draws out the pitfalls of pride and reminds readers that only with great humility and grace will life be transformed so that all creation can experience life to the fullest.

In Chapter 5, "Feeding the Hungry and Protecting the Environment," David Alexander notes that a tension exists today between farmers and those who are concerned about the harm that is done to the environment by modern agricultural practices. Out of this concern has grown an awareness of the need to develop innovative ways of producing agricultural crops while minimizing the impact of farming practices on terrestrial and aquatic ecosystems. Agricultural scientists now focus much of their attention on concepts such as "sustainable agriculture" and an "ecosystems approach" to farming as they seek to find new ways to feed and clothe the world's growing human population while protecting our fragile environment. Written from the perspective of a biologist, this chapter wrestles with protecting the land and its intrinsic beauty and goodness, its fertility and fruitfulness, and the biblical call to feed the hungry and clothe the naked (Isaiah 58; Matt 25:35-36). It also explores contemporary approaches to solving some of the problems associated with traditional agricultural practices.

Chapter 6, "Mental Cartography in a Time of Environmental Crisis," by Steven Kolmes, examines the mental cartography, i.e., the maps, images, designs, etc., of scientists, policy-makers, and consumers that have been forced to change dramatically in the last half century as a result of the environmental crisis. Where a half-century ago people may have viewed themselves as "outside" looking into the natural world, they have now come to realize that the human community is "inside," adjacent to the environmental crisis that many of us have produced. Where "the solution to pollution is dilution" once allowed dumping of toxic wastes into the world ocean, and agricultural pests were controlled with DDT, we are now recognizing the finite nature of this planet and attempting to replace chemicals as much as possible with knowledge of pest cycles and their inherent vulnerabilities. As global population soars and hunger gains ground in many parts of the world this chapter calls people to consider the pace at which scientists, consumers, and policy-makers need to reconstruct our mental maps of the world.

Political scientist Claude Pomerleau seeks to explain in Chapter 7, "Toward an Understanding of International Geopolitics and the Environment," the relationship between sustainable development and environmental ethics from a global perspective. Students of international politics have become increasingly concerned with environmental issues and their relationship to global and national security. During the Cold War ethics and power were examined in relationship to foreign policy and security. The chapter attempts to show how the environment and its protection have become a major issue in understanding the ethics of foreign policy and global interdependence.

Chapter 8, "Sustainability: An Eco-Theological Analysis," written by Russell Butkus, looks at the beauty and intrinsic goodness of all of creation. The chapter is an eco-theological analysis of the principle of sustainability and is aimed at bringing together a solidly scientific and theological understanding of this concept and its importance for continued life on the planet.

A creative contribution, Chapter 9, "The Stewardship of Natural and Human Resources," by Joyce Osland, Bruce Drake, and Howard Feldman, links the traditional notion of stewardship to the innovative process called "The Natural Step." This new process challenges organizations to examine and redesign the way they conduct business on the planet so that organizations are in better harmony with the economy of creation. Clear and detailed graphs and charts help to clarify the standards needed for sustainability in natural and human resources.

Drawing on insights from both psychology and sociology, Ardys Dunn contends in Chapter 10, "Development of Environmental Responsibility in Children," that children can develop an appreciation for the beauty of creation and can learn how to care for the natural world in a way that exemplifies both moral and ethical values. The chapter examines developmental theories related to moral behavior, establishes the relationship between moral development and environmental learning, outlines the development of an environmental consciousness, and uncovers the challenges facing educators and caregivers, and then offers practical and pedagogical suggestions on how to proceed with environmental education so that the children of today can become the sensitive and responsible adults they are meant to be within the divine plan of stewardship.

Chapter 11, "An Ecological View of Elders and Their Families: Needs for the Twenty-First Century," by Joanna Kaakinen, asserts that stewardship and care for another human being are something more than the physical relationship between humankind and the earth. Connection and connectedness of human beings one to another within the context of family are essential to the survival of the planet. The first section of this work presents an ecological framework in which to view family. The second part outlines specific challenges for elders and their families. The last section of the work suggests changes in beliefs, ideas, and paradigms regarding the aged, their families, and the environment that are necessary for successful adaptation in the twenty-first century. The major theme throughout this paper is the connection between people and the environment.

Composer, musician, and professor of music Kenneth Kleszynski considers the impact that the natural world has had on the creative process of musical composers throughout the centuries. In Chapter 12, "Symphonies of Nature: Creation and Re-creation," Kleszynski helps readers to see that musical composers have a profound awareness of, identification with, and sensitivity to the natural world, and write music that reflects these characteristics. The chapter examines the music of four interlinked composers: Ludwig van Beethoven, the progenitor of symphonic re-creation, Gustav Mahler, Jean (Jan) Sibelius, and Peter Maxwell Davies; each offers readers and listeners a glimpse into the spirit of the ultimate source of all creation.

Chapter 13, "A Sense of Place," by Frank Fromherz, is a heartwarming and heart-wrenching contribution that takes at its starting point the work and thought of Robert Bellah. In *Habits of the Heart* Bellah and colleagues spoke of a real community as a "community of memory," one that does not forget its past. Such a community will tell stories of achievements and stories of shared suffering, including dangerous memories of suffering inflicted, memories that call a community to alter ancient evils. Others have written about a "sense of place" and have suggested that a major sign of the times is a widely felt sense of displacement, uprootedness, and movement at a frenetic pace. Many people yearn for a sense of place, intuiting at times that a place can hold an intensity of meaning. There is a mutually enriching relationship between a sense of place and a community of memory, and it is that relationship that this contribution explores. Stories of collective history, told again and again by people of all generations, have the potential to evoke memories of the human family's relations with the land, rivers, particular places. As readers contemplate a particular place it may inspire their capacity to recollect the communities of memory that have shaped their character. This chapter ties these reflections to the biblical understanding of justice as fidelity to the demands of a relationship.

Chapter 14, "Hope Amidst Crisis: A Prophetic Vision of Cosmic Redemption," by Carol Dempsey, asserts that within the Israelite prophetic tradition there is the suggestion of a systemic connection between creation and redemption, specifically that the redemption of humankind is connected to the restoration of the natural world through divine promise. The chapter focuses on several passages from the biblical prophets' eschatological visions that can provide a basis for hope and a new paradigm for faithful living with grace and wonder.

The work reaches it finale with a brief epilogue that summarizes the book's main points while highlighting the distinctive contribution this work makes to the world of scholarship. The "Epilogue" outlines the various paradigm shifts that have occurred and must continue to occur if the spirit of transformation is to permeate all aspects of life.

Finally, this volume is dedicated to the memory of Thomas C. McGlinn, colleague and friend, who died suddenly and unexpectedly in the spring of 1998 in an avalanche while climbing Mt. Hood to enjoy, with other mountain climbers, the wonder and beauty of God's magnificent creation. Tom saw a world in a grain of sand and heaven in a wild flower, and he knew how to hold infinity in the palm of his hand and eternity in an hour. With you, Tom, we remember that

> The Earth is the Lord's and all that is in it,
>   the world, and those who live in it;
> for he has founded it on the seas,
>   and established it on the rivers.
> Who shall ascend the mountain of the Lord?
>   And who shall stand in his holy place?
> Those who have clean hands and pure hearts,
>   who do not lift up their souls to what is false,
>   and who do not swear deceitfully.
> They will receive blessing from the Lord,
>   and vindication from the God of their salvation.
> Such is the company of those who seek him,
>   who seek the face of the God of Jacob. (Psalm 24)

1

Stories from the Heart

"I will give them one heart
and put a new Spirit within them." (Ezek 11:19)

*T*he central and unifying organ for the people of the ancient biblical world was the heart. It was the source of all emotional, physical, and intellectual activities. The heart governed the people's ethical actions as well as their response to the divine Spirit whom they discerned to be in the midst of all creation. Living in the midst of chaos and devastation caused by the fall of the Southern Kingdom of Judah, the destruction of the Temple and the holy city Jerusalem, and the exile of the Israelites to Babylon and Egypt, the prophet Ezekiel offers words of comfort and hope. To a people scattered and broken in Spirit, God indeed will give one heart and put a new spirit within them.

This message of comfort and hope resounds in Paul's message to the Romans where he focuses on the Christ-event that is no longer anthropological but rather cosmological:

> I consider that the sufferings of this present time are not worth comparing with the glory about to be revealed to us. For creation waits with eager longing for the revealing of the children of God; for creation was subjected to futility, not of its own will but by the will of the one who subjected it, in hope that creation itself will be free from its bondage to decay and will obtain the freedom of the glory of the children of God. We know that the whole creation has been groaning in labor pains until

now; and not only the creation, but we ourselves, who have the first fruits of the Spirit, groan inwardly while we wait for adoption, the redemption of our bodies. For in hope we were saved. For who hopes for what is seen? But if we hope for what we do not see, we wait for it with patience. (Rom 8:18-25)

The image of the heart and the groaning of all creation are two themes in "Stories from the Heart" where the message of contemporary writers and poets continues to offer words of comfort and hope as all creation waits to be redeemed.

INTRODUCTION

> *"Because we have forgotten our kinship with the land . . . our kinship with each other has become pale. We shy away from accountability and involvement. It is a matter of living the circle."* [1]

In a post-modern American society the circle is not being lived. Ecologists and scientists like cell biologist Lewis Thomas urge biospheric accountability and sustainability: "it is up to us, if we are to become an evolutionary success . . . to become the consciousness of the whole earth. We are the planet's awareness of itself." [2] How can the humanities join the sciences in promoting this crucial awareness and evolutionary success? Eco-historian David Worster posits: "Historians, along with literary scholars, anthropologists, and philosophers, cannot do the reforming, of course, but they can help with the understanding." [3] Ecocriticism [4] pioneer William Rueckert, however, seeks a literary application that transcends understanding: "How can we apply the energy, the creativity, the knowledge, the vision we know to be in literature to the human-made problems ecology tells us are destroying the biosphere which is our home?" [5] This chapter examines literature's ecocritical potential not only to evoke sacred and personal awareness and connectedness, but also its "application" in biospheric action and stewardship.

Two perspectives drawn from ecocriticism will be highlighted: (1) the transformative capacity of literature to connect readers with sacred and personal eco-insights and global biospheric stewardship [6] and (2) the unique potential of contemporary American nature literature of the West, called hereafter landscape literature. [7] Excerpts from three such writers of the human and nonhuman landscape—Pattiann Rogers, Robert Michael Pyle, and Terry Tempest Williams—will be placed in dialogue with reader-response stories from several advanced writing students and from Karen Vaught-Alexander, author of this chapter and professor of English Studies.[8] These excerpts and the subsequently evoked reader responses will affirm the promise that ecocritical readings hold for inspiriting an ecospheric paradigm of community, respect, and justice—through ecoconsciousness, translated into Wendell Berry's individual "right livelihood."

ECOCRITICAL READINGS AND LANDSCAPE WRITING: TRANSLATIONS INTO "PURGATIVE-REDEMPTIVE BIOSPHERIC ACTION"

> *"The most important function of literature today is to redirect human consciousness to full consideration of its place in a threatened natural world."* [9]

In his 1978 landmark essay, "Literature and Ecology: An Experiment in Ecocriticism," Rueckert joins literature's aesthetic, social, textual, and ethical roles with the ecological visions of Aldo Leopold, Ian McHarg, Barry Commoner, and Garret Hardin—Rueckert's central ecocritical tenet being the "first Law of Ecology: 'Everything is connected to everything else.'"[10] Along with ecologists, bioregionalists, ecofeminists, environmental pyschologists, deep ecologists, and others, Rueckert calls upon literary scholars and teachers of literature[11] to evoke reader awareness of the biosphere through literature: to "translate literature into purgative-redemptive biospheric action."[12]

In an increasingly urban, post-modern American society, rather than feeling connected, individuals often experience separateness or estrangement from the human and non-human alike. Eco-critics look especially to nature or landscape literature to move such individuals from "ego-consciousness" to "eco-consciousness."[13] This "lived" interrelatedness—an understanding of and responsibility for a physical and spiritual kinship, a humility and respect for the sacred interdependence of all in Creation—Australian Aborigines call "Jukurrpa."[14] This chapter uses the term Jukurrpa to designate an evoked sacred and personal connectedness, which some individuals in today's society have lost or never had, and which ecocritical readings hold promise of restoring or creating.

Ecocritical readings connect. Writers "store" creative verbal and nonverbal energy into text for readers to "re-store." Readers mediate the aesthetic, emotional, and imaginative energy of literary text into personal and public meanings and actions. Ecocritical readings evoke.

Words go beyond words, transmuting into personal and public eco-consciousness and possible action.[15] The exterior becomes interior; the interior becomes exterior.[16] Texts, writers, and readers transact in open-ended dialogues, within and outside of texts of "lived" experience. Awakened memories and insights jolt readers into awareness and engagement with all that was the other. Metaphor[17] is crucial to ecocritical readings. Metaphors join the different. In ecocritical readings metaphors are catalysts in the first law of literary ecology: everything is connected. Readers are transformed; sacred and personal Jukurrpa is evoked.

Landscape literature embraces a series of eco-metaphors, inherent in the American West's experience of land and peoples. Landscape writing heralds a return to the "Sacred Hoop" of harmony, cooperation, and community, to a "One-ness."[18] Metaphors of anthropocentric, "Euro-centric," and gendered conquest, exploitation, and "otherness"—the rape of virgin forests, the land as maternal breast or womb, the "civilizing" of the noble savage, the taming of wildness and the natural for human progress—describe both human and non-human landscape.[19] While any literature can be read ecocritically, landscape literature is called the "literature of hope"[20] because as writer Barry Lopez contends this provocative literature may contribute to "the reorganization of American political thought"[21] for both the human and the non-human.

In the following excerpts from their writings Pattiann Rogers, Robert M. Pyle, and Terry Tempest Williams characterize the scope and intent of this "literature of hope." Woven into sections about each writer are examples of ecocritically-evoked reader responses from students and professor Karen Vaught-Alexander,[22] furnishing evidence of the transformative value of ecocritical Jukurrpa.

Pattiann Rogers: Witnessing the Sacred in the Everyday

Pattiann Rogers, who has been quietly writing of science and nature and the divine long before it was fashionable,[23] discerns wonderment in the everyday. A writer who profoundly and intensely experiences divinity in all around her, Rogers explains:

> The world provides every physical image and sensation we will ever need in order to experience the sacred. . . . If we could only learn to recognize it . . . just as we learn to see and distinguish with accuracy the ant on the trunk of the poplar, the Pole Star in Ursa Minor . . . just as we learn to hear the voices of our children, the creak of the floor at the lover's footstep. . . .

I believe that we move through the sacred constantly. . . . And perhaps the divine, the sacred, the holy, can only come into complete existence through our witness of them, our witness for them and to them. If this is so, then our obligations are mighty and humbling.[24]

She witnesses the sacred through unusually perspicacious metaphors: a wren trapped in a cathedral, a whale in a field of iris. Readers experience a redbird as their father and other humbling and awe-filling miracles of awareness, as in "Achieving Perspective":

Straight up from this road
Away from the fitted particles of frost
Coating the hull of each chick pea,
And the stiff archer bug making its way
In the morning dark, toe hair by toe hair,
Up the stem of the trillium,
Straight up through the sky above this road right now,
The galaxies of the Cygnus A cluster
Are colliding with each other in a massive swarm
Of interpenetrating and exploding catastrophes.
I try to remember that.[25]

In response, David Atherton recounts in his oral presentation to Rogers:

As you, like Emerson, stand on the bare ground, uplifted into infinite space, we step aside from a patriarch of nature, to hear a new-found maternal voice. . . .

. . . images cling to my mind. The horned toad lizard, a field of flowers, a slow-steady wind can trap you and elevate you by illuminating the commonplace. With power and magnitude, she juxtaposes the dissimilar. Rogers will take you from a chick pea to the Cygnus A cluster, a 40,000 light year journey, in four lines or less. The transition to light speed, soothed by the toe hair of an archer bug, interlace[s] the mystical and the scientific. In understanding, we have no choice but to observe our part in the whole.

For Atherton, reading Rogers creates a sacred and personal Jukurrpa. With this poem about the Oneness of life's drumbeat Rogers speaks to another student's heart:

But the heart must be the most
pervasive drum of all. Imagine

> hearing all together every tinny
> snare of every heartbeat
> in every jumping mouse and harvest
> mouse, sagebrush vole and least
> shrew living across the prairie;
> and add to that cacophony the individual
> staccato tickings inside all gnatcatchers
> kingbirds, kestrels, rock doves, pine
> warblers crossing, criss-crossing
> each other in the sky, the sound
> of their beatings overlapping. . . .[26]

For Bevyn Rowland a childhood awe returns; her adult, urban estrangement falls away. The reading is transformative; it is ecocritical Jukurrpa. Rowland writes her return:

> At the end of a short muddy road, off Oregon highway 26, stands an ancient natural monument—the majestic Sitka Spruce. As a child, I would visit my tree friend each time my mother and I journeyed to the beach. Two weeks ago, I journeyed back. Rogers stirred in me a memory of pressing my untrained ear to the trunk of that Sitka Spruce—hearing its pulse and seeing a quiet minuet of branches above me, connecting me to a forest of natural wonder. I had forgotten the heart beat of my Sitka. Behind the mechanical hum and roar of road noise, I heard the cacophony of her forest family. "Tickering rolls/of rain off the flat-leaves/and razor-rims of the forest" guide me to Sitka.
>
> We are all connected in this family of nature through cycles of life and death. The ordinary or the hideous to the resplendent and miraculous. Insight coupled with beauty-filled articulation of the spiritual and the uncontrived, Rogers bridges the ever-growing gap between the natural, preternatural, and the alienation of my modern existence.

Rowland's heightened connectedness with nature and the sacred in nature is wholehearted and profound Jukurrpa. Likewise, Rogers awakened my own heart to the sacred from which there is no retreat. I ponder in my class journal, "When I see a clump of Douglas firs to be bulldozed for a new parking lot on campus, how will I feel now? Will I not hear a chorus of protest from the trees, crickets, cucumber beetles, grey squirrels, blue jays, and my own awakened heart?"

Through the din of traffic jams, MTV, and five-minute sound bites, Rogers calls hearts and minds to join her in celebration of the Oneness of All Creation: "This kinship of being, of devotion to life, once recognized, demands respect for each living entity in its place."[27] Her poems and essays stand as witness to her respect and devotion; her gift of Jukurrpa further witnessed through the responses of Atherton, Rowland, and myself. I recorded in my journal Rogers' telling reply to a student, when she was asked why her writing does not call for environmental activism:

> I write the way I do because this is my work. My writing celebrates all that is natural and sacred. I could not write this way if I were protesting. Remember Thomas Moran the artist whose inspiring painting of the Grand Canyon is said to have moved politicians to begin our national parks system. That is how my poetry does its work. I leave other work to others.

Robert Michael Pyle: Standing as a Witness Tree for the Deforested Human and Non-Human Landscape

Choosing that other work is lepidopterist and writer Robert Michael Pyle. In *Wintergreen: Listening to the Land's Heart,* Pyle connects and critiques the deforestation and exploitation of both human and non-human landscape: a clearcut land, ravaged oyster beds, the hard-working loggers of the Willapa Hills. He celebrates nature's adaptive and resilient beauty even as he documents its cycle of senescence and regeneration. His prologue positions his respect and his critique:

> This is the plan of the book: to describe the Willapa Hills and the wildlife they support, both native and alien; to examine the impact of intensive forestry upon the land and its life; and finally to assay the ability of organisms (including ourselves) to survive in the aftermath of massive resource extraction. . . . Throughout, questions of biogeography, ecology, and evolution in the wet wintergreen world find their way into the text.

> As a disclaimer, I wish to be explicit in saying that no part of this book is to be taken as in any way condoning or abetting the sort of steep slope, clearcut logging that takes place in large parts of southwestern Washington. While much of what I have to say speaks in sympathetic terms of a community based largely on a logging economy, my sympathies lie with the people and the woods, not with the companies that have used them both with equal disregard.[28]

For those who live there, and those who do not, Pyle invokes the Northwest rain forest wet and wintergreen. Readers see, hear, feel, touch wintergreen—winter in the rain forests. Readers walk the forest service roads in Pyle's favorite stumpfields, "winter—wet, green, slowly growing, cool, fresh, rainy, dripping winter."[29] His words transport readers like Erin Bower to Grey's Harbor. Bower's response illustrates not only her impassioned eco-consciousness but a newfound urgency and responsibility for action:

> Pyle places me in this amazingly dense forest of words. He doesn't just tell me about its beauty; his words grow it. I am no longer an observer. I walk with Pyle in the "gauzy" spruce canopies and star-carpet floors of moss, bramble twine under my feet. I become a sword fern on the forest floor—"Sword ferns show no awareness of limits, shooting slick and riotous from the sword mat . . . five-foot fireworks imported from green seeing Oz. Sword fern: supplier in season of spores by the bagful, merchant in chlorophyll all the year round. Sword fern, trademark of the rain forest. Rain forest, wintergreen's apogee" (*Wintergreen* 289).
>
> I am transported from my concrete and asphalt world to the rain forest. I see what is there to preserve for my children's children. Pyle's vision to save the sword ferns, the loggers, and the old-growth stands becomes mine. It is not just about spotted owls or overly mature forests. We all will be diminished if we lose these wonderlands of green. His words take me home. If I were not here in Oregon I would be heartsick to return to the wintergreen of my spirit's landscape.

Bower's response to the exigency of the old growth timber debate resonates with her Jukurrpa. Tellingly, Pyle situates the Willapa Hills old growth debate as a conundrum of scientific, aesthetic, economic, and religious perspectives:

> Nearby is the very spot where John Muir liked to listen to the hermit thrushes broadcast what his friend John Burroughs called the "religious beatitude" of their song. . . . Everyone concerned knows that old growth furnishes a stunning, humbling, aesthetic experience. . . . But it also provides some of the best high-grade lumber, at the highest densities per acre, and therefore the highest priced stumpage to be found. And in most quarters, housing starts count more than the clutch success of owls. . . . But the fact that these big trees are out there just going to waste, dying and rotting, is quite another. Impelled by an anthropocentric view of resources from the start ("God put it there for us to use!"), they're driven wild.[30]

Pyle counters economic or anthropocentric views with those of stewardship and respect for the forests and the loggers through metaphor. One of his most powerful metaphors for deforestation is a "witness tree," the Umbrella Tree of the Willapa Hills, the last old-growth survivor, "standing high on its clearcut ridge" above the second-growth wolf trees. Spared twice, the witness tree stands alone as totem for what was.[31] With numbed sadness and deep pain Pyle landmarks past and present timber management by such survivor trees: "The big old wolf trees, while they still stand, stand for something. They can represent the senses we could still come to, too little, too late but at last. Or they can be seen as lonely monuments to our stupidity, cupidity and greed."[32] Pyle is not without hope: his vision co-evolutionary. Even in the Willapa's now diminished human and non-human landscape he predicts that a sustainable natural world could provide a sustainable economy and lifestyle for all:

> Wintergreen does tell a tale of resilience and a chronicle of toughness. Like an old forest, the towns of these hills are senescing—growing old, losing vigor. Whether senescence of human communities must lead to extinction or may (in a forest) forecast regrowth, I do not pretend to know. But when a green and pleasant land becomes run-down and ravaged, evolution takes over.

> The decisions being made now will determine whether nature takes back Willapa or agrees to share it with us on more equitable terms than we have accepted. Clearly Willapa is a metaphor for wasted lands everywhere. I hope that by framing some pictures of this green and damaged land, these essays will help a little in our efforts to coevolve with the rest of the living things of the planet.[33]

From reading Pyle, Ted Parent discovers his own metaphor for Jukurrpa, a spiritual "oneness," an ecospheric reverence, which like Erin's calls for action and change:

> Heaven and earth are one. "Amen." Nature has been left to become its own creator. "Who picks the pattern?" "Through the gut of worms, say I, lies heaven." Nature is Pyle's metaphor for God. Death and resurrection in nature lead to analogies for saving our human society. In approach to the second millennium, human society seems bent on self-destruction of the earth and its peoples for the material gain of a few. Pyle balances this pessimism. Pyle teaches me spiritual insights through a reverence for nature. Nature can enlighten and guide our decisions, as the divine of the here and now. Through Pyle and Nature I am reminded of the sacred nature of all life and my place in that. Pyle moves us to revere the forests,

butterflies and ferns of the Willapa—and by doing so calls into question present policies of land and economics.

As these responses from Bower and Parent show, and as ecocriticism predicts, Pyle evokes eco-consciousness. He stands as a "witness tree," marking the boundary of his vision of a co-evolutionary Jukurrpa.

Terry Tempest Williams:
Testifying Through Personal and Public Acts of Faith

Terry Tempest Williams, a naturalist and writer, unabashedly proclaims her personal passion and reverence for the sacredness in her Utah landscape:

> If the desert is holy, it is because it is a forgotten place that allows us to remember the sacred. Perhaps that is why every pilgrimage to the desert is a pilgrimage to the self. There is no place to hide and so we are found.

> In the severity of the salt desert, I am brought down to my knees by its beauty. My imagination is fired. My heart opens and my skin burns in the passion of these moments. I will have no other gods before me.[34]

The desert is her pilgrimage to the sacred and the self. That which is exterior becomes interior, intensely joined in spiritual Jukurrpa:

> I was raised to believe in a spirit world, that life exists before the earth and will continue to exist afterward; if the natural world was assigned spiritual values, then those days spent in wildness were sacred. . . . We learned at an early age that God can be found where you are, especially outside.[35]

Williams finds the most immediate spiritual world her "other" mother, the Earth. She, like Rogers, takes her readers there in homage and faith. How can they not respond?

> The heartbeats I felt in the womb—two heartbeats, at once, my mother's and my own—are the heartbeats of the land. All of life drums and beats, at once, sustaining a rhythm audibly only to the spirit. I can drum my heartbeat back into the Earth, beating, hearts beating, my hands on the Earth—like a ruffed grouse on a log, beating, hearts beating—like a bittern in the marsh, beating, hearts beating. My hands on the Earth beating, hearts beating. I drum back my return.[36]

My own heart responds. Reared on the sycamore-lined banks of Sunderland Creek, I know to seek a familiar and sacred heartbeat to sustain and connect my urban lifestyle:

> My tenant farmer grandfather's words echo, "Always stay close to the land, or you'll go hungry in your belly or your soul." Every spring growing up on the farm, I would join my grandfather and father in turning the earth, with hoe, handplow, and tractor. Every spring after, I still must dig my hands into the soil and plant. Even when all I could do was grow squash in cedar planters or tomatoes and eggplants in clay pots on my apartment's deck, I had to feel that life force, fingers in the soil, touching the seeds, nourishing my soul.

My farm experience links with Williams's experience of the desert. It evokes ecocritical Jukurrpa. But what will be the ecospheric consequences if places like her Utah desert or my central Indiana farmland are considered "blank spots on the map"?

> A blank spot on the map translates into empty space, space devoid of people, a wasteland devoid of people, a wasteland perfect for nerve gas, wet eye bombs and toxic waste. . . . The army believe that the Great Salt Lake Desert is an ideal place to experiment with biological warfare. . . . An official from the Atomic Energy Commission had one comment regarding the desert: "It's a good place to throw used razor blades."[37]

Disturbingly, government agencies and agendas find as little value in the Utah desert's human landscape: "When the Atomic Energy Commission described the country north of the Nevada Test Site as 'virtually uninhabited desert terrain,' my family and the birds at Great Salt Lake were some of the 'virtual uninhabitants.'"[38] Williams and her family, like many other Mormon and Native American "virtual uninhabitants," face dire repercussions:

> My father's memory was correct. The September blast we drove through in 1957 was part of Operation Plumbbob, one of the most intensive series of bomb tests to be initiated. The flash of light in the night in the desert, which I had always thought was a dream, developed into a family nightmare. It took fourteen years, from 1957 to 1971, for cancer to manifest in my mother—the same time Howard L. Andrews, an authority in radioactive fallout at the National Institutes of Health, says radiation cancer requires to become evident. The more I learn about what it means to be a "downwinder," the more questions I drown in.[39]

The other women in her family now dead of cancer, Williams herself has been initiated into "The Clan of One-Breasted Women." Reared in a Mormon culture focused on tradition and loyalty to authority, Williams wrestles with her growing antipathy to any government or any authority that would so exploit its own citizens and its land. Her writing becomes her refuge and an act of faith.

Certainly her story is not the only story of such exploitation, and neither is the one that hers evoked, my own family's experience as "virtual uninhabitants" in the soybean and cornfields, those hills and "hollers," of the Heartland:

> For Poppa to have a winter job so close to home was a welcome surprise. Dupont was working with a secret government project in its Newport heavy water facility. No one questioned what the project was. Perhaps out of patriotism (in the early 1960's "Commie" plots and early involvement in Vietnam made questioning unthinkable) but more likely because of the high-paying jobs promised.

> As job supervisor, Poppa would rush to triage every accident at the plant. There were more and more as the project continued. With his hazel eyes dilated, the whites reddened—he would walk slowly up the steps on those days. His forest green or slate gray J.C. Penney's work clothes would fray into rags later that night when washed. His kiss on those days had a strange acridity.

> I wanted to ask, but knew this job like others Poppa worked for Dupont was top secret. Like Mission Impossible. How exciting. Once I overheard Poppa telling Mom about what it was like: "Sometimes the pipe don't hold it and even the earth busts out in explosions of flames . . . then it's all consumed, jest clean gone; other times this invisible, eye-burning gas takes grown men to their knees. In a split second. They just pass out, gasping for air. I carried your brother Cecil out twice this week."

> Eventually Poppa developed some kind of pneumonia. It hung on most of that winter and was diagnosed by spring as lung cancer. An operation revealed that except for one scarred lobe, his lungs were mysteriously "dissolved." No cancer, but we would never know the cause for sure. No information for the doctor or for the law suit could be revealed, due to the top secret classification. Dupont and the government settled out of court. Of all those injured, Poppa was hurt the worst, receiving top compensation, $20,000 or so.

> After that, Dupont required workers to wear protective clothing and take special showers. Then they moved the project somewhere out West. We

moved too. We lived in Tucson for a few years while Poppa recuperated. The government gave him a real easy job there. Several years later, Poppa died. His heart gave out.

Are there really "blank spots" whose human and nonhuman landscape deserves to be exploited or sacrificed, as Williams and I have experienced? I think not. How many others can tell such stories? They cry out for justice.

In response Williams models one course of public action and service. She testifies before Congress about the Pacific Yew and its promise of taxol for cancer treatment. In *Testimony: Writers of the West Speak on Behalf of Utah Wilderness,* Williams and Stephen Trimble, along with twenty-one other writers, "put their love of the land into action" for Congress' 1995 debate on Utah wilderness lands: through "the power of story to bypass political rhetoric and pierce the heart. . . . We write as an act of faith." To write as an act of faith and love is truly an act of Jukurrpa.

Besides testifying and writing, Williams recounts her civil disobedience against those who still make the desert rumble with nuclear testing:

> I crossed the line at the Nevada Test Site and was arrested with nine other Utahans for trespassing on military lands. They are still conducting nuclear tests in the desert. Ours was an act of civil disobedience. . . . It was a gesture on behalf of the Clan of the One-Breasted Women. . . .
>
> The women could not bear it any longer. They were mothers. . . . A contract had been made and broken with the land. A new contract was being drawn by the women, who understood the fate of the earth as their own. . . . The time had come to protest with the heart, that to deny one's genealogy with the earth was to commit treason against one's soul. . . .
>
> As one officer cinched the handcuffs around my wrists, another frisked my body. She found a pen and a pad of paper tucked inside my left boot.
>
> "And these?" she asked sternly.
>
> "Weapons," I replied.[40]

Like Henry David Thoreau, Williams lives her words of protest. Her words are weapons ready to be beaten into plowshares of a "lived" Jukurrpa, a "right livelihood" as Wendell Berry calls it. The message is clear: Jukurrpa must be lived, not just written or read. This is an example of what eco-critical readings and landscape writings call purgative-redemptive biospheric action. This action is a movement toward eco-justice.

For Berry responsible stewardship for the "gift of good land" demands the everyday, often unrewarded or unnoticed practice of the skills of justice and charity:

> The divine mandate to use the world justly and charitably defines every person's moral predicament as that of steward. . . . And stewardship is hopeless and meaningless unless it involves long term courage, perseverance, devotion, and skill. This skill . . . has to do with everyday proprieties in the practical use and care of created things—with "right livelihood."[41]

CONCLUSION AND THEOLOGICAL REFLECTION

If the harmony and oneness of the Creator's divine pattern is not understood or is tampered with, stewardship falters. So if the first step for successful stewardship is to discern the divine pattern's harmony and oneness this paper speaks to one possibility for eco-consciousness. The divine pattern, through Jukurrpa, may be discovered in the Willapa Hills, the Utah desert, the toe hair of an archer bug, or the awakened human heart. Berry's next step is "right livelihood," the individual act of living Jukurrpa, an everyday testimony of faith. This is the "how"; this is the "application" of ecocritical Jukurrpa.

This is also "how" the humanities can join the sciences in promoting this crucial eco-consciousness for the evolutionary success. The landscape writers and the reader responses presented in this paper evidence hope-filled possibilities. Indeed, whether in the sciences or humanities, proponents of eco-consciousness and global biospheric justice will find remarkably persuasive and responsible stewardship in these literary "acts of faith." Stalwart and upright, they stand—"witness trees"—pointing to a redemptive Jukurrpa for all of creation.

Finally, the general message of this chapter is the creative power of the literary pen, particularly that style of literature called "ecocritical." In an age predominated by urban consciousness and the ravaged natural world ecocritical literature is an evocative medium that holds the potential capacity for reuniting humanity with creation, human and non-human. Drawing on the writings of Rogers, Pyle, and Williams, this essay specifically highlights the transformative power of ecocritical literature, especially nature-landscape literature of the North American West, to reconnect humanity with "sacred and personal insights" with the aim of provoking "purgative-redemptive biospheric action."[42]

But what is it about nature-landscape literature that holds this transformative capacity? First is the narrative medium itself and the evocative, or in theological language the revelatory power of the story that, with its use of image and metaphor, speaks directly to the heart. Accordingly in ecocritical literature the author suggests that "words go beyond words, transmuting into personal and public eco-consciousness and possible action."[43] Second, the narrative structure of nature-landscape writing has the power of evoking (or provoking) the reader's memory and imagination. Within the dialogical exchange between text and reader the essay declares that "Awakened memories and insights jolt readers into awareness and engagement with all that was the other."[44] Moreover, ecocritical writing is the "literature of hope" luring the mind and heart to imagine a better future, one that is just and sustainable. Finally, the narrative and anamnetic structure of nature-landscape literature holds the capacity to reconnect the reader with the sacred dimension of creation. As Terry Tempest Williams writes, "If the desert is holy, it is because it is a forgotten place that allows us to remember the sacred."[45]

There is an important theological dimension to narrative and memory as well. A number of years ago the renowned German theologian Johann Baptist Metz proposed memory and narrative, along with solidarity, as practical fundamental categories for theological reflection. According to Metz: "Theology is concerned with irreducible original experiences which, when they are articulated in language, reveal unmistakably narrative features."[46] A primary example is the biblical tradition itself beginning with the mythic-poetic stories of creation and culminating in the eschatological vision of creation's restoration and renewal. For Metz narrative is an essential medium through which memory is evoked. Memory, defined as the remembrance of suffering and freedom, can become "dangerous" because it can compel us to embrace action for justice and freedom.[47] In Metz's view narrative memory can function on three levels. On the individual level it refers to the personal stories of remembered suffering and freedom. On the socio-historical level it embodies the narrative remembrance of an entire group's struggle against oppression and non-identity. On the explicitly theological level it refers to the remembrance of God understood in Christian terms as the dangerous memory of the suffering and freedom of

Jesus Christ. Ultimately narrative memory in a theological context is an eschatological category of salvation pointing to a hoped-for future as yet unrealized. According to Metz "The Christian memory of suffering is in its theological implications an anticipatory memory: it intends the anticipation of a particular future of man as a future for the suffering, the hopeless, the oppressed, the injured and the useless of this earth."[48]

There is, however, an important distinction between Metz's understanding of narrative memory and the ecocritical literature of nature-landscape writing. For Metz memory and narrative are exclusively anthropocentric, rooted in the historical reality of oppressed people and their struggle for emancipation. Ecocritical literature, particularly the writings of Pyle and Williams, forces us to expand the meaning of dangerous memory and its narrative structure to encompass the suffering and longing for liberation of all creation—human and non-human. Pyle, for example, links "the deforestation and exploitation of both human and nonhuman landscape: a clearcut land, ravaged oyster beds, the hard working loggers of the Willapa Hills."[49] Williams, on the other hand, links the destruction of the natural world with the decimation of her own family fallen victim to the ravages of nuclear radiation and the cancerous experience of being "down-winders." These are all dangerous memories, stories of creation's suffering given voice in the writings of ecocritical authors. Moreover, this literature compels us to remember our unforgettable responsibility to labor for that day when all creation shall be redeemed.

NOTES: CHAPTER 1

[1] Terry Tempest Williams, *Refuge: An Unnatural History of Family and Place* (New York: Vintage, 1992) 137.

[2] Lewis Thomas, "Are We Fit to Fit In?" *Sierra* 67/2 (March/April 1982) 52.

[3] Donald Worster, *The Wealth of Nature: Environmental History and the Ecological Imagination* (New York: Oxford University Press, 1993) 27.

[4] Ecocriticism uses interdisciplinary theory to examine and critique literature's potential for evoking aesthetic, ethical, spiritual, socio-political consciousness of the human and nonhuman as well as for promoting subsequent action and justice for today's global crisis. To connect literary ways of knowing with those of ecology and other fields ecocriticism draws from ecology, biology, biogeography, environmental ethics, theology, psychology, anthropology, sociology, deep ecology, history, ecofeminism, linguistics, semiotics, cultural studies, American studies, structuralism, modern and postmodern criticism.

[5] William Rueckert, "Literature and Ecology: An Experiment in Ecocriticism," in Cheryll Glotfelty and Harold Fromm, eds., *The Ecocriticism Reader: Landmarks in Literary Ecology* (Athens, Ga.: University of Georgia Press, 1996) 121.

[6] The Australian Aboriginal term "Jukurrpa" will be used hereafter in this chapter to describe this transformative potential for creating eco-kinship. This embodies the evocative power of ecocritical reading and its potential "application."

[7] Landscape literature or writing and landscape writers will be used hereafter to refer to these twentieth-century American nature writers of the West and their works. While nature writing is the more common term some ecocritics prefer landscape, rather than nature writing, because of landscape's connotation of mutual influence and interaction between the human and the nonhuman. See John Brinckerhoff Jackson's *Discovering the Vernacular Landscape* (New Haven: Yale University Press, 1984) or Thomas J. Lyon, ed., *This Incomparable Land: A Book of American Nature Writing* (Boston: Houghton Mifflin, 1989) for further discussion. The term is used both for connotation and simplicity of reference in this chapter.

[8] In the fall semester 1995 the advanced writing class read the works of Terry Tempest Williams and collaboratively presented their responses to her. In the fall semester 1996 the advanced writing class read the works of Robert Michael Pyle and published their responses in a class pamphlet presented to him. In the fall semester 1997 the advanced writing class read the works of Pattiann Rogers and published their responses in a class pamphlet presented to her. The reader responses placed in dialogue with these writers will come from these sources. Karen Vaught-Alexander's responses come from her teaching journals kept for those classes during those years.

[9] Glen A. Love, "Revaluing Nature: Toward an Ecological Criticism," *The Ecocriticism Reader* 237.

[10] Rueckert, "Literature and Ecology," 112.

[11] His call has been answered. Beginning in the mid-1980s environmental literary studies emerged. In 1989 *The American Nature Writing Newsletter* began publication. In 1992 The Association for the Study of Literature and the Environment (ASLE) was founded. Currently ASLE sponsors a web page, an e-mail discussion group, a journal (*ISLE: Interdisciplinary Studies in Literature and Environment*), an annual annotated bibliography, and an annual membership directory with a graduate handbook. See Cheryll Glotfelty's introduction to *The Ecocriticism Reader,* "Literary Studies in an Age of Environmental Crisis," xv–xxxvii, for a comprehensive overview. See Stephen Greenblatt and Giles Gunn, *Redrawing the Boundaries: The Transformation of English and American Literary Studies* (New York: Modern Language Association of America, 1992) for this field in the literary canon.

[12] Rueckert, "Literature and Ecology," 121.

[13] Love, "Revaluing Nature," 232–33, 238.

[14] For further discussion of this awareness evoked through exteriority and interiority see Scott Slovic, *Seeking Awareness in American Nature Writing: Henry Thoreau, Annie Dillard, Edward Abbey, Wendell Berry, Barry Lopez* (Salt Lake City: University of Utah Press, 1992).

[15] The website for Jukurrpa is http://aboriginalart.com.au/culture/dreamtime/htm. See also n. 6 of this chapter.

[16] Rueckert, "Literature and Ecology," 110–11.

[17] The creative and evocative, as well as imaginative and spiritual potential of metaphor can be found in a number of sources. See Slovic, *Seeking Awareness,* as well as Annette Kolodny, *The Lay of the Land: Metaphor as Experience and History in American Life and Letters* (Chapel Hill: University of North Carolina Press, 1979), and J. Douglas Porteous, *Landscapes of the Mind: Worlds of Sense and Metaphor* (Toronto: University of Toronto Press, 1990).

[18] In Glotfelty and Fromm's *Ecocriticism Reader* see the essays by Leslie Marmon Silko and Paula Gunn Allen, as well as books on deep ecology by Bill Devall and George Sessions *(Deep Ecology: Living as if Nature Mattered* [Salt Lake City: G. M. Smith, 1985]) or Roderick Nash *(The Rights of Nature* [Madison: University of Wisconsin Press, 1989]), as well as other key perspectives in books by Belden C. Lane *(Landscapes of the Sacred: Geography and Narrative in American Spirituality* [New York: Paulist, 1988]), Edward O. Wilson *(The Diversity of Life* [Cambridge, Mass.: Harvard University Press, 1992]), or Jerry Mander *(In the Absence of the Sacred: The Failure of Technology and the Survival of the Indian Nations* [San Francisco: Sierra Club, 1991]).

[19] In Glotfelty and Fromm's *Ecocriticism Reader* see the essays by Lynn White, Jr., Christopher Manes, Harold Fromm, David Mazel, and Michael McDowell for general background. See Patrick D. Murphy, *Literature, Nature, and Other: Ecofeminist Critiques* (Albany: SUNY Press, 1995), Kolodny, *The Lay of the Land,* Irene Diamond and Gloria Feman Orenstein, eds., *Reweaving the World: The Emergence of Ecofeminism* (San Francisco: Sierra Club, 1990), and Clarissa Pinkola Estes, *Women Who Run with the Wolves: Myths and Stories of the Wild Woman Archetype* (New York: Ballantine Books, 1992) for additional reading.

[20] Taken from Ray Gonzalez's 1990 interview with Barry Lopez entitled "Landscapes of the Interior: The Literature of Hope." See Scott Slovic, "Nature Writing and Environmental Psychology: The Interiority of Outdoor Experience," in idem, *Seeking Awareness* 368.

[21] Barry Lopez, "Natural History: An Annotated Booklist," *Antaeus* 57 (Autumn 1986) 97.

[22] From this point onward throughout this section the voice behind the unidentified personal pronouns ("I," "my") belongs to the author of this chapter, Karen Vaught-Alexander. Her reflections on various pieces of writing are woven in with the students' reflections.

[23] Pattiann Rogers shared these thoughts during her presentation to the advanced writing class at the University of Portland, October 21, 1997.

[24] Pattiann Rogers, "Surprised by the Sacred," *U.S. Catholic* (March 1998) 27.

[25] Pattiann Rogers, *Firekeeper: New and Selected Poems* (Minneapolis: Milkweed Editions, 1994) 25.

[26] Ibid. 169.

[27] Rogers, "Surprised by the Sacred," 26.

[28] Robert Michael Pyle, *Wintergreen: Listening to the Land's Heart* (Boston: Houghton Mifflin, 1996) 3.

[29] Ibid. 283.

[30] Ibid. 183–85.

[31] Ibid. 174.

[32] Ibid. 198.

[33] Ibid. 3.

[34] Williams, *Refuge* 148–49.

[35] Ibid. 14.

[36] Ibid. 84–85.

[37] Ibid. 241–42.

[38] Ibid. 287.

[39] Ibid. 286.

[40] Ibid. 289–90.

[41] Wendell Berry, *The Gift of Good Land: Further Essays Cultural and Agricultural* (San Francisco: North Point Press, 1981) 275.

[42] See above, p. 3.

[43] See above, p. 4.

[44] See above, p. 4.

[45] Williams, *Refuge* 148.

[46] Johann Baptist Metz, *Faith in History and Society: Toward a Practical Fundamental Theology* (New York: Seabury, 1980) 206.

[47] Ibid. 109–10. On the notion of dangerous memory Metz writes: "there are dangerous memories, memories which make demands on us. There are memories in which earlier experiences break through to the centre-point of

our lives and reveal new and dangerous insights for the present. They illuminate for a few moments and with a harsh steady light the questionable nature of things we have apparently come to terms with, and show the banality of our supposed 'realism.' They break through the canon of the prevailing structures of plausibility and have certain subversive features. Such memories are like dangerous and incalculable visitations from the past. They are memories that we have to take into account, memories, as it were, with a future content."

[48] Ibid. 117.

[49] See above, p. 7.

2

New Ways of Knowing and Being Known

"Before I formed you in the womb I knew you,
and before you were born, I consecrated you;
I appointed you a prophet to the nations." (Jer 1:5)

*P*erhaps the most intimate word in the biblical world is *yādaʿ*, "to know." While it can be understood to mean knowledge of factual information, in the religious sense it is most often associated with knowledge that is not objective but rather subjective, relational, and deeply experiential. In Jer 1:5 the prophet proclaims that before God had made him God "knew" him. A relationship between God and creature had been established early on in the creation, long before the prophet's birth.

The psalmist in Psalm 139 picks up on Jeremiah's understanding of what it means to "know" and to "be known":

> O Lord, you have searched me
>   and known me.
> You know when I sit down and when I rise up;
>   you discern my thoughts from far away.
> You search out my path and my lying down,
>   and are acquainted with all my ways.
> Even before a word is on my tongue,
>   O Lord, you know it completely.

You hem me in, behind and before,
    and lay your hand upon me.
Such knowledge is too wonderful for me;
    it is so high that I cannot attain it. (vv. 1-6)

The understanding that Jeremiah and the Psalmist have about "knowing" and "being known" is brought forth in a new way in what follows in this chapter. What the ancient biblical people understood about life, God, and creation, and what it means to be in relationship with all these aspects is a knowledge that some scholars today are trying to recover and re-shape so that the struggle for integration and wholesomeness may give way to the vision and reality of a God-human-earth relationship. This relationship can only happen when the current theory of knowing and how people know—a theory steeped in the notion of objectivity that has long been hailed by science and other disciplines—is revisioned.

INTRODUCTION

Feminist critiques of science have much to offer people who want to think about their relationship to the environment and how to change it. Unfortunately these critiques are often misunderstood, especially by scientists themselves. There are several levels on which this misunderstanding occurs but they are all based in certain misconceptions about the feminist project and different assumptions about the power and force of language and metaphor. There is a prevalent view that *how* people say things is not nearly as important as *what* they say. Many feminists, though certainly not only feminists, hold that how people say things changes what they are saying and that how people say things conditions their views of the world and perpetuates prejudices of which they may not even be aware. There are no "simple turns of phrase;" they all say something about the way one conceptualizes things. For example, a student wrote in his journal that he was going to "kill" a paper that evening, by which he meant finish it. He was asked why he used the word "kill" since some people consider writing a paper a process of giving birth. In other words, his use of "kill" said something a lot deeper about his attitude toward the paper and probably toward writing and schoolwork in general. He responded that it was "just a saying." For the kind of analysis of interest in this chapter, and that is of interest to many feminists, among others, there are no *mere* sayings. The words one uses always bring with them a whole cartload of baggage. The reader who might reject this view is asked to consider it open-mindedly and thoughtfully rather than dismissing it from the outset.

Another objection related to this point stems from the fact that such a critique must be historical. This chapter will look at what the founders of modern science and of our scientific conception of the world laid in place through the language and metaphors they used. The fact that no contemporary scientist even reads people like Francis Bacon (1561–1626) may seem to make this entire critique irrelevant, but it actually makes it all the more important. Attitudes that derive from the way men like Bacon talked about the world, the self, and the self's relation to the world are ubiquitous in Western culture. It may well be that insofar as they are practicing science, contemporary scientists are as far from the conceptions of the seventeenth century as they could be. Nonetheless, in their everyday lives many people in the industrialized West continue to have an alienated relation to the world, and this alienation can be seen to have its source in the scientific revolution of the seventeenth century, all the good things that resulted from it notwithstanding. Uncovering these roots is the first step in moving beyond them and figuring out how to have a less alienated relation to the world—something everyone needs to have if the current environmental crisis is truly to be overcome.

The project of this chapter, then, is a feminist analysis of the seventeenth-century roots of current prevalent attitudes toward the world. These attitudes are bound up with the modern conception of knowledge and the way modern people know the world. In other words, it is bound up with the *epistemology* of the modern world. According to this epistemology, in order for there to be knowledge at all there must be a *knower* and an *object of knowledge.* The strict and absolute separation of subject (knower) from object (known) is the condition for the possibility of knowledge in the prevailing epistemology of the modern era. The seventeenth century, which is widely seen as the beginning of the modern era, marked not only the explicit beginning of the scientific revolution but also the explicit theorization of the knowing subject and its separation from the object of knowledge, the world. Soon knowledge could only be conceived of in such terms. The prevailing epistemology today, a view at the basis of science, is founded on this distinction, which was articulated perhaps most clearly by René Descartes (1596–1650).

The epistemology at the basis of the science of the modern era has been characterized by many as violent. Bacon's metaphors of violence have been pointed to as paradigmatic evidence of this. However a second theme, more subtle, even more pervasive, and probably from which it will be more difficult to free ourselves, has emerged: that of separation from the world as an epistemological ideal. Susan Bordo has described this as a "flight to objectivity" and sees it as characterized by the exclusion of subjectivity from inquiry and the separation of mind or reason from body and emotion. These separations also necessitated the separation of the human from nature (or, as philosophers tend to put it, the knowing subject from the object known). The world was foreign and alien to the knowing subject and needed to be "conquered," her secrets "penetrated," and she needed to be "tamed" and brought under the will of "man." In knowing nature "man" sought to control nature and make her bend to his will.[1] Notice the warlike terminology: there is no conversation or even negotiation with nature. To understand is to dominate, not to live in sympathetic harmony with or to care for, except possibly in the sense that one might care for one's possessions.

This chapter will explore these themes. The basic argument will be that as long as we speak within the dominant Western epistemological framework it will reinscribe our separation and alienation from nature. First I will trace out the theme of violence, as it is not only important to understanding certain prevalent attitudes toward nature and knowledge but will also help us to see more fully the theme of separation. I will then go on to discuss why this theme of separation, the radical disjunction of inner and outer, subject and object, is a continuing danger in attempting to come to terms with the current environmental crisis and to all of us wishing to improve our relationship to nature today. Finally, I will point to some recent work in the area of epistemology, or theory of knowledge, that might help us to work toward a new way of knowing more compatible with the ultimate goals of environmentalism.

Current attitudes toward knowledge and toward our relationship to the environment emerge from a mechanistic view of the world that began to be the basis for thought about the world beginning in the seventeenth century. Although there had been mechanists since ancient Greece, the predominant worldview had been an organic one right up through the Middle Ages and Renaissance to the beginning of the scientific revolution. While organic views were still articulated and continue to be so today, the view that gained dominance was one based on a mechanical view of creation and it is the basis of what we consider rationality today.[2] The framework of explanation that is based in mechanism comes with certain values. To see nature, or indeed any object to be known, as fundamentally a mechanism rather than an organism makes us value it differently and see our obligations both to it and to ourselves differently. This view of nature is also a view of our own bodies and ultimately of ourselves and our place in the world. To understand how this view emerged, to see its strengths as well as its weaknesses, we need to look at the view it replaced: the organic view of nature.

THE ORGANIC VIEW OF NATURE

The organic view of nature, as the name implies, views all of nature and the cosmos as an organism. This view held sway through the Renaissance and was still advocated by alchemists and hermeticists in the debates leading up to the founding of the Royal Society[3] in 1662. Medievals did not consider the mind or self as a wholly separate thing from the world but rather saw themselves as part of the world—as a microcosm within the macrocosm. Indeed, as Susan Bordo describes, for the medievals and the early Renaissance there is no radical disjunction between the "inner" reality and the "outward" appearance, but rather a close relation between the movement of the body and the movement of the soul. The medieval consciousness might be considered a "participating consciousness" for which the categories of inner and outer, self and world, human and natural were not rigorously opposed.

For those who held this worldview the notion of "Reason" resisted locatedness, that is, it could not be located "inside" or "outside" the human being. People did not feel themselves isolated inside their skins from the world outside to the same extent that people in the modern era do. They were "integrated or mortised into it, each different part of [them] being united to a different part of it by some invisible thread. In [his or her] relation to the environment, the [person] of the middle ages was rather less like an island, rather more like an embryo."[4] This has been called a "participating consciousness" because it is structured around a merger with nature rather than a detachment from it. In the alchemical and hermetic traditions of the Renaissance, participation was a genuine mode of knowledge. Indeed, the magic of these traditions was sometimes called "sympathetic magic" because one had to work in harmony with the world and feel sympathy for it. Of course one can only feel sympathy for living things, so this kind of attitude could only hold sway so long as it was held against the background of an organic worldview.

Despite the obvious appeal of this organic conception to those of us concerned about the environment today, it should be remembered that this conception did not prevent massive environmental destruction. This destruction occurred in part, at least, because no one understood the consequences of various actions. In other words, the epistemological methods of the organic view did not allow people to understand or even think about the larger impact of apparently sensible actions that in fact proved destructive. For example, in the late Middle Ages the increase in the European population led to more and more land being cultivated for crops and less for the pasturing of animals. Many forests were destroyed as well. As a result the soil rapidly became depleted as there was less manure to fertilize the soil and it was quickly overused. Crops became leaner and leaner and widespread starvation followed. In addition to deaths from starvation the malnourished population became increasingly susceptible to the plague and other diseases. The population then declined quickly, in some places by as much as 60 percent between 1315 and 1450[5] as a result. These are the kinds of things that a more modern scientific approach and its quite different epistemological methods would surely have prevented. This period of population decline, however, led to reforestation and ecosystem renewal, in some cases back to pre-plague states. While one might argue that in this way the earth took care of itself in the long run, the human cost is ethically unacceptable to most people and many would be uncomfortable with even temporary environmental devastation. Clearly, the organic view is not one that will guarantee an ethical relation to either the earth or one's fellow humans.

The organic view had many other limitations. For one thing, at least as it was articulated in the Middle Ages and Renaissance it was profoundly undemocratic and elitist. In the Middle Ages knowledge was to be found solely in ancient texts accessible only to the educated few (largely priests). In the Renaissance, as Carolyn Merchant describes,

> Knowledge and power could be obtained through a union with the understanding and intellect of God: "No one has such powers but he who has cohabited with the elements, vanquished nature, mounted higher than the heavens, elevating himself above the angels to the archetype itself, with whom he then becomes cooperator and can do all things." But power obtained by such methods was restricted to each individual. It was an experience that could not be shared or transferred except through initiation.[6]

By contrast one of the great values of modern science is that knowledge must be publicly available. Subjective experience, like that of the Magus or mystic, is worthless. Knowledge is objective and must be something that all can see for themselves, not something only those with certain spiritual purity or special initiation can see. Replicable, public experience is always to be preferred over the words of ancient texts or private experience. Indeed, some have argued that modern science is one of the cornerstones of democracy.[7]

THE MECHANISTIC WORLD VIEW

The scientific revolution saw the displacement of the organic worldview in favor of a mechanistic one. This view is still the prevailing one today, although signs of its waning can also be seen.

The mechanistic view was based on the idea that knowledge of the world is certain and consistent and that the laws of nature are immutable and, for early mechanists as well as for many later ones, imposed by God. Matter was made up of tiny particles and was passive and inert. Change was the result of the rearrangement of particles where motion is transmitted from one part to another through the laws of causation.

Seeing creation as a dead mechanism, mechanists were free from the ethical concerns of those who viewed creation as a living being. In coming to see the world as a mechanism people find that they are no longer bound by the controls over environmental exploitation that were bound up with the organic view of nature as alive, sensitive, and responsive to human action. While in the magical tradition of the Renaissance the manipulation of nature was an individual effort, under mechanism it became associated with "general collaborative social interests that sanctioned the expansion of commercial capitalism."[8] This philosophy was also closely connected to "an empirical philosophy of science and a concept of the human being as a designer of experiments who by wresting secrets from nature gained mastery over its operations."[9]

The central mechanist philosophers were Marin Mersenne, Pierre Gassendi, and René Descartes, but both France from 1620–1650 and England from 1650–1690 were at the center of the mechanical reconstruction of the cosmos. In both countries ideas associated with the organic worldview and with animistic and pantheistic philosophies were severely criticized.[10]

In debates prior to the founding of the Royal Society the decisive move that ensured the victory of the mechanists was made during the 1650s when such leading intellectuals as Robert Boyle, Walter Charleton, and Henry More abandoned their earlier sympathy for the organic view, which at that time was associated with hermeticism and alchemy, and became strong proponents of the newly published mechanical viewpoints of Gassendi and Descartes. At the end of the 1650s a number of churchmen, including some founding members of the Royal Society, waged a campaign against the alchemical "enthusiasts." The establishment of the Royal Society 1662 marked the institutionalization of the new science. From then on alchemical "enthusiasts" were not supported and were often attacked.

The image of creation that became important in the early modern period, the period in which mechanism developed, was that of a disorderly and chaotic realm to be *subdued* and *controlled*.[11] While the metaphor for creation prevalent in the Middle Ages was that of an organism, that of the modern era is of a machine or mechanism. At the same time writers in the sixteenth and seventeenth centuries tended to view both the natural world and society as a wilderness and to advocate control over the forces and fates dealt by creation.[12]

Whereas previously the body had been viewed as permeated and enlivened by an animating spirit, the view of the human person in this era was also that of a machine. This machine was governed by the soul as an external operator.

While the magical tradition operating within the organic view in the Middle Ages and Renaissance sought to control creation by working in harmony with it, the techniques of the magician were taken up in very different ways in the Early Modern era. This change can be seen most clearly in the work of Francis Bacon, one of the fathers of the scientific revolution and the inventor of the experimental method. While previously the need to dominate creation was not for the sole benefit of the individual magician but for the good of humanity, Bacon transformed the magus from creation's servant to its exploiter, and creation from a *teacher* into a *slave*.[13] The new scientific method advocated dissecting creation with a properly trained understanding. As Bacon said, creation can be "forced out of her natural state and squeezed and molded."[14] Bacon also equated knowledge with power. Creation is to be conquered, subdued, made to "betray her secrets." Scientific method combined with mechanical technology created a new system of investigation that unified knowledge with material power. As Bacon said, creation will betray "her secrets more fully . . . than when in enjoyment of her natural liberty."[15]

By the mid-seventeenth century cosmos, society, and the self were reunified under the metaphor of the machine. "In the mechanical world, order was redefined to mean the predictable behavior of each part within a rationally determined system of laws, while power derived from active and immediate intervention in a secularized world. Order and power together constituted control. Rational control over nature, society, and the self was achieved by redefining reality itself through the new machine metaphor."[16] This mechanical view of creation was now common-sense reality. Because creation was now a machine it was dead and inert. This framework, then, could be used to justify and legitimize the manipulation of the natural world. Indeed, Merchant and others have argued that the two are intimately connected. Furthermore, this conceptual framework had associated with it a framework of values based on power. This is fully compatible with the emerging commercial capitalism. Merchant summarizes the reshaping of the worldview as follows:

> The rise of mechanism laid the foundation for a new synthesis of the cosmos, society, and the human being, construed as ordered systems of mechanical parts subject to governance by law and to predictability through deductive reasoning. A new concept of the self as a rational master of the passions housed in a machinelike body began to replace the concept of the self as an integral part of a close-knit harmony of organic parts united to the cosmos and society. Mechanism rendered nature effectively dead, inert, and manipulable from without. As a system of thought, it rapidly gained in plausibility during the second half of the seventeenth century. Its ascendancy to status as a new worldview was achieved through combating some presuppositions of the older organic view of nature while absorbing and transforming others.[17]

Reality had become structured around order and power. This worldview was also a conceptual power structure. In the seventeenth century two different intellectual strains led to two different styles of science and two different modes of dominating nature. One, based on the medieval tradition of intellectualism (which placed primacy on God's logic and the divine intellect over the divine will), emphasized logic, order, and predictability. The other, emerging from medieval voluntarism (which placed primacy on God's will and immediate active power), emphasized power and activity.[18]

Perhaps what is most basic to the mechanistic view and to main-stream science is the idea that *things* rather than relations are the ultimate reality. Relations between things, for the early mechanists, are externally imposed by God in the form of natural laws. While scientists today leave out mention of God, the place of natural laws is, for many, the same as for these early mechanists.

While the first mechanist philosophers and scientists, such as Newton, are best known for their contributions in mathematics and mechanics, the mechanist research program has resulted in mechanical models of the self, society, and the cosmos in which relations are secondary and derivative and things are primary. As Carolyn Merchant sees it,

> . . . during the three centuries in which the mechanical world view became the philosophical ideology of Western Culture, industrialization coupled with the exploitation of natural resources began to fundamentally alter the character and quality of human life. Through popular scientific education, through commonsense empirical philosophy and natural religion, and through the spread of scientific, rationalizing tendencies to manufacturing, government bureaucracies and medical and legal systems, the mechanical science, method, and philosophy created in the seventeenth century have gradually become institutionalized as a form of life in the Western world.[19]

This worldview also presented a new epistemology, or theory of what it means to know something and what the best way is to go about achieving knowledge. This epistemology is often equated with the words "reason" and "rationality," but these words were used in different ways prior to the seventeenth century and have continued to be used to mean quite different kinds of things by philosophers such as G.W.F. Hegel. I will then, when I need to refer to this epistemology, call it "scientistic," by which I will mean the notion of reason and rationality equated with the rise of modern science.

THE EPISTEMOLOGY OF MECHANISM

The Renaissance was a time of great intellectual uncertainty. A new epistemological basis was necessary, for it had become clear that the senses were not a road to knowledge where knowledge means certainty. The question "how can I know anything?" became one that animated a great deal of thought in the sixteenth and seventeenth centuries.

Descartes, for example, developed what he believed to be a certain basis for knowledge, but he did so by removing himself from his untrustworthy senses. The mind alone was capable of achieving knowledge and the senses would only lead him astray. His epistemology, then, is one of a mind completely alien from the world—so alien, in fact, that he could not be sure that there was a world. He also, famously, believed that the body was nothing but a machine to which the mind is intimately, but not necessarily, attached. For Descartes "God sets up mathematical laws in nature as a king sets up laws in his kingdom."[20] God is outside the cosmos, operating the machine from out there, just as the soul operates the bodily machine.

Richard Rorty points out in his *Philosophy and the Mirror of Nature* that in Descartes a crucial departure is made from the Aristotelian and medieval epistemologies, from the notion of "mind-as-reason" to the notion of "mind-as-consciousness."[21] In the Middle Ages, Aristotle's view that there are two modes of knowing corresponding to the two ways that things may be known was still prevalent. These two modes of knowing are *sensing,* which is the province of the body and is of the particular and material, and *thought* (or reason), which is of the universal and immaterial. For Descartes, however, both these modes of knowing become subsumed under the category of *penser* (literally "to think"), "which embraces perceptions, images, ideas, pains, and volitions alike."[22]

Rorty indicates that in Greek there is no way to divide conscious states from events in the external world.[23] "Reason," for the Greeks and medievals, was a human faculty that resisted metaphors of locatedness. It was neither "inside" nor "outside" the human being. For Descartes, however, "consciousness" "was the quality of a certain sort of event— the sort of event distinguished from all other events precisely by being 'located' in 'inner space' rather than the external world."[24]

The construction of thought as "inner" gave rise to new epistemological dilemmas: How do I verify my judgment that what is "inside," that is, my modes of thought, is similar to or conforms to things outside me? What Descartes refers to as the "natural attitude" assumes that my ideas are like the things outside of me, but that is the source of, indeed, the principle of error. One has no certain basis for making such an assumption.

Here we see the problem of subjectivity emerge in philosophy. Bordo defines subjectivity as "the notion of influences proceeding from 'within' the human being—not supplied by the world 'outside' the perceiver—which are capable of affecting how the world is perceived."[25]

For Descartes and Galileo subjectivity is what stands between the knower and an accurate perception of the world.

> It is via the imagery of an untrustworthy "inner space" that the "mind" is born in the sixteenth and seventeenth centuries. It makes its initial appearance not as "mirror," the internal reflection of things "as they are," but as subjectivity—the capacity of the knower to bestow false inner projections on the outer world of things.[26]

The old metaphysical dichotomy of change/permanence is played out in a new form in the sixteenth and seventeenth centuries, an epistemological form with the new categories of bias/neutrality becoming the central worry of philosophers. "Since the 'colors' that the mind bestows on objects vary from person to person, a 'neutral' view of the object is impossible."[27]

One of the things that had been lost in the period immediately preceding the scientific revolution was the sense of being at home in the world. At this time "infinity had 'opened its jaws' and the medieval universe—once 'as safely enclosed as a cot in the nursery or a babe in the womb'"[28]—had been burst asunder. Many authors consider this, and not the "Copernican Revolution," to have been the most profound result of the scientific transformations of the modern era. As Bordo points out, the change from a heliocentric to an acentric system raised the radically disturbing possibility that "there is no intelligible cosmic system at all, no center of orientation, and, therefore, no spiritually proper 'home' for anything."[29] But while there is no home, no "place," in the world, there is simple location. The universe is now cold and indifferent and the newly separate self is "simply located" within it. The response to this sense of alienness in the world might be most easily summed up by Pascal: "Through space the universe grasps me and swallows me up like a speck; through thought I grasp it." Yet this alienness points to another attitude as well, that of "man" against nature. As Bordo explains,

> if the impersonal, arbitrary universe of the early modern era is capable of physically "swallowing" him, like a random bit of ontological debris, he is nonetheless capable of containing it and subduing it—through comprehension, through the "grasp" of the mind. As in much of early modern science and philosophy—in Bacon, most dramatically—the dream of knowledge is here imagined as an explicit revenge fantasy, an attempt to wrest back control from nature.[30]

But for Descartes it is not possible for a finite intelligence to comprehend an infinite universe. He instead develops the possibility of *pure* thought, of *pure* perception. "Such perception, far from embracing the whole, demands the disentangling of the various objects of knowledge *from* the whole of things, and beaming a light on the essential separateness of each—its own pure and discrete nature, revealed as *it* is, free of the *distortions* of subjectivity."[31]

Knowledge, then, requires a knower purified of all bias, perspective, and emotional attachment. This can only be achieved through a transcendence of the body and all its distractions, which only serve to obscure our thinking. In his *Rules for the Direction of the Native Intelligence* Descartes gives us explicit instructions for how to achieve this. His *Meditations on First Philosophy* could be seen as a guide to, and example of, this transcendence of the body.

This new Cartesian model of knowledge is grounded in *objectivity* and "is capable of providing a new epistemological security to replace that which was lost in the dissolution of the medieval world-view."[32] Such a view of knowledge tends to hold that what cannot be categorized cleanly deserves no place in the universe. It allows for no ambiguity or dissonance, but rather orders the world according to firm, clearly articulated categories. Susan Bordo sees this quest for objectivity as

> capable of transforming the barren landscape of the modern universe into a paradise for analysis, dissection, and "controlled" experimentation. Its barrenness, which filled Pascal with such existential dread, is, of course, precisely what makes it capable of being "read" mathematically and taken apart with philosophical accuracy—and moral impunity.[33]

For Descartes the "known" is conceived as that realm in which the distorting effects of human interest and activity are eliminated, and in which fixity and purity rule. In the sixteenth and seventeenth centuries earthly science, insofar as it is trustworthy, is equated with "spectatorship" and the passive reception of ideas rather than participation. In the work of Descartes we find the official philosophical birth of the notion, prevalent to this day, that the mind is a "mirror of nature."[34] Descartes emphasizes the ideals of *submissiveness* and *receptivity* to the "true native rays" of things. Achieving this receptivity, however, requires that the mind first purify and cleanse *itself* of "idols" and "false preconceptions." Evelyn Fox Keller describes Francis Bacon's project in similar terms:

> To receive God's truth, the mind must be pure and clean, submissive and open. Only then can it give birth to a masculine and virile science. That

is, if the mind is pure, receptive, and submissive in its relation with God, it can be transformed by God into a forceful, potent, and virile agent in its relation to nature. Cleansed of contamination, the mind can be impregnated by God and, in that act, virilized: made potent and capable of generating virile offspring in its union with Nature.[35]

The mutual exclusivity of mind and body has important consequences. While Plato and Aristotle viewed the "soul" as a principle of life, for Descartes the "life" of the body is a matter of purely mechanical functioning. Indeed, he sees the difference between the body of a living man and that of a dead man to be analogous to the difference between a clock that is wound up and running well and one that is broken and unable to work. The knower, for Descartes, is without a body. As such not only does it have "no need of any place,"[36] but it actually *is* "no place." Precisely because the knower is not, insofar as s/he is a *pure* knower, trapped in a body, s/he does not bring a *perspective* to knowledge, does not bring any biases, but is rather completely neutral and unbiased. S/he has, as one might put it, "a God's eye view" of the objects of knowledge, or as the twentieth-century philosopher Thomas Nagel puts it, "a view from nowhere." This is the ideal of objectivity in the Cartesian tradition. Susan Bordo points out that

> not only, in this way, is the spectre of "subjectivity" laid to rest, but the very impersonality of the post-Copernican universe is turned to human advantage. For impersonality has become the mark of the truth of the known. Resistant to human will, immune to every effort of the knower to make it what *he* would have it be rather than what it "is," purified of all "inessential" spiritual associations and connections with the rest of the universe, the clear and distinct idea is both compensation for and conqueror of the cold, new world.[37]

Bordo suggests that one might even see the possibility of objectivity Descartes describes as a kind of *rebirth*.[38] In freeing oneself from the senses one is born again, this time as an objective observer and knower. One's first birth is as a separate entity, no longer continuous with the universe as humans were in the Middle Ages. The second birth, freeing one of the senses and therefore of all bias, secures the boundaries between the "inner" and the "outer," between self and world.

By separating the spiritual and the corporeal into two utterly distinct substances Descartes also makes the natural world and the human world completely separate. The world, nature, is totally devoid of mind and thought. Nature can only be grasped by measurement rather than by sympathy. One can now look to a "cool, impersonal, distanced cognitive relation to the world. At the same time, the nightmare landscape of the infinite universe has become the well-lighted laboratory of modern science and philosophy."[39]

By the time Immanuel Kant was writing, more than one hundred years after Descartes, the separation between subject and object was no longer something to be established or discovered, as it was for Descartes; it is rather the *foundation* of human cognition. For Kant knowledge *depends* upon this distinction between subject and object. Without it knowledge simply is not possible. What could it mean to *know* something if there is no knower and no separate object to be known? This is even a question when it comes to *self*-knowledge. To know oneself one must make oneself into an object—an object of knowledge. Since Kant, unless there is this absolute separation there is no knowledge at all. To say that we know something is to first separate ourselves from it. What Descartes described and argued for has now become the very condition for the possibility of knowledge. The consequences of this, both to the natural environment and to *everything* on which the mind brings its knowing faculty to bear, should by now be clear. The project of coming to know the world, of coming to *know* anything, is one that keeps us apart from it. And the goal of objectivity, as it is understood in the Cartesian tradition, places a very strong *value* on this. To the extent that we are not separate from the objects we study we are, at the very least, biased and, depending on how unseparated we are from the objects, we might not be said to have any sort of knowledge at all. This ultimately leaves our understanding onesided and partial and brings with it attitudes and values that seem to be at odds with the goals of environmentalism. It would appear that what is needed is a new epistemology, a new vision of knowledge and of objectivity.

NEW KINDS OF OBJECTIVITY AND KNOWLEDGE

Contemporary feminist writers have argued that one should look for a natural foundation for knowledge not in detachment and distance but in closeness, connectedness, and empathy. For them the failure of connection, not the blurring of boundaries, as the scientistic view would have it, is the principal cause of breakdown of understanding. This view, of course, is not new and echoes many aspects of the way of knowing that characterized the organic view. These traits have often been linked to the feminine both by defenders of the organic view in the

Renaissance, such as Paracelsus, and by some feminists today. The scientistic view has similarly been linked to the masculine both by the defenders of mechanism and the scientific method such as Bacon and by some contemporary feminists. Up through the nineteenth century, and even far into the twentieth, this equating of these two kinds of knowing with masculine and feminine was used to keep the feminine in its own sphere. With the ascendancy of mechanism and its accompanying epistemology "feminine" modes of knowing were excluded from the realm of knowledge altogether. To count as knowing something at all one must adopt the masculine attitude and epistemology of the mechanistic Cartesian view. While some have argued that the only way to overcome the Cartesian view, which leaves us so separate from the world, is to establish the philosophical and scientific legitimacy of alternative modes of knowing in the public arena, this is not enough. These modes of knowing must be united with the more "masculine" modes in every person so that no one is strictly a thinker of one kind or another. A first step, of course, is to establish the legitimacy of alternative modes of knowing, but that would not be enough.

What is proposed here is a speculative view of rationality that would reunite reason and emotion, mind and body, subject and object, reflection and action, theory and practice into a *mediated* unity rather than the immediate one that characterizes much of traditional organic thinking. This unity would involve recognizing that one always brings oneself to the inquiry in which one is engaged and would embrace this rather than trying to escape from it. By recognizing this people of the modern standpoint can move to what Sandra Harding has called "strong objectivity," because while they now recognize that they inevitably and always bring themselves to the inquiry people can now, and indeed must now, listen to others and hear and see their perspectives. This view of rationality would necessitate that inquiry always ultimately be group inquiry where many diverse individual standpoints are brought to bear on the object under study. While science, as it is practiced today, is a social activity, its epistemology assumes a single rational mind that if everyone follows the right procedures anyone can attain. The scientistic stance eschews the value of standpoints in knowledge as *subjectivity and bias.* The sort of rationality proposed here would also necessitate a kind of *involvement* with the objects of study rather than dispassionate observation.[40] Moreover, this notion of rationality could no longer hold the individual thinker as the primary locus of knowledge, but would have to recognize the community as that locus. This will also involve rejecting and overcoming a certain kind of hubris that goes with traditional notions of objectivity—the kind of hubris that can lead to the assumption that *my* perspective is *all* perspectives because I brought none of *myself* to this study, because I was *objective*. The attitude we need to adopt might be called "effective humility."

This "effective humility" has been present, but marginalized and suppressed, in the Western philosophical tradition for at least the last 2500 years. It was first and perhaps best expressed by Heraclitus who said that in order to know the whole, the true, the universal, the Logos, "one must talk about everything according to its [particular] nature, *how* it comes to be and how it grows. People have talked about the world without paying attention to the world or to their own minds as if they were asleep or absent minded." The overcoming of traditional "scientific" objectivity and the development of a strong objectivity, or what Evelyn Fox Keller calls "dynamic objectivity," thus involves a kind of self-forgetting or momentary *letting go* of the self, even while one recognizes what the self brings to the inquiry and the object. But it must also be a *momentary* self-forgetting, for were it a permanent self-loss there would be no knowledge at all, indeed no thought of which one could speak. In other words it is not suggested that the self/world distinction be simply done away with. Rather, the suggestion is that it be part of a dynamic movement and that the *conversation* required when only communities can be truly objective knowers requires both a self-forgetting and a kind of self-confidence. There is a sense in which the Cartesian tradition and the "masculine" way of knowing to which it gives rise promote weak selves—there is a certain loss of self that is feared. This is why the lines between the "inside" and the "outside" must be drawn so strongly. This new way of knowing will require strong selves—selves strong enough to yield to other selves in a community of inquiry, seeing all the standpoints brought to bear on the object of study, and to the object itself.

One might see the epistemological shift suggested here as one from "epistemic capitalism" to "epistemic communism." This chapter has already discussed the link between the growing commercial capitalism and the mechanical worldview. "Epistemic capitalism" would be characterized by the view that knowledge and thinking are things one does alone and involves a concomitant strong notion of intellectual private property. "Epistemic communism" would be based on the idea that all knowledge, even self-knowledge, is a social rather than individual achievement, that thinking is not something to be done alone, and that objectivity can only be achieved through the open sharing of ideas and standpoints. This is not to say that all perspectives would be accepted uncritically in a sort of mushy relativism wherein all ideas are equally valuable; rather it would mean that all ideas would be examined by the community and all standpoints taken seriously when a group is engaged in the endeavor of trying to know something. It would involve the hard work of listening to those who may be uncredentialled and have nonstandard forms of knowledge and this is where the need to validate other ways of knowing becomes a necessary precursor to the larger epistemological change suggested here.

Evelyn Fox Keller, for example, defines objectivity as "the pursuit of a maximally authentic, and hence maximally reliable, understanding of the world around oneself."[41] In advocating "dynamic objectivity" to reach this goal Keller aims at "a form of knowledge that grants to the world around us its independent integrity but does so in a way that remains cognizant of, indeed relies on, our connectivity with that world." It involves a *disentangling* of the subject from the object rather than *severing* the subject from the object. The capacity for this "requires a sense of self secure enough to tolerate both difference and continuity." She considers dynamic objectivity to be

> a pursuit of knowledge that makes use of subjective experience . . . in the interests of a more effective objectivity. Premised on continuity, it recognizes difference between self and other as an opportunity for a deeper and more articulated kinship. The struggle to disentangle self from other is itself a source of insight—potentially into the nature of both self and other. It is a principal means for divining what Poincaré calls "hidden harmonies and relations." To this end, the scientist employs a form of attention to the natural world that is like one's ideal attention to the human world: it is a form of love.[42]

The epistemological stance of those working in the sciences today is one in which "the scientific mind is set apart from what is to be known, i.e., from nature, and its autonomy is guaranteed . . . by setting apart its modes of knowing from those in which the dichotomy is threatened."[43] What one needs if one is to approach a problem scientifically are autonomy, separation, and distance. There must be a radical rejection of any commingling of subject and object. By following the methods laid out by the founders of modern science, by adopting this kind of epistemology, one is supposed to attain a cleaner, purer, more objective and disciplined epistemological relation to the world.

Keller uses as her example of this different way of knowing biologist Barbara McClintock, who felt an emotional connection to the corn she studied. She had, as the title of Keller's biography of her suggests, *A Feeling for the Organism*. One could also look to primatologist Jane Goodall or anthropologist Tanya Luhrmann as examples of scientists who have established connections to their objects of study that have prompted some to accuse them of losing objectivity, but that have given them a much deeper understanding of their subjects than the methods that ensure "objectivity" would allow. However, for a model scientist who has striven for this kind of unity with the world while maintaining his scientific stance when necessary it is perhaps more appropriate to look closer to home at the epistemological spirit of the physicist to whom this volume is dedicated. In the very way he lived his life Tom McGlinn united love and knowledge in the way Keller seems to be suggesting. For him knowledge was not about gaining power over nature, but rather understanding nature because it is so incredible and wonderful. This understanding took place not only on the more Cartesian level of learning natural laws and how they applied to various phenomena but also on the emotional and personal level of dwelling in the world and becoming one with it. For him, for example, part of the joy of fly fishing was to become one with the river. Mountain climbing was not about the challenge of man or woman against nature; it was rather about existing with the mountain, knowing it on its own terms, feeling it, and being a part of it—to be filled with wonder at it. One loses oneself temporarily that way, though one returns to oneself later to reach understanding that is communicable, in McGlinn's case not just as a physics professor but also as one with a sense of wonder at the world. Rather than knowledge as power, for him knowledge was a form of love. That is the spirit scientists and all people need to bring to their efforts to know differently and one reason why dedicating this book to his memory is so appropriate.

As this example shows, the standpoint of connection would involve not just knowing, but also *feeling* the object. Connection occurs not primarily on the cognitive level, but on the affective and emotional levels.

There are certain dangers involved in any specific description of a world characterized by this new epistemology. Utopian thinking can foreclose unforeseen possibilities and we need to remain open to all the potential. Since this epistemology is not yet operative in a way that would impact a general ethics one can only broadly conceive of what the impact on ethics would be. It becomes more difficult because the metaphors one might use for this kind of connectivity are already infected with presuppositions of modern epistemology. One can, however, see that the feelings of empathy and connectivity that cause us to wince when a person one cares about, or anyone with whom one can empathize, is hurt would give us a different relation to creation if one winces when *it* is hurt. Just as in people the hurt is sometimes necessary (e.g., in setting a broken leg), so too it may be necessary in dealing with the natural world and with people from whom one is more removed. If people feel that same kind of empathy that they do for particular other people, however, far more care and consideration will be given to one's actions.

This feeling of empathy could not involve a reversion to a feeling of oneness with the world in the absence of any separation at all, for then people would not be aware of the possible harm they cause. On the other hand, the traditional epistemological position, by excluding so many standpoints, does not achieve the objectivity it purports to and is unable to reach an awareness of all the harms a particular action might bring about. One must feel the other, the object of knowledge. In this there is no separation between the knower and the known. When one returns to oneself to decide upon a course of action one brings a more intimate knowledge with him or her. This knowledge is not simply cognitive, but deeper and fuller—a felt knowledge. One does not simply know that one is connected to all of creation in the sense of assenting to the proposition "I am connected to all of creation." Rather one feels and lives this connection. Many people experience this deeper knowledge in a passing way when they say that a novel or an experience "changed their lives." Usually it is not that they learn some proposition they did not know before. It is instead that they *feel* the truth of it. Sometimes people articulate this as going from *believing* something is true to *knowing* that it is true. Yet this kind of knowing seems to violate the rules of rational discourse in that no one who has not had a similar experience can know what you know. They can "know" the proposition and assent to it, but the deeper knowledge can be shared only, if at all, through such things as literature, not through logical or empirical proof. Unfortunately to the modern mind this tends to sound flaky and mystical, but that too may be a part of modern epistemology that needs to be overcome.

Some have argued that the need to *dominate* nature we see so clearly in the writings of early modern philosophers and scientists such as Bacon and Poincaré arises out of anxiety and impotence in the face of a nature that seems powerful, vast (even infinite), and chaotic. What about the epistemological style that grew out of this? Those who practice it may well not feel anxious or impotent and their goal may well not be to dominate nature. Nonetheless the epistemology that those in the west have all grown up with, the "correct" way to go about finding things out, to go about attaining knowledge, emerges from this. People, albeit unintentionally, adopt an epistemology as a result of their education that often leads them to places they do not intend to go and at which they may not even realize they have arrived. Indeed, they may think that they are not going there at all. But the danger of working with this prevailing epistemological structure, even when one engages in environmental science or ecology, is that, to borrow a turn of phrase from *The Godfather,* "just when we think we're out, it keeps dragging us back in."

Susan Bordo and others believe that newer modes of thinking and conceptions of rationality, intelligence, and "good thinking" offer more humane and more hopeful approaches to science and ethics. The suggestions offered in this chapter as to how they may impact action and thus ethics support this view. Yet there is certainly considerably more work to be done to make such new approaches a reality. This is a challenge that philosophers today and in the future must work to meet if we in the West are not to continually replicate the environmental problems that already exist in other forms by continuing to engage in knowing the world in ways that separate us from it, and that continually make a radical separation between the inside and the outside, between consciousness or self and world, between knower and object known. Until those within the Western tradition are able to work within a new epistemological framework, or at least to recognize the limitations of the one within which we currently operate, we will continually be dragged back into the habit of separation and so to the same basic mistakes that led to the environmental crisis the world now faces. At the very least people must become aware of the epistemology within which they work and think so that they may be aware of the dangers and mistakes to which it predisposes them.

CONCLUSION AND THEOLOGICAL REFLECTION

Several theological reflections emerge from this chapter. Part of the contemporary project of dealing with our environmental problems has been the effort of uncovering the historical antecedents to our current crisis. The question, "How did we humans get ourselves into this environmental fix?" continues to be a legitimate issue of inquiry. This chapter, from a historical-philosophical view, boldly argues that the epistemological foundation of modern science is partly responsible for our environmental crisis. Tracing the historical developments to Bacon and Descartes, the author suggests that the emphasis on "objectivity" and the strict dichotomy between subject and object had the unforeseen consequences of accelerating or exacerbating the human species' growing estrangement from the natural world. From a theological viewpoint one could say that the emergence of modern science, with its canon of objectivity, assisted in the transformation of the pre-scientific experience of the natural world as creation into the post-modern experience of nature as an object for scientific scrutiny. In so doing science, in combination with a host of other human endeavors including religion, has inadvertently contributed to our alienation from the natural world.[44]

The solution proposed herein is the development of a new mode of knowing that is more feminine in nature and characterized by four distinguishing attributes. First, this new epistemology emphasizes "connectivity" and involvement between knowing subject and what is known. In other words, knowledge is the byproduct of an engaged and relational approach to the natural world. Second, the community out of which knowledge arises is the "primary locus" and ultimate arbiter of genuine knowledge. Third, this epistemological approach to the natural world is an expression of love. That is, knowing the world is a passionate enterprise and there is a legitimate role for the affections. Finally, this paradigm for knowledge has ethical implications. A relational approach to knowing the natural world can easily translate to empathy with and concern for it leading to a sense of moral obligation and duty.[45]

This epistemological alternative to the objective, bifurcating tendency of traditional scientific knowledge bears striking similarity to the notion of "knowing" in the Hebrew worldview of the Old Testament. *Yādaᶜ* is the Hebrew verb "to know." Within the Hebrew thought-world *yādaᶜ* does not connote objective intellectual knowledge. Rather it is a form of knowledge that is "from the heart" and is deeply experiential. According to Thomas Groome *yādaᶜ* is more by the heart than by the mind, and the knowing arises not by standing back from in order to look at, but by active and intentional engagement in lived experience.[46] The relational and experiential character of *yādaᶜ* is probably best observed in its usage for making love and friendship (see Gen 4:1, 25; Ps 31:18). Knowledge in this context is the result of intimate personal relatedness. Furthermore, *yādaᶜ*, when linked to the "knowledge of the

Lord," embodies ethical action. Groome writes that "knowledge of the Lord demands active acknowledgement of the Lord, and that in turn requires obedience to God's will."[47] In other words, to know God is to do God's will and in the doing of God's will God is known.[48]

The cultural backdrop of this biblical epistemology is a worldview of interrelatedness, what Douglas John Hall has referred to as an "ontology of communion."[49] In this perspective God, human, and earth are, "according to biblical faith . . . inextricably bound up with one another."[50] The relationality or connectivity of creation is reflected in the ancient Hebrew understanding of knowing. The task in the modern era of the twenty-first century is to recapture, if possible, this old yet new posture of knowing creation.[51]

NOTES: CHAPTER 2

[1] The gendered pronouns are no accident. Nature was conceived as female and the metaphors used to describe the male scientist knowing her reflect a misogyny deep in the culture of the time, one that helped women to be there to be conquered and controlled by men lest their chaotic nature cause havoc otherwise. Bacon even went so far as to talk of a "virile" and "masculine" science as an ideal in his work *The Masculine Birth of Time.*

[2] It is not at the basis of some large areas of science today, such as community-level ecology, chaos theory, and epiphenomena. Nonetheless, because it structures our attitudes toward knowledge *per se* it has a continuing influence on even those who in their scientific practice do not appear to be mechanistic.

[3] The Royal Society, originally known as the Royal Society of London, was founded as an organization to defend and promote the "new science" based on experiment rather than appeals to authority. It continues today to promote the natural and applied sciences and has as its mission to recognize excellence in science, promote independent, authoritative advice to government, inform public debate on science, encourage research and its application, foster public understanding of science, and act as a forum and focus for discussion of issues relating to the wider scientific community.

[4] Owen Barfield, *Saving the Appearances: A Study in Idolatry* (New York: Harcourt Brace & World, [1965?]) 78, as quoted in Susan Bordo, *The Flight to Objectivity: Essays on Cartesianism and Culture* (Albany: SUNY Press, 1987) 53.

[5] Carolyn Merchant, *The Death of Nature: Women, Ecology and the Scientific Revolution* (San Francisco: HarperCollins, 1980) 48.

[6] Ibid. 109.

[7] See, e.g., Malcolm W. Browne, "Scientists Deplore the Flight from Reason," *New York Times* (June 6, 1995).

[8] Merchant, *The Death of Nature* 111.

[9] Ibid.

[10] Ibid. 125.

[11] Ibid. 127.

[12] Ibid. 129.

[13] Ibid. 169.

[14] Ibid. 172.

[15] Ibid.

[16] Ibid. 193.

[17] Ibid. 214.

[18] Ibid. 217.

[19] Ibid. 288.

[20] René Descartes to Marin Mersenne, 1630, as quoted in Merchant, *The Death of Nature* 205.

[21] Bordo, *The Flight to Objectivity* 49–50.

[22] Ibid. 50.

[23] Richard Rorty, *Philosophy and the Mirror of Nature* (Princeton: Princeton University Press, 1979) 47.

[24] Bordo, *The Flight to Objectivity* 50.

[25] Ibid.

[26] Ibid. 51.

[27] Ibid. 52.

[28] Arthur Koestler, *The Sleepwalkers* (New York: Grosset & Dunlap, 1959) 19.

[29] Bordo, *The Flight to Objectivity* 71.

[30] Ibid. 75.

[31] Ibid. 76.

[32] Ibid.

[33] Ibid. 78.

[34] Ibid. 88.

[35] Evelyn Fox Keller, *Reflections on Gender and Science* (New Haven: Yale University Press, 1985) 38. Bacon is arguing for the birth of what he calls "masculine science."

[36] René Descartes, *Philosophical Works.* Vols. I and II, edited by Elizabeth Haldane and G.R.T. Ross (Cambridge: Cambridge University Press, 1969) 101.

[37] Bordo, *The Flight to Objectivity* 95.

[38] Ibid. 97.

[39] Ibid. 99.

[40] Evelyn Fox Keller gives a striking example of this in her biography of biologist Barbara McClintock (Evelyn Fox Keller, *A Feeling for the Organism: The Life and Work of Barbara McClintock* [New York: W. H. Freeman, 1983]).

[41] Keller, *Reflections on Gender and Science* 117.

[42] Ibid.

[43] Ibid. 79.

[44] Regarding the role of religion see the now famous (or infamous) essay by Lynn White Jr., "The Historical Roots of Our Ecologic Crisis," in Ian G. Barbour, ed., *Western Man and Environmental Ethics* (Reading, Mass.: Addison-Wesley, 1973) 18–30. In the article, written in 1967, White claims that the Judeo-Christian tradition is the primary cause of our environmental crisis.

[45] This model of epistemology has much in common with Aldo Leopold's "The Land Ethic." In his philosophical-ethical extrapolation from the science of ecology Leopold writes: "We abuse land because we regard it as a commodity belonging to us. When we see land as a community to which we belong, we may begin to see it with love and respect." For a concise treatment of the land ethic see Aldo Leopold, *A Sand County Almanac and Sketches Here and There* (New York: Oxford University Press, 1949) 201–26.

[46] Thomas Groome, *Christian Religious Education* (San Francisco: Harper & Row, 1980) 141.

[47] Ibid.

[48] This idea forms the very heart of Hosea's prophetic discourse in Hosea 4:1-3 where he proclaims that there is "no knowledge of God in the land." The consequence is moral chaos, which, interestingly, causes the land to mourn, and everything that dwells in it to languish.

[49] Douglas John Hall, *Imaging God* (Grand Rapids: Eerdmans, 1986) 119.

[50] Ibid. 129.

[51] It is significant to note that in biblical Hebrew there is no separate word for nature referring to the natural order outside humanity. According to Bruce Birch, "We are already implying a dichotomy in our use of the word nature that the Hebrews did not recognize. Each order has its name but all (human and nonhuman, animate and inanimate) were part of the single creation of God." See Bruce C. Birch and Larry L. Rassmussen, *The Predicament of the Prosperous* (Philadelphia: Westminster, 1978) 118.

3

An Islamic Perspective on the Environment

"The Lord God took the human being and put the person in the garden of Eden to till it and keep it." (Gen 2:15)

*T*he biblical account of the creation story in Genesis 1–2 reveals to readers that one of the first tasks given to human beings by God is to till and care for the land. This brief verse from Genesis has been foundational for developing an understanding of the concept of stewardship in many Jewish and Christian circles today. However, respect and care for the earth and all its creatures do not represent a vision and challenge germane to Judaism and Christianity alone. It is central to the Islamic tradition and sacred writing as well, as evidenced by the Qur'an 2:164.

> Behold! in the creation of the heavens and the earth; in the alternation of the night and the day; in the sailing of the ships through the ocean for the profit of humankind; in the rain which Allah sends down from the skies, and the life which He gives therewith, to an earth that is dead; in the beasts of all kinds that He scatters through the earth, in the change of the winds, and the clouds which they trail like their slaves between the sky and the earth; here indeed are signs for people who are wise.

INTRODUCTION

In a discussion of the Islamic perspective on the environment and its preservation the Islamic theory of knowledge and a Muslim's approach to problem-solving should be considered first. The reason for doing this at the outset is to delineate the differences between the rationalistic and reductionist approaches of Western thinking on the one hand and the more holistic and "organic" Islamic thinking on the other.

It is now well documented in the literature of various disciplines that Eastern thinking is shaped by global and all-encompassing perspectives while Western thinking is considerably more linear in its approach to problem-solving. It is this difference in worldviews that has given rise to different paths taken by the nations of the East versus those of the West in their different approaches to science and technology throughout the ages.

The Islamic theory of knowledge removes contradictions between science, philosophy, and religion. The holy book of Islam, the Qur'an, requires Muslims to seek knowledge to serve two purposes, one divine and the other mundane. The divine purpose is to study nature as the handiwork of Allah (God), looking at the universe carefully and minutely to become cognizant of the hand that guides and controls all worldly happenings. The mundane purpose is to use this knowledge for the benefit of humankind and to subjugate the forces of nature for this purpose. Thus a proficiency in pure and applied sciences as well as a firm grounding in religion and philosophy are prerequisites for being a "knowledgeable" person in the Islamic way of thinking. Indeed, for a Muslim science, philosophy, and religion are like three concentric spheres, one fitting inside the other. The smallest sphere represents science, which deals with the quantifiable and the measurable, the intermediate one philosophy, and the largest sphere religion, which encompasses the study of philosophy and its progeny, science.

Islam thus brought a more organic and integrated view of knowledge and achieved a balance between the deductive and inductive methods of acquiring knowledge. This was quite different from the Greeks, for example, who were enamored of the deductive method and thus influenced the minds of generations after them in a pro-deductive fashion. The history of Europe from the early Greeks to the beginning of the seventeenth century is a long and continuous tale of the neglect of observation and experimentation and the exaltation of pure reflection and discursive reasoning over everything else. This tendency, though extremely useful in the early stages of human civilization, proved to be a hindrance when physical sciences reared their head. It was at this time that Francis Bacon (1561–1626) felt the need for a new instrument of inquiry—*Novum Organum*—to replace the old instrument of inquiry, the *Organum* of Aristotle. This new approach depended heavily on experimentation and empirical observations and was quite similar to what the Muslims had been doing for the past several centuries in various fields of inquiry.

The term "Islamic Science" embraces a wide spectrum of intellectual activity, from the study of plants to algebra, carried out over more than a millennium by many races and peoples spread over a good part of the globe from Spain and Morocco to Central Asia. Its extensive influence upon the Latin and Renaissance West has, in the last two centuries, caused many studies in European languages to be devoted to the various facets of Islamic science.

The unifying perspective of Islam has never allowed various forms of knowledge to be cultivated independently and there has been a certain hierarchy of knowledge in which every form of knowledge, from that of material substances to the highest metaphysics, is organically interrelated, reflecting the unity of Reality itself. Thus the study of nature for a Muslim is not the study of small "shards" of reality but an exercise in contemplating the whole reality, looking at all the connections between these smaller pieces and how they fit into this "organic whole."

ISLAMIC ENVIRONMENTAL ETHICS

Islamic environmental ethics, like other forms of ethics in Islam, is based on clearly defined legal foundations that Muslims hold to be formulated by Allah. Thus there is no dichotomy or split between what is "legal" and what is "ethical," since they are essentially the same. This concept is quite different from the process used in some other cultures where the laws may be based on humanistic philosophies, as for example in the British penal code. The Arabic word used for the law is "Shari'ah," which literally means "source of water." Since water is the "source of all living things," as the Qur'an proclaims, so Shari'ah is the lifeblood that contains both legal rules and ethical principles for living a "good life" in a moral and spiritual sense. This is borne out by the division of Shari'ah relevant to human action into the following five categories:

- Wajib (Obligatory Actions): Actions a Muslim is required to perform.
- Mandub (Devotional and Ethical Virtues): Actions a Muslim is encouraged to perform. Nonobservance of these actions, however, incurs no liability.

- Mubah (Permissible Actions): Actions in which a Muslim is given complete freedom of choice.
- Makruh (Abominable Actions): Actions that are morally, but not legally wrong.
- Haram (Prohibited Actions): All those actions and practices that are forbidden by Islam.

In Islam, then, the conservation of the environment is based on the notion that all individual components of the environment were created by Allah for the sustenance of humankind and other creatures on this planet and that there is a meticulous and optimum balance between these components. The Qur'an makes powerful references to this "due balance" at various places in its text. For example:

> And the earth We have spread out like a carpet; set thereon mountains firm and immovable; and produced therein all kinds of things in due balance. And We have provided therein means of subsistence for you, and for those for whose subsistence ye are not responsible. [Qur'an, 15:19-20]

The legal and ethical reasons for protecting the environment can thus be summarized as follows:

1. The environment is Allah's creation and to protect it is to protect its value as a sign of the Creator. It is interesting to note here that the Arabic word "Ayat" is used to connote both the verses of the Qur'an and "the signs" of the Creator all around. Hence, in order to gain wisdom one must look at and study both kinds of signs.

2. The various parts of nature are in continuous praise and supplication of their Creator although human beings may not be able to understand their form of supplication. As the Qur'an describes it:

   > "The seven heavens and the earth and all that is in between praise Him, and there is not such a thing but sings His praise; but ye understand not their praise. Lo! He is ever Merciful and Forgiving." [Qur'an, 17:44]

3. All laws of nature are laws made by Allah and based on the absolute continuity of existence and utmost balance in nature. Attempts to break this natural law of Allah (Sunnah) must be prevented.

   > "Everything with Him is measured." [Qur'an, 13:8]

   > "There is not a thing but with Us are the stores thereof, and We send it not down save in appointed measure." [Qur'an, 15:21]

4. The Qur'an explains at many places that humankind is not the only community living on this planet and that it shares this abode with other living things that also form their own communities.

> "There is not an animal in the earth, nor a flying creature flying on two wings, but they are peoples like unto you." [Qur'an, 6:38]

Passages like these in the Qur'an simply mean that while the human race may have the power to change or even destroy this fragile planet at this time it actually shares this home with a lot of other "peoples" and "communities" that are as worthy of respect and protection as the human community.

5. Islamic environmental ethics is based on the concept of justice (*'adl*) and equity (*ihsan*) in all kinds of relationships.

> "Lo! Allah enjoins justice and kindness." [Qur'an, 16:90]

Hence the tradition limits even the benefits to the human race derived at the expense of animal suffering.

6. The environment is not in the service of the present generation only. Rather it is the gift of Allah to generations of all creatures, past, present, and future. This can be understood from the general meaning of the following verse:

> "He it is Who created for you all that is in the earth." [Qur'an, 2:29]

The word "you" here refers to all ages—past, present, and future—with no limits put on time or place.

7. No other creature is able to perform the task of protecting the environment. Allah entrusted the human race with the duty of vice-regency, a duty so difficult and onerous that no other creature would accept it!

> "Lo! We offered the trust unto the heavens and the earth and the hills, but they shrank from bearing it and were afraid of it. And man assumed it!" [Qur'an, 33:72]

So, as can be seen from the foregoing points, ethics in Islam is not based on separate, scattered virtues but is part of a total, comprehensive way of life that controls and guides all human activity. Islamic ethical values are based not on human reasoning, as Aristotle claimed, nor on what the society imposes on the individual, as Emile Durkheim thought, nor on the interests of a certain class or group of people, as Marxists maintain. In each of these instances values are affected by circumstances. In Islam ethical values are those without which neither the individual nor the society at large can be sustained. This position is based on the basic tenets of Islam according to which the human being has been created by Allah and hence He alone knows fully the nature of humankind. Thus Allah alone is in a position to prescribe the right kind of behavior that is congruent with human nature.

According to the Islamic way of thinking, then, the role of the human race on this planet is that of a caretaker and responsible husband of all the creatures and the world's resources. This whole system was created "in due balance" and it must remain so after the wave of human activity has passed by. Islam does permit the utilization of natural resources that Allah has provided for the benefit of humankind, but this utilization must not be at the scale we see today, which seems to be pointing in the direction of total destruction and plunder. Overindulgence and squandering are strongly discouraged in Islam. As the Qur'an says:

> "O children of Adam! Look to your adornment at every place of worship, and eat and drink, but be not prodigal.
>
> Lo! He loveth not the prodigals." [Qur'an, 7:31]

In this passage "eating and drinking" refers to the utilization of earthly resources, but this utilization is not without controls. The various components of this mosaic of resources have to be used and protected in such a way that they continue to provide sustenance for the generations to come. In other words, Islam voted for "sustainable development" many centuries before this term became popular.

One *hadith* (saying of the prophet Muhammad) drives this point home in a very succinct way. He once said: "When doomsday comes, if someone has a palm shoot in his hand, he should plant it." This *hadith* points to the crux of Islamic environmental ethics. Even when all hope is lost planting should continue, for planting is good in itself! Moreover, planting should be done to continue the process of life even if one does not have any hope of deriving personal benefit from it.

The concept of charity in Islam goes together with sustainable development as well, since charity is not only for the present generation but also for those who will follow in due time. A story about the second caliph of Islam, Umar ibn al-Khattab, elucidates this point. He once noticed that an old man in the community had neglected his land. Umar asked why he was not cultivating his land and received the answer, "I am old and expect to die soon." Hearing this, Umar insisted that he should plant it and provided the physical help himself which the old man needed to cultivate the land.

ENVIRONMENTAL ETHICS IN PRACTICE

As stated in the earlier sections of this chapter, Islam brings an integrated approach to science, technology, environmental issues, and indeed to life. This attitude, when it was practiced to its fullest extent, had a great influence on the development of individual Muslim communities and their policymaking. Two concepts will be mentioned here as examples of how a community of Muslims is supposed to bring sustainable development into everyday practice by observing some simple rules.

The first concept is the idea of *"hima,"* which is essentially the protection of certain zones from the encroaching demands on resources. This idea, which has existed from the time of Prophet Muhammad, involves strict regulations by which a certain unused piece of land may be termed as "protected" and set aside for the welfare of the people. This area can then be used for purposes such as a wildlife refuge, limited grazing by the cattle of poor people, etcetera.

The second concept is that of *"harim,"* which is along the same lines as *hima* in that it is an inviolable zone that may not be used or developed unless specific permission is granted by the state. This zone or *harim* is usually defined in conjunction with wells, natural springs, underground water channels, rivers, and the like. Apparently this protective zone would keep pollution and contamination of the water table to a minimum since the administration of *harim* was done in a careful and strict manner in the Muslim communities of the past. It should be noted here that until recently the achievements of Western science and technology so mesmerized Muslim nations that every new invention was welcomed with enthusiasm without any regard to its environmental impact.

Lately, however, many outstanding intellectuals from several Muslim nations have spoken against this blind faith and have asked Muslims to reexamine these situations in the light of traditional wisdom. Phrases like "appropriate technology," "Islamic science," and the like are being used more and more to describe a departure from the conventional Western science where science rules supreme and is not "bothered" by the philosophical or religious angles.

THE BIRTH AND DEATH OF A PLANET

The Qur'an has passages scattered throughout the text that deal with the creation and eventual death of the planet Earth. Whether this "death" of the planet is only symbolic, referring to our making it unin-habitable through our own actions, or is a real cataclysm in which Earth will cease to exist as we know it, only time will tell. But it is important to bring in the Qur'anic concepts here in the hope that the reader will find it alarming enough to look deeper into our relationship with the rest of creation and this fragile abode called "Earth."

First one needs to look into how the creation of the universe and Earth is described in the Qur'an. Some of the relevant passages are quoted here without any attempt to expand much on the Qur'anic text.

> "Your Lord is Allah Who created the heavens and the earth in six days." [Qur'an, 7:54]

The "days" here are explained at various places in the Qur'an as "very long periods" (thousand years, fifty thousand years, etc.).

> "Say: Do you disbelieve Him Who created the earth in two periods? Do you ascribe equals to Him? He is the Lord of the Worlds. He set in the earth mountains standing firm. He blessed it. He measured therein its sustenance in four periods, in due proportions, in accordance with the needs of those who ask for sustenance. Moreover, He turned to heaven when it was smoke and said to it and to the earth: come willingly or un-willingly! They said: we come in willing obedience. Then He ordained them seven heavens in two periods, and He assigned to each heaven its mandate by Revelation. And We adorned the lower heaven with luminar-ies and provided it a guard. Such is the decree of the All Mighty, the Full of Knowledge." [Qur'an, 41:9-12]

It should be kept in mind that the Qur'an is not implying some sort of a sequence of events in these verses. Rather it is mentioning the states of the heavens and earth at the time of creation and how life and other things might have evolved on this planet in gradual stages. Some other verses that refer to the early stages of creation and the expanding uni-verse are as follows:

> "Do not the Unbelievers see that the heavens and the earth were joined together, then We clove them asunder and We got every living thing out of water. Will they not then believe?" [Qur'an, 21:30]

> "The heaven, We have built it with power. Verily, we are expanding it." [Qur'an, 51:47]

There are many more verses that go deeper into the creation of other heavenly bodies, such as the moon and the sun and other astronomical phenomena. But for the sake of brevity this discussion is limited to the verses already mentioned. After this auspicious beginning of the universe and the earth Allah sends down His bounty "in due balance" and provides "subsistence to you and to those for whose subsistence ye are not responsible." Such is the imagery that a Muslim brings to his/her appreciation for the bounties of this earth and its beauty. There is a sense of awe and a deep respect and love for the creatures on this planet and the things provided for them by Allah.

Unfortunately the belief in technology and "techno-fixes" for the gravity of the environmental problems that we face is so profound that very few people are willing to look into the more obvious and much less risky ways of combating these "mega-problems." Not too many people, for example, suggest cutting down on the hedonistic levels of consumption in the developed countries. People have total faith in a system that promises continuous "progress" and quantum jumps in the standards of living for the coming generations. In spite of all the statistics and data now available that make it abundantly clear that we cannot go on with a "business as usual" attitude about the environment, the earth, and our relationship to it a great majority of people are still going about living their lives in the same old ways of consumption and waste.

It is time for a paradigm shift. It is time to step back and look around us with that sense of awe that is due to this "beautiful blue marble" and find a sense of connection and our place in the scheme of things. Otherwise, who knows?—the Qur'anic predictions about the death of this planet may come true earlier than one would think or would like to believe. As the Qur'an says:

> "They see the Day (of reckoning) indeed as a far-off event. But We see it quite near. The Day that the sky will be like molten brass, and the mountains will be like wool." [Qur'an, 70:6-9]

> "When the sun, with its spacious light, is folded up, when the stars fall, losing their luster, when the mountains vanish (like a mirage)." [Qur'an, 81:1-3]

> "When the sky is cleft asunder; when the stars are scattered; when the oceans are suffered to burst forth; and when the graves are turned upside down; Then shall each soul know what it hath sent forward and what it hath kept back. O man! what has seduced thee from thy Lord, Most Beneficent?" [Qur'an, 82:1-6]

CONCLUSION AND THEOLOGICAL REFLECTION

It is appropriate to conclude this chapter with a beautiful passage from Seyyed Hossein Nasr's article entitled "Islam and the Environmental Crisis" in *Spirit and Nature: Why the Environment Is a Religious Issue:*

> The solution of the environmental crisis can come about only when the modern spiritual malaise is cured and there is a rediscovery of the world of the Spirit, which, being compassionate, always gives of Itself to those open and receptive to Its vivifying rays. The bounties of nature and its generosity to the human race are there as proofs of this reality, for despite all that we have done to destroy nature, she is still alive and reflects on her own ontological level the love and compassion, the wisdom and the power, which belong ultimately to the realm of the Spirit. And in this crisis of unprecedented proportions, it is nature as God's primordial creation that will have the final say.[1]

Huston Smith writes, "Islam is the most difficult religion for the West to understand." [2] This is due in large measure to the unfortunate fact that the relationship between the Christian West and Islam has been punctuated over the last fourteen hundred years by profound suspicion and hostility. The global environmental crisis may, however, provide a unique opportunity for interreligious dialogue and collaboration. From a theological perspective the destruction of the natural world reveals a fractured relationship between humans and the earth and is at its foundation a religious problem. Many of the world's religious leaders believe that the solution to the crisis lies not only in a wiser use of science and technology but in new earth-centered spiritualities and religious forms of practice that address the alienation within the household of God. Ironically the world's environmental problems may offer Christians and Muslims a ray of hope and a "silver lining" in what is otherwise a very dark cloud, to achieve a greater degree of mutual understanding as we continue life together in the twenty-first century.

"An Islamic Perspective on the Environment" ought to remind Christians, especially Catholics, of the significant step forward accomplished at the Second Vatican Council on the relationship between the Church and non-Christian religions. The bishops declared that "the Catholic Church rejects nothing of what is true and holy in these religions."[3] In a specific reference to Islam the bishops wrote: "The church has . . . a high regard for the Muslims" and urged Christians and Muslims: "let them together preserve and promote peace, liberty, social justice and moral values."[4] The theological and ethical nature of the environmental crisis provides Christians and Muslims with the "common cause" of safeguarding the natural world and promoting ecological justice. A solid basis for dialogue on this global issue exists in a common view of creation and stewardship.

For Christians and Muslims the theological foundation for protecting the natural world is grounded in a shared view of creation. This essay declares that "the environment is Allah's creation and to protect it is to protect its value as a sign of the Creator."[5] Consequently creation—because God created it—is endowed with inherent goodness and value. Moreover, the multiple forms of creation are "signs of the Creator all around."[6] Compare this to the U.S. Catholic bishops' assertion that creation is a "sacramental universe—a world which discloses the creator's presence by visible and tangible signs."[7] The view that creation is a sign of God offers Christians and Muslims a shared theological point of reference: that creation is a primary medium through which God is disclosed and encountered.

In addition to their common understanding of creation Christians and Muslims also agree on the role or vocation of humanity within the order of creation. According to Islam "Allah entrusted the human race with the duty of viceregency" and accordingly "the role of the human race on this planet is that of a caretaker and responsible husband of all the creatures and its resources."[8] This corresponds to the Judeo-Christian notion of stewardship, which also mandates ethical responsibility for earth and its creatures. The U.S. bishops write, "As faithful stewards, fullness of life comes from living responsibly within God's creation. . . . stewardship places upon us responsibility for the well-being of all God's creatures."[9] The commonality of vision between Christians and Muslims toward creation and the human role therein provides a potential commonality of purpose as humanity grapples with the global environmental crisis. This shared vision ought to establish a mutual basis for collaboration in the human responsibility of protecting and restoring the integrity of creation.

NOTES: CHAPTER 3

[1] Steven C. Rockefeller and John C. Elder, eds., *Spirit and Nature: Why the Environment Is a Religious Issue* (Boston: Beacon, 1992) 84–108.

² Huston Smith, *The World's Religions* (San Francisco: HarperCollins, 1991) 221.

³ "Declaration on the Relationship of the Church to Non-Christian Religions," in Austin Flannery, ed., *Vatican Council II: The Basic Sixteen Documents* (Northport, N.Y.: Costello, 1996) 570–71.

⁴ Ibid. 571–72.

⁵ See above, p. 49.

⁶ Ibid.

⁷ "Renewing the Earth," *Origins* (December 1991) 429.

⁸ See above, pp. 50–51.

⁹ "Renewing the Earth," 429.

4

Christian Values, Technology, and the Environmental Crisis

"You have given them dominion
over the work of your hands." (Ps 8:6)

*C*ontemplating the wonder of God and the dignity of the human creature, the psalmist proclaims:

When I look at your heavens, the work of your fingers,
    the moon and the stars that you have established;
what are human beings that you are mindful of them,
    mortals that you care for them?
Yet you have made them a little lower than God,
    and crowned them with glory and honor.
You have given them dominion over the works of your hands;
    you have put all things under their feet,
all sheep and oxen,
    and also the beasts of the field,
the birds of the air, and the fish of the sea,
    whatever passes along the paths of the seas.
O Lord, our Sovereign,
    how majestic is your name in all the earth! (Ps 8:3-9)

One of the key phrases in this text is "dominion." Human beings are to exercise dominion over the works of God's hands, and here "dominion" does not suggest "domination"; rather it connotes "care" and "respect." Human beings are to care for creation—human and non-human life—in the same way that God graciously cares for all creation as described so beautifully in Ps 104:1-30.

This attitude of "dominion" is nurtured by four virtues: simplicity, moderation, frugality, and gratitude. Together this attitude and way of life pose a challenge to the contemporary technological world and its environmental crisis.

INTRODUCTION

Much has been said about the environmental problems that threaten not only the integrity of the biosphere but also the wellbeing of future generations. In his January 1, 1990 homily Pope John Paul II asserted that the world is threatened "by a lack of due respect for nature, by the plundering of natural resources and by a progressive decline in the quality of life."[1] Contaminated waterways, polluting smokestacks, deforestation, toxic dumpsites, and oil-covered animals are all graphic reminders of the environmental damage human beings have done to the earth.

The litany of causes of environmental damage is becoming increasingly familiar to some: urbanization, growing population, overconsumption, economic growth, affluence, poverty, conflict, and ignorance of the interrelatedness of the global ecosystem. What is not as frequently acknowledged is that the relationship of humans to the rest of creation has changed dramatically since the turn of the twentieth century. According to Larry Rasmussen the power of human technology to significantly alter planetary life systems is the highlight of that change. Together with the explosion of both human population and consumption, technology has sufficient power to "destroy the material conditions of human and other life."[2] It is Rasmussen's view that "for the first time, our power to destroy outstrips the earth's power to restore."[3]

The potential of technology to affect all life in unprecedented ways raises large and complicated ethical issues. As Christians who are citizens of an affluent, technologically advanced society we[4] are asked to re-examine our lifestyles, behaviors, and attitudes to see how we can participate in resolving this environmental crisis. What values and attitudes must we change to stop the destruction of the environment? What type of persons must we become to protect and to restore the environment? An important emphasis in any discussion of the solution to the ecological problem is personal responsibility and accountability. No solution is complete unless we take a serious look at the values, character, lifestyles, and actions of individuals.

This essay explores these ethical dimensions. It begins with an overview of the impact of technology on life in this century. This is followed by a discussion of the problems created by the technological revolution. The final section deals with the Christian[5] values that can guide a person to live responsibly in a rapidly changing world.

THE CHALLENGE OF TECHNOLOGY

Before examining how technology has affected nearly every aspect of human life it seems useful to define the word itself. Simply stated, technology means applied science. According to George Grant technology is not just another area of knowledge such as physics, biology, or chemistry, since it includes the means used to make things happen. The word technology captures the ability of human beings to utilize advances in scientific knowledge to develop new tools, devices, and processes to work our will on the world around us. In fact, this century has seen an explosion of new technologies. Examples include nuclear power, reproductive technology, the jet airplane, the giant crane, the computer—and the list is growing.[6]

It would be a mistake to assume that technological changes are confined to this century. Humans have always attempted to introduce new technologies that made life easier, more comfortable, and more efficient. The introduction of the wheel, the building of a printing press, and the invention of the cotton gin are but a few of the examples that one could cite. What is new is that we have created an even closer unity between science and technology. Grant observes that

> modern civilization is distinguished from all previous civilizations because our activities of knowing and making have been brought together in a way which does not allow the once-clear distinguishing of them. In fact, the coining of the word "technology" catches the novelty of that co-penetration of knowing and making.[7]

With this close alliance the twentieth century has experienced rapid and massive technological development. Its impact is felt at every level, for good or ill. At the social level it has transformed how our primary institutions, whether they be military, government, or economic, function. At the personal level it has opened up new possibilities for the satisfaction of human needs and wants. Reproductive technologies allow infertile couples with ample financial resources to fulfill their desire to have a child. Airplanes and cars provide easy and quick transportation. Albert Gore succinctly captures the significance of these new possibilities when he declares that

> every ambition, every hunger, every desire, every fear, and every hope now resonate in the human heart with more powerful implications for the world around us. Ancient habits of thought now carry new significance because of our power to transform even the boldest thought into action.[8]

With a rapidly expanding array of new tools and technologies we can more easily fulfill our dreams and intentions.

Technology has proven to be useful. According to O. B. Hardison Jr. its usefulness leads us today to accept technological development almost without thought.[9] The desire for comfort and control impels us to accept without much examination every new device or gadget. We need them for our survival. Furthermore, this attitude of acceptance is coupled with an expectation that there will be additional advances in technology. We have fallen victim to a kind of pride that causes us to believe that our power to create is unlimited. We assume that in the near future we will create new and better tools and technologies that will make our lives easier and will resolve our present problems.

THE PROBLEM OF TECHNOLOGY

It is well known that technological developments have raised significant ethical questions. While technology at least in principle can be morally neutral, it is obvious that it complicates our reflection on our ethical lives and decision-making. First, technology has the potential to reinforce certain attitudes and values, specifically a particular view of creation[10] and a dangerous technological pride. Second, technology and its development contribute to the environmental problems we face today.

As we rely more and more on technology we have substantially changed how we view our relationship to creation. According to Albert Gore

> the more we rely on technology to mediate our relationship to nature, the more we encounter the same trade-off: we have more power to

process what we need from nature more conveniently for more people, but the sense of awe and reverence that used to be present in our relationship to nature is often left behind.[11]

The loss of awe and reverence is primarily responsible for the view that creation is nothing more than a collection of resources to be used for our benefit. The intrinsic value of creation is ignored. The price we pay for such a perception is high. As our desire to consume increases and as we ignore the strains placed upon the natural world to meet our desire to consume we do significant damage to creation itself.

Likewise, our desire at times to manipulate creation for our purposes has become so prominent that we have lost our connection to creation. Our approach to technology has emphasized ways to dominate creation rather than ways to work with creation. Gore argues that "technology has vastly magnified our various abilities to manipulate nature far beyond the extent to which it has thus far magnified our abilities to conserve and protect nature."[12] In his analysis he points out that we have developed many new ways to enhance our capacity to acquire what we need from the natural world, but our ability to protect the earth against unintended negative consequences is still underdeveloped.

Technology's destructive impact on creation is often accompanied by denial: denial of the negative consequences, denial of the limits of technology, and denial of our estrangement from the rest of creation.[13] We have been successful at controlling aspects of creation, but the cost of that success is our connection to creation. This has motivated some theologians, such as James Nash, to introduce the notion of ecological sin, defined in part as

> the arrogant denial of the creaturely limitations imposed on human ingenuity and technology, a defiant disrespect or a deficient respect for the interdependent relationships of all creatures and their environments established in the covenant of creation, and an anthropocentric abuse of what God has made for frugal use.[14]

Technology has also reinforced a kind of technological pride. There is a tendency in our culture to believe that the solution to every technologically induced problem is more technology. As Gore remarks, "it is as if civilization stands in awe of its own technological prowess."[15] Our confidence in our ability to develop technology to counteract bad environmental effects "tempts us to lose sight of our place in the natural order and believe that we can achieve whatever we want."[16] This confidence is a form of pride, a pride rooted in the belief that our power may be unlimited.[17]

Last, technology brings with it certain unintended consequences. Oftentimes, the unforeseen consequences are the result of our ignorance of the interrelated nature of the global ecosystem. The environment is threatened by what has been called "technological drift." In describing this phenomenon Langdon Winner writes,

> A multiplicity of technologies, developed and applied under a very narrow range of considerations, act and interact in countless ways beyond the anticipations of any person or institution. . . . As the speed and extent of technological innovation increase, societies face the distinct possibility of going adrift in a vast sea of unintended consequences.[18]

At times some unforeseen benefits result, as was the case in the Gulf of Mexico. According to Vincent Barry,

> Much to everyone's surprise, the operational docks, pipes, and platforms [of offshore oil rigs] provided a more beneficent place to which lower forms of life could be attached than the silt-laden sea ever did. As a result, oil drilling in the Gulf of Mexico has greatly increased the commercial catch in the area.[19]

Unfortunately, more frequently the unforeseen consequences due to ignorance are negative. A good example would be the indiscriminate use of pesticides,[20] but there are many others.[21]

In the government publication *Sustainable America: A New Consensus* it is reported that environmental damage may also be the result of technological and development decisions made "when information is too sketchy to anticipate their full consequences."[22] The decline of Pacific salmon runs would be an example.[23] Furthermore, unforeseen negative consequences can even be the result of technological innovations whose purpose is to remedy technologically induced environmental problems. William Blackstone cites as an example the effort to solve the pollution problems caused by coal-fueled power plants by changing to nuclear power plants. The solution itself created new and different environmental concerns.[24]

CHRISTIAN VALUES AND THE ENVIRONMENT

The United States Catholic bishops' document *Renewing the Earth* challenges its readers to examine the values found in the Judeo-Christian tradition if they truly desire to help resolve the environmental crisis. Such a challenge forces us to address two questions: what values in our present technological culture must we give up if we wish to cease doing damage to the environment? and what values need to be accented as we act as citizens, consumers, workers, and investors in the midst of an ecological crisis?

These two questions will assist us in getting a clearer picture of who we are, who we ought to be, and what we ought to do. To state the issue in its simplest terms, our first overriding concern is our "character." According to Rodney Clapp "every culture or way of life requires a certain kind of person—a character with fitting attitudes, skills, and motivation—to sustain and advance the good life as that culture knows it."[25]

Depending upon the way of life we wish to follow, we must strive to become a particular kind of person, a person with certain values, attitudes, and intentions. If our goal is to live as one with the earth we will need to form a character consistent with that goal. This requires the development of certain moral values and the rejection of other values promoted by our technological culture.

Our second concern, what is the right thing to do, also involves values. The primary task of ethics for any Christian is the endeavor to remain faithful to the person and work of Jesus. John Howard Yoder, in his book *The Priestly Kingdom,* asserts that each generation faces the task of attempting to be faithful to the beliefs and values of Jesus in its own historical context. In each ethical dilemma Christians address the difficult chore of discerning which action best embodies the values of Jesus.[26] For our purposes this means that we are called to apply our values to the ethical issues associated with the environment.

The intention here is to list and describe some of the core Christian values that can guide our character formation and our decision-making, especially as this relates to technology. The focus will be on those values that bear most directly on issues related to the environment.

Simplicity, Moderation, Frugality, and Gratitude

In the United States those of us who are consumers have been taught to pursue the immediate and ceaseless satisfaction of our wants and desires. Advertising is the prod; technology supplies the means. Many factors contributed to the development of this mindset, but advertising, especially through its new technological sources (television, radio, and even film), is the most important. According to Rodney Clapp, advertising underwent a fundamental change in the twentieth century. Until the late nineteenth century the purpose of advertising was mainly informational. It catered to preexisting needs and supplied information, much like a news story, about when and where a product would be available. Since the turn of the century the focus of advertising has changed. It is now used not only to persuade consumers to buy a particular product but also to create new needs. Clapp, to reinforce this latter point, quotes the *Thompson Red Book on Advertising:* "Advertising aims to teach people that they have wants, which they did not recognize before, and where such wants can be best supplied."[27]

Advertising has helped to make many of us consumers with a certain set of qualities and values. One value we have been taught is the immediate satisfaction of unbounded desire. Advertising has, in Clapp's words, served as an important shaper of an "ethos . . . that would have (us) constantly yearning for new products and new experiences."[28] Never satisfied for long, we want more and more, and we want it immediately. This contributes to a new kind of addiction, an addiction to the consumption of more and more products created by technological innovations.[29]

A second value taught us by advertising is that human fulfillment is attained through acquisition and consumption. Advertising tutors us to believe that the good life consists in pampering ourselves in a life of selfishness. Gore, in his analysis of industrial civilization, raises the same concern: "the pursuit of happiness and comfort is paramount, and the consumption of an endless stream of shiny products is encouraged as the best way to succeed in that pursuit."[30] This false promise of fulfillment will ultimately serve to distract us from the search for real meaning and purpose in our lives.

As an antidote to these two values Christianity teaches the worth of living a simple life. This value involves moderation, frugality, and gratitude. Moderation is necessary to counteract the tendency of our consumer mindset to proliferate wants. Without moderation our lives would become an endless search for new material pleasures without any consideration given to the damage they cause. Through moderation we learn that not everything we want is a necessity. This is important in a society that suffers from what some have called the "expectation syndrome." It is common in our society to consider what is a luxury in one generation to be a necessity in the next generation. Computers, dishwashers, microwaves are but a few examples. These items are useful and efficient, but it is debatable if they are necessary for survival. Practicing moderation can help us learn what is truly essential and what really is an item for convenience or comfort.

The Christian notion of frugality emphasizes the prudent use of the earth's resources to meet the necessities of life. James Nash designates frugality as one of the "ecological virtues" that, if practiced, can make ecological integrity a reality. On frugality Nash writes: "As the antithesis of consumerism and prodigality, it thrives on the control of consumption, the reduction of waste, and comprehensive recycling."[31] As individuals who consume a large share of the world's resources we are asked voluntarily to use a balanced and restrained approach to these resources. Frugality can be described as thrift. "It means, as the current slogan says, living lightly on the earth."[32] In the words of Paul VI, we need to learn to be a society that "intelligently conserves rather than needlessly consumes."[33]

A spirit of gratitude is also a mark of the simple life. Gratitude involves the acknowledgement and appreciation of the simple, basic things we do have. According to Clapp our consumer culture tempts us with a dissatisfaction rooted in what we do not have. There is a tendency for us always to yearn for another item that will satisfy a perceived need. It is at these moments that we need to remember and be grateful for those things we do have. Clapp offers a very practical suggestion here. We should make a list of the basic things we have enjoyed that day, but have taken for granted. Gratitude serves as a kind of spiritual discipline to calm our urge to fulfill our every whim.

Justice and Concern for the Future

A third set of values associated with the character of the consumer is self-centeredness and self-indulgence. We as consumers are schooled to think first of ourselves and our needs. According to Clapp this preoccupation with meeting our needs is reinforced through an explosion of new products, new conveniences, and new experiences now available to us as a result of technological advances. He notes, for example, that the average supermarket now carries 30,000 products, as opposed to 9,000 in 1976. While the vast array of choices is not all bad, it does lead us to see ourselves simply as individuals who, in freedom, are left to choose among many options for our happiness. Clapp quotes Alan Ehrenhalt, who asserts that

> too many of the things we do in our lives, large and small, have come to resemble channel surfing, marked by a numbing and seemingly endless

progression from one option to the next, all without the benefit of a chart, logistical or moral, because there are simply too many choices and no one to help sort it out.[34]

We are so trained to go from one choice to the next that we sometimes fail to question if our choices are significant and if this is the way of life we wish to choose.[35]

Self-centeredness and self-indulgence have created in many of us a habit of consuming larger and larger quantities of the earth's resources. The United States as an affluent, technologically advanced society has an unparalleled rate of consumption and waste generation. *Sustainable America: A New Consensus* indicates that we consume 4.5 billion metric tons of material annually to produce the goods we feel we need or want.[36] By the authors' estimates we are the leading producers of garbage and industrial waste. According to one source the volume of our production of waste is so high that 15,000 out of the 20,000 landfills in existence in 1979 are now filled to capacity.[37] Our overindulgence has led to serious environmental damage.

In his reflections on the ecological crisis John Paul II argues that any solution requires a serious reexamination of our values. As an antidote to self-centered overindulgence, the value of justice and a concern for future generations must become a part of everyday life. Only with such a focus in life can the human community move beyond self-interest to a genuine concern for the common good.

One antidote to self-centered overindulgence and its effects on the environment is the Christian value of justice. It is fundamentally unjust that the overconsumption of a few leads not only to the major portion of environmental degradation but also to greater burdens being placed upon the poor.[38] This raises significant issues in terms of social and environmental justice. When we speak of justice it is essential that we use a more comprehensive notion than that found in Anglo-Saxon jurisprudence, social philosophy, and moral traditions. According to Larry Rasmussen, their focus regarding justice is on individual liberty and/or equality.

> As an ideal, justice as liberty has meant guaranteeing the widest range of individual choice commensurate with such choices for others, while justice as equality has meant guaranteeing a comparative allotment of goods, services and opportunities at a humane level for the largest number of citizens possible.[39]

Justice defined as liberty and equality is too human-centered since it "restricts justice to matters of human welfare alone, directly and indirectly."[40]

A more helpful understanding of justice begins with an awareness that justice pertains to humans and non-humans alike. The "neighbor" to whom we owe justice is not limited to creatures in human form but includes "all that participates in being, organic and inorganic."[41] Rasmussen continues his analysis by defining justice as right relatedness. By this he means that it is "the rendering, amid limited resources and the conditions of a still chaotic world, of whatever is required for the fullest possible flourishing of creation in any given time and place."[42] Justice, as the fullest possible flourishing of all creation, would require us to take seriously the sustainability, or in other words the condition of life to survive and thrive, of all that is on this planet.

Such a notion of justice counters our addiction to the technological consumption of the earth's resources. Instead of focusing on how the wealth of the natural world can further our ends we should remember that all forms of creation are owed justice. Animals, plants, trees, water, as well as those in poverty, to name a few, are basic units with the right to survive and flourish. Therefore we have a responsibility to investigate and give consideration to how our actions as consumers and our nation's technological innovations affect anyone or anything on this earth. No longer can we disregard the damage done to the environment and the suffering of the poor.

Closely tied to justice is a second antidote: concern for the future. Our overindulgence has led to a depletion of resources and an explosion of pollution that threaten the capacity of humans and non-humans to survive and thrive. We have let our desire to satisfy our wants in the present blind us to the future consequences of our actions. We make decisions and act, at times, as if all resources belong totally to the present generation. Furthermore, economic logic heavily discounts the value of resources for future generations. Since economic logic tends to downplay qualities that are not quantifiable, according to Willis Harman, it "discounts the future, which is a formalized way of saying that the well-being of future generations doesn't count."[43]

In response to this "discounting" both secular and religious documents have emphasized the necessity of considering the future while making decisions in the present. In 1972, for example, the Bruntland Commission accented the need for "intergenerational equity." It is fundamentally unjust for us to succumb to short-term pressure and fail to acknowledge our responsibility for the future. If, as Rasmussen claims, justice entails a duty to ensure that the planet as a whole can survive and thrive, then this duty cannot be limited to the present. Any decision in the present concerning the introduction of technological innovations must be made with an awareness of its impact on the sustainability of future humans and nonhumans alike. In speaking of the "neighbor" to whom justice is due, Rasmussen declares that the neighbor embraces "all participants in being . . . present, past, and future."[44]

In practical terms concern for the future will lead to a way of life that seeks to preserve and restore creation. Manuel Velasquez offers a partial list of actions that may prove beneficial to maintaining a healthy global ecosystem:

> This would mean that we should preserve wildlife and endangered species; that we should take steps to ensure that the rate of [depletion of] fossil fuels and of minerals does not continue to rise; that we should cut down our consumption and production of goods that depend on non-renewable resources; that we should recycle nonrenewable resources; that we search for substitutes for materials that we are too rapidly depleting.[45]

There is no manual on what we should do to maintain the integrity of creation, but a good starting point would be, as suggested in the previous section, to adopt a lifestyle of simplicity, frugality, and gratitude. Furthermore, we need to protect creation by developing our abilities to safeguard the natural world against unintended consequences of our actions. Instead of focusing on our abilities to manipulate creation, we would do better if we intensified our efforts to learn how to identify potential environmental damage resulting from our technological endeavors.

Humility

In a technological culture pride often becomes part of our character. As indicated earlier, one manifestation of pride stems from an overconfidence in our ability to use our technological prowess not only to fulfill our needs but also to counteract bad environmental effects by developing new technology. We are in awe of our power, a power we view as unlimited. Pride also manifests itself in the unwillingness to acknowledge the fallibility of our knowledge and our judgment. As we try to act on complicated global issues we tend to overestimate our capacity to discern the consequences of our proposed innovations. Finally, pride reveals itself in our belief that we are superior to creation. Creation is "below us" since it is often seen solely as raw material to be manipulated into consumer goods or creature comfort.

Christianity's emphasis on humility is an essential antidote to the kind of hubris found in a technological culture. In *Renewing the Earth* the Catholic bishops capture a key aspect of humility when they speak of the need to "honestly admit our limitations and failings."[46] Humility reminds us that human power and knowledge are limited and subject to misuse. It calls for us to get an accurate measure of our strength, for when we perceive our "weakness" we will be less prone to place our trust in our power and devices to resolve the environmental crisis on our own. A second lesson to be learned in humility involves the correction of the perception that we are "above" the rest of creation. Humility, to use C. S. Lewis's words, entails a willingness to give up the center. It helps us to recognize not only our dependency on creation but also the interdependence of all creation.

CONCLUSION AND THEOLOGICAL REFLECTION

To be active participants in resolving the environmental crisis we must undertake a three-pronged strategy. First, we must be willing to examine critically and to transform the values, attitudes, and intentions that form the core of our own character. The American bishops are correct when they suggest that "we need a change of heart to save the planet for our children and generations not yet born."[47] This will not be easy. We have been shaped, sometimes even unwittingly, by a culture whose "values" contributed to the environmental damage. To be transformed, we need to strip ourselves of the values associated with human acquisitiveness and power. In their place are proposed a series of values and virtues associated with the Christian tradition. It is important to remember here that a particular kind of character is needed if we wish to pursue a way of life whose goal is to live as one with the earth.

Second, we must commit ourselves to making ethical choices consistent with our values. According to James Burtchaell, our daily actions, much like a ritual, reveal the values that are the core of our existence. We are challenged to highlight and celebrate our commitment to restore and maintain the integrity of creation by promoting and defending our emerging ecological values in the midst of difficult and sometimes complex environmental issues. This may cause us some frustration, because there is no way to outline what we should do specifically in any given situation, yet the values that should guide us are clear: simplicity, frugality, moderation, concern for the future, and especially justice, defined as the fullest possible flourishing of all creation, should set the tone of any ethical discussion.

Third, we must break our addiction to every new technological advance. As David Hopper states, "technological innovation continues to accelerate and there is no thought or suggestion of its slackening its pace."[48] With each new advance there exists the potential danger of profound, unintended environmental damage. Instead of focusing on our capacity to manipulate the natural world we are called in humility to intensify our efforts to identify the consequences of our proposed technological innovations.

More importantly, technology must be given a new focus, a new direction. In our present age the good life is often seen as the pursuit of happiness and comfort, and the consumption of new products provided by technology is encouraged as the best way to succeed in that pursuit. Our fascination with technology and the new has distracted us in our search for real meaning and purpose in our lives. According to Hopper, the human community must be reminded of the Christian call for a wider redemptive purpose.[49] This entails a commitment on our part to the goal of preserving and healing the natural order. It is in the context of this commitment that we must be prepared to question the course of technology and to assess its impact on creation.

Only with great humility and grace do we venture to tackle the task of applying our emerging ecological values to difficult and complex ethical issues associated with the environment and technology. It takes practice.[50] Only through daily practice can we acquire the skill and the courage necessary to live a simple and humble life in an age of greed and self-centeredness.

Finally, there is no doubt, as this chapter clearly attests, that the current environmental health of the earth has had a major impact on axiological and ethical considerations.[51] From an axiological point of reference many human beings are asking new questions regarding the value of the natural world. This chapter asserts that in spite of all its advantages technology has contributed to the devaluation of creation to "nothing more than a collection of resources to be used for our benefit."[52] When we are consumed with the instrumental use of the natural world "the intrinsic value of creation is ignored."[53] For the first time in the history of moral discourse, ethicists and theologians are asking these new questions: Do we humans have moral obligations and duties to the natural world? Do we have moral obligations and duties to future generations of humans and non-humans not yet born? This chapter testifies to the fact that these new axiological and ethical questions have created an entirely new terrain of ethical discourse as humanity urgently attempts to map of way of living on the planet that is just and sustainable.

As an ethical palliative to the consumerist and technological abuse of the natural world, this essay advocates a return to several longstanding values—simplicity, moderation, frugality, gratitude, humility, and justice—that are historically consistent with the Benedictine tradition. The Rule of St. Benedict, interpreted from a contemporary environmental perspective, may offer a communal paradigm for living these countercultural values—something that could be defined as a new asceticism. Humility, for example, is primary in the Rule and a countervalue to the arrogant human will to power that is at the very basis of the contemporary human predicament. Benedictine humility recognizes that humanity shares an inherent bond with the rest of creation. Terrence Kardong, O.S.B., reminds us that "the etymology of the term [humility] reveals its connotation: humus means 'soil.'"[54] Whether viewed from the perspective of biblical creation theology or neo-Darwinian evolution, human beings are creatures of the earth and humility reminds us of this forgotten solidarity with the rest of creation.

Frugality, perhaps the most significant value proposed herein, is also a Benedictine virtue. The Rule of Benedict is permeated with direct and indirect references to frugality. This is particularly true of the section governing the administration of the monastery and includes Benedict's teaching on communal living and the non-ownership of private property, the distribution of goods according to need, and the appropriate use of food and drink; here Benedict writes: "Frugality should be the rule on all occasions" (*RB* 39). According to James Nash the virtue of frugality also incorporates the values of moderation and simplicity of lifestyle, hallmarks of the Benedictine way.[55]

The values proposed in this chapter are presented with fresh insight and interpretation in light of our environmental exigencies, as an "antidote" to the profligate ways of the commodity culture. For these values to have impact they will have to be internalized and acted upon by committed individuals who understand them as expressions of an earth-centered spirituality. To be maintained and sustained with consistency —in the face of an affluent North American culture—they will also require communal support. The Benedictine tradition offers a countercultural model that is a potential solution to the predicament of the prosperous.

NOTES: CHAPTER 4

[1] John Paul II, *The Ecological Crisis: A Common Responsibility* (Washington, D.C.: U.S. Catholic Conference, 1990) 1.

[2] Larry Rasmussen, *Earth Community, Earth Ethics* (Maryknoll, N.Y.: Orbis, 1996) 4.

[3] Ibid. 5.

[4] The use of the pronoun "we" is intentional. The author of this chapter includes himself in the category of affluent Christians living in a technologically advanced society. The chapter focuses upon the need for rich Christians to come to terms with the consequences of their having been shaped, sometimes even unwittingly, by a culture whose "values" contribute to the environmental problem.

[5] The stress on Christian values in this chapter is due to the fact that the author wishes to examine what the Christian tradition has to say to those living in a technologically advanced society. This is not intended to prevent conversations with others who are not members of the Christian faith. Rather it is intended as a contribution to any discussion of the particular kind of character that is needed if human beings desire to live as one with the earth.

[6] A more detailed discussion of the ideas in this paragraph is found in John Popiden, "The Problem of Technology and Morality," unpublished paper, pp. 3–4.

[7] George P. Grant, "Thinking about Technology," in idem, *Technology and Justice* (Notre Dame: University of Notre Dame Press; Toronto: Anansi, 1986) 12.

[8] Albert Gore, *Earth in the Balance* (New York: Plume, 1993) 205.

[9] See O. B. Hardison, Jr., *Disappearing through the Skylight: Culture and Technology in the Twentieth Century* (New York: Viking Penguin, 1989) 83–84.

[10] Creation is a theological rather than a scientific term. It means "all things together, in, with, and before God, all things in their totality and in their differentiation as an expression of the divine life." (Rasmussen, *Earth Community, Earth Ethics* 105). He argues that "creation" may be used as a synonym for nature if nature is understood as "a luminous expression of sacred power, life, and order" (p. 105).

[11] Gore, *Earth in the Balance* 203.

[12] Ibid. 214.

[13] Gore (*Earth in the Balance* 233) uses the notion of a dysfunctional civilization to accent the danger of denial. While this civilization heightens our addiction to consuming the earth's resources, it also maintains a conspiracy of silence concerning the impact of technology on the environment. He reminds us that "just as the unwritten rules in a dysfunctional family create and maintain a conspiracy of silence about the rules themselves, even as the family is driven toward successive crises, many of the unwritten rules of our dysfunctional civilization encourage silent acquiescence in our patterns of destructive behavior toward the natural world."

[14] James A. Nash, *Loving Nature: Ecological Integrity and Christian Responsibility* (Nashville: Abingdon, 1991) 119.

[15] Gore, *Earth in the Balance* 206.

[16] Ibid. 206–207.

[17] In the early Church pride was defined as the human desire to be like God, not in righteousness, but in power. See Matthew Baasten, *Pride According to Gregory the Great* (Lewiston, N.Y.: Edwin Mellen, 1986) 13–51.

[18] This quotation from Langdon Winner is taken from David Hopper, *Technology, Theology, and the Idea of Progress* (Louisville: Westminster/John Knox, 1991) 75.

[19] Vincent Barry, *Moral Issues in Business* (3d ed. Belmont, Calif.: Wadsworth, 1986) 407.

[20] Rachel Carson in her classic book *Silent Spring* warned of the dangers of pesticides. Subsequent studies have confirmed her worst suspicions. For example, studies have indicated that pesticides can affect the reproductive capacity of animals and cause brain damage and cancer in humans. Another study has noted that workers such as crop dusters have exhibited dull reflexes and mental instability due to constant exposure to certain pesticides. For a fuller discussion see Barry, *Moral Issues in Business* 407.

[21] David Hopper offers chlorofluorocarbon spray containers, refrigeration units, styrofoam insulation, and nuclear power plants as other examples of technological developments that precipitated unintended negative consequences. See Hopper, *Technology, Theology, and the Idea of Progress* 16–22, 75. James A. Nash (*Loving Nature* 25–28) also provides an extensive list of how technology contributes to the pollution of the environment.

[22] President's Council on Sustainable Development, *Sustainable America: A New Consensus* (Washington, D.C.: U.S. Government Printing Office, 1996) 110.

[23] The decline of the wild salmon population began with overfishing in the middle of the nineteenth century. Logging, livestock and farming practices, and the introduction of dams accentuated the decline of salmon stock. Interestingly, the creation of fish hatcheries would become one of the problems

in preserving the wild salmon population. When they were created few realized that fish produced in hatcheries were inferior and lacked some of the necessary survival skills. As a result the mixing of hatchery salmon with wild stock led to the weakening of practically all the salmon population.

Despite efforts from various parties there has still been a decline in the Columbia River basin's salmon and steelhead runs. According to the *Corps of Engineers Fish Passage Report* the following numbers of salmon were counted in the years 1991 and 1995: Chinook (274,622 vs. 243,450), Steelhead (274,545 vs. 161,976), Sockeye (76,481 vs. 12,676), and Coho (64,057 vs. 22,794). Information provided may be found at the website http://www.pond.net/michele/summary.html.

[24] See William Blackstone, "Ethics and Ecology," in W. Michael Hoffman and Jennifer Mills Moore, eds., *Business Ethics: Readings and Cases in Corporate Morality* (New York: McGraw-Hill, 1984) 361.

[25] Rodney Clapp, "Why the Devil Takes Visa," *Christianity Today* 40/11 (October 1996) 26.

[26] See John Howard Yoder, *The Priestly Kingdom* (Notre Dame: University of Notre Dame Press, 1984) 2–12.

[27] Clapp, "Why the Devil Takes Visa," 25.

[28] Ibid.

[29] Albert Gore (*Earth in the Balance* 222) compares some people's need for higher and higher levels of consumption to the "rush" experienced by drug addicts. He writes, "over time, a drug addict needs a progressively larger dose to produce an equivalent level of exhilaration; similarly, our civilization seems to require an ever-increasing level of consumption." For a fuller discussion see ibid. 220–22.

[30] Ibid. 222.

[31] Nash, *Loving Nature* 65.

[32] Ibid.

[33] Paul VI, "Message of Paul VI for the World Day of Environment," in Vincent P. Mainelli, ed., *Official Catholic Teachings: Social Justice* (Wilmington, N.C.: Consortium Books, 1978) 452.

[34] As quoted in Clapp, "Why the Devil Takes Visa," 29.

[35] In his analysis of technology David Hopper (*Technology, Theology, and the Idea of Progress* 74) echoes the theme of this paragraph. He argues that technology has allowed many people to move from one choice to the next without providing them with a deep meaning for their lives. Technology offers people at any moment a temporary hope that soon evaporates into disillusionment. He writes: "technology's distractions are short lived: a new style, a new convenience, the passage of some time and then boredom, and the search for something new." For a full discussion of this theme see ibid. 73–75, 94–95.

[36] *Sustainable America: A New Consensus* 142.

[37] Gore, *Earth in the Balance* 151.

[38] Manuel Velasquez argues that the external costs of pollution are borne largely by the poor. He writes, "pollution may produce a new flow of benefits away from the poor and toward the well-off, thereby increasing inequality." For an extensive discussion of the impact of pollution on the rich and the poor see Manuel Velasquez, *Business Ethics* (2d ed. Englewood Cliffs, N.J.: Prentice Hall, 1988) 245–46.

[39] Rasmussen, *Earth Community, Earth Ethics* 260.

[40] Ibid.

[41] Ibid. 261.

[42] Ibid. 260.

[43] Willis Harman, "Business as a Component of the Global Ecology," *Noetic Sciences Review* 19 (Autumn 1991) 19.

[44] Rasmussen, *Earth Community, Earth Ethics* 261.

[45] Velasquez, *Business Ethics* 256.

[46] "Renewing the Earth," *Origins* 21/7 (December 12, 1991) 432.

[47] Ibid.

[48] Hopper, *Technology, Theology, and the Idea of Progress* 72.

[49] For a fuller discussion of this point see ibid. 112–15, 126–28.

[50] For an excellent discussion of the necessity of daily practice see Pat Fellers, "Practice the Skills You Want to Achieve," *Catholic Sentinel* 125/20 (May 20, 1994) 16.

[51] Axiology is defined as the study of the nature of values and the process of human valuation.

[52] See above, p. 62.

[53] Ibid.

[54] Terrence G. Kardong, o.s.b., "Ecological Resources in the Benedictine Rule," in Albert J. LaChance and John E. Carroll, eds., *Embracing Earth: Catholic Approaches to Ecology* (Maryknoll, N.Y.: Orbis, 1994) 165.

[55] Nash, *Loving Nature* 65.

5

Feeding the Hungry and Protecting the Environment

For the Lord your God is bringing you into a good land, a land with flowing streams, with springs and underground waters welling up in valleys and hills, a land of wheat and barley, of vines and figs trees and pomegranates, a land of olive trees and honey, a land where you may eat bread without scarcity, where you will lack nothing, a land whose stones are iron and from whose hills you may mine copper. You shall eat your fill and bless the Lord your God for all the good land that he has given you. (Deut 8:7-10)

Then the righteous will answer him, "Lord, when was it that we saw you hungry and gave you food, or thirsty and gave you something to drink? And when was it that we saw you a stranger and welcomed you, or naked and gave you clothing? And when was it that we saw you sick or in prison and visited you?" And the king will answer them, "Truly I tell you, just as you did it to one of the least of these who are members of my family, you did it to me." (Matt 25:37-40)

T he words of Deuteronomy and Matthew resound with blessing and responsibility that call all people today to embrace a spirit of gratitude and generosity as a way of life and ethical practice. In the ancient biblical world the Jewish people understood that the land and all its natural resources belonged to God and was given to them as a gift to be cared for, shared, and cherished. In the Gospel of Matthew the gospel writer depicts Jesus instructing his listeners that to be righteous means to care for one another through concrete deeds of justice and compassion. The messages of Deuteronomy and Matthew find a home and strike a chord in the world today wherein exists a tension between world hunger and agricultural practices. On the one hand agriculture produces needed food, but on the other hand it causes harm to the gift of land. What is needed, then, is a new vision of stewardship that cares for both people and the land. This chapter lays out some crucial human and environmental problems and then offers a new vision for dealing with such problems.

LAYING OUT THE ISSUES: WORLD HUNGER

As the number of people inhabiting the Earth expands, it becomes increasingly difficult to heed Jesus' call to feed the hungry and provide clothing and shelter to the homeless. The United Nations Food and Agriculture Organization estimates that 841 million people currently suffer from inadequate access to food.[1] Most of these starving people live in the developing countries of Africa, Asia, and Latin America, where one person in five endures chronic hunger.

"Food inadequacy" is defined as the intake of fewer calories than the average adult requires for normal daily activities.[2] A calorie is a measure of the amount of energy available in food, so a person suffering from food inadequacy does not have the energy to work, play, grow, or think as would a healthy person with an adequate diet. Food inadequacy is closely related to the concept of "undernutrition," except that undernutrition takes into account the additional energy needed to fight infection and to compensate for the malabsorption of nutrients during periods of intestinal illness. These are important considerations because undernourished people are more susceptible to disease and often have inadequate access to health care and community disease prevention.

The concept of undernutrition also takes into account the higher energy requirements of children and pregnant women. Children are particularly susceptible to disorders associated with a poor diet because of the high energy demands of growth and development. The most common form of nutritional deficiency in children is a lack of protein,[3] resulting in a condition known as *kwashiorkor*. The name of the condition comes from a Ghanaian term that describes "the evil spirit that infects the first child when the second child is born."[4] This description reflects the deficiency symptoms that appear in older children when they are weaned from mother's milk (an excellent source of protein) so that younger children may nurse. *Kwashiorkor* is characterized by stunted growth, scaly skin, lesions that fail to heal, a belly swollen with edema (fluid secretion due to low blood protein), high susceptibility to infection, and a condition known as "wasting." Wasting occurs when the body digests its own tissues to obtain the protein that is needed to maintain vital functions.

An insufficient number of calories in the diet produces a condition known as *marasmus,* which has many of the same symptoms as *kwashiorkor* because diets lacking in calories are invariably deficient in protein as well.[5] Marasmic children are disturbingly thin and have a slow metabolism, low resistance to infection, and often a subnormal body temperature due to the lack of body fat for insulation. Their heart and other muscles are weak and brain development is often impaired by the lack of adequate nutrition during the critical first six months of life.

An estimated 190 million children worldwide are underweight (low weight for their age), 230 million are stunted in growth (low height for their weight), and fifty million are "wasted" (low weight for their height) due to inadequate nutrition.[6] Considering the additional energy requirements of children and adults suffering from frequent infections, assessments of food inadequacy probably underestimate the true prevalence of undernutrition in the world.[7]

In addition to requiring a minimum number of calories in food, most of which are obtained from carbohydrates, people also require specific nutrients in the form of proteins, vitamins, and minerals. A person whose diet lacks one or more essential nutrients is said to be malnourished. If a person's diet consists primarily of carbohydrate-rich grains such as rice, millet, or corn, which lack these essential nutrients, the person will suffer physically and mentally regardless of the number of calories consumed. An estimated two billion people subsist on diets that are deficient in iron[8] and 1.6 billion are at risk of iodine deficiency,[9] a condition that causes brain damage and mental retardation. Forty million children do not receive adequate amounts of vitamin A, a nutrient that is essential for all stages of growth and development.[10] Vitamin A deficiency causes impaired vision and hardening of mucous membranes in the respiratory and intestinal tracts, which increases susceptibility to infection. It also impairs the growth of teeth and bones and can lead to paralysis when the brain and spinal cord are restricted by stunted development of the skull and spine.

FOOD PRODUCTION AND POPULATION GROWTH

The widespread hunger currently plaguing the world is largely due to an inequitable distribution of food rather than insufficient agricultural food production. The developed countries of North America and Europe produce and consume most of the world's food, while vast numbers of people in developing countries suffer from undernourishment and malnutrition. Alan B. Durning describes the situation this way in his report on poverty for the Worldwatch Institute:

> Americans spend five billion dollars each year on special diets to lower their calorie consumption, while 400 million people around the world are so undernourished, their bodies and minds are deteriorating. As water from a single spring in France is bottled and shipped to the prosperous around the globe, nearly two billion people drink and bathe in water contaminated with deadly parasites and pathogens.[11]

National governments and non-government organizations are making concerted efforts to improve food production and distribution throughout the world. The United Nations and World Health Organization sponsored an International Conference on Nutrition in 1992[12] and a World Food Summit in 1996[13] that produced formal World Declarations on "Nutrition" and "World Food Security" and policy guidelines and strategies for "National Plans of Action" to eliminate hunger and reduce all forms of malnutrition. These organizations, along with numerous private organizations such as Food for the Hungry and Bread for the World, have achieved some success in reducing world hunger, but the challenge of feeding the hungry becomes more difficult with each passing year.

It appears that government and non-government organizations are losing ground in the effort to maintain food production and distribution at levels that are adequate to feed the growing human population. Agricultural productivity peaked during the 1980s and 1990s, while the human population continued to grow, resulting in a fourteen percent decrease in per capita food production since 1984.[14]

The current worldwide human population is now more than 5.7 billion.[15] The Food and Agriculture Organization projects that the population will increase to 9.8 billion by the year 2050.[16] A report by the World Hunger Program at Brown University estimated that if food supplies were equitably distributed the record food harvest of 1985 would provide a minimal vegetarian diet for about six billion people, the projected world population in the year 2000.[17] This estimation assumes that no grain is diverted to livestock or poultry for meat and dairy products. If all people consumed a diet similar to that of North Americans and Western Europeans, about one-third of which consists of animal products, only 2.5 billion people could be adequately fed. These estimates suggest an imminent and catastrophic shortage of food.

Projections by the Food and Agriculture Organization are not as alarming but still illustrate the need for immediate measures to cope with the demand for food in the near future. The Food and Agriculture Organization estimates the biological carrying capacity of the Earth (the maximum population that can be supported by available resources) to be about fifty billion people.[18] To support this number of people would require that every resource be used for human subsistence, with none left over for amenities such as cars, televisions, or air conditioners, and no plots of land set aside for gardens, parks, or wilderness. Life without these amenities is unimaginable for those who have become accustomed to a higher standard of living, yet this is the future humanity faces if nothing is done to limit population growth. A more reasonable objective would be to stabilize the human population at a level well below the biological carrying capacity of the Earth.

Delegates at a United Nations summit meeting in Cairo in 1994 suggested a world population of eight billion people as a number that could be reasonably sustained by current agricultural technology.[19] At the current rate of growth the human population will reach eight billion by the year 2020. To achieve zero population growth within the next twenty-five years will require immediate changes in the social and economic structure of many countries. Most developed countries have stable or near-stable populations already, so it is the developing nations that are being asked to make these changes. Developing countries are understandably wary of wealthy and powerful nations that try to impose changes that would profoundly affect their cultural, religious, and social traditions. Furthermore, the problem of population growth is also compounded by the rate of consumption of resources.

One cannot predict what technological advances might make it possible to increase food production in the years to come. In 1798 the English scientist Thomas Malthus predicted that the world would soon experience unprecedented famine because food production would be unable to keep up with the rate of human population growth.[20] He could not foresee the extraordinary technological advances of the twentieth and twenty-first centuries that miraculously increased agricultural productivity. Similar advances may come from genetic engineering or other technological breakthroughs, but we cannot count on it. Even with the possibility of new technologies, consumers and policy makers must face the reality of physical and biological limits on the amount of food that can be produced and the amount of damage that the environment can endure in the process. It would be wise simply to hope that farmers can maintain the current level of agricultural productivity and that government and non-government organizations can achieve a more equitable distribution of food in the coming years without imposing irreparable harm on the environment.

INTENSIVE AGRICULTURE AND THE GREEN REVOLUTION

Global food production has almost tripled since the end of World War II,[21] a phenomenon commonly referred to as the Green Revolution. Food and fiber production increased sharply during the 1950s, 1960s, and 1970s with the development of high-yield hybrid crops, chemical fertilizers and pesticides, and specialized farm machinery. Agricultural yields subsequently leveled off in North America and Europe as the new technology of the Green Revolution achieved its maximum productivity.

Attempts to transfer this new technology to developing countries have achieved some success, but not without setbacks and new challenges. High-yield crops that thrived in temperate climates withered in the intense sun and drowned in the torrential rains of tropical countries, while expensive fertilizers and pesticides were lost to leaching and runoff. The development of new crop varieties bred for tropical climates and the introduction of new agricultural practices helped overcome some of these difficulties and enabled many countries in South America and Asia to increase food production as their populations grew.

Serious social and economic problems have accompanied these increases in agricultural productivity, however, and the effects on the tropical environment have the potential to significantly alter the global climate. The cost of improved seed, fertilizers, pesticides, and farm equipment made the new technology available to only the most affluent farmers in developing countries. The increased yields and profits that they enjoyed, and the falling price of commodities that accompanied the bountiful harvests, widened the economic gap between the wealthiest and poorest farmers in these countries.[22] To offset the cost of the new technology and reduce trade deficits with developed countries much of the most productive agricultural land in developing countries was devoted to cash crops such as coffee, tea, and cocoa for export. This left less arable land available for food production for the people of these countries.

AGRICULTURE AND THE ENVIRONMENT

Habitat Destruction: Agriculture on any scale is unavoidably harmful to the environment. The dynamic balance of a natural ecosystem is disturbed when a plot of land is cleared, tilled, and planted with a crop. Small disturbances can be tolerated without far-reaching effects. The civilizations of South America, Africa, and Europe were not affected when the Mesopotamians inadvertently poisoned their crops with salt that accumulated in their irrigated fields. Larger disturbances, or the combined effects of many small disturbances, can have more widespread consequences. This was made painfully evident by the recent severe flooding of the Mississippi River in the midwestern United States. With the growth of agriculture in this area over the past one hundred years, ninety percent of the wetland habitats adjacent to the Mississippi River were drained to produce acres of rich farmland.[23] Initially the loss of a few wetland habitats had little effect on the river ecosystem. As one wetland after another was converted to farmland, however, the ecosystem lost its capacity to absorb heavy rainfalls and a large geographic area became susceptible to massive flooding.

Habitat destruction in the tropics could have even greater consequences. A substantial portion of the increase in agricultural productivity in many developing countries has been achieved by carving new farmland out of tropical forests. The loss of hundreds of thousands of species of plants and animals that inhabit these biologically rich areas could adversely affect the quality of life for all humankind. The loss of medicinal plants, for instance, may severely limit our ability to treat many debilitating and life-threatening diseases. One-fourth of all pharmaceutical drugs, including seventy percent of all cancer drugs, come from tropical rainforests.[24]

Global climate could be significantly altered by the effects of deforestation on carbon dioxide fixation and transpiration. Carbon dioxide is "fixed" when plants remove the gas from the atmosphere and use it to synthesize the sugars they need for growth. Global warming has been attributed, at least in part, to human activities such as the burning of fossil fuels, which increases the concentration of carbon dioxide in the atmosphere.[25] Eliminating a major "consumer" of carbon dioxide by destroying tropical forests could significantly increase the rate of global warming.

Transpiration is the movement of water from soil through the roots, stems, and leaves of plants into the atmosphere. Enormous volumes of water are transpired by lush tropical forests, forming moist air masses that provide rainfall to vast geographic areas. The climate of the south-western United States, for instance, is influenced by the movement of air masses from Amazon rainforests, fourteen percent of which have al-ready been destroyed by human intrusion. Significantly altering this source of warm, moist air could modify climate patterns throughout the Western Hemisphere.

Energy Consumption: The loss of native habitats is just one example of the adverse effects that agriculture can have on the environment. Conventional, high-yield agriculture requires intensive inputs of en-ergy, most of which is derived directly or indirectly from fossil fuels. The inorganic fertilizers that replaced the manure, compost, and peat used in traditional agriculture require an abundant supply of cheap oil to be produced economically. Nitrogen fertilizers, for instance, are pro-duced under intense pressure by a high-temperature process fueled by natural gas. These fertilizers are used in massive quantities because ni-trogen is the nutrient whose deficiency most often limits plant growth and productivity.

The pesticides[26] used to combat weeds, insects, and molds are also products of the petrochemical industry, as are the fuels needed to oper-ate tilling, planting, and harvesting equipment and the pumps that op-erate large irrigation systems. Intensive agriculture currently consumes approximately eight percent of the world's oil.

Diminishing Soil Quality: Conventional agriculture also damages soil structure and depletes the soil of essential nutrients. To maintain the fertility, water-holding capacity, and aeration needed for healthy plant growth, a soil needs to contain a blend of small particles (clays), larger particles (silt and sand), and stable aggregates of these particles. The small clay particles provide extensive surface area for the adsorp-tion of mineral nutrients and water. The larger silt and sand particles, along with stable aggregates, increase pore size in the soil, thereby im-proving drainage and aeration. Repeated tilling with heavy farm equip-ment breaks down aggregates and compacts the soil, resulting in poor drainage, reduced plant productivity, and increased erosion. Grazing and trampling by large herds of cattle have similar effects on soil structure.

Each time a crop is harvested, the nutrients absorbed by the plant are removed from the soil and must be replaced with more fertilizer for the next crop. Most inorganic fertilizers replace the nutrients that are needed in the greatest quantity—nitrogen, phosphorus, and potassium—but do not replenish micronutrients such as iron, copper, manganese, and molybdenum. After several growing seasons the depletion of micronutrients from the soil may limit crop production.

The removal of plant cover at harvest also contributes to the loss of topsoil by erosion and exposes the soil to direct sunlight that increases soil temperature. As soil temperature rises microorganisms rapidly degrade residual soil organic matter. Organic matter plays a key role in stabilizing soil aggregates and retaining water and mineral nutrients, so microbial degradation of this component of the soil significantly reduces soil quality.

Draining Aquifers: Increasing crop yields has increased the demand for water to sustain plant growth. Many crops are grown on marginal lands with limited or erratic rainfall and can consistently yield productive harvests only when irrigated throughout much of the growing season. The source of water for irrigation may be a nearby river or stream, but often it is groundwater that is pumped to the surface by wind- or fuel-driven pumps. Groundwater is extracted from a saturated underground layer of porous stone or gravel known as an aquifer. If water is removed from an aquifer more rapidly than it can be replaced by percolation from above or lateral recharge from adjacent areas it will eventually be pumped dry. This situation exists in many irrigated agricultural lands, notably the midwestern and southwestern United States. Agricultural land from South Dakota to Texas is sustained by water pumped from a vast aquifer known as the Ogallala aquifer. Water is currently being removed from this aquifer at eight times the rate of recharge.[27] The loss of this natural resource would cripple a region that yields fifteen percent of the corn and wheat, twenty-five percent of the cotton, and forty percent of the beef produced in the United States.[28]

Agricultural Pollution: Pollution can be defined as the contamination of soil, water, or air with undesired amounts of natural or synthetic substances. Many of the pollutants associated with intensive agriculture are chemicals that stimulate the growth of populations or communities in an ecosystem. Fertilizers, when applied at levels above those that are needed to achieve optimum yields, can pollute streams, lakes, and ponds adjacent to farmland. Excess nitrogen and phosphorus, in particular, can wash out of agricultural fields and stimulate the growth of aquatic plants and microorganisms in nearby bodies of water.

The influx of these nutrients increases the rate of eutrophication, a natural process in which the luxuriant growth of algae and aquatic plants near the surface of a lake or pond and the accumulation of organic sediment at the bottom gradually fill in the lake bed and convert the lake to a marsh or meadow. This process requires thousands of years under natural conditions but can occur much more rapidly with a steady influx of inorganic nutrients. As eutrophication proceeds microscopic organisms consume dissolved oxygen in the cool bottom waters of the lake as they decompose organic matter in the sediment. When the concentration of dissolved oxygen falls below a critical level many species of fish and other aquatic animals die. This ultimately affects the waterfowl and other wildlife in the lake ecosystem that feed on aquatic animals.

Pesticides are used during every phase of crop production in conventional agriculture. Herbicides are needed to control weeds in the field, especially early in the growing season when fast-growing weeds can overwhelm seedling crops. Many of the hybrid crop species that have been bred for maximum yield of fiber or grain compete poorly with native plants for water and nutrients in the soil. Almost half of the pesticides used in the United States are herbicides to control weeds in agricultural fields and urban lawns.[29] Various other pesticides are used to protect fruit, grain, and seed from spoilage before they are delivered to market.

Insecticides are needed to prevent insects from devouring crops in the field, and the breeding of genetically uniform crop species has increased farmers' dependence on chemicals to control these pests. Prior to the development of such crops agricultural fields would be planted with crops in which each plant differed genetically from other plants in the field, just as each individual in a human population differs from other individuals. Each variety of plant possessed a different set of defense mechanisms to protect itself against insects and other pests. In this situation some varieties would be susceptible to attack by a particular pest while other varieties would be resistant. Large monocultures of genetically identical plants with the same defense mechanisms do not have this buffering capacity. If a pest can overcome the defenses of that one variety of plant it can rapidly decimate a field.

The reliance on pesticides to maintain current levels of agricultural productivity is immense. It is estimated that one-third of the annual harvest was lost to competition from weeds, insect damage, and spoilage before pesticides became a staple of intensive agriculture. The widespread use of pesticides has not reduced the extent of crop damage, but it has made it possible to maintain losses at about one-third of the annual harvest as yields increased sharply.[30] Agricultural losses with current cropping practices would be much greater without the use of pesticides or an equally effective means of weed and insect control.

An ideal pesticide should quickly kill the organism it is intended to eliminate, then rapidly break down to harmless products. Selectively killing the target organism prevents the pesticide from harming crops, livestock, wildlife, or natural predators of the pest. Rapid breakdown ensures that pesticide residue does not accumulate in the environment. Long-lasting chemicals are more likely to harm surrounding habitats by leaching into groundwater or spreading through agricultural runoff and more likely to hasten the development of resistant pest populations. A small portion of the pest population almost always survives each treatment with a pesticide. The longer the chemical persists in the environment, or the more frequently it is applied, the greater is the opportunity for this segment of the pest population to proliferate and become predominant.

A pesticide with all of these desired qualities has not yet been developed, so pesticide use will always produce some degree of harm in agricultural areas. Careful and appropriate use of pesticides can minimize their impact on the environment and prolong their effectiveness.

SUSTAINABLE AGRICULTURE

> *Whatever our accomplishments, our sophistication, our artistic pretension, we owe our very existence to a six-inch layer of topsoil— and the fact that it rains.*
>
> Anonymous, *The Cockle Burr*

No one is more aware of the truth and meaning of this statement than a farmer. Farm families live close to the land and fully appreciate how profoundly our lives are affected by the forces of nature. A farmer's livelihood is directly affected by rainfall, runoff, soil erosion, and pest infestations. Farmers understand the cost of intensive agriculture and the damaging effects that it has on the land, and many are receptive to new agricultural practices that minimize the impact of farming on the environment, as long as those practices are economically feasible.

The past two decades have seen a growing interest in the development and implementation of agricultural practices that are environmentally sound, economically viable, and less dependent on fossil-fuel energy.[31] This new approach is known as "sustainable agriculture" to emphasize the focus on developing farming methods that can be practiced for years to come without depleting natural resources, destroying native ecosystems, exhausting energy reserves, or crippling a farmer's ability to produce a marketable crop and avoid financial ruin.

Intensive agriculture, as it is currently practiced in North America and Europe, is not sustainable. In terms of energy consumption alone it is estimated that if every country farmed like the United States all known oil reserves would be depleted in about twelve years.[32] Intensive farming has yielded remarkable increases in agricultural productivity, but it has also led to the decline of family farms, disintegration of rural communities, and displacement of farm laborers. Since 1950 almost half of the family-owned farms in the United States have gone out of business and have been consolidated into large corporate farms, many of which are owned by insurance or pension companies.[33] More than half the food produced in the United States comes from fewer than ten percent of the nation's farms, and the United States Department of Agriculture predicts that by the year 2000 half of the nation's food will be produced by just one percent of its farms.[34] None of these trends can continue without serious social, economic, and environmental consequences.

Sustainable agriculture should not be equated with "organic farming." Organic farming is a form of sustainable agriculture that relies entirely on organic products for fertilization and pest control. Products such as manure, compost, and peat are used as fertilizers, and various plant extracts are used as pesticides. This type of farming is economically viable on a small scale, but it cannot produce enough food to feed the world's rapidly growing human population.

Sustainable agriculture does not preclude the use of inorganic fertilizers and pesticides when needed, but seeks to minimize this type of input and to integrate other techniques to maintain a high level of productivity. The strategy is to substitute renewable resources or labor for non-renewable resources whenever feasible and to minimize the use of energy-intensive materials and equipment while maintaining productivity and profitability.

Soil Quality: One of the keys to maintaining productivity is to maintain soil quality. A healthy soil produces vigorous plants that are less susceptible to pest damage and competition from weeds. Farming practices that reduce soil quality increase the need for water, fertilizer, pesticides, and energy to maintain crop yields. Several techniques, some of which have been used for thousands of years, can be integrated into conventional farming operations to improve or maintain soil quality. Plowing across a slope rather than in the direction of the slope, a technique known as contour plowing, reduces runoff and soil erosion by impeding the flow of water downslope. Plowing less frequently (no-till or minimum-till farming) maintains soil structure by limiting the destruction of soil aggregates and reduces soil compaction by heavy farm equipment. Regular additions of compost or manure and covering the soil with mulches also enhance aggregate stability by adding organic matter to the soil, reduce water loss by evaporation, and help to maintain a diverse community of soil microbes, all of which improves soil fertility. Winter cover crops protect against soil erosion, and if a nitrogen-fixing crop such as clover or vetch is sown it can be plowed into the soil to add essential nutrients before the next growing season.

Crop Diversity: Selection of appropriate crops for a particular area is also an important component of sustainable agriculture. Crop species that are well adapted to the local climate and soil conditions require fewer inputs to produce a marketable harvest. Cultivating a variety of crops helps to protect a farm against fluctuating yields and market prices. Farms that raise a single crop (monoculture farms) are simpler to manage, but the failure of a crop due to nutrient deficiency, harsh weather, disease, pest infestation, or a saturated market can be economically devastating, and monocultures are more susceptible to these types of failures. Each plant species has specific requirements for growth and extracts the nutrients it requires from the soil. Planting the same crop season after season depletes the soil of those nutrients and increases dependence on fertilizers. This type of farming also allows plant pathogens and insects that feed on the monoculture crop to establish large populations.

Alternating crops between growing seasons (crop rotation) or cultivating a variety of crops each season (polyculture) helps to maintain soil fertility, suppress weeds, and limit the proliferation of plant pathogens and insect pests. If crops are alternated, the type of plant that is available for pathogens or insects to attack changes regularly. Unless a pest can attack many different species its population will decline with each rotation. Polyculture produces similar results by limiting the area covered by each crop species. It is difficult to plant and harvest polyculture fields with modern farm equipment, however, so this type of farming is more likely to be practiced in areas where labor is plentiful and farm equipment is not used extensively.

Integrated Pest Management: Integrated pest management employs a variety of strategies to minimize losses due to pest damage without relying exclusively on environmentally hazardous pesticides. One strategy that has been very successful in certain situations is biological control of plant pests. A natural predator or antagonist of the pest species is introduced to keep pest populations small and minimize crop damage. A classic example of this type of pest control was the introduction of ladybugs to control scale insects in California orange orchards in the 1880s. Within one year after the release of the ladybugs the California orange crop was saved from a devastating infestation, and the same species of ladybug continues to protect California orchards to this day. This type of biological control can also be accomplished by providing a habitat that favors the development of natural predator populations. Groundcovers planted in orchards and vineyards, for instance, provide a habitat for arthropods that feed on insects.

Several species of bacteria, fungi, and viruses have been used effectively to control insect pests on a variety of vegetable crops, fruits, shade trees, and ornamental plants, and selected species of bacteria are currently being investigated as potential soil inoculants to protect crops against plant pathogens. Genetic engineering has created the possibility of transferring the bacterial genes that produce insecticidal toxins into plants to make the plants themselves resistant to insect pests.

Despite a number of successful applications, biological control has not had widespread success. Even when this strategy is effective it does not eliminate all crop damage. Nonetheless, biological control can be economically beneficial when the losses due to crop damage amount to less than the cost of applying chemicals for pest control. Biological control is also more pest-specific and longer lasting than chemical pesticides. Broadspectrum insecticides may kill beneficial insects, such as the natural predators of a pest species and bees that pollinate crops, as well as the target species. Resistance to most pesticides is readily acquired within a few years after the chemical is first used, whereas natural predators and antagonists can effectively control pest populations for longer periods of time.

Another pesticide-free method that has been used effectively to control insects is the introduction of sterile strains of the pest species in infested areas. Sterile individuals mate with the native population but do not produce offspring. With time this can significantly reduce pest populations.

Crop rotation, polyculture, and a technique known as trap cropping can also be used to control insects. In trap cropping a small area within an agricultural field is planted before the main crop and treated with a chemical attractant such as an insect pheromone (a sexual attractant). As the trap crop grows it attracts large numbers of the pest species in the area. The trap crop is then treated with a concentrated dose of insecticide to eliminate the pest and discarded. This leaves a relatively small population of surviving pests to damage the main crop. Trap cropping minimizes the area treated with pesticide and produces a crop with no pesticide residue.

This is just one of the innovative ways in which insecticides can be used in integrated pest management schemes. The goal is not necessarily to eliminate pesticide use entirely but to use these chemicals in more creative and efficient ways that minimize environmental hazards, reduce cost, lower energy consumption, and prolong effectiveness. Common strategies include less frequent and widespread use of pesticides and the use of different classes of chemicals in combination or in series to delay the development of resistant pest populations.

CONCLUSION AND THEOLOGICAL REFLECTION

People of conscience throughout the world, particularly those whose values and beliefs are grounded in the teachings of the world's most influential religions, must accept the responsibility to care for the multitudes of poor, starving families who desperately need assistance to obtain adequate food, clothing, and shelter. International hunger relief efforts by governments and non-government organizations have succeeded in reducing world hunger by a small margin in recent years, despite continued growth of the human population. A survey conducted by the Food and Agriculture Organization from 1969 to 1971 estimated that at that time 918 million people had inadequate access to food.[35] By the time of the 1979 to 1981 survey the number had declined to 906 million.[36] The current number of 841 million is based on the results of the 1990 to 1992 World Food Survey.[37] The decline in the number of inadequately fed people over the past twenty years is remarkable when one considers that the world population has increased by 1.5 billion during that period.

Success in reducing world hunger has been accomplished by improving agricultural practices and converting more land to agricultural use in developing countries and by improving the worldwide distribution of food. High levels of productivity must be maintained to feed the growing human population, but the destruction of native habitats and the practice of intensive agriculture cannot be sustained. The challenge is to find more creative, energy efficient, environmentally sound ways to produce food and fiber. Ultimately growth of the human population must be contained or the world will experience unprecedented poverty, hunger, disease, and political and social upheaval.

The developing countries of the world provide a great opportunity to implement sustainable agricultural practices in regions where it is critical to maintain or increase the current level of food production. Intensive agriculture is not deeply entrenched in these countries as it is North America and Europe, and most developing countries do not have the economic resources to support it. What they do have is an abundant supply of laborers in need of work to provide their families with food and shelter, and in tropical regions an enormous variety of native plant species that can be cultivated and harvested for food.

An estimated 30,000 plant species have edible parts, yet only twenty cultivated species currently provide ninety percent of the world's food supply.[38] Many of these widely cultivated species are native to temperate regions and do not adapt well to a tropical climate. Tropical ecosystems, on the other hand, are the most biologically diverse ecosystems in the world and contain an immense variety of edible plants that are well adapted to the local climate and superior to many cultivated species in growth rate and productivity. E. O. Wilson eloquently describes the potential that these plant species offer as a source of food for the human population in *The Diversity of Life*:

> Waiting in the wings are tens of thousands of unused plant species, many demonstrably superior to those in favor. One potential star species that has emerged from among the thousands is the winged bean *(Psophocarpus tetragonolobus)* of New Guinea. It can be called the one-species supermarket. The entire plant is palatable, from the spinach-like leaves to young pods usable as green beans, plus young seeds like peas and tubers that, boiled, fried, baked or roasted, are richer in protein than potatoes. The mature seeds resemble soybeans. They can be cooked as they are or ground into flour or liquefied into a caffeine-free beverage that tastes like coffee. Moreover, the plant grows at a phenomenal pace, reaching a length of 4 meters in a few weeks. Finally, the winged bean is a legume; it

harbors nitrogen-fixing nodules in its roots and has little need for fertilizer.[39]

A crucial benefit of promoting the use of native plant species for food is that it provides an economic incentive to limit the destruction of the natural habitats of these plants. An encouraging example of this is the demonstration that harvesting edible fruits, oils, latex, and medicines from tropical rainforests can be as profitable as, and in the long term more profitable than one-time logging of the forests for timber export. This practice has succeeded in selected regions of Brazil and Peru and has the potential to succeed in other locations.[40] Tangible economic benefits such as these are more likely to persuade governments and individuals of the need to preserve the rich biological diversity of these regions than the most eloquent descriptions of the intrinsic value of natural habitats.

Implementing the transition to sustainable agriculture in North America and Europe will be much more difficult. American and European farmers have become economically dependent on the high yields that can be achieved through intensive agriculture, and consumers are accustomed to low prices and abundant supplies of food. The average American family currently spends less than ten percent of its income on food,[41] a lower percentage than any culture at any time in history, while a billion or more people in developing countries spend up to seventy percent of their income on food.[42]

Widespread implementation of sustainable agricultural practices in developed countries will require changes in the hearts and minds of producers, consumers, and government officials as well as the development of innovative, environmentally sound technologies. A key element in the success of sustainable agriculture is the willingness of consumers to pay higher prices for products that are less plentiful. Consumers can profoundly influence producers, retailers, and policymakers by demonstrating a preference for products that are produced in a sustainable manner. Policymakers can, in turn, encourage the development of sustainable agriculture through commodity, price support, and tax policies. While most North American farms continue to practice intensive agriculture, it is estimated that fifty thousand to one hundred thousand farmers in the United States have converted largely or entirely to sustainable agriculture.[43] Crop yields are generally lower on sustainable farms but net income is comparable to conventional farms because of the lower expenditures for fertilizers and pesticides and the higher prices that can be obtained for "organically grown" produce.

Another key element in sustainability will be increased reliance on human labor as an alternative to energy-intensive machinery. Consumers and government officials must be willing to support programs that encourage adequate wages, safe working conditions, health benefits, and economic stability for farm laborers, and economic policies that support rural community development and protect family farms.

Curiosity, ingenuity, and industriousness have made humans the dominant species on Earth. As a species we have learned to recognize patterns and cycles in nature, to domesticate animals, and to cultivate plants for a reliable supply of food. We have used our knowledge and cleverness to add comfort and convenience to our lives, and in the process have acquired the illusion that we are separate from the natural world and capable of controlling it as we see fit. Humans are an integral part of nature, though, not its "master." We have the same biological needs and frailties as any other species, including those that our activities are driving to extinction by the tens of thousands every year. The destructive practices that we currently use to feed, clothe, shelter, comfort, and entertain ourselves cannot be continued for much longer. Scientists who specialize in investigating and understanding the complexity of the natural world and humanity's place in it are virtually unanimous in proclaiming that we are in the midst of an ecological crisis, with precious little time to alter our course. We must make difficult choices now to provide for a livable world in the future. Anita Gordon and David Suzuki clearly describe the challenge facing humanity in *It's a Matter of Survival:*

> If the human species is genuinely exceptional, it will be shown by what we do in the coming decade. No other species has been able to anticipate limits and deliberately avoid a catastrophe by taking appropriate action ahead of time. We have to face the reality of what scientists are telling us. We have a stake in what happens because our children will inherit what we leave them. But until we truly accept the reality that this planet may soon become unlivable, we'll only make gestures.[44]

With each year that passes, the choices facing humanity become fewer and more difficult. We must change our view of the natural world and our place in it, and use our ingenuity now to secure a livable world for our children. If we have the courage and determination to make the difficult choices there is hope for the future.

Finally, "Feeding the Hungry and Protecting the Environment" is a reminder of the essential function of farming and the agricultural enterprise for human survivability. While modern agriculture—at least since the "green revolution"—has been extremely productive, the industrial approach to farming, known as "intensive agriculture," has in recent years been increasingly scrutinized for its negative environmental impact. This chapter provides a clear summary of those ecological problems such as habitat destruction, diminishing soil quality, depleting aquifers and pollution. Wendell Berry concurs with this assessment. Reflecting on the high cost of American agriculture he writes that "the costs are in loss of soil, in loss of farms and farmers, in soil and water pollution, in food pollution, in the decay of country towns and communities, and in the increasing vulnerability of the food supply system."[45] These intensively driven agricultural problems are immeasurably compounded by the fact of rapidly growing human population and the specter of world hunger. How will humanity feed growing numbers of people when current agricultural practices are increasingly determined to be ecologically questionable? The solution proposed herein is the switch to sustainable methods of agriculture.

Theologically, the ecological necessity of sustainable farming raises the culturally and biblically relevant notion of stewardship. As the Judeo-Christian tradition attempts to redefine itself in the midst of environmental crisis the appeal to the biblical roots of stewardship is increasingly frequent in church documents and eco-theological treatises. There are, however, voices within the tradition who look unfavorably upon the reappropriation of biblical stewardship. Some argue that the term is overly anthropocentric and is no longer an adequate metaphor for what ought to be a more ecocentric or egalitarian relationship between the human and non-human world. Some like Jay McDaniel find the notion of stewardship "troublesome" because "it promotes a paternalistic approach of humans to the Earth and animals."[46] In similar fashion Elizabeth Dodson Gray, representing a feminist critique, argues that "stewardship is still steeped in hierarchy and paternalism . . . [and] leaves these illusions of hierarchy, ownership and dominion safe in our heads and hearts."[47] These criticisms are understandable given the anthropocentric "dominion" (Gen 1:26-28) view of stewardship.

There are, however, other possible interpretations of biblical stewardship that are less anthropocentric and more organic. Furthermore, critics tend to ignore the fact that the steward principle appears throughout the biblical tradition and cannot, therefore, be easily jettisoned. Moreover, the concept of stewardship has wide cultural appeal particularly within North American agricultural communities.

The theological justification of stewardship as the practice of sustainable agriculture is best achieved by drawing upon the second creation account where in Gen 2:16 the human beings are to cultivate *(ʿābad)* and care *(shāmar)* for the garden. According to Walter Brueggemann, *ʿābad* and *shāmar* suggest the vocation or work of a gardener or shepherd.[48] Phyllis Trible claims that the verb *ʿabad* means to serve. She says, "It connotes respect, indeed, reverence and worship."[49] In her view "To till the garden is to serve the garden; to exercise power over it is to reverence it. Similarly, to keep *(šmr)* the garden is an act of protection, not of possession."[50]

The imagery here is not monarchic; rather it is agricultural and organic and strongly suggests that human beings have the vocation and responsibility to be earth keepers. This interpretation of stewardship provides a theological basis for farming and the agricultural endeavor. More importantly, however, this essay offers a very specific and concrete ethical framework for defining the stewardship of farming in an era of environmental problems: the practice of sustainable agriculture. Agricultural stewardship—appropriate cultivation and care for the land— must be sustainable focused "on developing farming methods that can be practiced for years . . . without depleting natural resources, destroying native ecosystems, exhausting energy reserves, or crippling a farmer's ability to produce a marketable crop and avoid financial ruin."[51]

NOTES: CHAPTER 5

[1] *Sixth World Food Survey* (Rome: Food and Agriculture Organization of the United Nations, 1996).

[2] Ibid.

[3] M. deOnís et al., "The Worldwide Magnitude of Protein-Energy Malnutrition: An Overview from the WHO Global Database on Child Growth," *WHO Bulletin* 71 (1993) 703–12.

[4] Eleanor Whitney and May Hamilton, *Understanding Nutrition* (St. Paul: West, 1977) 125.

[5] Ibid.

[6] See M. deOnís et al., "The Worldwide Magnitude of Protein-Energy Malnutrition."

[7] See *Sixth World Food Survey* (n. 1 above).

[8] *World Food Summit Report* (Rome: Food and Agriculture Organization of the United Nations, 1996).

[9] *Global Prevalence of Iodine Deficiency Disorders* (Micronutrient Deficiency Information System Working Paper Number 1 [Geneva: World Health Organization/United Nations Children's Fund/International Council for Control of Iodine Deficiency Disorders, 1993]).

[10] *Global Prevalence of Vitamin-A Deficiency* (Micronutrient Deficiency Information System Working Paper Number 2 [Geneva: World Health Organization/United Nations Children's Fund, 1995]).

[11] Alan B. Durning, "Ending Poverty," in Lester R. Brown, project director, *State of the World 1990: A Worldwatch Institute Report on Progress Toward a Sustainable Society* (New York and London: W. W. Norton, 1990) 135.

[12] International Conference on Nutrition, Rome, December 1992.

[13] World Food Summit, Rome, November 1996.

[14] William R. Rees, unbroadcast portion of an interview for the Canadian Broadcasting Corporation radio series "It's a Matter of Survival." Quoted by Anita Gordon and David Suzuki, *It's a Matter of Survival* (Cambridge, Mass.: Harvard University Press, 1990) 92–93.

[15] See *Sixth World Food Survey* (n. 1 above).

[16] Ibid.

[17] Quoted by Anita Gordon and David Suzuki, *It's a Matter of Survival.*

[18] See *Sixth World Food Survey.*

[19] Mark B. Bush, *Ecology of a Changing Planet* (Upper Saddle River, N.J.: Prentice Hall, 1997) 197.

[20] Thomas Malthus, *An Essay on the Principle of Population as It Affects the Future Improvement of Society* (London: J. Johnson, 1798).

[21] Lester R. Brown et al., *Vital Signs 1994: The Trends that Are Shaping Our Future* (Washington, D.C.: Worldwatch Institute, 1994).

[22] Mark B. Bush, *Ecology of a Changing Planet* 232.

[23] Ibid. 61.

[24] Gordon and Suzuki, *It's a Matter of Survival,* and Edward O. Wilson, *The Diversity of Life* (Cambridge, Mass.: Harvard University Press, 1992) 283–85.

[25] Gordon and Suzuki, *It's a Matter of Survival* 143, 195.

[26] "Pesticide" is a general term that refers to any chemical that is used to kill a crop "pest" such as a weed, insect, nematode, fungus, bacterium, or virus. More precise terms are used for chemicals that control infestations by specific types of pests. For instance, "insecticides" are used to kill insects, "herbicides" are used to kill weeds, and "fungicides" are used to kill fungi.

[27] Gordon and Suzuki, *It's a Matter of Survival* 79.

[28] Bush, *Ecology of a Changing Planet* 229.

[29] Ibid. 252.

[30] See Gordon and Suzuki, *It's a Matter of Survival* 173.

[31] Gail Feenstra et al., University of California Sustainable Agriculture Research and Education Program, http://www.sarep.ucdavis.edu/concept.htm (University of California, Davis, 1997).

[32] Bush, *Ecology of a Changing Planet* 236.

[33] Ibid. See also Sheldon Krimsky and Roger Wrubel, *Agricultural Biotechnology and the Environment* (Chicago: University of Illinois Press, 1996) 244.

[34] Bush, *Ecology of a Changing Planet* 227–28.

[35] See *Sixth World Food Survey* (n. 1 above).

[36] Ibid.

[37] Ibid.

[38] Wilson, *The Diversity of Life* 287.

[39] Ibid. 289.

[40] Ibid. 323.

[41] Bush, *Ecology of a Changing Planet* 226.

[42] Gordon and Suzuki, *It's a Matter of Survival* 87.

[43] Bush, *Ecology of a Changing Planet* 238.

[44] Gordon and Suzuki, *It's a Matter of Survival* 237.

[45] Wendell Berry, *Home Economics* (San Francisco: North Point Press, 1987) 128.

[46] Jay B. McDaniel, *With Roots and Wings* (Maryknoll, N.Y.: Orbis, 1995) 91.

[47] Elizabeth Dodson Gray, "Come Inside the Circle of Creation: An Ethic of Attunement," in Frederick Ferré and Peter Hartel, eds., *Ethics and Environmental Policy* (Athens, Ga.: University of Georgia Press, 1994) 27.

[48] Walter Brueggemann, *Genesis* (Atlanta: John Knox, 1982) 46.

[49] Phyllis Trible, *God and the Rhetoric of Sexuality* (Philadelphia: Fortress, 1978) 85–86.

[50] Ibid.

[51] See above, p. 88.

6

Mental Cartography in a Time of Environmental Crisis

"I call heaven and earth to witness against you today that I have set before you life and death, blessings and curses. Choose life so that you and your descendants may live. . . ." (Deut 30:19)

I n his address to the Israelite community the great lawgiver and prophet Moses encourages the people to choose life, which meant loving God, walking in God's ways, and observing God's commandments, decrees, and ordinances (Deut 30:16). In the context of today's world, one that faces environmental problems on a global scale, Moses' words could become a mantra, "Choose Life," as the human community struggles to reconstruct its mental map so that it can chart a new course that will ensure life for the present and future generations of creation.

INTRODUCTION

If the environmental situation of today were likened to a family vacation, the global population of humanity would be sitting in an automobile on the shoulder of a curving and narrow lane. As dusk approaches, with the engine temperature warning light blinking, the challenge for the family is to unfold a complicated roadmap to try to find its way. All the elements of this image match the current state of our species as the twenty-first century unfolds. We cannot see where we need to go directly so we are forced to rely on indirect methods like maps or satellite images, or demographic models, or long-range meteorological projections. Taken in its entirety the map of our situation turns out to be exceedingly complex, and the warning light is blinking. Each year satellite images show the shrinking of tropical rainforests and the seasonal thinning of the ozone layer in the Antarctic spring. Demographic projections indicate an upcoming surge in population as the under-fifteen-year-olds of the developing world mature physically. The long range meteorological models now predict unstable precipitation patterns associated with rising atmospheric CO_2 levels that may have considerable adverse impact on global agriculture.

The metaphor of a map is a powerful one for me because it so closely matches the nature of scientific knowledge. A map is representative information rather than a direct experience of the reality about which it informs us; it can more or less accurately indicate locations and possible routes, but it cannot tell us where we ought to go. A map can also often be awkward of access because of its size and complexity as we strive to unfold its meanings in a limited space like a car or a limited span like a human life.

How have we, the human family, arrived at our present location? We, the family, have been relying on an outdated mental map. In fact, the map we used became outdated as we were driving. The mental map common in Western civilization fifty years ago needs to be examined. The last half century has seen changes in environmental circumstances so great that unless we make a special effort to recall the world of the 1950s it no longer comes to mind as relevant. But in fact our journey toward our present environmental crisis began in earnest fifty years ago, and unless we recall and reevaluate our direction we have little hope of being able to take the turns needed to extricate ourselves from our current destination.

THE MAP OF HUMAN POPULATION GROWTH

Fifty years ago the planet we share seemed a much less crowded place. To people in the western world overpopulated places seemed few and "far away" then, and distances seemed much larger. It also seemed that the western world had vast unharvested resources, i.e., agriculture, metals, fossil fuels, and lumber, available for human use. This was a naïve understanding of where we were located on the curve of population growth. To date global human population is approximately 6.0 billion in contrast to 3.0 billion in the 1950s and 1.6 billion in the 1900s.

How could such enormous changes take place so quickly? The nature of population growth and the possible remedies for overcrowding are best understood in mathematical terms because it is the inexorable nature of logarithmic equations (like the one described below) that faces the human community today.

The simplest expression of how any species of organisms grows under ideal conditions[1] is: *population increase in numbers per season = rN* where "r" is what scientists call the intrinsic rate of increase and "N" is the number of organisms in the preceding generation. The intrinsic rate of increase is determined by the number of offspring that a typical pair of a species might produce. It would be a larger number for any species that had a short generation time or a large number of offspring per generation. Thus "r" would be very large for mosquitoes,[2] rather large for rabbits, and much less for humans. A further example of the equation is as follows.

Imagine a pair of rabbits, in a temperate and richly vegetated climate, where a female might produce three litters of six kits apiece in a year. These are, in fact, realistic numbers. Given that a pair of rabbits can therefore produce eighteen kits in a year, further imagine that the original pair quietly die as a result of their efforts. This situation would lead one to say that the original "N" (population size) was two, while the intrinsic rate of increase (r) was nine offspring on average per rabbit, since the female bears eighteen offspring and the male bears none. In the course of time if all their offspring survive and reproduce at a rate similar to the ancestral pair, and if the offspring born in every generation were to follow the typical rules of mammalian gender determination (half male and half female), then their population growth would look like this:

- generation 1, number of rabbits = 2; generation 2, number of rabbits = 18;
- generation 3, number of rabbits = 162; generation 4, number of rabbits = 1,458;
- generation 5, number of rabbits = 13,122; generation 6, number of rabbits = 118,098;
- generation 7, number of rabbits = 1,062,882; generation 8, number of rabbits = 9,565,938;
- generation 9, number of rabbits = 86,093,442; generation 10, number of rabbits = 774,840,978;
- generation 11, number of rabbits = 6,973,568,802.

In eleven generations the original pair of rabbits has produced enough descendants to exceed the present human population of the earth. Note that the numbers increase from generation to generation and that the amount of increase is increasing in each generation. For example from generation 9 to 10 the increase is 774,840,978 − 86,093,442 = 688,747,536 rabbits. From generation 10 to 11 the increase is 6,973,568,802 − 774,840,978 = 6,198,727,824.

Human population growth throughout the centuries has almost matched the sort of unlimited growth equation described above.[3] With the development of modern hygiene, vaccines, and agriculture came the partial release from some factors contributing to human mortality. Hence the species increased in numbers at an enormous rate. Why have census bureaus not noticed the rapid increase in numbers until recently? Why was the mental map of the 1950s world so different from that of the 1990s world? The expanding rate of increase over time of an unlimited growth pattern suggests that there is an apparent sudden "jump" late in the game, even though that jump is part of a previously existing pattern of increase that built up quietly. In fact, human population increase rates have slowed very slightly in the last half decade, but given the rate from which they are slowing and the population level we have already achieved it may be that this slowing will have a minimal effect as our numbers nonetheless shoot upwards. Whether the rabbits achieved a level of 6,973,568,802 in their eleventh generation or slowed slightly to 6,500,000,000, their twelfth generation would still be enormous. The human species may now be in the same position.

Natural populations do not grow in an unconstrained fashion because of limiting factors, i.e., predators, disease, lack of water, lack of food, lack of shelter, accumulation of toxins, etc., that increase mortality as population density increases. In the real world population growth follows a more complex logistic growth equation that incorporates an expression that reduces growth rates progressively as a population approaches the maximum carrying capacity an environment can indefinitely support.[4] However, we humans cannot rely on a logistic growth equation to provide us with a humane or admirable solution to population growth. The mortality factors described by the logistic growth equation are harsh in their reality. Factors such as war over the control of declining resources, pestilence as public hygiene deteriorates, and human expansion into rain forests bring us into contact with new diseases like Ebola virus, and we encounter famine as agriculture falls short of population growth.[5] These factors suggest a powerful ethical imperative for humans to make appropriate decisions about their own population growth before the mortality factors of the logistic growth equation make the decision.

THE MAP OF ATMOSPHERIC CO_2

It is common knowledge that the great industrial growth that had taken place by 1950 was, in fact, increasing atmospheric CO_2 (carbon dioxide) levels.[6] This fact was unknown then, and there was no sign that global temperatures were increasing because of the CO_2-driven greenhouse effect. Nor was it known that climatic patterns were altering in a systematic direction. Atmospheric CO_2 levels had risen silently from 280 parts per million [ppm] in the preindustrial era, a time when humans subsisted by hunting, fishing, or farming, to 315 ppm in mid-century when the industrial revolution had completely changed how most humans lived. Currently they are 360 ppm. As far as climate was concerned no one suspected that anything else was taking place other than normal climatic fluctuations like the often-mentioned "twenty-year cycle."

To some extent it is true that the present climatic changes caused by increasing CO_2 levels are nothing new. Fossil and geological records indicate frequent dramatic climatic changes on the earth. Glaciers and ice ages have come and gone; the woolly mammoths and the dinosaurs before them were subjected to things like warming cycles and sun-eclipsing impacts of enormous colliding objects. Mass extinctions are a periodic and dramatic element of the fossil record, and there is no doubt that some of them were driven by natural climatic alterations on a global level. There are, however, two distinctions between all previous climatic cycles and the change in global climate now taking place due to changes in the atmospheric CO_2 levels. The first distinction is that the current change in global climate is anthropogenic: it is caused by humans. The second distinction is that we are now present on the planet, and even the most dispassionate observer would have to allow humans a special interest in climate-driven human extinction as a possibility distinct from other plant and animal extinctions. As a species we humans are now here on the planet, and we do not want to go extinct.

At this point in human history many North Americans continue to take great satisfaction not only in the size and acceleration of their personal vehicles but also in the size of their air-conditioned homes. However, anything that burns fossil fuels contributes to the destabilization of the earth's climate, and current CO_2 levels indicate that satisfaction is short-lived as some of our choices progressively change the earth in such a way as to pass on a more difficult and less hospitable planet to our children and their children. The human family needs a new mental map to relate personal choices to factors like CO_2 levels in the global environment. The basis of that map was written thirty years ago. An article entitled "The Tragedy of the Commons" by Garrett Hardin[7] used a metaphor of a community of humans who all focused on their own short-term individual interests. This community shared a communal grazing area for livestock, and simple adherence of each individual to his or her own short-term economic interests caused the community to overuse their grazing resource to the extent that everyone was eventually impoverished by long-term overgrazing. The ability of our atmosphere to absorb CO_2 from all our individual uses of combustible fuel parallels this metaphor closely.

The human community remains at this point now. The atmosphere carries away the exhaust fumes of cars, furnaces, and fuel-burning power plants only to distribute those waste gases instead of destroying them. There has been no decrease either in total human generated carbon dioxide emissions from fossil fuels used in the northern hemisphere or in slash-and-burn agriculture in the southern hemisphere.[8] Hardin suggested that the tragedy of the commons could only be overcome by privatizing the resource involved or by government regulation that set limits on human activities related to that resource.[9] The atmosphere is not a candidate for privatization. One needs to look from this vantage point to understand the current international debate about treaties to limit CO_2 outputs. In later discussions in this chapter about other forms of pollution it is worth bearing in mind that lakes, rivers, oceans, and groundwater all represent different types of commons.[10]

THE MAP OF ATMOSPHERIC OZONE

If someone had approached another person on the street in the 1950s and asked that person if he or she knew that above the earth was a thin layer of ozone that shielded all life on the planet from the damaging effects of ultraviolet radiation, a perplexed stare might have been the only response. If the hypothetical informant were asked if he or she had ever heard of the potential environmental risks inherent in widespread use of chlorofluorocarbons (CFCs), the industrial gases used as refrigerants and spray can propellants, the response would have been bewilderment. Neither stratospheric ozone depletion nor CFCs were part of the human mental map of the 1950s, although the process that caused the depletion of the ozone layer had already begun.

Until the late 1920s ammonia was the refrigerant used in industrial cooling systems. Household and automobile air conditioning systems were essentially nonexistent. Ammonia is a toxic and potentially highly dangerous refrigerant. Industrial chemists searched to find a safer substitute.[11] What was invented in the late 1920s as an answer was CFCs, and it was believed at that time that CFCs were harmless, nontoxic, chemically inert, and inexpensive to produce. Most of that was true. Europeans and North Americans began to use CFCs as propellants in spray cans. However, these CFCs were so stable and inert chemically that they did not break down, and once released into the atmosphere they exist for decades or centuries.

In the late 1970s, realizing that massive global release of CFCs might pose an eventual risk to the atmosphere, various nations began to ban CFCs from use in aerosol cans. CFCs did continue to be used in applications for which no alternative product was available, and literally hundreds of thousands of tons per year continued to be employed as refrigerants, solvents, and so forth.

In 1985 the British Antarctic Atmospheric Survey found a huge seasonal ozone hole over the South Pole. The ozone levels dropped sharply during the Antarctic spring (September and October). This was the result of decades of previous ozone thinning. The Antarctic ozone hole became the most obvious manifestation of a global ozone-layer thinning. Most estimates indicate that each one percent decrease in the ozone layer will produce a two to three percent increase in human skin cancers such as basal cell carcinomas, squamous cell carcinomas, and malignant melanomas. If this process could be reversed, many people would benefit.

To the credit of the world community's ability to respond rapidly to the environmental challenge, a new mental map for ozone was developed quickly for such ventures. In 1989, eighty-one nations met and agreed to phase out CFC production by the end of the twentieth century and to replace the CFCs with less damaging classes of chemicals. Subsequent to that meeting accumulating evidence of the rapidity and extent of ozone depletion led to the adoption of an even shorter timeline; CFC production was to be banned by the mid-1990s. Currently CFC production is greatly reduced globally, but there is still the problem of illegal CFCs being produced and smuggled internationally. Alternative technologies using other materials are being developed to permanently replace CFCs. At present atmospheric CFC levels have been stabilized although their long residence time means that stratospheric ozone levels are still decreasing and are not expected to recover to their earlier levels for some decades.

The case of ozone layer thinning is an example for everyone to contemplate. It was a circumstance in which a limited environmental problem to which a focused technical remedy was possible posed an obvious direct health risk to humans. The international community was able to come together rapidly and agree upon a mental map that indicated not only where we are but also where we need to go. Whether that process can be replicated to deal with broader problems whose resolution would call for more significant revisions in people's lifestyles and personal behavior remains to be seen.

THE MAP OF PESTICIDES

Humankind has always struggled with pest species attracted by the concentrated food supplies offered by our agricultural products. Millennia ago the Sumerians burned sulphur in storehouses to rid grain of vermin. Ancient Greeks mention this process in their epic poems. In the year 1865 an anonymous person discovered the metal-salt insecticide "paris green," and people began using it. Many pesticides of this type were based on heavy metals such as lead arsenate and calcium arsenate, a combined total of 156,000,000 pounds of which were sprayed in the U.S. in 1943.[12] There is often a misapprehension that modern pesticides ushered in an era of environmental contamination with toxins that was preceded by pleasanter times. The cessation of the widespread distribution of heavy-metal-based pesticides was doubtless a good thing, although there have been considerable problems with reducing the toxicities of the materials that have replaced them.

The widespread use of modern pesticides began in the Second World War. DDT first came into use in 1939. This was a material that provided the Allied forces a considerable advantage since they had sole access to it for controlling the insect vectors of epidemic diseases that always hover in the wings waiting for warfare or other catastrophes to loosen the grip of public hygiene programs. As soon as the war ended the use of modern pesticides began worldwide.

Synthetic organic insecticides, beginning with DDT, were a new and hopeful technology in the late 1940s and 1950s. Although the first troubling signs of the rapid emergence of insecticide resistance were noticed by agricultural scientists, Rachel Carson had yet to publish *Silent Spring* and alert the general populace to the dangers posed to vertebrates by the accumulation of synthetic organic materials in human bodies. The bald eagles and brown pelicans did not yet have their calcium metabolism altered. When that alteration happened they laid eggs with shells so thin that the incubating parents crushed their offspring. But in those earlier decades "biological magnification" was a phrase that might have meant looking at a bug through a lens.

However, in the latter part of the 1950s and the early 1960s it became clear that DDT was not a safe panacea. Residues of DDT and its metabolites like DDE began to persist for many years in the environment. Because of their lipid solubility they bioaccumulated, beginning at low levels in plankton and tiny fish and then at higher levels in larger predatory organisms. The waters of Lake Michigan soon had DDT levels that could be measured in parts per trillion. The fish in the lake had levels in their bodies in the parts per million range. Rachel Carson's book documented this process,[13] and the general public began to realize that pesticides with suitable biodegradability needed to be developed. Although it remained a widely used pesticide elsewhere in the world, DDT was banned in the United States.

The situation today, with the widespread application of synthetic organic compounds to the environment, is a complicated one. Many people have become categorically opposed to all chemical pest control. They do not realize, however, the necessary role of effective pest control in preventing starvation worldwide. Many others take pesticides and herbicides too much for granted and hire lawn-care companies to regularly spray cocktails composed of fertilizers and potentially harmful pesticides and broadleaf weed herbicides on their lawns. Meanwhile pesticide and herbicide exposure has become an occupational hazard for farmers, and cancers like chronic leukocytic leukemia and non-Hodgkins lymphomas have been linked to long-term exposure to pesticides by those who apply them. It has been suggested that children allowed to play on recently chemically sprayed lawns or exposed to pesticides due to home use may be at increased risk for some cancers. Much research, however, remains to be done on this question.[14]

Agricultural scientists have devised new classes of pesticides with considerably shorter environmental persistence, e.g., organic phosphorus compounds, carbamates, and botanicals that are derived from compounds that plants use to protect themselves from insect attack. Other means of pest control are being developed and deployed, such as the application of insect hormones that distort pest insect development, or the use of augmented levels of natural predators or pathogens to kill the pest species without chemicals.

Today most consumers are demanding cosmetically perfect apples that in many regions need to be sprayed ten to twelve times a year to avoid any spots. These consumers do not seem to reflect on the fact that a few spots cannot kill anyone, and the overuse of agricultural chemicals can cause death. Another example is golf courses. They are generally maintained so that rather than the putting greens having enough chemicals applied to them to make them carpet-like, long stretches of fairway are heavily sprayed. People continue to have synthetic organic pesticides and herbicides sprayed frequently on the lawns that they subsequently let their children wrestle and play on. The human community needs to mature in its perspective on pesticide and herbicide use. They need to determine where applications are worthwhile and then attempt to reduce the casual exposure to such materials.

THE MAP OF OTHER POLLUTANTS

A half-century ago, when the human race began an accelerated journey toward an environment contaminated with a bewildering array of chemicals, it was believed that humans were producing a quantity of pollutants that would remain harmless as long as they were distributed evenly throughout the environment. After all, the ocean was deep, the air moved over large areas of agricultural and forested land as well as cities and factories, and the release of materials from any one site seemed paltry compared to the immense scale of the physical world. Nevertheless, some events that should have been warning signs had taken place. For example, there had been some killer smogs like the one caused by industrial processes in Donora, Pennsylvania that killed twenty people in 1948. There was also the infamous London smog of December 4–10, 1952 that killed an estimated four thousand people because of a combination of cold, damp, stagnant air and the subsequent increase in heating fuel use in homes heated largely with coal. During this smog London's traffic needed to use headlights at noon.[15] However, these were local rather than global events. Gases and liquid effluents produced by industry were generally released high atop smokestacks that let the wind carry them away, or poured via outflow pipes into rivers, lakes, or the ocean. In either case the rhyme "the solution to pollution is dilution" was taught to school children, who soon came to believe in dispersal of pollutants rather than in reductions of pollutant output as a responsible means of dealing with potentially harmful industrial and domestic wastes. Of all the human thought about the natural world of the 1950s this idea may be, in retrospect, the most simple-mindedly optimistic of the lot. It is not that nature has no capacity to cleanse itself of wastes produced by human activities; it is just that the cleansing capacity of nature is finite, and the combination of human numbers and our demand for the production of an enormous variety of consumer goods has overwhelmed that regenerating capacity and produced a crisis of toxic accumulations within all that is breathed, drunk, and eaten.

If categorizing pollutants is a way to help make sense of what is presently going on, one could list several broad categories: (1) naturally occurring materials, often benign to our health in low concentrations, that are increasing in concentration due to human activities; (2) materials like heavy metals that are mined and concentrated by human activities, and have negative impacts on human health; (3) materials that never existed in nature before humans invented the molecules in laboratories and then began to synthesize them in bulk in chemical factories; and (4) radioactive wastes. I will describe these categories of compounds individually in some detail.

1. Naturally Occurring Materials

Naturally occurring materials, often neutral to our health in low concentrations, are increasing in concentration due to human activities and include the following:

(a) The CO_2 in the atmosphere already discussed, rising silently but steadily by midcentury.

(b) Sulphur compounds in the air and water that are released periodically by processes such as volcanic eruptions and by the organisms that produce hydrogen sulfide (H_2S, the "rotten egg" smell). By the 1950s sulphur compounds were already being released in large quantities in the acid runoff water from coal mines[16] and in the sulphur dioxide (SO_2) liberated from coal-fired power plants, smelters, and other industries. Also by this time acid rain[17] was a recognizable problem in parts of Europe and in some Scandinavian rivers that were acidifying and losing their salmon populations. However, only more recently have we recognized the geographically much broader problem of acid rain over large areas of eastern North America, Europe, and Asia. Developments are mixed because as domestic use of coal for home heating has declined the global thirst for electricity has soared even more quickly than global population levels,[18] so that a quadrupling of human population levels from 1860 to 1991 was accompanied by a ninety-three-fold increase of our energy use. This has been translated into a great multiplication of coal-fired power plants. In wealthy countries like the U.S. scrubbers to reduce emissions of SO_2 have been effective, while in rapidly developing economies like China SO_2 emissions are increasing as a large number of less sophisticated power plants burning coal are brought on line every year. While the technology to reduce SO_2 emissions exists, the cost of this technology is limiting its application.

(c) Nitrogen oxides emissions are associated with the passage of lightning bolts through the nitrogen and oxygen molecules in the atmosphere, and in the manufactured world with petroleum combustion. Nitrogen oxides, which come in several chemical forms, join SO_2 as the major sources of acid rain and contribute greatly to urban smogs. The air quality crisis of the 1970s in Los Angeles led to emission control devices that reduced the per-auto releases of air pollutants, but this decrease has been offset by the increasing number of automobiles. After the oil supply crisis of the 1970s it seemed that automobiles might become smaller and more fuel efficient. In more recent years an increase in sales of less-fuel-efficient larger vehicles has reversed that trend.

(d) Petroleum has now begun to enter the biosphere, and especially the oceans, in catastrophic quantities. Almost a third of marine petroleum pollution is caused by open-sea bilge pumping and tank cleaning practiced by the shipping industry[19] and by the transportation via accident-prone oil tankers demanded by an increasingly oil-hungry world. A great amount of oil pollution also enters the oceans through rivers and direct dumping of wastes into the ocean by human activities inland. The numbers here are sobering. The tens of millions of pleasure boats owned by people around the world are estimated to release 520,000 tons of oil and oil products into the atmosphere and another 260,000 tons leaked into the water. The combination of those figures is over twenty times the volume of the famous Exxon Valdez spill of 1989.[20]

Simple mathematics indicates the potential for pollution that the numbers of consumers in the developed world represent. Given over 250,000,000 Americans, if one percent of those people dumps three oil changes of four quarts apiece into a storm sewer system each year the combined release annually equals seven and one half million gallons.

This hypothetical but reasonable calculation produces a number nearly equal to the eleven million gallons that the Exxon Valdez released into Prince William Sound, Alaska. Yet current trends indicate that marketing efforts are being successful in moving Americans away from purchasing modest-sized cars and toward less fuel efficient sport-utility vehicles and light trucks. These vehicles cannot help but exacerbate problems with petroleum pollution in both transport and use.

2. Heavy Metals

Materials like heavy metals that are mined and concentrated by human activities and have negative impacts on human health include:

(a) Mercury. This is a liquid metal that, at room temperature, volatilizes readily into an odorless and colorless gas. It has always been found in areas where mercury-rich rocks occur but it is now released in large quantities by some sectors of the chemical industry, in some forms of gold mining, and by the burning of coal. In the 1950s such magazines as *National Geographic* and *Life* featured stark photographs of crippled Minamata disease victims from Japan. In Minamata Bay a vinyl chloride factory released large amounts of mercury near a fishing community. These photographs sensitized many people to the dangers of mercury poisoning.[21] Today, the increasing number of coal-fired power plants makes local mercury release into the atmosphere an increasing problem, as does the use of mercury in some forms of mining for gold.[22]

(b) Lead. Another metal, lead was formerly not something of great concern with respect to human health. Now, however, it has been recognized as a problem. Ironically, the Romans knew about lead poisoning centuries ago. Despite this knowledge insufficient advances have been made in eradicating lead pollution in the last half of the twentieth century. Lead has become an increasingly important pollutant and has increased perhaps a thousandfold in the present global atmosphere due to the use of leaded gasoline that came into widespread use during the last fifty years but is now banned in many countries. Lead enters drinking water anywhere lead pipes or copper pipes are held together with lead solders. Lead is also in paint that had a tragically sweet taste to many inner city children who have been permanently injured by eating paint flakes from deteriorating surfaces. It is worth noting that much of the acute juvenile lead poisoning now taking place in this country is due to the work of some well-meaning parents who attempt to remove older leaded paint instead of covering it over. These parents do not realize that their attempts often spread lead as a finely divided dust if they remove the old paint with a belt sander or volatilize it with a hot paint gun. In communities with many older homes painted before 1978 juvenile lead poisoning due to inexpert parental attempts to remove leaded paint is still sometimes tragically common. The banning of leaded gasoline in the U.S. over the last two decades has had a positive effect on atmospheric lead pollution, but lead emissions continue at an estimated level of two million metric tons per year globally. This is about two-thirds of all metallic air pollution. Sadly, there are many places in the world where leaded gasoline remains in use.[23]

3. Human-Made Materials

Materials that never existed in nature before humans invented the molecules in laboratories and then began to synthesize them in bulk in chemical factories are too many for more than a cursory listing of a few commonly discussed chemical categories to be presented here. Pesticides have already been discussed. Few people probably realize what an enormous change the last half century has seen in the number of other sorts of synthetic organic chemicals that are devised solely by human minds and produced solely by human hands.

From the 1950s to the 1990s the American Chemical Society registered over ten million new chemicals. While most of these never come into widespread use, about seventy thousand chemicals are in common use throughout the planet by various industries.[24] The great majority of these have never undergone rigorous testing for their effects on human health. This is because they are intended for use in industrial plants and are not meant to be released. Only food additives, pesticides, medicines, and herbicides are given more than a minimal testing for their toxic or carcinogenic potential. However, even a cursory inspection of the reports in newspapers shows that whether by tank truck accident, railway spillage, or accidental release directly from a site of synthesis or storage many industrial chemicals do, in fact, enter the environment and come into contact with people. Some of these synthetic organic compounds include trichloroethane, dioxins, and polychlorinated biphenyls.

(a) Trichloroethane (often called TCE). This and other industrial degreasers were used to clean industrial machinery in the 1950s but were not recognized as serious potential sources of groundwater contamination at that time. They are now one of the most common categories of pollutants of groundwaters and have been implicated in liver cancers in laboratory animals and in leukemia in children. TCE has been found everywhere from municipal drinking water wells in New York and Massachusetts to the groundwater of the San Gabriel Valley in California. Millions of people in the U.S. are exposed to TCE at some level in their drinking water.

(b) Dioxins. These are a class of approximately seventy-five synthetic organic compounds produced as virtually unavoidable byproducts in the production of synthetic organic herbicides and related chemicals, in the bleaching of paper at all but the most modern (chlorine-free) paper mills, and in the incineration of household wastes at incinerators or "trash to electricity" power plants. There is no doubt that some dioxins were being produced in the 1950s. The advent of the modern petrochemical industry in the last half century, however, led to situations like that of Times Beach, Missouri, a town of about 2,400 people that had to be entirely abandoned and bulldozed because of dioxin-contaminated oil sprayed on the local roads to control dust. Dioxins may well be the most toxic of the human-made chemicals, causing cancers and failures of the hormonal, immune, and reproductive systems. There is great concern at present about dioxin production in waste incinerators, especially in countries like Japan where areas for landfills are highly limited and a large proportion of domestic waste is incinerated. Health risks for those who live near such facilities are increasingly being recognized.

(c) Polychlorinated Biphenyls (PCBs). These are a class of organic compounds composed of two six-carbon rings with more than one chlorine atom attached. These compounds were in use in the U.S., to some degree, by the 1950s. Subsequently the emergence of the modern petrochemical industry caused, for a time, a heavy use of these compounds. They became the "workhorses" of the chemical industry. PCBs occurred everywhere from carbon paper to the transformers that look like elevated gray trash cans on neighborhood power lines. More than half a million tons of PCBs were produced and employed in the U.S. Production of PCBs has now ceased in this country due to rising environmental concerns. However, they remain in the environment as common, if not ubiquitous pollutants, found in waters, soils, and the tissues of freshwater fish and other animals.[25] It is often PCB levels that cause warnings to be issued about the consumption of predatory fish like salmon, trout, and bass that biologically magnify PCB levels due to their consumption of smaller organisms and to the fat-soluble nature of these chemicals. It is very difficult for fish or human bodies to eliminate

PCBs from our systems once these soluble chemicals have been absorbed.

4. Radioactive Wastes

Radioactive wastes from the peaceful generation of electricity and the preparation for nuclear holocaust form a topic of such complexity and controversy that it can only be mentioned here. Radioactive wastes are the result of the optimistic use of fission reactors from the 1950s onwards and the reprocessing of nuclear materials used to make weapons. The total extent of global nuclear contamination is not fully understood, but it is certain that it is vast. At the Hanford site in Washington state, where most of the weapons-grade plutonium for American weapons was once produced, and where nuclear power generation goes on now, approximately 425 million curies of radioactive waste and materials are stored. More than thirty million curies of radiation were released to the Columbia River between 1944 and 1987. While little is known of the situation in the former Soviet republics, what is known indicates that their nuclear waste problems are much worse than those in the United States. The cleanup of nuclear wastes will be a challenge for generations of people to come.[26]

THE MAP OF BIODIVERSITY

There is nothing new about humans altering their environment to supply their wants and needs. People need shelter, food, warmth in winter, water for crops and for drinking and cleansing. Supplying these things to large numbers of people has always involved processes like chopping down forests for firewood and building materials, and mining ores. However, the sheer number of humans who are now harvesting the world's resources threatens to eliminate natural ecosystems in a way unlike anything seen in human history. When natural ecosystems vanish, so do the plants and animals that inhabit them.

In much of the Northern Hemisphere the natural landscape was already eliminated by 1950. Examples are the prairies of North America, now almost all converted to rich farmland, and the forests of Great Britain, now logged for fuel and lumber. But in this instance fate has been perhaps more generous than was deserved. The Northern Hemisphere habitats converted to human use had been ones that contained only a fraction of the earth's biodiversity, while great tracts of tropical forest remained unaltered. Understanding why the sheer number of species in the tropics so far exceeded the numbers in the temperate zone involves a discussion of continental drift, the relatively recent glaciation of Northern Europe and America, and the corresponding lack of a similar climatological event in South America, Africa, and much of Asia. While there is no room here to develop this topic at length, suffice it to say that in terms of human history most of the plant and animal species that existed were located in the tropical rainforests, due to the natural events of the preceding few hundred thousand years. As a yardstick to measure by, ten to fifteen percent of the world's species were present in North America and Europe, with enormously higher numbers of native species in Central and South America, Asia, Africa, and Australia. Malaysia had over 8,000 native species of flowering plants, South America has perhaps 200,000 such species, while Great Britain had 1,400.[27] Thus in 1950 the amount of natural habitat in areas where the numbers of native species were the lowest were the ones most severely reduced. The vast tracts of tropical forests, often undescribed and unnamed by scientists, still remained intact for most of the terrestrial species on the earth.

The massive population growth of the last fifty years has taken place disproportionately in tropical countries and has resulted in the loss of tropical forest habitat. Therefore unique species of plants and animals that live nowhere else have disappeared at an almost unimaginable rate. Deforestation in the tropics is partially due to fuel needs for heating and cooking and building needs. Deforestation is also necessary for clearing tropical lands in the slash-and-burn agricultural system that produces fields fertile enough to produce crops. But the land remains fertile for only a few years due to a thin layer of topsoil in tropical forests. Much of this slash-and-burn agriculture is subsistence farming, some of which supplies the apparently insatiable appetite of developed nations for inexpensive hamburgers. It is estimated that at present between 800 million and 1,200 million hectares of tropical forests remain, with perhaps 11.1 million hectares entirely eliminated annually and another 10 million hectares extremely disrupted by human activity.[28] Given the present population growth rates in tropical countries and the level of consumer demand in the developed world for materials like tropical hardwoods and ground beef it seems most probable that tropical forests, except for the small percentage contained in national parks, will be entirely eliminated in between one hundred and two hundred years.

Is tropical biodiversity really that important to people who live in the temperate zone? While a thorough development of this theme requires the book-length efforts made recently by notable authors,[29] a few points can be made here. People depend on plants and animals found in nature for food, and many more edible plant species exist in the tropics than the developed world now employs to feed itself. Given the continual human struggle against insect species and plant diseases that are introduced in areas where our crops have never encountered them before, the loss of edible tropical species greatly diminishes researchers' capacity to develop novel answers to problems of world food supply. Similarly, more than half of all prescription medicines, including some of the most effective anti-cancer drugs, heart medicines, and antibiotics, were originally derived from living organisms. The vast and as yet unstudied diversity of the tropics, especially of its plant life, doubtless contains thousands of biological compounds that could cure serious human diseases and improve the quality of human lives. Researchers will never find these materials if the species involved are lost before they can be evaluated for their potential pharmaceutical properties. Childhood leukemia, once almost invariably fatal, is now one of the most curable cancers thanks to alkaloid compounds from the rosy periwinkle of Madagascar. Tropical forests contain plants that cleanse the atmosphere far more effectively than the same surface area of farmland would, and the rising CO_2 levels will only be exacerbated by the loss of these forests. Finally, and most significantly, there is a peace and beauty in nature that has a special quality of love contained within it.

Scientific studies of the loss of oceanic biodiversity have been much less numerous than studies of terrestrial habitats, but this is also clearly taking place. Numerous global fisheries are in decline due to overexploitation; whale population levels have been greatly reduced because of whaling (still carried on by some nations under a thin guise of scientific research); portions of the Great Barrier Reef of Australia closest to input sources of human pollution are suffering widespread coral death; and even the number of species of single-celled algae seems to be in decline. Oil pollution, pesticide runoff in rivers, ocean dumping of garbage, and other processes are beginning to cause deterioration of the web of life in the world's oceans. Humans must improve their handling of wastes and curb some of their appetites if the creatures of the world's oceans are not to diminish as their terrestrial counterparts have begun to do.

E. O. Wilson, one of the prophetic voices telling humans about the state of our world today and our future if we continue to act as we have, estimates that humans are driving twenty thousand species per year into extinction.[30] While there are doubtless several million species of plants and animals presently on our planet their numbers are not infinite, and they each possess their own unique and unduplicatable characteristics. We cannot claim ignorance about what we are doing. We, as a world community, need to make imaginative and strenuous efforts to find ways for the burgeoning population of the earth to be supported without wholly deforesting the tropics or degrading the oceans, and without that kind of effort the future of the majority of earth's species is clear.

THE EMERGENCE OF AN ENVIRONMENTAL MAP, OR HOW ECOLOGY INFORMS THE REST OF OUR THOUGHT

The 1950s, when the human race fully embarked on the developmental journey that led to the current environmental crisis, was an era of great enthusiasm and great naïveté. The First World War, the Great Depression, and the Second World War were over. DDT was still generally considered a new miracle in insect control; penicillin was a new miracle in disease control; effective vaccinations for widespread diseases were clearly on the rise globally; and it was generally held in the Western world that nuclear fission reactors would provide the cheap, safe, reliable source of power for nothing less than a revolution in human living standards. Each era has a worldview of its own, and the pervasive optimism of much of Western society in the 1950s blinded many people to the environmental crisis that was to come so soon. Many people were worried about Cold War issues; some people were concerned with segregation and others with the decline of American cities. Yet if there is such a thing as a communal expression of a time, then the expression of the 1950s was relief that the difficult first half of the twentieth century was finished. People were optimistic about what science could do for humankind.

Prior to the twentieth century environmental thinkers in Western society were active, but their work did not much alter the mindset of most Americans. John Muir, first president of the Sierra Club, had an important influence in the establishment of the National Park system in the U.S. in the era of President Theodore Roosevelt. The National Park Movement,[31] however, was about putting aside areas for protection rather than about altering how people thought about their use of resources in a more general sense. Parks were places set aside from day-to-day life.

This idea was, perhaps, important but limited in scope. It was not until environmental problems began to be manifest closer to the places where people live their daily lives that the modern environmental movement began. A sampling of the books that ushered in the current era of environmental thought includes *A Sand County Almanac and Sketches Here and There,* published by Aldo Leopold in 1949. In this work Leopold articulated the environmental ethic prophetically: "A thing is right when it preserves the integrity, stability, and beauty of the biotic community. It is wrong when it does otherwise." In another work, *Round River,* published after he died fighting a prairie fire, he had written:

> Conservation is a state of harmony between men and land. By land is meant all of the things on, over, or in the earth. Harmony with land is like harmony with a friend; you cannot cherish his right hand and chop off his left. That is to say, you cannot love game and hate predators; you cannot conserve the waters and waste the ranges; you cannot build the forest and mine the farm. The land is one organism. Its parts, like our own parts, compete with each other and co-operate with each other. The competitions are as much a part of the inner workings as the co-operations. You can regulate them—cautiously—but not abolish them.[32]

Leopold went on to develop the idea that the "small cogs and wheels," as he called them, things like soil microbes and native grass species, were the sort of vital basics of what the human community needs to conserve in nature. Furthermore, focusing on large "show pieces" for conservation rather than trying to treat all of the ecosystem gently was a great failure of understanding at that point in American conservation.

Following Leopold's writings, Rachel Carson's *Silent Spring,*[33] published in 1962, had an enormous impact on the American imagination. Her evocative portrait of the dangers of widescale pesticide use and of the eventual probability of a spring with no songbirds to be heard, struck a chord (or perhaps the possible lack of a chord) in many people's communal imagination. This was close to home indeed because it was the tree outside one's window, whose branches might be occupied or not. There emerged a nagging fear that anything that was devastating to the birds around us could not be benign to human bodies.

After Rachel Carson numerous gifted writers and speakers took up the torch of environmental issues. Garrett Hardin's contribution about the tragedy of the commons[34] has already been mentioned. Many others have added their voices to the topic. The combined import has been that every issue of our lives, every decision we make, is an environmental choice. We either use the environment up quickly or we choose a more modest path of development and consumption moment by moment.

Barry Commoner[35] provides a synthetic discussion, from a scientific vantage point, of the choices presented to modern society by alternative technologies. He likens the relationship of Western consumer society to the environment to a war. He writes:

> It is true, of course, that the householder who discards nearly two hundred pounds of plastic trash annually has struck a blow against the ecosphere. But often the householder has no choice; after all, milk is no longer sold in returnable glass bottles. Moreover, the decision to produce the plastic in the first place was not made by the householder, nor does the householder benefit from the profits that motivated that decision. That power and that motivation reside with the corporate managers— the generals who order the assault, unwittingly, on the biosphere. This narrow segment of society makes the decisions that obligate the rest of us to participate in the ecological war. And it is the corporate generals who reap the short-term—and short-sighted—economic benefits.

Happily, while much of the corporate world may be acting as Commoner suggests, there are now the beginning signs of the possibility of change even there. A prime example is the Natural Step process, recently brought to North America from Sweden where it originated. This process provides business leaders with a motivation for change, specifically, the eventual loss of competitive position among businesses that neglect to get themselves ahead of the upcoming tightening of environmental legislation as the environmental crisis becomes plainer and plainer to see. It is a process that involves four quantifiable system conditions that can help business leaders to move their companies incrementally towards environmental responsibility. In the chapter in this volume entitled "The Stewardship of Natural and Human Resources," Joyce Osland et al. discuss the Natural Step program in detail.[36]

One more thread remains to be woven into the developing cloth: the link between environmental concerns and theological concerns. It is appropriate to mention that the *Sierra Club Bulletin* was the first place in which Wendell Berry's essay, "The Gift of Good Land" (originally 1979; reprinted in the 1981 volume with the same title) appeared. In this essay Berry wrote: "I wish to deal directly at last with my own long held belief that Christianity as usually presented by its organizations, is not earthly enough—that a valid spiritual life, in this world, must have a practice and a practicality—it must have a material result."[37] He later stated:

To live, we must daily break the body and shed the blood of Creation. When we do this knowingly, lovingly, skillfully, reverently, it is a sacrament. When we do it ignorantly, greedily, clumsily, destructively, it is a desecration. In such desecration we condemn ourselves to spiritual and moral loneliness, and others to want.[38]

THE TWIN PILLARS OF OUR ENVIRONMENTAL CRISIS, AND WHERE WE ARE

The twin threats to the continuation of human life are overpopulation and overconsumption. Overpopulation, one of the pillars supporting this crisis above our collective heads, becomes obviously awful when it reaches a certain level. At the point the drinking water begins to be scarce and foul, the air hurts to inhale, food becomes scarce, and privacy and shelter are hard to find, any normal human will be able to recognize that something is seriously wrong. In the last two decades we have seen numerous national governments begin to acknowledge that overpopulation is a threatening process. Therefore some governments have been taking steps to limit population growth, whether by informational campaigns, health care education, or tax incentives and disincentives designed to limit family size. The great danger here is that the staggering number of humans who have not yet had children provides a considerable amount of inertia to the growth of world population. There are so many people under fifteen on the planet (perhaps forty percent of the populations of some of the most crowded nations) that there is an inevitability, to some degree, of continued population growth regardless of anything else. Global human population growth is like an enormous truck that has gained speed moving down a steep hill, and the question of limiting it before we overwhelm ourselves with our sheer numbers is like the problem of managing to turn on a curve at the bottom of the hill. It will take great efforts for us to make that turn, but the fact that world leaders are recognizing that the efforts are important moves this to the realm of possibility. Our mental map might note this curve ahead as an "acknowledged challenge, threatening but being addressed in many places."

It is the pleasant nature of overconsumption that may pose the greatest threat to our collective survival. Just as living in the midst of overpopulation is transparently awful, living in the midst of overconsumption is a pleasant condition, at least for those with financial resources to expend. If the pollution and toxic wastes associated with manufacturing can be kept away from the majority of the population of consumers, and in view of the excitement associated with new goods and services (like electronics and information technology), masking the depletion of resources due to environmental degradation (e.g., world fishery declines matter less to most North Americans than digital televisions) there is little incentive for overconsumers to change their ways. World leaders have not yet acknowledged that overconsumption is a basic problem that has the potential to destroy our ecosystems. They merely respond to specific instances of pollution as though reduction of a single effluent made sense out of a broader context of reducing our overuse of the world's resources. In fact it makes no sense at all to talk about reducing CO_2 emissions in isolation from the level of our consumption of consumer goods. This, however, is how we are presently acting with regard to many specific results of overconsumption. For many members of Western societies the mental maps of overconsumption are now blanks labeled "terra incognita" perhaps embellished a bit like the maps of old explorers who imagined grotesque monsters lurking beyond the margins of known seas. However, in this instance the monsters are all too real. The refusal to recognize that what is needed is a fundamental alteration in how people regard high levels of personal consumption poses, perhaps, the greatest threat to the human family's ability to maintain itself in any form we would care to see.

CONCLUSION AND THEOLOGICAL REFLECTION

The metaphor of the present human being sitting on the shoulder of a curving and narrow lane as dusk began to fall, with the car's temperature warning light blinking insistently, creates something of a soothing picture. A more honest metaphor would be to acknowledge that the entire human species is actually moving at a great velocity on that selfsame road of limited visibility, trying simultaneously to steer and to unfold a changing map needed to find the path to any acceptable destination. Thus every moment that we move forward we are leaving more and more options for turns away from our present path behind us. When we as a global community do decide to turn aside from our path it will matter a great deal how many of the remaining options are still ahead of us and how many have been irrevocably passed. It seems likely that the more attractive options are the turns that our present course will pass by first. The later we decide to make a change in course, the poorer the set of alternative paths that will still be ahead of us. That the warning lights are blinking is unmistakable. It is up to us to understand the current environmental situation, to persist in making the scientific and moral dimensions of our present course the topic of public and private debate, and to insist on changes sooner rather than later. An ability to intelligently anticipate the probable and harmful changes in the circumstances of this planet calls for energetic employment of our capacities to think and reason. This is our responsibility, and it is also our gift to the planet, to all creation.

Finally, utilizing cartography as its primary image, this chapter guides us through the major environmental issues with which humanity and the entire biosphere are faced as we experience life in the twenty-first century. The signposts on the journey reveal a spectrum of environmental challenges and threats that create a rather disconcerting portrayal of Earth's current state of environmental health. From atmospheric conditions that threaten us with global warming and ozone depletion to pesticide and pollutants to collapsing biodiversity, this essay provides a "prophetic" warning that can not be ignored. Furthermore, this scientific reading of the environmental "signs of the times" strongly suggests that we, the human species, are in need of a new compass and a new future direction if disaster is to be averted.

But why should theology be concerned with such issues? The answer, at least within the Roman Catholic tradition, lies in the Second Vatican Council's "turn to the world" as a legitimate concern for theological praxis. With its reference to "reading the signs of the times" Vatican II initiated a shift in theological method that requires theology to attend to historical developments and issues. Moreover, the Judeo-Christian tradition holds that creation and history are sources of God's self-disclosure and it is consequently the ongoing task of theology to discern the significance and meaning of such events as our environmental crisis and its impact within creation and history. That is precisely what the U.S. Catholic bishops attempt to accomplish in their 1991 statement, *Renewing the Earth*. They begin their reflection with the "Signs of the Times," writing: "At its core the environmental crisis is a moral challenge. It calls us to examine how we use and share the goods of the earth, what we pass on to future generations and how we live in harmony with God's creation."[39]

What can theology deduce from this scientific assessment of the signs of the times? The overriding message is clear: we as a species are not living in harmony with God's creation. The disturbing artifacts of our past and current socioeconomic praxis strongly suggest that the human-earth relationship is fractured. Our treatment of the earth indicates that we are alienated or estranged from our home. This reflection immediately calls to mind the notion of sin and how that primary theological concept requires expansion in the face of ecological destruction. To that end James Nash proposes the engaging notion of "ecological sin," which reflects our failure as responsible stewards of the earth. In *Loving Nature* Nash writes:

> Ecological sin is expressed as the arrogant denial of the creaturely limitations imposed on human ingenuity and technology, a defiant disrespect or a deficient respect for the interdependent relationships of all creatures and their environments established in the covenant of creation, and an anthropocentric abuse of what God has made for frugal use.[40]

NOTES: CHAPTER 6

[1] For the mathematically inclined this expression is a discrete approximation of what is really a continuous function based on a derivative. For further discussion see Edward O. Wilson and William H. Bossert, *A Primer of Population Biology* (Sunderland, Mass.: Sinauer and Associates, 1977).

[2] There is a Buddhist Sangha, a religious community, whose numbers informally voted that mosquitoes did not count as "sentient beings." Thus the mosquitoes were eligible to be swatted. This was directly related to their excessive intrinsic rate of increase.

[3] For further discussion see Joel E. Cohen, "Population Growth and Earth's Carrying Capacity," *Science* 269 (1995) 341–46, and Mark B. Bush, *Ecology of a Changing Planet* (Upper Saddle River, N.J.: Prentice Hall, 1997).

[4] See Wilson and Bossert, *A Primer of Population Biology* (n. 1 above).

[5] Neil Gaiman and Terry Pratchett, *Good Omens* (New York: The Berkley Publishing Group, 1990), provide a contemporary vision of the four horsemen. Gaiman and Pratchett suggest that pestilence retired in 1936 after the invention of penicillin only to be replaced immediately by pollution. While the book is a work of entertainment rather than scholarship it is worth noting changes in people's shared view of reality that reflect what is happening in today's world.

[6] See Bush, *Ecology of a Changing Planet*, and William P. Cunningham and Barbara Woodworth Saigo, *Environmental Science: A Global Concern* (4th ed. Dubuque, Iowa: William C. Brown, 1997).

[7] Garrett Hardin, "The Tragedy of the Commons," *Science* 162 (1968) 12–43.

[8] See Bush, *Ecology of a Changing Planet*, and Cohen, "Population Growth and Earth's Carrying Capacity."

[9] See Hardin, "The Tragedy of the Commons."

[10] See Garrett Hardin and John Baden, eds., *Managing the Commons* (San Francisco: W. H. Freeman, 1977).

[11] See Bush, *Ecology of a Changing Planet,* and Cunningham and Saigo, *Environmental Science.*

[12] See Robert Metcalf, "An Abbreviated History of Insecticide Toxicology," in Jean Adams, ed., *Insect Potpourri: Adventures in Entomology* (Gainesville, Fla.: Sandhill Crane Press, 1992).

[13] Rachel Carson, *Silent Spring* (Boston: Houghton Mifflin, 1962).

[14] See S. Bhatia and J. P. Neglia, "Epidemiology of Childhood Acute Myelogenous Leukemia," *Journal of Pediatriac Hematology and Oncology* 17/2 (1995) 94–100, and R. A. Lowengart et al., "Childhood Leukemia and Parents' Occupational and Home Exposures," *Journal of the National Cancer Institute* 79/1 (1987) 39–46.

[15] See Daniel Botkin and Edward Keller, *Environmental Science. Earth as a Living Planet* (2d ed. New York: John Wiley, 1998).

[16] Acid mine drainage actually depends not only on the exposure of the material previously buried in the earth to air and water but also on the action of the bacterium *Thiobacillus thioxidans.* Even in this sort of circumstance nature manages to maintain a living foothold. In fact, the chemical reactions that the bacteria carry out to support their lives are a crucial step in the liberation of a large amount of acid runoff from the mines.

[17] "Acid rain" was a term first coined by scientist Robert Angus Smith in England in the 1850s during the Industrial Revolution to describe the cause of the environmental degradation surrounding the great steel city of Manchester. At that time it was a local phenomenon related to large amounts of coal being burned in the city and its surrounds. Increased use of fossil fuels has transformed this from a local problem to one enveloping large portions of continents.

[18] See Cohen, "Population Growth and Earth's Carrying Capacity."

[19] See Michael McKinney and Robert Schoch, *Environmental Science, Systems and Solutions.* Web Enhanced Edition (Sudbury, Mass.: Jones and Bartlett, 1998).

[20] Ibid.

[21] Mercury poisoning should not be met with complacency. The effects are serious, as witnessed by the 1980s outbreak of Minamata disease in the White Cloud Indian Reservation in British Columbia, Canada. The problem there was runoff from a mine causing local fish to carry very heavy loads of mercury in their tissues. A similar release of about ten metric tons of mercury from a pulp and paper mill in Dryden, Ontario, from 1963–1970 permanently dam-

aged native peoples eating fish from the Wabigoon-English River system. For further discussion see Cunningham and Saigo, *Environmental Science.*

[22] Ibid.

[23] Ibid.

[24] See Donald Kaufman and Cecilia Franz, *Biosphere 2000: Protecting Our Global Environment* (2d ed. Dubuque, Iowa: Kendall/Hunt, 1996).

[25] See Daniel Chiras, *Environmental Science: A Systems Approach to Sustainable Development* (5th ed. Belmont, Calif.: Wadsworth, 1998).

[26] See Glenn Zorpette, "Hanford's Nuclear Wasteland," *Scientific American* (May 1996) 88–97; Roy Gephart and Regina Lundgren, *Hanford Tank Clean Up: A Guide to Understanding the Technical Issues.* PNL-10773 (Richland, Wash.: Pacific Northwest National Laboratory, 1997); and Bette Hileman, "Energy Department Has Made Progress Cleaning Up Nuclear Weapons Plants," *Chemical and Engineering News* 74 (July 1996) 14–20.

[27] See Cunningham and Saigo, *Environmental Science.*

[28] Jeffrey A. McNeely, et al., *Conserving the World's Biological Diversity* (Washington, D.C.: International Union for Conservation of Nature and Natural Resources, World Resources Institute, Conservation International, World Wildlife Fund-US, and the World Bank, 1990).

[29] See Edward O. Wilson, *The Diversity of Life* (Cambridge, Mass.: Harvard University Press, 1992).

[30] Ibid.

[31] See John Muir, *On National Parks* (Boston: Houghton Mifflin, 1901).

[32] See Aldo Leopold, *Round River,* ed. Luna B. Leopold (London: Oxford University Press, 1953).

[33] See Carson, *Silent Spring.*

[34] See Hardin, "The Tragedy of the Commons," and Hardin and Baden, eds., *Managing the Commons.*

[35] Barry Commoner, *Making Peace with the Planet* (New York: Pantheon, 1990).

[36] See below, pp. 168–92.

[37] See Berry, *The Gift of Good Land: Further Essays Cultural and Agricultural* (San Francisco: North Point Press, 1981).

[38] Ibid.

[39] "Renewing the Earth," *Origins* (December 23, 1991) 425.

[40] James Nash, *Loving Nature: Ecological Integrity and Christian Responsibility* (Nashville: Abingdon, 1991) 119.

7

Toward an Understanding of International Geopolitics and the Environment

In days to come
  the mountain of the Lord's house
shall be established as the highest of the mountains,
  and shall be raised up above the hills.
Peoples shall stream to it,
  and many nations shall come and say:
"Come, let us go up to the mountain of the Lord,
  to the house of the God of Jacob;
that he may teach us his ways
  and that we may walk in his paths."
For out of Zion shall go forth instruction,
  and the word of the Lord from Jerusalem.
He shall judge between many peoples,
  and shall arbitrate between strong nations far away;
They shall beat their swords into plowshares,
  and their spears into pruning hooks."
Nation shall not lift up sword against nation,
  neither shall they learn war any more;
but they shall all sit under their own vines and under their own fig
    trees,
  and no one shall make them afraid;
for the mouth of the Lord of hosts has spoken. (Mic 4:1-4)

*T*he vision of the prophet Micah offered the people of his day great hope as it looked forward to a time of peace and security. Swords would be turned into plowshares, spears into pruning hooks, and each nation would sit under its own vines and fig trees without fear of harm.

Heard in the context of international geopolitics and the environmental problems that face all nations today, the vision of Micah calls people to a deeper consciousness, namely that to effect global change all nations will have to participate fully in the choice to use power to create policies and structures that will ensure quality of life for both human and non-human instead of choosing to use power to secure the domination and control of one nation over and against another. The capacity of nations to work together in the political, social, and economic spheres is directly related to their ability to work together on the environmental concerns that cross all hemispheres and time zones. The Mican vision of peace and security offers an impetus for change so that what is prophetic can come to pass as the human community works toward an understanding of international geopolitics and the environment.

INTRODUCTION

The emergence of global environmental politics has been one of the most significant developments of the second half of the twentieth century for political scientists on both the local and global levels. Since the end of the Cold War a rigidly polarized political framework has been transformed into something that is much more fluid and complex. This transformation has challenged both specialists and ordinary citizens to rethink their understanding of basic policy issues. This chapter examines the major trends in global and local policies as a result of environmental needs and challenges. Furthermore, this chapter also examines the many challenges of environmental issues facing those who try to formulate global policies. Many specialists have entered the environmental arena, challenging policymakers to redefine political, social, cultural, religious, and economic issues. As a result, it is necessary to identify the major institutional actors—many of them new—that link global, national, and local politics, and to formulate an appropriate framework for explaining environmental issues as they influence the political sphere. Finally, specific policy responses to the new environmental challenges will be discussed.

The study of environmental issues and related political regimes has become a complex endeavor replete with controversial challenges within the discipline of international relations. The environment and its protection have influenced the way we understand and do politics on all levels and in all areas. There are many controversies among students of international relations because of the contradictions and ambiguities that characterize the new and fast-changing data from science, economics, and other disciplines. Until recently, environmental issues touched only a few persons from developed countries, but it is now rare for diplomats and politicians, from rich, developed countries as well as from poor ones, not to be concerned with a wide range of such issues. There are many disagreements among analysts over the meaning and direction of global environmental politics. These disagreements arise over theories that are to be used to explain and control the fast and profound changes in development theory and policies and their significance for sustainable development. Sustainable development, an approach to international assistance that gives primary importance to sustained self-help, has also been strongly influenced by environmental issues.

The global macrotrends that shaped the second half of the twentieth century are essential prerequisites for understanding the importance of environmental studies within the discipline of international relations. The following trends are crucial for understanding the problems that face the specialists who formulate policies in the environmental arena: (1) the rapid and unexpected growth of industrial and energy production in developing countries, (2) the recent and rapid growth of population and increase in life expectancy, (3) the revolutionary—an appropriate word here—developments in the technologies of communication and transportation, in both military and civilian applications, and finally, without trying to be wholly inclusive, (4) the continued state of global disorganization (many still prefer to call this anarchy) in which the approximately 189 nation-states of this earth shape global politics. Experts continue to speak of a disconcerting "mismatch" between the political structure of nation-states and the orderly development of environmental regimes considered essential for a safe and secure future.[1]

Specialists who study power politics from the perspective of state security have often expressed their malaise with the language of ethics and morality when discussing policies from the perspective of state security. However, theologians and ethicists have for some time been examining the importance of moral values in international politics, especially for understanding the area of human rights and the environment.

The fact of the emergence of global norms for human rights and for the protection of the global commons has begun to seep into the workshop of political practitioners and theoreticians. Traditional international politics have been dominated by experts who specialize in the theory and application of military and state power. For them, debates were limited to philosophers and social scientists who specialize in the arcane language of balance of power, deterrence, and security. However, with the growing complexity of this interdependent world the study of the environment, human rights, global civic society, and related economic issues has become as relevant to the study of international relations as the high politics of war and peace as reflected through alliances and the application of military power.[2]

IDENTIFYING THE MAJOR GLOBAL ACTORS

Many agents are involved in the formulation of environmental policy. The major ones are the nation-states, intergovernmental organizations, and global non-governmental (civilian) organizations such as Amnesty International, as well as more specialized regional organizations like the Union of Concerned Scientists. We examine these three categories of actors below.

Nation-States

The interactions of nation-states with each other still constitute the bulk of what is called international relations. Their struggles for status and identity often lead to conflict but usually require cooperation. Until recently issues of development, security, environment, and human rights were considered to be a monopoly of sovereign states. This monopoly as a characteristic of sovereign states is being challenged by non-state actors and organizations. Some challenges, including those of ethnic groups, come from within the state. Other challenges such as those from churches, human rights organizations, and business organizations come from beyond the state's sphere of sovereignty.

It is almost a truism to say that the traditional power of the nation-state has been severely constricted by global markets. Those are the same market, political, and ideological forces that collapsed communist regimes in Central Europe and brought new life to local politics in

China. The Nike "swoosh" and the Sony Walkman® have done as much in their own way to weaken traditional state power as terrorism and weapons of mass destruction.[3] The growing body of multilateral agreements and international regulations is transforming the older form of "cowboy leadership" that had characterized international relations during the Cold War. More than brute power and military force are required to succeed in this new interdependent environment.

There are still, however, many countries in both the developed and developing world that too quickly resort to force and intimidation when environmental and human rights issues block their interests.[4] Interestingly enough it is not always the powerful states such as the so-called G-7 economies (United States, Canada, Japan, Germany, Italy, France, and the United Kingdom) that provide the most creative leadership for global environmental issues. Small states with marginal or small economies such as Costa Rica, Norway, Sweden, and Finland have authored imaginative proposals for solving environmental problems, showing more creativity than many larger and richer states.

Gareth Porter and Janet Welsh Brown[5] have shown that domestic economic and political issues strongly influence the role that different states assume in the arena of environmental politics. Large states like India, Indonesia, Brazil, and Mexico have resisted adopting environmental policies because of organized domestic pressure groups. While a small nation like Costa Rica has become a model for innovative programs to protect the rain forests, it is significant that influential Western countries such as the United States, France, and Germany have powerful and influential international lobbies to protect the environment. Rich countries like the U.S. and Canada have established relatively tough controls on pollution. As a result, large populations with smaller GNPs like those of India and China will soon become the dominant polluters. These developing nations have not been in the forefront of environmental reforms. Regardless of the level of development at which countries find themselves, they often still consider the political costs too high for the environmental payoffs.

Intergovernmental Organizations (IGOs)

The United Nations is the principal intergovernmental organization promoting global environmental policies. Some U.N. organizations relate directly to environmental issues from a general or specialized perspective. They are the U.N. Conference on Environment and Development (UNCED); U.N. Environment Program; U.N. Conference on the Human Environment; and the Committee on Trade and Environment of the World Trade Organization (formerly known as GATT). Other organizations have important implications for environmental issues even though that is not their primary purpose. They are the U.N. Development Program; U.N. Conference on Sustainable Development; World Bank; World Health Organization; and World Meteorological Organization. UNCED emerged as a U.N. vanguard for seeking global agreements on environmental issues in 1992 at the Rio Conference (also known as the Earth Summit), which produced a comprehensive set of recommendations on issues relating to environment and development that is now known as "Summit 21." One of the special objects of the conference was to reach a global agreement on the management of the world's forests. However, no agreement was reached. Instead a series of comprehensive but non-binding recommendations emerged. The U.N. leadership discovered to its dismay that even though the world's powerful nations want solutions they can be blocked by relatively weak, developing nations. The U.S. wanted a forest management convention that would protect the world's forests, but Indonesia, Brazil, and Malaysia refused to cooperate.[6]

The latest attempt to reach a comprehensive agreement on a global environmental issue was the Kyoto (Japan) Summit in December 1997, organized by the U.N. and attended by 159 countries. Participants divided into two camps, those who wanted a modest, incremental, and flexible arrangement for curbing gas emissions, and those who wanted a powerful document with comprehensive and specific standards. While most participants probably recognized that global warming should be taken seriously, only developed countries were willing to set costly quotas. The final agreement provides an interesting study in international environmental diplomacy. Although only thirty-four developed countries agreed to reduce gas emission by seven to eight percent by the year 2012 (the U.S. by seven percent and the European Union by eight percent), *The Economist* nevertheless called it "the most ambitious feat of environmental diplomacy ever attempted."[7] However, it is doubtful that the United States Senate will ever ratify this agreement, and it is even more doubtful that the level of gas reduction will ever be met even by those who ratified the agreement. Most developing countries did not ratify.

The leaders of developed countries have long disagreed on the cost and feasibility of limiting greenhouse gases and on the benefits of different policies. Before Kyoto, U.S. diplomats proposed a limited and gradual reduction that returned to 1990 levels by the year 2010. Germany insisted that new technology was available allowing a significantly higher reduction. For the U.S. that seemed unrealistic. Germany has reduced its emissions since 1991 by twelve percent. However, some believe that this is principally due to upgrading the polluting factories of East Germany.

Nonetheless, scientists are now predicting that the commercial use of PEM-cell (proton-exchange-membrane) engines in cars and other vehicles together with the application of photovoltaic power and wind power could significantly alter predictions of climate changes during the twenty-first century.

Non-Governmental (Civilian) Organizations (NGOs)

Many citizens' organizations are involved with government agencies and business corporations in planning and formulating policies that affect the quality of life in the area of the environment. These include many non-profit private organizations that have established global links in order to formulate more effective local policies. Some of the best-known and most effective of these organizations are The World Wildlife Fund (with headquarters in Geneva and agencies in the U.S. and twenty-eight other countries), the European Environmental Bureau, the Sierra Club, the National Audubon Society, the National Wildlife Federation, the Environmental Defense Fund, World Watch Institute, the World Resources Institute, the Union of Concerned Scientists, and Greenpeace. These organizations, taken collectively, have helped influence the formulation of global environmental policies in two ways. First, they have helped to assemble data bases and provide a better understanding of issues. At times they even formulate new legislation and propose more creative frameworks for understanding the relationship among global regional interests, environmental issues, and global agreements. Second, they lobby governments and other organizations to become more sensitive to environmental issues. They also organize educational campaigns, boycotts, and lawsuits. Although some of these organizations (such as the Sierra Club and the National Audubon Society) have been functioning for most of this century they have become a significant new element influencing policy on the global level. Multinational corporations have also organized into pressure groups in order to maximize their influence in the policy arena.

FOUR FRAMEWORKS THAT EXPLAIN THE POLITICS OF THE ENVIRONMENT

There are four suggestive frameworks—societal, economic, security, and moral—for understanding the global politics of the environment. Such frameworks offer useful perspectives on the politics of global environmental issues. They help us to focus on social relationships, market strategies, policies of national and global security, and the role of religious and secular ethics in ways that incorporate environmental issues.

The Societal Framework puts persons and their social interactions with the environment at the center of the discussion. The issue here is not primarily how productive the market can be. It is assumed that the earth contains enough resources to sustain the present population and even a larger number of people. Nor does this perspective necessarily consider the issue of population in terms of calamitous pressure on earth's resources. Rather, those who argue from this perspective believe that the most significant and relevant discussion is centered on the bonds of community and culture. Because humans are inseparable from their environment the appropriate framework is the human one, and that will inevitably include the environment and its protection.

All societies have developed a specific set of attitudes toward the environment. Optimists focus on the positive benefits that science already has bestowed on the planet.[8] They believe that the expanding world economy (along with the doubling of a population estimated at 5.8 billion in 1997) will not spell disaster. They see progressive improvement of the environment in the long run. They acknowledge that the arbitrary disappearance of many species is increasing at an alarming rate and should be reversed in the long term; they also agree that the rapid increase in global warming and the expansion of the ozone hole are concerns, but they do not see them as causes for panic and ill-considered solutions. The optimists focus on the speed and nature of past improvements in the human condition and on the potential benefits of science to help humans understand and improve the ecosystem. This perspective points to the growth of populations with extended life cycles, the elimination of diseases, the improvement of communications and transportation, and the growth of large cities as sophisticated centers of economic exchange and culture.

Not everyone sees the flexibility and adaptability of the social system with such optimism, however. If the earth has a limited carrying capacity humans will eventually use up the nonrenewable resources and face the problem of a collapsing ecosystem. There may be a delay in the negative impact on the environment, but eventually the human community will suffer. Some specialists have predicted that the earth will soon reach its carrying capacity, and they call for extreme efforts at population control.[9]

While some see population as the single biggest problem facing the world in the next century, others believe that the gap in wealth and health is the most serious problem and that this is a cultural and moral issue. These problems are not just a matter of natural resources and geography. Social, cultural, and moral traits often determine basic differences within and between rich and poor countries.[10]

The Economic Framework provides a perspective that is more focused and specific than the societal one. The economic perspective places market relationships at the center of any future global planning. Liberal economists believe that the political role of states should be reduced to that of regulating the global system and restricting the natural tendency of politicians to interfere with market forces. They believe that economics is the appropriate framework for thinking about environmental policy, and furthermore that the current global structure will facilitate constructive environmental policies. Is the population growing too quickly in the global South? One suggested response is to change immigration policies and allow the global North to absorb the excess until economic strategies help to adjust the gap between North and South. It has even been claimed that falling fertility rates in developed nations like Italy and Germany may produce a new set of problems for the future.[11]

Not all economists agree with such an optimistic assessment. Some offer a radical criticism of the existing economic order.[12] They see the integration of the global economy, the existing—some would say growing—disparity between the rich nations and the poor nations (the latter containing the majority of the world's population), and the power of multinational corporations as priority problems that need to be resolved with global structural changes. Only after structural disparities have been resolved can environmental issues be properly addressed. Both the liberal economists and the radical economists warn against focusing so narrowly on environmental issues as to inhibit economic development and lose sight of the centrality of economic issues. They would point to the growing problems with forests in Brazil and Indonesia. Efforts to reduce burning and stripping of forests in these countries have failed because economic issues were not properly addressed.

The Security Framework focuses on the political dimension of the global system. The advocates of this approach focus on security as a global term that includes social, economic, and political aspects.[13] Like the advocates of economic interdependence first, those who focus on security argue that the principal task of government and civilian leaders and related institutions is to reinterpret security from a global perspective. They argue that competition for power (whether military, political, or economic) will inevitably lead to conflicts and war, violence and terrorism, unless global environmental problems are addressed in a comprehensive, collective framework. This has been emphasized by numerous commissions of experts but one of the most convincing formulations comes from the Brundtland Commission (also known as the World Commission on Environment and Development) that was established by the U.N. General Assembly in 1987. Thus, without denying that arms control is an essential component of this global approach to security they point out that finding a solution to global warming, ozone depletion, and water and forest degradation is fundamental to future security and indispensable for effective and sustained development. This framework acknowledges a high probability of tragedy for the global commons unless a majority participates, and not just a few local actors or individual tree enthusiasts.

The Moral Framework. The role of morality in politics has been powerfully influenced in the U.S. by the political realists who have always insisted that in the context of national security (especially during the Cold War) there is no morally good or bad policy, only security and survival. "Good" policies are those that assure global survival and national security. "Bad" policies do not. George F. Kennan articulated this policy most effectively when he wrote that a sovereign state is legitimate when it guarantees the "blessings of military security, material prosperity and . . . the pursuit of happiness. For these assumptions the government needs no moral justification. . . ."[14] Furthermore, since there are no globally accepted moral standards each government defends its policies within its own moral framework.

Since environmental issues increasingly require a global framework for satisfactory solutions on the economic, political, and social levels it is appropriate that a comprehensive response to global issues must also include the relationship between environmental change, social justice, and morality. The political institutions that are instrumental in guaranteeing security and happiness and (increasingly) environmental health are rooted in religious cultures. Even in so-called secular environments the origins of political life are patently religious. Morality was instrumental in legitimizing capitalism, just as it is now challenged with its humanization. Morality also expresses and shapes the basic self-understanding and values of so-called "socialist" societies (where the collective good is considered more important than individual self-expression).

The reform movements of Central Europe and Russia originated in concerns for human rights and environmental issues that were rooted in Christian, Jewish, and Muslim understanding of the world and in the ethical values that shaped the understanding of humans in that world. Even in China, Cuba, Vietnam, and North Korea the moral underpinnings of the governments that still claim to represent the common good rest on complex ethical systems that are older than Christianity, Judaism, and Islam. While it has become commonplace for scholars to relate contemporary political institutions to their cultural origins, it is still rare to situate environmental issues within a moral framework. One author in this collection explains how the Christian understanding of simplicity, humility, and justice can help us understand ecological problems and guide the policy process.[15] As severe environmental disasters and breakdowns become more common (the nuclear meltdown at Chernobyl in the then-Soviet Union, the total ecological destruction of the Aral Sea in Russia, the massive deforestation of Brazil and Indonesia, the disappearance of species in Borneo and Central America, to name some examples), governments and international organizations will have the capacity to address and correct them only if they consider the moral implications of such calamities and enlist the powerful support of religious organizations in their efforts.

ENVIRONMENTAL CHALLENGES AND PROPOSED POLICY RESPONSES

There are three categories of challenges facing any diplomat or member of an environmental regime who wishes to formulate effective environmental legislation: fundamental disagreements, the gap between rich and poor nations, and international law. The first category consists of the fundamental and basic disagreements over the speed and intensity of environmental degradation and the estimated cost of an effective policy. The second category consists of the challenge posed by the continued disparity between the rich nations of the North and the poor nations of the South, and the relative responsibility of nations to work for a solution. The disparity between rich and poor nations establishes serious obstacles to effective legislation.

The third category of challenges is in the field of interdisciplinary studies and international law. Even those few global regimes created to respond to environmental issues that have been codified into international law (Law of the Sea, for example) are not very effective. There is a huge disparity between the formulation of the theories and the application and enforcement of international law. Many developing nations have argued that they cannot be expected to bear the cost of environmental protection until they have reached a high level of development. They intend to be free riders. There is need for an agreement among nations to enforce a uniform code of behavior with allowance for levels of development and considerations of social justice.

Disagreements over Objectives and Solutions

Disagreements over the meaning and direction of environmental degradation and the realistic cost of effective solutions are intense and widespread. It is impossible to calculate the rate and intensity of development of the economies of China and India (which represent one third of the earth's human population) and how their economic growth and development might affect the overall emission of harmful gasses. The rapid and sustained efforts of developing countries to industrialize without attending to pollution will be one of the most daunting challenges to the creation of effective environmental regimes in the next century. Just as the developed world begins to make some technological progress the "brown coal industries" springing up in developing nations are adding vast new pollution inputs. For citizens of these countries the choice is often pollution or starvation. Faced with such options, they will choose pollution, regardless of their economic or moral convictions.

The U.S. continues to be the country that offers the most powerful leadership for environmental agreements and yet presents the greatest obstacle to serious environmental negotiations.[16] For example, the United States has refused to ratify the Basel Convention (1989) on the transfer of hazardous wastes, and it opposed the Convention on Biodiversity at the Rio Conference of 1992. Finally, the U.S. dragged its feet and then reluctantly pledged its support for the Global Environmental Facility.

A limited but practical approach to resolving disagreements has resulted from the negotiations over the Global Environmental Facility

(GEF), initiated by European countries in 1991 and sponsored by the World Bank. The GEF proposes to sponsor and develop technical and scientific assistance for projects that would reduce environmental degradation with minimum harm to the economies of both rich and poor countries. After years of haggling over the institutional direction and administrative control of GEF by leaders of rich and poor nations a satisfactory solution was reached. The resolution of many differences between rich donor nations and poor receiving nations over a specific environmental area suggests that a realistic framework can be established.[17]

Disparities

The disagreements that arise over global environmental policies, their cost and financing, are strongly affected by the continued disparity between the post-modern nations like the U.S., Canada, and the countries of the European Union on the one hand and the developing and almost-modern nations like Mexico, Brazil, Chile, India, Korea, and Turkey on the other. Although there is disagreement over the nature and origins of this disparity no one denies that the relative differences in power and development of nations are major factors influencing negotiations over the environment. The World Bank has become a leader among multilateral institutions negotiating environmental standards. That was not always the case. After decades of criticism by environmentalists the World Bank implemented some policy changes in 1995 that may allow it to redirect resources to environmental programs.[18]

One response to this problem of North-South disparity in the arena of forest depletion is the Joint Implementation Plan (JIP). This proposal was initiated by the U.S. and seeks to privatize global pollution in order to protect the forests of developing countries. The JIP uses market strategies to encourage industries of rich countries (who may be serious polluters) to invest in protecting threatened forests of poor countries. They do this by paying pollution taxes that will then be used to support projects designed to save forests. One such project was initiated in Costa Rica and the funds have been used to support workers who survive on forest products.

International Law and Global Understanding

As global solutions are sought for a growing number of economic, environmental, and political problems international law and global understanding increase in importance. International protocols will become a regular part of domestic policymaking. For any multilateral environmental agreement to succeed, domestic laws must be transformed to conform to their global counterparts. However, the task of formulating a coherent and consistent body of international law that will be respected and enforced is still at a very early stage.

The Environmental Law Center of the International Union for the Conservation of Nature (IUCN) is a civilian organization with an effective global network consisting of many scientists, lawyers, and specialists in related fields. Although IUCN focuses specifically on wildlife conservation and the disappearance of species it serves as a model for coordinating resources and strengthening the role of international law in the environmental arena.

CONCLUSION AND THEOLOGICAL REFLECTION

This chapter has tried to show how environmental issues have begun to influence public policy on many levels. The future quality of human communities depends on the capacity of policymakers not only to find a new relationship between the national and international actors and the global ecosystem but also to introduce an ethical framework for such policies. A group of scholars and specialists has recently called for a new ethical framework for the formulation of policies in the global marketplace.[19] For global specialists who became politically aware during the Cold War it may appear to be very idealistic to think that the growing awareness of the global environmental crisis will introduce a new era of ethical concerns. The above analysis would warn us away from too much optimism. The same unethical framework that produced the excesses of the Cold War remains with us. That framework allowed policymakers to contaminate some of the best wilderness areas of the planet and thereby threaten the very existence of our ecosystem, all in the name of defending a higher set of values.

Now the most urgent task before policymakers consists in developing a new ethic for global policies before the ecosystem collapses under the weight of progress and economic development. Can scientists, professionals, and environmentalists cure the diseases facing this ecosystem? Perhaps "cure" should be preceded by "care." In order to discover effective cures we may first have to rediscover a new relationship of care for the environment. Care, as distinct from cure, depends on reclaiming the truth that our best values are beauty and holiness. Unless we experts realize that the survival of the environment is not measured only by production and growth but also by fruitfulness and care, policies are unlikely to change from those of the past. A pragmatic and realistic approach to environmental problems should include more than power and control. When the environment becomes once again as sacred as life itself the language of optimism versus pessimism may be replaced with that of hope for effective policies that will treasure and protect the ecosystem well into the twenty-first century.

Finally, the environment, from a global geopolitical perspective, presents us with the typical good news/bad news scenario. The good news is that for the first time in the history of humanity we have come to recognize that environmental devastation is not simply a local or regional problem but a global phenomenon, and we are responding to this awakening. International conferences like the Earth Summit of 1992 in Rio and the Kyoto Summit on global warming in 1997 are good examples of this response. The U.N. in particular has taken the lead in this area with the U.N. Environment Program and the U.N. Conference on Sustainable Development that produced *Our Common Future.* This document virtually standardized the language of "sustainable development" overnight. Also on the good news side has been the creation of international agreements on the environment like the Montreal Protocol (1987) which sought to limit and reduce the production of ozone-harming chlorofluorocarbons (CFCs). This first-of-its-kind international treaty seems to be working as a recent scientific report indicates that the quantity of CFCs in the stratosphere has stabilized and is decreasing.[20] All of these positive developments suggest the practical and global movement toward what the U.S. Catholic bishops have called the "planetary common good."[21]

Then there is the bad news, which this essay has tried to summarize. First there is the reality of serious international disagreement on the speed, intensity, and cost of ecological destruction. This was most recently exemplified in the lack of agreement over global warming issues at the Kyoto conference. Second, there is the economic disparity between the developed nations of the North and the developing nations of the South. This "Gordian knot" evokes the unavoidable observation that, globally, ecological solutions are inextricably connected to socio-economic justice. In his 1990 World Day of Peace address Pope John Paul II declared that "proper ecological balance will not be found without directly addressing the structural forms of poverty that exist throughout the world."[22] The U.S. Catholic statement *Renewing the Earth* (1991) and the U.S. Presbyterian document *Hope for a Global Future: Toward Just and Sustainable Human Development* (1996) also support this view. If the full weight of theological insight and judgement is brought to bear on this international problem the weight of the burden and responsibility for reaching a solution to the North-South impasse must fall on the wealthy nations of the North. After all, they account for a minority of the world's population but consume the vast majority of the earth's resources and consequently produce the lion's share of the world's pollution.[23] It is crucial that the churches of the North continue and increase their efforts to persuade developed nations to take progressive leadership responsibility in forging new and creative forms of international solidarity that alleviate structural poverty and ecological destruction.

The globalization of economic life and ecological problems indicated by this essay also challenges the standard understanding of the common good. The notion of the "planetary common good," introduced in *Renewing the Earth,* has a great deal of merit in this regard provided we remember that the planetary common good, from an ecological and theological perspective, must incorporate all of creation, human and non-human. Globally the primary hurdle for the twenty-first century will be achieving an integrated balance between socio-economic justice for developing communities and ecological justice for all life on planet Earth.

NOTES: CHAPTER 7

[1] Seyom Brown, *International Relations in a Changing Global System* (New York: St. Martin's Press, 1997) 87.

[2] For example, compare international relations texts from the 1940s and 1950s such as Hans J. Morgenthau, *Politics among Nations* (3d ed. New York: Knopf, 1956) with more recent texts such as Bruce Russett and Harvey Starr, *World Politics. The Menu for Choice* (4th ed. New York: W. H. Freeman, 1992) or Barry B. Hughes, *Continuity and Change in World Politics: The Clash of Perspectives* (2d ed. New York: Prentice Hall, 1994).

[3] Nicholas Boyle, *Who Are We Now? Christian Humanism and the Global Market from Hegel to Heaney* (Notre Dame, Ind.: University of Notre Dame Press, 1998). For a relevant discussion of the transformation of the power of the state see the chapter entitled "After History," 70–93.

[4] Gareth Porter and Janet Welsh Brown, *Global Environmental Politics* (2d ed. Boulder, Colo.: Westview, 1996) 36.

[5] Ibid. 33–39.

[6] Ibid. 115–27.

[7] For a summary of the conference see *The Economist* (December 13, 1997) 13.

[8] Dennis Avery, "The Myth of Global Hunger," *The World and I* (January 1997), reprinted in Theodore D. Goldfarb, ed., *Taking Sides. Clashing Views on Controversial Environmental Issues* (8th ed. Guilford, Conn.: Dushkin Publishing Group, 1998) 359–63. See also Julian L. Simon, "More People, Greater Wealth, More Resources, Healthier Environment," a version from *Economic Affairs* (April 1994) reprinted in Theodore D. Goldfarb, ed., *Taking Sides. Clashing Views on Controversial Environmental Issues* (7th ed. Guilford, Conn.: Dushkin/McGraw Hill, 1997) 187–96.

[9] See Lester R. Brown, "Analyzing the Demographic Trap," in idem, project director, *State of the World 1987: A Worldwatch Institute Report on Progress Toward a Sustainable Society* (New York: W. W. Norton, 1987) 20–37.

[10] David S. Landes, *The Wealth and Poverty of Nations* (New York: W. W. Norton, 1998).

[11] Barbara Crossette, "How to Fix a Crowded World: Add People," *New York Times* Week in Review (November 2, 1997) 1.

[12] André Gunder Frank and other dependency theorists are not concerned with environmental issues. They would look primarily to resolve economic disparities. See André G. Frank, "World System in Crisis," in William R. Thompson, ed., *Contending Approaches to World System Analysis* (Beverly Hills: SAGE, 1983) 27–42.

[13] See, e.g., Jessica Tuchman Mathews, "Redefining Security," *Foreign Affairs* 68/2 (Spring 1989) 167–77.

[14] George F. Kennan, *At a Century's Ending. Reflections 1982–1995* (New York: W. W. Norton, 1996) 274.

[15] Matthew Baasten, "Christian Values, Technology, and the Environmental Crisis" (see above, pp. 58–76). See also Fen Osler Hampson and Judith Reppy, eds., *Earthly Goods: Environmental Change and Social Justice* (Ithaca, N.Y.: Cornell University Press, 1998).

[16] Konrad von Moltke, "Institutional Interactions: The Structure of Regimes for Trade and the Environment," in Oran R. Young, ed., *Global Governance: Drawing Insights from the Environmental Experience* (Cambridge, Mass.: M.I.T. Press, 1998) 256.

[17] M. J. Peterson, "International Organizations and the Implementation of Environmental Regimes," in *Global Governance,* 115–51.

[18] David Reed, "The Environmental Legacy of Bretton Woods: The World Bank," in *Global Governance,* 227–45.

[19] Dorinda G. Dallmeyer and Albert F. Ike, eds., *Environmental Ethics and the Global Marketplace* (Athens, Ga.: University of Georgia Press, 1998).

[20] The encouraging news comes from a draft report (to be published in early 1999) of the World Meteorological Organization, the weather agency of the United Nations. See the news report "Damaged Atmosphere Begins to Heal," *The Oregonian* (October 1, 1998).

[21] "Renewing the Earth," *Origins* (December 12, 1991) 429.

[22] John Paul II, *The Ecological Crisis: A Common Responsibility* (Washington, D.C.: U.S. Catholic Conference, 1990) 4.

[23] A good case in point is the energy consumption of the U.S. With six percent of the world's population, the U.S. consumes approximately thirty percent of the world's energy. The U.S. also produces fifty percent of the world's toxic waste and twenty-five percent of the world's carbon dioxide emissions. According to Daniel Chiras, "on a per capita basis Americans consume more than twice as much energy as the people of Japan and Western Europe and about 16 times more per capita than the people of the developing nations." See Daniel D. Chiras, *Environmental Science: Action for a Sustainable Future* (4th ed. Redwood City, Calif.: Benjamin/Cummings, 1994) 243–44.

8

Sustainability: An Eco-Theological Analysis

O Lord, how manifold are your works!
In wisdom you have made them all;
the earth is full of your creatures.
Yonder is the sea, great and wide,
creeping things innumerable are there,
living things both small and great.
There go the ships,
and Leviathan that you formed to sport in it.
These all look to you
to give them their food in due season;
when you give to them, they gather it up;
when you open your hand, they are filled with good things.
(Ps 104:24-28)

With a spirit of exuberance the psalmist expresses delight in the great diversity of creation and then goes on to affirm God as the caretaker of all that has been created. The picture here is one of a benevolent and compassionate God who remains in relationship with all that was divinely created. These five verses are part of a larger picture that depicts the diversity of creation and God's care for it (vv. 1-35). Both human and non-human forms of life are the recipients of God's graciousness.

In Gen 1:26-27 of the Genesis 1–2 creation story one hears about the creation of human beings who were made in the image of God, according to God's likeness, and then given dominion over all that was created beforehand (v. 26). For the ancient biblical people, to be created in God's image, according to God's likeness, implied that they had a task, namely to bless, to co-create, and to be caretakers of creation. Essentially they had a share in God's work (see also Gen 2:15). How God cares for creation is described by the psalmist in Psalm 104. Thus the biblical text offers the human community a sacred charge: to embrace all creation in a spirit of justice and compassion while being ever respectful of its intrinsic goodness, which must be sustained and supported through ethical praxis.

INTRODUCTION:
ECONOMIC DEVELOPMENT AND THE
RHETORIC OF SUSTAINABILITY

The quagmire of global ecological crisis is quickly becoming a sobering phenomenon. Many scientists believe that the litany of environmental problems with which we have become familiar—resource depletion, deforestation, soil erosion, species extinction, global warming, toxic pollution, etc.—are all symptoms that the human species is living unsustainably on the earth. Furthermore, many of those same scientists are convinced that at 6 billion the human population, combined with our global environmental problems, has already exceeded the carrying capacity of this planet. Carrying capacity is a standard parameter in ecological investigation and is usually defined as the maximum population that any particular ecosystem can indefinitely support on a sustainable basis without irrevocably damaging the ecosystem upon which populations depend. According to Daniel Chiras, an environmental scientist, carrying capacity is composed of "at least four factors: food production, living space, waste assimilation and resource availability."[1] Because our predicament is local and global, William Rees and Mathis Wackernagel argue that carrying capacity must be understood as "the maximum rate of resource consumption and waste discharge that can be sustained indefinitely without progressively impairing the functional integrity and productivity of the relevant ecosystems wherever the latter may be."[2] Given the current human population and its worrisome rate of growth, combined with the environmental damage already accrued, we can say that the current course of humanity is unsustainable because it is exceeding the carrying capacity of planet Earth.

Another way of considering our predicament of unsustainability is from the perspective of economics. The word itself is derived from the Greek *oikos,* meaning, in Larry Rasmussen's words, "earth as a vast but single household of life."[3] In this view our global human economy is out of "synch" with what Wendell Berry calls the "Great Economy" of nature. Berry writes that "the human economy, if it is to be a good economy, must fit harmoniously within and correspond to the Great Economy; in certain important ways, it must be an analogue of the Great Economy."[4]

The growing agreement that our human economy is unsustainable within the Great Economy of earth has catapulted the language of sustainability into mainstream cultural discourse. Once a notion on the periphery, it is now used with increasing frequency by members of scientific, religious, political, and even economic institutional circles. A number of disparate definitions of sustainability abound, adding to its often ambiguous and mercurial nature.[5] Nevertheless, sustainability is usually employed as an adjective qualifying such terms as economic growth, development, society, and world. The implication common to all of these usages is that these institutional realities—economy, society, and world—are currently unsustainable and must be transformed if humanity and, in the view of some, the earth and all its living creatures, are to have a viable future.

If a single definition has gained center stage it would have to be the one proposed by *Our Common Future,* the 1987 report of the U.N. World Commission on Environment and Development. That document defined sustainable development in the following manner:

> Sustainable development is development that meets the needs of the present without compromising the ability of future generations to meet their own needs. It contains within it two key concepts:
>
> - the concept of "needs," in particular the essential needs of the world's poor, to which overriding priority should be given; and
>
> - the idea of limitations imposed by the state of technology and social organizations on the environment's ability to meet present and future needs.[6]

There is no doubt that this definition of sustainable development and the report as a whole signify a major historical breakthrough in recognition of the current state of our unsustainable human economy and its global organization. From within a milieu of ethical sensitivity *Our Common Future* clearly articulates the severity of anthropogenic environmental devastation. It addresses the wasteful consumption of the world's affluent in juxtaposition with the dehumanizing poverty of many in developing nations and how these realities are rendered still more complex by the specter of continued population growth. To remedy this unsustainable course it calls for new modes of international co-operation and new modes of economic calculation (by internalizing the "externalities" of classic economic theory) with the overall aim of proposing a possible vision for sustainable global economic development. *Our Common Future* with its accompanying definition of sustainable development is rapidly becoming the baseline for our current understanding of sustainability and is appearing with growing frequency in mainstream environmental textbooks, political documents, and institutional Church statements on the environment. For example, in February of 1996 President Clinton's Council on Sustainable Development issued its report, *Sustainable America, A New Consensus.* In it they adopted verbatim the definition of sustainable development proposed by the Brundtland Commission. It is interesting to note that the borrowed quotation defining sustainable development leaves out *Our Common Future*'s two key concepts of priority for the essential needs of the world's poor and the idea of limitations. Nevertheless, the "Vision Statement" of *Sustainable America* says,

> A sustainable United States will have a growing economy that provides equitable opportunities for satisfying livelihoods and a safe, healthy, high quality of life for current and future generations. Our nation will protect its environment, its natural resource base, and the functions and viability of natural systems on which all life depends.[7]

While space prevents critical analysis, the vision and the overall document are, as far as they go, both admirable and forward-looking.

In the religious domain, the U.S. Catholic bishops' statement *Renewing the Earth* (1991) calls for comment. For the first time in a U.S. Catholic document the notion of sustainability appears with frequent regularity. While the statement does not offer an explicit definition or make reference to the Brundtland Report, the notion of sustainability appears approximately sixteen times, ten of which are linked to economy, agriculture, or development. Other references are to world policy and only one to "ecological diversity," by which the authors mean biological diversity. In other words the clear focus and emphasis on sustainability in *Renewing the Earth, Sustainable America,* and *Our Common Future* is on human-centered economic development and growth.

This issue has been taken up by a vocal minority of dissenters, some of whom have argued that the notion of sustainable development is oxymoronic. The heart of the critique is the contradiction between notions of sustainability and prevailing assumptions about economic growth and development, assumptions that are largely uncritiqued and unchallenged by those who utilize the Brundtland and similar definitions of sustainable development. After providing a sobering portrayal of human unsustainability—caused in large measure by the current organization of the global economy—*Our Common Future* goes on to declare that

> if large parts of the developing world are to avert economic, social, and environmental catastrophes, it is essential that global economic growth be revitalized. In practical terms, this means more rapid growth in both industrial and developing countries. . . .[8]

Growth on the order of three to four percent in industrial countries and a minimum rate of five to six percent in developing countries is proposed by the report. According to Larry Rasmussen the proposal to revitalize growth in both industrial and developing nations "is oddly askew of the earlier analysis, where growth and consumption in richer regions are the problem. Now they are suddenly key to the solution."[9] Rasmussen continues his reflection on this contradiction by observing that ". . . how growth-driven economies are made compatible with biospheric sustainability in a world where the scale of human activity relative to the biosphere is already too large is anything but clear, and may be impossible."[10] This is the crux of the matter for many dissenters, particularly the new breed of ecological economists like Herman Daly who believe the prevailing notions of economic growth and development in effect since the end of World War II remain unquestioned and unaltered. These underlying economic assumptions ignore or minimize the inherently exploitative dynamics of global capitalism as well as the drastic changes that will have to occur in the affluent "North" if rates of consumption and growth are to be reduced to sustainable levels. Essentially the dominant notion of sustainable development means, in Rasmussen's analysis, "economic activity as qualified by environmental considerations in such a way as to secure sustainable economic growth."[11]

Other problems exist with dominant notions of sustainability, particularly with the persistent anthropocentrism and utilitarian valuation of nature underlying these definitions. The U.S. Presbyterian document, *Hope for a Global Future,* succinctly names this concern when it declares that

> other key elements of sustainable development seem ethically dubious, notably the sovereign right of nations to exploit their resources, the exclusively human-centered orientation of most versions of sustainable development, and the simplistic objective of "sustainable economic growth."[12]

The overwhelming emphasis in these dominant notions of sustainability is on human economic development, and while environmental considerations are important they are clearly secondary to the utilitarian uses of nature for human purposes. The intrinsic value of nature is largely missing and the sustainability of ecosystems is valued not for the systems themselves and the living organisms that reside there, but for the sustenance and fulfillment of human need. From a deep ecological perspective these reigning notions of sustainable development are "shallow," that is, they are reformist at best and lack the awareness of the fundamental socioeconomic changes required for authentic sustainability to become a reality.

Due to the anthropocentric and utilitarian bias inherent in typical definitions these approaches do not give enough attention to the ecological dynamics and principles necessary for a genuine understanding of sustainability. They are, as a rule, ecologically deficient. In addition to ecological assessment these standard notions of sustainability must be assessed theologically. They tend to reduce creation to nature and thereby contribute to its commodification. Within dominant economic practice the integrity of creation is, according to Rasmussen, "simply ignored, even when violated."[13] As the Presbyterian statement, *Hope for a Global Future,* makes obvious, religious traditions cannot accept definitions of sustainability without sufficient critique and analysis. The modest aim of this chapter is, consequently, a preliminary attempt to offer an eco-theological analysis of sustainability with the overall objective of proposing an understanding of sustainability that is ecologically and theologically adequate. For the time being, however, an acceptable definition of sustainability is Larry Rasmussen's from his insightful book *Earth Community, Earth Ethics* in which he defines it as "the capacity of natural and social systems to survive and thrive together indefinitely. It is also a vision with an implicit earth ethic. Both sustainability and its earth ethic follow from creation's integrity and a picture of earth as *oikos.*"[14]

SUSTAINABILITY IN AN ECOLOGICAL PERSPECTIVE

According to Robert Ricklefs, "maintaining a sustainable biosphere requires that we conserve the ecological processes responsible for its productivity."[15] This is precisely the common weakness of most accepted notions of sustainable development: they are not adequately grounded in the ecological processes of earth's ecosphere upon which all human economies depend. As suggested in the previous section, this is because the focus and emphasis is on sustainable economy, not sustainable ecology. Yes, they do give attention to environmental problems but not to the extent that the commonly held definition of sustainable development is consistent with what Wendell Berry calls an "analogue of the Great Economy" of creation. Attending to the principles of ecological sustainability can assist in enlarging current notions of sustainability and thereby render them more adequate and authentic. However, before we address these insights from ecological investigation several preliminary comments about ecology and ecosystems are in order.

Ecology is a relatively new and evolving field of scientific inquiry. As research and analysis become more refined and sophisticated, ecologists are less confident in their ability to predict nature and its fluid dynamism. What may indicate homeostasis, that is, a process of dynamic equilibrium in one local ecosystem, may not translate to others. Likewise, what leads to sustainability in one may not apply at all to others, particularly if they are very different. This variability is due to a large extent to the nature and complexity of ecosystems themselves. In *The Diversity of Life* E. O. Wilson hypothesizes two possible extreme scenarios in the creation and evolution of ecosystems. At one extreme there is the ecosystem characterized by total disorder. In this scenario species are "free spirits." According to Wilson,

> their colonization and extinction are not determined by the presence or absence of other species. Consequently, according to this extreme model, the amount of bio-diversity is a random process, and the habitats in which the various species live fail to coincide except by accident.[16]

The other extreme is the ecosystem that is perfectly ordered and predictable. In this scenario "species are so closely interdependent, the food webs so rigid, the symbioses so tightly bound that the community is virtually one great organism, a superorganism."[17] In this case if an ecologist knew of only one resident species he or she could predict and determine all accompanying species. Ecologists, however, reject both extremes. According to Wilson ecologists

> envision an intermediate form of community organization, something like this: whether a particular species occurs in a given suitable habitat is largely due to chance, but for most organisms the chance is strongly affected—the dice are loaded—by the identity or the species already present.[18]

The nature of ecology and its focus of inquiry (ecosystems) are such that no fixed laws yet exist as they do in chemistry and physics. Nevertheless Wilson indicates that there are "principles that can be written in the form of rules or statistical trends."[19] The interest in this section is the principle of ecological sustainability that might assist in proposing an ecologically adequate notion of sustainability. The reader should bear in mind that disagreement exists on the exact number and content of these principles but not to the degree that they cannot be utilized.

We here propose for consideration a modified version of Daniel Chiras' six biological principles of ecosystemic sustainability. Those principles are conservation, recycling, renewable resources, restoration, population control, and adaptability,[20] to which should be added solar energy and bio-diversity. Chiras recognizes that "species diversity is essential to sustainability."[21]

The earth itself is a "closed system," that is, all the necessary ingredients to support and sustain life—except one, namely solar energy—are available in the thin outer layer of earth we call the biosphere or ecosphere. Sunlight is the only—but absolutely essential—ingredient that comes from outside. Chiras suggests that we imagine earth as a terrarium where "all the materials necessary for life, such as oxygen are contained within and are used over and over."[22] No system can function without an energy source and earth is no exception. Sunlight is the primary and initial source of energy for all of earth's major ecosystems both terrestrial and aquatic, with the exception of ecosystems located in deep oceanic trenches. According to Nebel and Wright solar energy "is fundamental to sustainability for two reasons: it is both nonpolluting and nondepletable."[23]

The flow of energy within ecosystems begins with input from the sun, without which life would not be possible or sustainable. Sunlight is then "captured" by photosynthetic organisms such as green plants, which compose the basis of all food webs. Autotrophic (self-feeding) plants support the entire biosphere through the photosynthetic process because they alone of all of earth's living organisms are capable of directly absorbing solar energy. However, plants absorb only one to two percent of the total solar energy received by earth. Chiras writes that "the entire living world is built on this small fraction of sunlight."[24]

Conservation is the next principle of ecological sustainability. Fundamental to this is the first law of thermodynamics, otherwise known as the conservation of energy. Simply put it means that energy, which in our case begins with the sun, cannot be created or destroyed but can be transformed or converted to other forms of energy. In the flow of energy through the system energy is conserved, that is, energy input equals energy output. This fundamental concept is popularly known as the "no free lunch" principle of nature, meaning you can't get something for nothing or, in other words, you can't acquire more energy out of a natural system than is put into it. Because of this conservation, as a principle of sustainability, means two things; there is no waste in nature, and natural resources, that is, forms of energy, are used efficiently. Chiras writes that "natural ecosystems persist because organisms in them use only the resources they need and often they use them with efficiency."[25] He goes on to declare that "waste of the magnitude in human society is almost unheard of in nature. In fact, the evolution of life in many regions of the Earth hinged on the emergence of structural and functional characteristics that permit organisms to use resources with efficiency."[26]

Related to conservation is the principle of recycling. Ecosystems are sustained because they use and reuse material resources again and again—which is precisely why ecosystems are efficient. Within the Great Economy of nature, energy and material resources flow from plants (producers) to animals (consumers). These essential nutrients flow in a cyclical manner or, in other words, they are recycled. According to Nebel and Wright recycling is a fundamental principle for two reasons: "It prevents waste, which would cause problems, from accumulating . . . and . . . it assures that the ecosystems will not run out of essential elements."[27] The continual recycling of nutrients, particularly carbon, phosphorus, and nitrogen, is essential for ecosystemic health and sustainability. Nebel and Wright state:

> If we reconsider the natural law of conservation of matter, which says that atoms cannot be created, destroyed nor changed, we can see that recycling is the only way to maintain a dynamic system, and the biosphere has mastered this to a profound degree.[28]

Connected to the process of nutrient recycling is the concept of renewable resources. The main point here is that the cyclical flow of nutrients within ecosystems is renewable. The biosphere of earth is sustained because it is dependent upon and utilizes renewable material resources. Chiras states that "Natural systems . . . persist because they rely principally on renewable resources . . . such as air, water, plants, and animals that regenerate via biological or geological processes."[29] The underlying dynamic of renewable resources is the regenerative and restorative capacity of nature, provided that natural or human-caused trauma or damage is not irreparable. This leads to the process of restoration, the next principle of ecological sustainability.

Restoration refers to the natural ability of ecosystems to repair damage. Like our own capacity "to heal," mechanisms exist in nature that allow the restoration of ecosystems after serious trauma from natural phenomena like fire and volcanic eruption and from human encroachment—provided it is not overly extensive. In the western United States recent examples of this would be the eruption of Mount St. Helens in 1980 and the massive fire in Yellowstone National Park in 1988. Natural regeneration in both areas of devastation is well under way in a process called secondary ecological succession. According to Chiras secondary succession "is the sequential development of biotic communities after the complete or partial destruction of an existing community."[30] The natural process of restoration has generated a new sub-discipline of ecology called restoration ecology, which studies the recovery of ecosystems and how humans might promote that process.[31] Essential to the notion of sustainability is the capacity to restore and repair the damage to important ecosystems caused by human negligence and irresponsibility. Central to this undertaking are conservation biology and restoration ecology.

Following restoration is the important principle of population control. Natural ecosystems are sustained because they contain a complex set of biotic and abiotic checks and balances that maintain equilibrium between the population size of species and the carrying capacity of ecosystems. Through such mechanisms as growth and reduction factors and the notion of environmental resistance populations of organisms are maintained within ecosystemic limits determined in large measure by food supply and other available resources. In other words, to use Chiras' colloquial way of stating it, "a natural system of checks and balances keeps organisms from eating themselves out of house and home."[32] This complex set of biotic and abiotic factors tends to produce a process of dynamic equilibrium or homeostasis which in turn sustains the ecological integrity of ecosystems.

As the Introduction to this paper suggested, current human population and its predicted growth curve are deeply troublesome to ecologists, many of whom see this complex as a major symptom of human unsustainability.[33] However, as a major contributing factor to this scenario the overall impact of population growth does not stand alone but must be factored along with accompanying rates of resource consumption and the waste (pollution) produced by consumption. To calculate and clarify this worrisome dynamic ecologists use the Population-Resource-Pollution Model.[34] To take the United States as an example: its current population combined with its consumption of resources makes it the most overpopulated country in the world. Combining this with the magnitude of waste we produce makes us one of the most unsustainable cultures on the planet. In other words we are living beyond our means and this sobering fact ought to raise serious questions regarding our hope of building a just and sustainable future.[35]

The final ecological principle is paired: adaptability and bio-diversity, both of which fall under the overarching process of evolution. It is commonly held among biologists that the process of evolution by natural selection produces two major results: the modification of existing species, known as adaptation, and the creation of new species (technically called speciation), contributing to bio-diversity. E. O. Wilson writes that "An undeniable trend of progressive evolution has been the growth of bio-diversity by increasing command of earth's environment."[36] Some ecologists believe that there is a direct correlation between bio-diversity and the stability of certain ecosystems. Although this is not a proven or universal "law," the general sentiment is that the higher the species diversity the greater is the stability of the system. Chiras writes: "no one knows for sure whether diversity creates stability. However, we do know that simplifying ecosystems by reducing species makes systems less stable and more vulnerable to outside influence."[37]

Adaptations, particularly favorable ones, increase the chances of species to survive and reproduce. These modifications also produce species better suited, that is, adapted to their environment. According to Chiras "natural systems persist because of the capacity of organisms within them to change in response to changing environmental conditions. . . ."[38] Both adaptability and bio-diversity are key components in the evolution of life on earth and essential ingredients in sustaining the planet's biosphere. The beauty of nature's evolutionary creativity in producing vast and multifaceted life forms on earth must be set in stark contrast to the unprecedented rate of anthropogenetic extinction currently occurring. It is tragic to think that species are being lost before they are even known. Theologically this must be recognized as a grievous affront to the integrity of God's creation.

This brief overview of the basic principles of ecological sustainability ought to provide an ecological baseline for measuring the adequacy of notions of sustainability. Current dominant concepts of sustainable development do not, as a rule, incorporate these principles to the degree they should and consequently render them inadequate. An authentic vision of sustainability must, in Wendell Berry's words, "fit harmoniously within and . . . correspond to the Great Economy" of nature; only then will our vision of a just and sustainable world be truly viable. However, while ecological justification and analysis of the reigning notions of sustainability are essential, they are not sufficient particularly for religious communities shaped and identified by the Judeo-Christian tradition. Theological analysis and justification are also required.

SUSTAINABILITY THEOLOGICALLY CONSIDERED

Theologically the basis and justification for sustainability can be approached in a number of ways. This section proposes that at the very least the notion of sustainability must be grounded within the nexus of ancient Israel's theology of creation and redemption and the eschatological horizon of faith known in the New Testament as the Reign of God. We should begin this task by acknowledging an important distinction between an ecological-scientific understanding of sustainability and a Judeo-Christian one. In the scientific paradigm the natural universe is observed much as the ancient Greeks looked upon it: that is, the cosmos is a self-sustaining and perpetuating reality. In other words the principle of sustainability is inherent in the natural process itself or, stated in another way, it is ecocentric. In the theological view of biblical faith the universe—more appropriately referred to as creation—does not stand alone but is continually sustained by the creative power of God. From a theological point of view the notion of sustainability is not ecocentric but profoundly theocentric. That faith-constructed worldview is rooted in Old Testament creation theology.

The theological justification of sustainability begins quite simply with the biblical recognition that the entire created order has its origins in the sovereign and creative power of God. Biblical creation theology addresses a primary cosmic issue: the origination of a cosmos; the beginning of all things. But the creation of the cosmos is not a singular event; it is an ongoing process. According to Bernhard Anderson the Hebrew verb *bārāʾ*, frequently used in creation texts, "refers to a *creatio continua.*"[39] Anderson writes that "creation is not just an event that occurred in the beginning, at the foundation of the earth, but is God's continuing activity of sustaining and holding everything in being."[40]

The idea of *creatio continua* is also linked to the biblical view that the entire cosmos is totally dependent and contingent upon God. In contrast to the Greek view the cosmos in the Hebrew perspective is not a self-sustaining or self-perpetuating reality. The cosmos requires the ongoing sustaining power and presence of God or it will return to its chaotic state. From this view the entire biosphere, human and non-human, shares the radical equality of creatureliness. All that exists does not exist on its own but is dependent on and grounded in the sustaining and creating power of God.

These theocentric creation themes are also found in ancient Israel's Wisdom tradition. In Wisdom literature, however, they receive interesting theological development. In Israel's sapiential tradition, Woman Wisdom (*ḥokmâ*), the personification of divine and human wisdom, preexists the creation of the cosmos. In Proverbs the imagery suggests, according to Leo Perdue, that Woman Wisdom is a "preexistent architect who designs and builds the cosmos."[41] Besides being God's instrument for creating the cosmos Woman Wisdom also sustains it. Perdue writes: "Divine wisdom is closely associated with the power to create and sustain the cosmos. . . ."[42] While the creation theology of Wisdom literature clearly reaffirms the sovereignty of God as creator, the emphasis appears to be on God sustaining, perpetuating, and maintaining the regularity and order of the cosmos through the presence of Woman Wisdom.

The notion of order or the orderliness of creation is central to biblical creation theology and relevant to a theological understanding of sustainability. In the biblical text creation does not occur *ex nihilo* but results in God creating order out of primordial chaos. In the mytho-poetic creation narrative of Genesis 1 creation unfolds with God creating order out of watery chaos. The order is a structured spatial unity. For Rolf Knierim biblical creation theology perceives the world "as a universal system, a cosmos, in which every realm has its proper place and function including humans."[43] The meaning and purpose of this cosmic order is, in Knierim's view, "life and represents the support system for life."[44]

Bernhard Anderson's reading of the Genesis text is consistent with Knierim's assertion. Anderson suggests that the structured order "out of chaos" is the creation of an *oikos,* that is, a home or habitat for God's manifold creatures. In his view Genesis 1 represents a sequential move-ment "from heaven to earth, which increasingly becomes an orderly habitation."[45] According to Anderson's interpretation the emphasis of the text does not fall so much "on anthropology, that is the supremacy of humanity, as on ecology, that is the earthly habitation that human beings share with other forms of 'living being' *(nepeš ḥayyâ)."*[46] It should be noted that in this pre-scientific text all the abiotic and biotic components for a thriving ecosphere are present. While it would be hermeneutically unsound to read too much ecology into Genesis 1 the text does nevertheless reveal that ancient Israel was well aware of the "eco-logical" ordering of creation necessary to support and sustain life. In their view the lifegiving and sustaining order of creation is God's design.

The theme of order is by no means limited to Genesis. For example, there are significant parallels between the Genesis account of creation and Psalm 104, an important Wisdom-creation psalm. Both texts indi-cate that all living creatures are given their proper place and function within the order of creation. However in Psalm 104, differently from the Genesis account, the ordering of creation is the work of Wisdom. Furthermore a predominant theme in this psalm, as indicated by vv. 10-18, is the "sustainability" of creation by Woman Wisdom. The orderly design of creation and its proper maintenance and sustenance are in the hands of Woman Wisdom who is immanently present in the created order. It would not be inappropriate to suggest therefore that the sus-tainability of the natural world, observed by ecologists as inherent to the natural process, is from a theological perspective also intrinsic to creation through the power and presence of divine Wisdom.

Within the Wisdom tradition, however, the order of creation is not simply physical but moral as well, requiring ethical behavior to sustain the harmonious working of creation. The root word for "order" in Hebrew is *ṣedeq,* meaning "justice" or "righteousness." According to H. H. Schmid righteousness "is not understood narrowly as a legal mat-ter, but as universal order, as comprehensive salvation."[47] The *ṣaddîq* is the "righteous one" who, in practicing justice, maintains the wholeness and integrity of creation. Consequently within the Wisdom tradition humanity, through the mediation of Woman Wisdom, becomes co-creator with God in the continuous responsibility of sustaining the order of creation.

In addition to establishing the ethical dimensions of world order Woman Wisdom also renders creation intelligible within human limits. Woman Wisdom will instruct the seeker of wisdom to discover the magnificent design of creation through study and rational reflection, and even to come to "know" God. What this suggests is a kind of "natural theology" insofar as creation reveals God and serves as the medium for divine instruction. In Perdue's words, "Wisdom . . . is also analytical and constructive reason that both observes and posits coherence and order, whether in reference to elements of nature or in the persuasive arguments of moral discourse."[48]

Biblical creation theology, particularly as it has taken shape in ancient Israel's Wisdom tradition, can provide a potential link between an ecological and a theological understanding of sustainability. Three immediate points of connection come to mind. First, the ecological principles of sustainability are part of and intrinsic to the "order" of creation. Ecology understands these principles as the inherent mechanisms whereby nature flourishes and is sustained. In a theological view these principles of sustainability are part of the design of creation and reflect, even reveal the working of divine wisdom in the ordering and sustaining of creation. Second, the order of creation is rendered intelligible through Woman Wisdom. By study and rational reflection one can discover the magnificent design of creation. A theological "reading" of ecology suggests that it is an example of this kind of rational endeavor. Through observation and rational reflection, ecology has deduced a number of principles or mechanisms through which ecosystems are ordered and sustained. Are these principles the "wisdom" of the natural world? Is it not true that the "wisdom" of ecology is telling us a great deal about the potential disorder, even chaos that living out of harmony can engender? The crux of our human predicament is that our economy is not an "analogue" of the Great Economy of creation. Ecology has assisted us in coming to "know" this wisdom.

Finally, the order of creation, from the view of wisdom-creation theology, is also a moral order. Humans have an ethical responsibility in sustaining the order of the created world. The science of ecology ever since Aldo Leopold indicates that there are ethical implications that can be deduced from ecological investigation. In other words, the laws and forces of nature that impact the structure and dynamics of ecosystems —what we might interpret theologically as the "order of creation"— strongly suggest ethical implications for the way humans ought to live on the earth. Chiras names this the "sustainable ethic," consisting of three ethical norms: "(1) The earth has a limited supply of resources, and they're not all for us; (2) humans are a part of nature, subject to its laws; and (3) success stems from efforts to cooperate with the forces of nature."[49] The biblical wisdom-creation tradition provides us with a theological backdrop for recognizing the ethical implications of sustainability from an ecological viewpoint. While this is essential, it is not theologically sufficient. The eschatological horizon of ancient Israel's redemption theology must also be considered for further justification of sustainability.

There are two components of ecological sustainability that lend themselves to eschatological reflection. The first is the notion of restoration. The principles of ecological sustainability require that damaged ecosystems be restored and current healthy ones maintained. Ecological restoration is consistent with the biblical vision of eschatological redemption understood as the restoration and renewal of creation—all creation, human and non-human. Rooted in the Old Testament, especially in the prophetic tradition, is the view that there exists an intrinsic link between creation and redemption. According to Old Testament scholar Carol J. Dempsey, "the redemption of humankind is connected to the restoration of the natural world through divine promise."[50]

The second "eschatological" theme in most definitions of sustainability is the responsibility for the future. The Brundtland Commission defined sustainable development with a focus on the ability of "future generations to meet their own needs." Ecologists believe sustainability is a necessity because, in Chiras' words, "our future depends on creating and maintaining a healthy well-functioning global ecosystem."[51] The eschatological horizon of biblical faith incorporates a hopeful, redemptive future for both anthropocentric and ecological concerns. The future vision of *shalom* includes social and ecological justice against the all-encompassing backdrop of restoring and renewing the integrity of creation.

The future hope of redemption originates within the prophetic eschatological vision and any number of major and minor prophets, including Isaiah, Jeremiah, Ezekiel, Hosea, Joel, and Amos, could be cited to substantiate this claim. This task, however, is beyond the scope of this chapter. Nevertheless, Dempsey provides an exquisite and concise set of conclusions in her summary analysis of prophetic eschatology and the future hope of redemption. She writes:

> The Israelite prophets show us through their writings the following points: (1) there is indeed an inherent link between redemption and

creation, specifically that redemption of humankind is connected to the restoration of creation either through cause or effect; (2) the redemption of humanity and the restoration of creation are divinely promised; (3) the divine promise of redemption and restoration leads to a vision of a new creation embraced by justice, righteousness, and peacefulness, and ordered by harmonious relationships.[52]

From this perspective the work of sustainability can be understood as the ethical praxis in hopeful anticipation of the future restoration and renewal of creation. It reflects the ethical commitment of justice and righteousness for both human and earth for the purpose of sustaining and maintaining the integrity of creation.

For Christians the eschatological hope of cosmic redemption culminates in Jesus' proclamation of the coming of God's reign. The notion that eschatological redemption incorporates the restoration and renewal of all creation is not new to the Christian tradition even though until recently—because of ecological exigencies—it has been largely overlooked and ignored. According to H. Paul Santmire what he calls the "ecological motif" is strongly present in the ancient theologies of such thinkers as Irenaeus and Augustine. However only recently, due in large measure to our predicament of unsustainability, has the ecological dimension of redemption been recovered.

Jürgen Moltmann's books *God and Creation* and *The Coming of God* are representative of the contemporary retrieval of the ecological motif in redemption. Moltmann concurs with the biblical vision that eschatological redemption incorporates both human and nature. He writes:

> Because there is no such thing as a soul separate from the body, and one humanity detached from nature—from life, the earth and the cosmos—there is no redemption for human beings either without the redemption of nature. The redemption of humanity is aligned towards a humanity whose existence is still conjoined with nature.[53]

In his theological analysis of creation in redemption Moltmann develops what he calls a "tripartite" concept of creation: *creatio originalis,* corresponding to God's initial creation, *creatio continua,* meaning God's continued sustaining of creation, and *creatio nova,* referring to the eschatological consummation of creation.[54] Moltmann writes that "the symbols 'kingdom of God,' 'eternal life' and 'glory' are ways of describing the eschatological goal of God's creation."[55] In *creatio continua,* God's work is the sustaining and preserving of original creation, but

God's historical activity of maintaining creation is anticipatory, that is, a preparation for its final transformation. Moltmann writes that "God's historical activity is then eschatologically oriented: it preserves the initial creation by anticipating the consummation and by preparing the way for that consummation."[56] The disclosure in history of God's Reign in and through the life, death, and resurrection of Jesus initiates the restoration and renewal of creation as the kingdom of God. Moltmann asserts: "It is theologically necessary to view created things as real promises of the kingdom; and it is equally necessary, conversely, to understand the kingdom of God as the fulfillment, not merely of the historical promises of the world, but of its natural promises as well."[57]

The sustainability of earth, both now and in the future, receives its theological justification from the biblical vision of creation and redemption. First and foremost sustaining, preserving, restoring, and renewing creation is the work of God. This is a theocentric vision. Human beings, however, have an ethical responsibility to participate in this great design of and for creation. The wisdom of God immanent in the created order of nature calls us to sustain, preserve, and restore the integrity of creation seriously threatened by human unsustainability. Before we conclude this analysis it is imperative to recall that a theological vision of sustainability must address both ecological and human concerns. The Judeo-Christian vision of creation and redemption understands the ecological and anthropological dimensions of sustainability as integral. The weakness of both ecocentric and anthropocentric definitions of sustainability is the tendency to emphasize one dimension over and even against the other. A theologically authentic perception of sustainability must account for and address the injustice to all creation, both humanity and nature.

CONCLUSION AND THEOLOGICAL REFLECTION

Based on the analysis presented here, a new definition for sustainability now emerges: sustainability is the ethical praxis of restoring and maintaining the integrity of creation in the hopeful anticipation of the coming of God's reign. There are four essential components to this notion of sustainability: ecological, social-anthropological, theological, and ethical.[58]

Primary to the notion of sustainability must be preserving and maintaining the ecological integrity of earth's biosphere because our *oikos* has value in and of itself, not simply because of its instrumentality.

This means measures must be taken to safeguard the ecological processes of earth as well as repairing those ecosystems damaged by human
abuse for the purpose of sustaining all life, human and other kinds, on
this planet. Furthermore, the intrinsic value of earth requires us to protect and maintain the abiotic (air, water, land) components of earth's
ecosphere without which life would not be possible.

Urgent and special measures, however, must be taken to halt the rate
of anthropogenetic extinction that seriously threatens the planet's biodiversity. While it is exceedingly difficult to estimate the total loss of
species worldwide, E. O. Wilson's calculations of the loss of species in
the world's rain forests—the richest source of bio-diversity on earth—
suggest that "the number of species doomed each year is 27,000. Each day
it is 74 and each hour it is 3."[59] If current trends remain intact we may
very likely witness the sixth-greatest collapse of life on earth within our
lifetime. Wilson concludes his assessment of threatened bio-diversity
with this dire statement: "Clearly we are in the midst of one of the great
extinction spans of geological history."[60]

In addition to preserving earth's ecological processes, restoring and
maintaining the integrity of creation means incorporating the ecological principles of sustainability, as outlined in the second section of this
chapter, into our operative definitions of sustainability. This requires
attention to the ecosystem dynamics of conservation, recycling, renewable resources, restoration, adaptability/biodiversity, and solar energy.
These mechanisms of the Great Economy of creation must be reflected
in the world's economies if we humans are going to pursue and realize
an authentic vision of sustainability.

Finally, the ecological dimension of sustainability requires us to
educate for ecological consciousness and responsibility. While all
human institutions have a stake in this it is particularly incumbent on
religious communities to embrace this task. This will not be easy. Many
rank-and-file members of religious communities, particularly within
the Judeo-Christian tradition, do not see ecological education as relevant to their notions of religious education. Yet Pope John Paul II is on
the mark when he states that "an education in ecological responsibility
is urgent: for oneself, for others, and for the earth. . . . Churches and
religious bodies . . . have a precise role to play in such education."[61]

The second essential component of the proposed definition of sustainability is socio-anthropological. In other words, operative notions
of sustainability must account for and address the systemic and integral
link between ecological degradation and socioeconomic injustice that

has become institutionalized at both local and global levels. As Larry Rasmussen states, "Both poverty and affluence threaten and degrade basic life-support systems, albeit in wildly different degree."[62] It is fundamentally unjust that the approximately 1.1 billion affluent, a minority of the world's population most of whom reside in the northern hemisphere, consume the majority of the earth's resources and produce the vast majority of the world's unassimilated and often toxic waste. By some estimates the affluent of the world are responsible for about seventy percent of the earth's ecological degradation.[63] Alleviating this vexing and persistent threat to earth's sustainability will require major transformation of local and global economic infrastructures. In other words, pursuing the dominant vision of sustainable economic development will not produce a just and sustainable world or future. An alternative vision of sustainability must be pursued. One such possibility is what Rasmussen calls sustainable communities. The difference, according to Rasmussen, between typical notions of sustainable development and sustainable communities is that

> conventional sustainable development qualifies economic growth with a view to ecological sustainability while the alternative vision [sustainable communities] tries to increase local economic self-reliance within a framework of community responsibility and ecolgical balance. The latter's attention is to webs of social relationships that define human community, together with ecosystem webs and the regenerative capacities of both human and ecosystem communities.[64]

What Rasmussen proposes as sustainable communities sounds remarkably similar to what some environmentalists call bioregionalism, where local community structures such as economic, social, and political institutions are organized according to the local or regional biotic community (i.e., ecosystem) or biome. As Rasmussen suggests, the focus is on preserving the integrity of both human and natural communities as an integral process. Due to the abysmal historical failure of economic development to alleviate human poverty there is no reason to believe that commonly held notions of sustainable development will produce both human and ecological sustainability. The alternative vision of sustainable communities offers more hope of addressing the inherent link between social and ecological justice.

The third dimension of sustainability proposed herein is fundamentally theocentric. It is grounded in biblical faith that God is the creator, sustainer, restorer, and renewer of creation. The integrity of creation is first and foremost a theological category. In Rasmussen's words creation means "all things together, in, with, and before God, all things in their totality and in their differentiation as an expression of the divine life."[65] Restoring and maintaining the integrity of creation is based on the eschatological horizon of Judeo-Christian faith that redemption includes humanity and nature, and that humanity and nature will be rescued and made whole by God. This vision and hope of future *shalom* is best symbolized by the central theme in Jesus' proclamation—the Reign of God. In powerful and appealing biblical imagery this symbol lures us forward to embrace a future where creation is perpetually sustained in deep and abiding relationships between God, human, and earth.

This theological vision is not, however, "cheap grace." It requires the hard work of ethical commitment to the praxis of sustainability. The ethical dimension of sustainability is perhaps the most important and the most difficult because it still requires fundamental changes in attitude and behavior, particularly for the world's affluent. The current rate of resource consumption in the "North" is unethical and unsustainable. Socioeconomic and ecological justice—intrinsic to the ethical dimensions of sustainability—require that the "voracious consumerism of the developed world" be dramatically curtailed.[66] In addition to consumption, human population growth must also be addressed and curtailed. The implications for ignoring these ethical issues are potentially disastrous.

The key ethical issue of sustainability is that it embraces both the work of social and ecological justice as integral in restoring and maintaining the integrity of creation. This ethical praxis is grounded in and anticipatory of the eschatological coming of God. This is not some veiled Pelagianism. In the language of the Second Vatican Council the praxis of sustainability makes "ready the material" of the kingdom and recognizes that the "fruits" of our labor will endure in the final reign of God. In the last analysis the praxis of sustainability is an earth ethic that recognizes and acts upon the fundamental commitment that all life, and that which supports and sustains it, is intrinsically good and that we embrace it in the perpetual dance of creation.

NOTES: CHAPTER 8

[1] Daniel D. Chiras, *Environmental Science: Action for a Sustainable Future* (Redwood City, Calif.: Benjamin/Cummings, 1994) 110.

[2] William R. Rees and Mathis Wackernagel, "Ecological Footprints and Appropriate Carrying Capacity: Measuring the Natural Capital Requirements of the Human Economy," in AnnMari Jansson, et al., eds., *Investing in Natural Capital: The Ecological Economics Approach to Sustainability* (Washington, D.C.: Island Press, 1994) 362–90.

[3] Larry L. Rasmussen, *Earth Community, Earth Ethics* (Maryknoll, N.Y.: Orbis, 1996) 91. For an excellent analysis of *oikos* and its derivative terms see the chapter entitled "Ecumenical Earth," 90–97.

[4] Wendell Berry, *Home Economics* (San Francisco: North Point Press, 1987) 59.

[5] For a sample of various definitions see Chiras, *Environmental Science: Action for a Sustainable Future* 6.

[6] *Our Common Future* (Oxford and New York: Oxford University Press, 1987) 43. The U.N. World Commission on Environment and Development is often called the Brundtland Commission for its Chair, Gro Harlem Brundtland of Norway.

[7] *Sustainable America: A New Consensus* (Washington, D.C.: U.S. Government Printing Office, 1996) iv.

[8] *Our Common Future* 89.

[9] Rasmussen, *Earth Community, Earth Ethics* 134.

[10] Ibid.

[11] Ibid. 148.

[12] *Hope for a Global Future: Toward Just and Sustainable Human Development* (Louisville: The Office of the General Assembly, Presbyterian Church, U.S.A., 1996) 76.

[13] Rasmussen, *Earth Community, Earth Ethics* 124.

[14] Ibid. 127.

[15] Robert E. Ricklefs, *The Economy of Nature: A Textbook in Basic Ecology* (New York: W. H. Freeman, 1997) 616.

[16] Edward O. Wilson, *The Diversity of Life* (Cambridge, Mass.: Harvard University Press, 1992) 163–64.

[17] Ibid.

[18] Ibid.

[19] Ibid.

[20] Chiras, *Environmental Science: Action for a Sustainable Future* 10–11.

[21] Ibid.

[22] Ibid.

[23] Bernard J. Nebel and Richard T. Wright, *Environmental Science* (Upper Saddle River, N.J.: Prentice Hall, 1996) 66.

[24] Chiras, *Environmental Science: Action for a Sustainable Future* 36.

[25] Ibid. 10.

[26] Ibid.

[27] Nebel and Wright, *Environmental Science* 66.

[28] Ibid.

[29] Chiras, *Environmental Science: Action for a Sustainable Future* 10.

[30] Ibid. 65.

[31] Perhaps one of the most significant success stories in restoration is the case of the Pacific sea otter, a species nearly hunted to extinction. Because it was a keystone species the threatened disappearance of the sea otter had a dramatically negative effect on the entire aquatic ecosystem off the western coast of the United States. With the assistance of strong public support conservation biologists were able to restore the sea otter and with it the original habitat and biodiversity. See Edward O. Wilson, *The Diversity of Life* 164–65.

[32] Chiras, *Environmental Science: Action for a Sustainable Future* 11.

[33] Estimates and scenarios for human population growth vary but a common one suggests that at present growth rates human population may reach ten to twelve billion before stabilizing sometime during the latter half of the next century. For more information see Nebel and Wright, *Environmental Science* 140ff.

[34] See Chiras, *Environmental Science: Action for a Sustainable Future* 95–96.

[35] The human population issue cannot be ignored particularly within Roman Catholic circles. Predictions of future population growth combined with the Church's continued prohibition of artificial means of birth control make this an issue deserving urgent attention. Some ecologists believe that if humans do not control their current rate of birth, nature will, with far more devastating consequences.

[36] Wilson, *The Diversity of Life* 188.

[37] Chiras, *Environmental Science: Action for a Sustainable Future* 63.

[38] Ibid. 11.

[39] Bernhard W. Anderson, *From Creation to New Creation* (Minneapolis: Fortress, 1994) 89.

[40] Ibid.

[41] Leo G. Perdue, *Wisdom & Creation: The Theology of Wisdom Literature* (Nashville: Abingdon, 1994) 91.

[42] Ibid. 326.

[43] Rolf Knierim, "Cosmos and History in Israel's Theology," *Horizons in Biblical Theology* 3 (1981) 75.

[44] Ibid. 83.

[45] Anderson, *From Creation to New Creation* 139.

[46] Ibid.

[47] H. H. Schmid, "Creation, Righteousness, and Salvation," in Bernhard W. Anderson, ed., *Creation in the Old Testament* (Philadelphia: Fortress, 1984) 107.

[48] Perdue, *Wisdom & Creation* 332.

[49] Chiras, *Environmental Science: Action for a Sustainable Future* 10.

[50] Carol J. Dempsey, "Hope Amidst Crisis: A Prophetic Vision of Cosmic Redemption" in this volume, pp. 269–84, at 270.

[51] Chiras, *Environmental Science: Action for a Sustainable Future* 10.

[52] Dempsey, "Hope Amidst Crisis: A Prophetic Vision of Cosmic Redemption," (below, p. 279).

[53] Jürgen Moltmann, *The Coming of God* (Minneapolis: Fortress, 1996) 260.

[54] Jürgen Moltmann, *God in Creation* (San Francisco: Harper & Row, 1985) 55, 208ff.

[55] Ibid.

[56] Ibid. 210.

[57] Ibid. 63.

[58] For the components of sustainability proposed herein I am very dependent on Larry Rasmussen's analysis of the "integrity of creation" in which he suggests six characteristics. He also reminds us that the World Council of Churches gave us the phrase, "the integrity of creation." See *Earth Community, Earth Ethics* 98–107.

[59] Wilson, *The Diversity of Life* 280. For a fairly comprehensive and disturbing scientific analysis of the loss of biodiversity see his ch. 12.

[60] Ibid.

[61] John Paul II, *The Ecological Crisis: A Common Responsibility* (Washington, D.C.: U.S. Catholic Conference, 1990).

[62] Rasmussen, *Earth Community, Earth Ethics* 103.

[63] Ibid. 104.

[64] Ibid. 131.

[65] Ibid.

[66] The language here is borrowed from the U.S. Catholic bishops' statement "Renewing the Earth," *Origins* 21/7 (December 12, 1991) 430.

9

The Stewardship of Natural and Human Resources

Then God said, "Let us make humankind in our image, according to our likeness; and let them have dominion over the fish of the sea, and over the birds of the air, and over the cattle, and over all the wild animals of the earth, and over every creeping thing that creeps upon the earth." (Gen 1:26)

One of the key words in this passage is "dominion," which is meant to imply "care," especially care for the most vulnerable in creation. Today the most vulnerable are found in both the human and non-human dimensions of life and therefore the exercise of dominion—good stewardship—is to care for natural resources and human resources. This integrated view of stewardship is made possible through the Natural Step Process, which is discussed in detail in this chapter.

INTRODUCTION

Authors from diverse disciplines have come together to write this book on contemporary environmental issues and their ethical implications. What is the key thread tying these readings together? It is a series of warnings: a set of wake-up calls to humanity. This chapter focuses on a concern for humankind's overall economic environment. Business organizations are indeed making progress in their understanding and professed relationships to their natural environment. In a systemic environment, however, progress in one area must be balanced by progress in others. A balanced ethic is required not only in our relationship with natural resources but also in our relationship with human resources.

Stewardship of the planet's natural resources is absolutely critical to the survival of both our organizations and the economy in general. Yet stewardship of natural resources cannot exist in a vacuum. It is imperative that we have a balance: that organizations recognize their equal responsibility for stewarding their human resources. Thus the purpose of this chapter is twofold: to illustrate the paradigm that seems to be emerging as the guiding framework for organizations as they manage their relationships with the natural environment, and to develop a comparable framework to guide business firms in their relationship to their human resources.

DEFINING STEWARDSHIP

In the biblical context, stewardship refers to humankind's responsibility for carefully husbanding God's gifts. In Gen 1:26 God says "Let us make humankind in our image . . . and let them have dominion over the fish of the sea, and over the birds of the air, and over the cattle, and over all the wild animals of the earth, and over the creeping things that creep upon the earth." This role is further clarified in Gen 2:15: "The LORD God took the earth creature and put it in the garden of Eden to till it and keep it."

The term "stewardship" has evolved since its early biblical use. Today the term is commonly used by both the business and academic communities to refer to our relationship to natural resources. The premise of this essay is that the concept of stewardship needs to be extended beyond the natural environment to include the relationship between organizations and their human resources.

Currently the concern for stewardship of human resources is found primarily in the field of leadership, where it implies a willingness to serve rather than control others and to be accountable for the well-being of the larger organization:

> Stewardship is to hold something in trust for another. Historically, stewardship was a means to protect a kingdom while those rightfully in charge were away, or, more often, to govern for the sake of an underage

king. The underage king for us is the next generation. We choose service over self-interest most powerfully when we build the capacity of the next generation to govern themselves.[1]

This chapter explores an exemplary approach to stewardship of natural resources and argues for the need to develop comparable models that sustain human resources in light of the increasing demands facing organizations and their employees.

STEWARDSHIP OF NATURAL RESOURCES

If one were to map on a continuum the typical human responses to social issues the result might look like Figure 1 below. This model[2] suggests that positions on environmental initiatives range from adamant opposition to equally adamant advocacy of protecting the environment. Thus stewardship behaviors are found in the values closer to the right endpoint of the continuum.

Figure 1. Values Guiding Environmental Behavior

Adamant Opposers	Pragmatic Opposers	Manipulators	Espousers	Pragmatic Believers	Adamant Protectors

Society holds a range of values regarding business's responsibilities to the environment. The popular preconception is that values tend toward the left side of Figure 1, yet the truth is that business people can be found at each point along the continuum. The two groups at the right end of the continuum, our stewards of the earth's resources, include many business people who believe in and act in accordance with the precepts of environmentalism. These are the *pragmatic believers* who seek to balance strong beliefs with realistic economics and the *adamant protectors,* or true believers, who support all environmental causes as a matter of principle. Many of the "early adopters" of environmental business practices are found in these groups.[3]

The middle groups along this continuum include *espousers* and *manipulators.* The first group espouse environmental values but do not act them out in their work lives. Unlike *manipulators* they may sincerely believe in underlying environmental values but fail to carry through in terms of actual behavior. Common excuses for their lack of consistency are the arguments that environmental safeguards are too expensive or constitute a disadvantage when a company is confronted with global competitors operating in countries with little or no environmental consciousness or regulations.

The other group in the middle consists of *manipulators.* These are the people who "do the right thing" strictly for ulterior motives. This group includes those business people who have jumped on the environmental bandwagon and are doing their best to "look green." Their true motive is to increase their sales and market share with customers and stockholders who believe in environmentalism. This practice of "greenwashing" involves symbolic rather than substantive action[4] and generates cynicism on the part of observers who recognize the manipulative nature of this posturing.

The left end of the continuum includes two groups that oppose environmental regulations and initiatives. Their resistance may stem in part from a lack of awareness. For example, they may fail to understand and subsequently acknowledge their role in environmental degradation. *Pragmatic opposers* are more likely to consider short-run economic considerations and a limited set of stakeholders (themselves and their stockholders) to whom they feel responsible. They frequently maintain that environmental protection is too expensive. A more strident political philosophy distinguishes *adamant opposers* from their pragmatic counterparts. This group is the most likely to take an individualistic stance and rebel against all forms of government or community intervention that threaten their business growth and profits.

According to William E. Halal the groups at both ends of the continuum cause problems: ". . . the primary obstacle to environmental progress today is a clash between two groups of believers who obscure the complex nature of the problem: one side is intent on protecting the environment at great cost to human welfare, while the other side is intent on growth at great cost to the environment."[5] These groups are criticized for fueling the polarization that frequently surrounds environmental issues.

Paradoxically, misunderstanding and conflict may also arise when one group takes multiple positions along the environmental value continuum. In business, for example, one division of a company may be highly proactive with regard to the environment while other divisions are involved in "greenwashing" or even aggressive lobbying of Congress to remove regulations.[6] Company environmental policy may differ markedly regarding which environmental impacts are addressed and which are ignored. Groups that take varied stances are often criticized for being inconsistent, thus reducing their credibility in disputes with parties that hold more uniform positions. Distorted perceptions may follow. When conflicts arise there is a common tendency to intensify those elements on which parties disagree. Areas where there is common ground are ignored, and positive contributions are downplayed. As a result of these negative shifts in perceptions, dialogue and problem solving become blocked. Critics may chastise an entire corporation or industry rather than recognizing and building on the positive efforts that are being undertaken. Clarifying these perceptions and discovering the common ground are important steps toward improving dialogue on environmental issues.

THE CHANGING SOCIAL CONTRACT AND GROWING U.S. ACCEPTANCE OF ENVIRONMENTALISM

Although there are business people at all points along the continuum, there has been a shift toward the right side. This movement reflects an increasing concern about environmental issues on the part of many U.S. citizens that is evident in the new social contract. A social contract is an implicit agreement between two parties that recognizes their mutual expectations about the terms of their relationship. The social contract regarding the environment in the United States has expanded to include the stewardship of natural resources. Some describe this change in ecological awareness as a historic shift in consciousness comparable to the religious consciousness of old and the technological consciousness of the Industrial Age.[7] For example, Willis Harman defines it as a fundamentally different philosophy, a "global mind change" that envisions the entire Earth as a sacred creation imbued with spiritual meaning.[8] Like all social contracts the concern for environmentalism is now reflected in the social, political, and economic systems, of which business is a part. It is this change in the social contract rather than regulation per se that is the key factor behind greater environmental concern on the part of business.

Although the United States is far behind many European countries with regard to the three R's (reduce, reuse, recycle) there is a greater consciousness and more behavioral change than existed in the past. As noted in the Wirthlin Worldwide Report, "environmentalism has become deeply rooted in the U.S. national psyche. Since its extremist beginnings thirty years ago, environmentalism has matured, gaining popular support and becoming part of the mainstream. . . . It's not just about saving whales and rain forests anymore."[9] Likewise Halal writes: "people now grasp the profound reality that the Earth is a unified global organism supporting an intricate web of life . . . the planet is a great living being in its own right. And if all life is intimately connected, then humans share a family-like relationship with other species."[10]

Other sources cite a similar trend in business. In 1993 eighty-one percent of business executives thought protecting the environment was necessary and reasonable.[11] These statistics reinforce Andrew Hoffman's primary thesis that there has been a sea change in the last thirty-five years in the way business views the environment.[12] In the 1960s environmental concerns were viewed as a fringe threat. Now they are perceived as a competitive advantage. The sources of pressure for environmental management evolved from industry-based pressure to government regulation and finally to environmental activists, investors, insurance companies, and competitors.[13]

As a result companies have shifted from a reactive stance of resistance to a more proactive stance of actively managing environmental concerns. Environmental stewardship has come to the forefront as a potential competitive advantage. In 1995 Michael Porter, the world-famous strategy guru, attempted to settle the environmentalism-competitiveness debate by arguing that environmental protection was not a threat but an opportunity that could increase a firm's competitive advantage.[14] Environmentalism is no longer a "necessary evil" or a "cost of doing business" defined by government regulation. Instead "it is now becoming part of the 'rules of the game,' as defined in the 1990s by an ever-increasing group of institutional constituents."[15]

SUSTAINABILITY AND NATURAL RESOURCES— THE NATURAL STEP PROGRAM

Sustainable development is defined as meeting the needs of present generations without compromising the ability of future generations to meet their own needs. The moral basis for sustainability is the ethical position that destroying the future capacity of the Earth to support life is wrong. The scientific basis for sustainability recognizes that people, and their economic and social activities, are an integral part of the ecosphere. It is the ecosphere and its ecosystems that support human societies and economies, not the reverse. Thus human societies should be designed in a way that does not compromise natural systems.

One effort to promote sustainability and safeguard both natural and human resources is an innovative program called The Natural Step, based upon the belief that humans can survive and prosper only by working within the natural cycles of the Earth. The Natural Step was founded in 1988 by Swedish oncologist Karl-Henrik Robèrt, who was motivated by an anomaly he observed in his work with children suffering from cancer. The parents of these children frequently mentioned that they would do anything to save their children, even sacrifice their own lives. In contrast Sweden as a whole was fairly complacent about taking steps to eradicate the environmental causes of cancer. Disturbed by this passive stance, Robèrt began a process of dialogue and consensus building with scientists that later spread to business and the rest of Swedish society.

Fifty scientists were asked to identify and agree upon the basic system needed for sustainability. A consensus developed around four basic, non-negotiable system conditions. These comprise the fundamental principles of The Natural Step program and serve as questions to be asked throughout the organizational decision-making process. For example, before adopting a waste disposal system a business would ask itself the four questions that accompany the following descriptions of The Natural Step principles as outlined by Doug Hinrichs:

1. Substances from the Earth's crust must not systematically increase in the ecosphere. This means that fossil fuels, metals, and other minerals must not be extracted at a faster pace than their slow redeposit and re-integration into the Earth's crust. This requires a radically reduced dependence on mined minerals and fossil fuels. Businesses must ask themselves this question: "Do we systematically decrease our economic dependence on underground metals, fuels, and other minerals?"

2. Substances produced by society must not systematically increase in the ecosphere. Nature cannot withstand a systematic buildup of substances produced by humans. This means that substances must not be produced at a faster pace than they can be broken down and integrated into the cycles of nature or deposited into the Earth's crust. The question for businesses is: "Do we systematically decrease our economic dependence on persistent unnatural substances?"

3. The physical basis for productivity and diversity of nature must not be systematically diminished. Nature cannot withstand a systematic deterioration of its capacity for renewal. In other words, societies cannot harvest or manipulate ecosystems in such a way that productive capacity and biodiversity systematically diminish. This requires that all people critically examine how they harvest renewable resources and adjust consumption and land use practices to be well within the regenerative capacities of the planet's ecosystems. The question for businesses is: "Do we systematically decrease our economic dependence on activities that encroach on productive parts of nature, for example over-fishing?"

   4. *For the three previous conditions to be met, there must be fair and efficient use of resources with respect to meeting human needs.* Their satisfaction must take precedence over the provision of luxuries, and there should be a just resource distribution. This is necessary for ensuring the social stability and cooperation required for making the changes in due time that will ensure sustainability. The question for businesses is: "Do we systematically decrease our economic dependence on using an unnecessarily large amount of resources in relation to added human value?"[16]

   The Natural Step has gained widespread popularity in Swedish municipalities and among multinationals such as IKEA Electrolux and Scandi Hotels. The program has also spread to the United Kingdom, New Zealand, Canada, Australia, the Netherlands, and the United States and has been adopted by over 170 companies throughout the world.[17] According to early adopters of The Natural Step, the program helps these companies to achieve the following benefits, as outlined in *The Natural Step* pamphlet:[18]

   • Reduce operating costs and environmental risk.
   • Stay ahead of regulatory frameworks and protect long-term investments.
   • Enhance the organization's standing among stakeholder groups including customers, suppliers, and employees.
   • Incorporate environmental concern into the culture of the workplace.
   • Spark creativity among employees, especially those in product and process design.
   • Differentiate their products and services and build brand image.

AMERICAN EXAMPLES OF THE NATURAL STEP

   The leading proponent of The Natural Step in the United States is Ray Anderson, founder of Interface, Inc., of Atlanta, Georgia, the largest carpet company in the world.[19] Anderson had an epiphany when he read Paul Hawken's *The Ecology of Commerce.*[20] Hawken maintains that we need to control the creation of harmful waste rather than simply focusing on waste disposal.[21] In keeping with this line of thought Anderson developed a new mission for his company that aimed at one day creating zero pollution with zero oil consumption while simultaneously advancing the interests of all involved in the company's endeavors —investors, employees, and customers. With the help of environmental consultants and The Natural Step format his employees examined their work processes and designed less wasteful ways of producing carpet. For example, Interface originated the idea of installing carpet tiles under a "perpetual lease" program: for a monthly rental fee Interface removes deteriorated individual tiles and recycles them into new carpet. This is less wasteful than the general industry practices of replacing an entire carpet that is only worn in heavy traffic areas and not recycling old carpet.

As a result of these innovations the company saved $25 million from 1995–1997 and predicts another $50 million in savings in the short-term future. Furthermore, many other businesses want to buy carpet from a green vendor, so Interface's market share has also increased. Interface's concerns are not limited to the environment, however: the company believes that employees are an integral part of nature, too. In an industry noted for bad working conditions, Interface's mill is relatively quiet, odor-free, and sunny.[22]

Another example of The Natural Step in action is the Collins Pine Company, a forest-products firm headquartered in Portland, Oregon. The Collins family began operations in 1855.

> Because of our long connections to the land, we have worked hard at being prudent stewards earning a reputation for integrity and quality. As a family-owned business, we have our own vision and commitment to the forest, seeing it as an entire ecosystem not for short-term profits but for its long-term viability, sustainability, and socio-economic benefits to the community. We believe forests must be appreciated and protected for their own sake, as well as for those who use them.[23]

Environmental experts independently certify the Collins Pine forests, and its wood products come with a label that states, "This wood was harvested from a Well-Managed Forest." Collins Pine does not clear-cut its lumber. Instead, foresters mark for cutting only the individual trees that are ready for harvesting. They leave debris on the forest floor to protect the habitat of birds and animals. Their logging roads are far enough away from streams to prevent run-off. They have mixed species forests with trees of varying ages as in a natural forest rather than single age monospecies. The company has educated its workforce in The Natural Step principles, and before making any decisions employees must answer the four fundamental questions. This strategic change has brought Collins Pine into contact with environmentalists they never would have met in the generally polarized lumber-environmentalist world.

Collins Pine has worked hard to be a good neighbor by supporting the communities in which it operates.

> The company gives the public liberal access to its forests. It directly and indirectly supports local land-use consensus-building groups made up of all types of individuals, including preservationists. Collins Pine encourages research and educational projects on its forest land, supports schools and hospitals, and through its long-term commitment to stable employment, it is recognized as a contributor to community economic stability.[24]

In a typical remark an employee commented: "This is a wonderful company. The Collins family is . . . just great to work for and that's why you don't see very high turnover. They are concerned for their employees and the environment."[25] Nevertheless, the company occasionally faces tough tradeoffs. Confronted with the higher costs associated with sustainable forestry, the company had to outsource some sawing and hauling work previously done by employees. Despite the tradeoff Bill Howe, their forest manager, stated: "We believe in being prudent stewards in a long-term sustained way."[26]

The family's sense of stewardship for both natural and human resources translate into less emphasis on maximizing short-term profit than is found in most publicly held companies. Observers, as well as the company itself, believe that its commitment to sustainable forestry ensured its survival when many other lumber companies failed. Like Interface, Collins Pine has prospered from its focus on environmental protection and stewardship.

STEWARDSHIP OF HUMAN RESOURCES

The last principle of The Natural Step focuses on human resources. In this context sustainability "encompasses a holistic concept of human welfare that recognizes the primacy of nature and all living beings over the exclusive pursuit of economic betterment."[27] What trends are observed when the topic shifts from the sustainability of environmental resources to the sustainability of human resources? When organizational practices are examined are there similar problems, emerging social expectations, and viable models for sustainability or human flourishing in healthy organizations?

Certainly the idea of flourishing is implicit in the concept of stewardship. In protecting the general environment a steward within an organizational context is responsible for ensuring the health, well-being, and enhancement of the firm's human resources. Thus a steward's role is to oversee and guide the flourishing and development of the employees at all levels within an organization. For the purposes of this discussion a distinction is made between flourishing on the job and flourishing throughout a person's career. Flourishing on the job pertains to the personal satisfaction and well-being associated with a specific job situation. Flourishing in a career context pertains to the continued development of skills and achievement of personal fulfillment. In both cases, flourishing involves establishing a proper balance among work, family, community roles, and spiritual spheres of life.

Scope of the Problem

While gains in all aspects of employment have been made since the early industrial revolution, there are several patterns in employment relationships emerging in the last ten years that raise growing concerns about a decrease in the potential for human flourishing in the workplace. These changes, particularly downsizing, re-engineering, and the creation of boundaryless organizations, have impact both on jobs and on career outcomes.

A. Flourishing on the Job. One way to assess human resource utilization is to monitor the time and energy demands placed on individual employees relative to the time spent in family and community endeavors. Ironically, recent progress in the environmental arena has been accompanied by a greater willingness in the last decade to exploit human resources. The weakness of labor unions, fears about job security, and the pressures of the global economy, compounded perhaps by the current tendencies toward deregulation, have left some U.S. employees without much protection for their "non-work" time. According to one source "the average employed American now spends the equivalent of an additional month a year more on the job compared with twenty years ago."[28] A 1994 survey found that the average work week of executives is fifty-nine hours.[29] There has been a thirty-seven percent increase in the number of professionals and managers working forty-nine hours or more a week.[30] In contrast the average weekly hours for production workers have hovered between thirty-four and thirty-five in 1997–1998 with an average weekly overtime of 4.6 to 4.9 hours for the same period.[31] In part the greater workload is attributed to:

- Mergers that displace thousands of workers;
- "Right-sizing" efforts that leave fewer employees to do their own work as well as that of their fired colleagues;
- Incentive programs that encourage and reward workers for cannibalizing the rest of their lives for the sake of financial payoffs or future promotions;
- Companies resorting to "forced" overtime at times when production demand is up rather than hiring additional workers and having to pay them benefits.

The 1997 Teamsters' strike against United Parcel Service provides a vivid example of the last trend. The Teamsters demanded more full-time jobs, better wages and pensions, and a safer workplace.[32] In particular they wanted the company to limit its use of part-time workers. Since the last labor contract was signed in 1993 the union claimed that eighty-three percent of the workers UPS hired were part-timers, who earn less and get fewer benefits than full-time employees. According to the union ten thousand part-time workers actually work full-time schedules of thirty-five hours a week or more.

It is increasingly difficult to balance work and non-work roles since the number of dual-career families and families with a single working parent has increased substantially. There has not been an offsetting increase in the amount of day care and related family support to restore a balance between work and non-work responsibilities.

The increased hours spent at work and extensive downsizing may be beneficial to owners and stockholders in the short run, but if we consider all the stakeholders involved as well as the costs to individual workers, their families, and their communities the picture is less positive. One consequence is burned-out employees who have less time to devote to their families, relationships, and spiritual life. Another consequence is the underutilization of people who cannot find comparable employment after being downsized or who are underemployed in temporary or part-time work. Common social problems can be traced in part to these consequences—neglected children who become involved in delinquency and drugs, marriages that fall apart when career demands outweigh family considerations, self-destructive behavior or family violence that occurs when unemployed adults lose self-esteem and direct their frustration inward or onto their families. A less visible but equally important cost is the decreased time available to overworked employees for volunteer work, community involvement, and church activities. Anecdotal evidence suggests that flourishing on the job is not occurring in many organizations.

B. Flourishing in Careers. The traditional career model contained the goal of continuing skill development and upward advancement over a long-time career primarily associated with one organization. However, as signaled in the titles of recent books such as *The Career Is Dead*[33] and *The Boundaryless Career,*[34] the traditional model has been replaced by a starker reality. During the 1980s 3.4 million jobs were cut from Fortune 500 firms.[35] These included prior exemplars of long-term employment such as IBM and AT&T. Following restructuring, delayering, downsizing, and related practices of the last decade, announcements of sizable job layoffs are now commonplace, generating little emotional reaction in the public press. Both the public and employees have come to accept the new reality that the likelihood of long-term careers in any one firm is no longer assured.

Not only has the longevity of a career been altered, but also the very assurance of full-time status is problematic for increasing numbers of workers as new forms of organizing shrink the number of essential full-time positions and expand part-time and contract positions. More and more workers may find that they have been marginalized into non-career tracks. Douglas Hall and Philip Mirvis cite studies of reduced career opportunities, reduced health benefits and pensions, increased work hours and lower take-home pay, and increasing cynicism about the quality of work life.[36] Some downsized workers never find replacement jobs or are underemployed in areas outside their expertise or in part-time work that does not provide benefits. Social problems also result from the loss of face and bitterness people experience when their planned careers are disrupted. A systemic view of employment patterns indicates that the business sector's infatuation with downsizing in the 1980s and 1990s has resulted in some people's being overworked while others are underutilized, an inefficient use of human resources that harms both individuals and society as a whole.

The Changing Social Contract Regarding Work and Careers

As the facts of organizational life change, the new situations gradually shape social attitudes about what can and should be expected in work relationships. Several commentators see marked shifts in these expectations in light of current business practices. Managers have come to accept downsizing, outsourcing, rapid response times, adaptability, and uncertainty as facts of life. What in the past were deep relational contracts are now being replaced with shorter-term limited transactional contracts.[37] With the recognition of the lexicon of core competencies as a foundation of corporate competitive strategies, careers will be increasingly driven by the competencies a person can acquire.[38] Employees are increasingly pressured to develop multiple competencies and to shorten the cycle time for mastering new competencies.[39] The extreme case no longer seems farfetched: the transactional nature of relationships "has shrunk to what Jack Welch, CEO of General Electric, has called a one-day contract, in which all that counts is the current value that each party contributes to the relationship."[40]

Robert H. Rosen and Lisa Berger present a summary of the new type of psychological contract between employees and organizations:

> From the corporate view, the new contract recognizes that employers can no longer offer lifetime jobs, guaranteed advancement, or kindly paternalism. Economic survival demands that they be able to expand and contract quickly and be flexible enough to respond to changing markets and emerging opportunities . . . so employers must offer a new contract that gives the company flexibility, but at the same time presents employees more chance for personal and professional growth. Employees will accept the new contract only with the proviso that their employers are honest, open, and fair with them and they have a larger say in their jobs.[41]

The terms of the new psychological contracts are not very reassuring. Employees are encouraged to adopt a new model of "protean" and "boundaryless" careers in which the responsibility for managing careers is shifted from organizations to individuals.[42] Employees are to master new skills and develop networks of relationships that facilitate ease of movement across organizational boundaries. Career identity as well as relationships are to be more flexible, fluid, and multifaceted. However, this model may be viable only for a limited number of highly competent and well-adjusted individuals. Some social scientists remain pessimistic about the average person's ability to successfully master the cognitive demands and identity adjustments of these new relation-ships.[43] What may be needed is a different type of psychological con-tract or at the very least a different approach to how we steward our human resources. In this regard The Natural Step model may be the foundation needed to build a relationship ethic that enables organiza-tions to interact successfully with their human resources as we see them doing with their natural resources.

Human Resource Sustainability

The four standards for environmental sustainability from The Natural Step program can provide an initial framework for examining how organizations are currently impacting their human resources. Figure 2 presents four human resource standards comparable to The Natural Step's principles. The first standard represents human resources practices that take place primarily within organizations. The second standard expands the organization's responsibilities to include working with other external groups to provide support mechanisms for employ-ment systems in a community or region. The third standard reflects a need for understanding and responding to the natural adjustment and development needs of individual employees. The final standard raises important issues of equitable utilization and fair treatment of employ-ees within work settings.

Figure 2.
Standards for Sustainability in Natural and Human Resources

Natural Resource Sustainability	Human Resource Sustainability
1 **Substances from the Earth's crust must not systematically increase in the ecosphere.** This means that fossil fuels, metals, and other minerals must not be extracted at a faster pace than their slow redeposit and reinte-gration into the Earth's crust.	1 **Human resources must not be de-pleted faster than they can be re-invigorated by the organization's support mechanisms.** Human re-sources practices should not push employees past a natural breaking point at which productivity, creativ-ity, morale, and well-being begin to decline. Time demands placed on individuals must reasonably balance work, family, and community sus-tainability.

2 **Substances produced by society must not systematically increase in the ecosphere.** Nature cannot withstand a systematic buildup of substances produced by humans. This means that substances must not be produced at a faster pace than they can be broken down and integrated into the cycles of nature or deposited into the earth's crust.	2 **Human resources must not be depleted at a faster rate than society's support mechanisms can reinvigorate them and reintegrate them into productive organizational and societal roles.** Work conditions and benefits should sustain long-term employability and health.
3 **The physical basis for productivity and diversity of nature must not be systematically diminished.** Nature cannot withstand a systematic deterioration of its capacity for renewal. In other words, societies cannot harvest or manipulate ecosystems in such a way that productive capacity and biodiversity systematically diminish.	3 **Demands placed on human resources must not surpass the developmental and regenerative capacities of employees and supporting social systems within organizations.** Organizations should develop practices that are sensitive to individual differences in capacity for developing new competencies, self-identities, and professional commitments.
4 **For the three previous conditions to be met, there must be fair and efficient use of resources with respect to meeting human needs.** Their satisfaction must take precedence over the provision of luxuries and there should be a just resource distribution. This is necessary for ensuring the social stability and cooperation required for making the changes in due time that will ensure sustainability.	4 **Organizations must be efficient and effective in their use of human resources and must be just in their dealings with all employees.** Organizations must balance reasonable demands for higher productivity with equitable rewards to all employees for their contributions. In seeking to become more strategically adaptable, organizations must be fair in all aspects of employment and share in the social costs of changing career practices.

Rule 1: Internal Human Resource Practices

Human resources must not be depleted faster than they can be reinvigorated by the organization's support mechanisms. Jeffrey Pfeffer, in an article entitled "Producing Sustainable Competitive Advantage Through the Effective Management of People,"[44] argues that good employment practices fall into three categories outlined below in Figure 3. These practices enhance both flourishing on the job and career development. Pfeffer notes that it may take a long time to achieve these support systems but the benefits are likely to be substantially more enduring.

Figure 3. Internal Human Resource Practices

Human Resource Development Activities	Training and skill development Cross-utilization and cross-training Symbolic egalitarianism Wage compression Promotion from within Information-sharing
Trends Toward Self-Management	Employee ownership Participation and empowerment Self-managed teams
Administrative	Employment security Selectivity in recruiting High wages Incentive pay

Other practices could be added to the list to further balance the demands placed on employees. These could include provisions for flex-time, job sharing, day-care facilities, and alternative career paths. Internal job information systems, mentoring, and Employee Assistance Programs also provide further professional and personal support.

Rule 2: External Human Resource Practices
Sustaining Viable Employment Systems

Human resources must not be depleted at a faster rate than society's support mechanisms can reinvigorate and reintegrate them into productive organizational and societal roles. This rule recognizes that business organizations have responsibilities beyond simply treating existing employees well. Organizations are part of larger employment systems and thus need to cooperate with others both in terms of the intake from and out-placement of employees into these systems. For example, businesses can cooperate with other institutions in enhancing educational opportunities to provide employees with the necessary skills to successfully enter the work force. Organizations also have responsibilities to help provide safety nets for those who are involuntarily displaced from their careers through downsizing, closures, and other shifts in business operations.

Manuel London cites numerous examples of societal support mechanisms that are greatly enhanced by collaboration with business organizations.[45] Figure 4 describes three examples. Others include entrepreneurship training, job clubs (support groups that help members find jobs), and joint Union/Management Retraining programs.

Figure 4. Examples of Societal Support Mechanisms

Michigan JOBS Project: designed to help unemployed workers seek jobs, prepare for rejection, and overcome or limit their feelings of depression. Provided participants with support and a positive learning environment to acquire job search skills while inoculating the participants against common setbacks that are a part of the job-seeking process. Goals of the project were to prevent the depression that often results from unemployment and to promote high-quality re-employment, thus contributing to individual growth.

Retraining for Displaced Engineers at SUNY-Stony Brook: established a government-funded retraining program for displaced engineers from the defense industry. Participants learned how to enhance career behavior, increase their knowledge of technology management, and do what they could to create jobs for themselves.

The Center for Commercial Competitiveness at SUNY-Binghamton: the goal was to work with displaced workers and regional industries to generate employment opportunities by creating new products and services.

Rule 3: Practices Supporting the Regenerative Capacities of Employees

Demands placed on human resources must not surpass the developmental and regenerative capacities of employees and supporting social systems within organizations. This is emerging as a new area of responsibility for employers. While new employment expectations are placing greater weight on employees managing their own careers and stretching to develop new competencies, there is a limit to how much and how fast employees can adjust. Although the words "resilience" and "hardiness" are appearing much more frequently on lists of desired employee traits, not much is known about normal human capacities for readjustment. Programs that recognize individual differences in acquiring new skills, particularly for experienced employees, need to be developed. By analogy to natural cycles of renewal within ecological systems, organizations need to understand and develop practices that help employees adjust to new professional identities and commitments within boundaryless careers.

Rule 4:
Practices Supporting Equity and Fairness in Employment Matters

Organizations must be efficient and effective in their use of human resources and must be just in their dealings with all employees. How efficient or wasteful companies are with regard to human resources depends in part on the laws of supply and demand. When there is excess supply organizations are less considerate of how resources are used, since these resources are relatively easy to replace. In times of scarcity organizations are likely to make more efficient use of both types of resources, but this may mean overtaxing the productive capacity of ecosystems as well as human systems. In the last decade when jobs were scarce, employers "burned out" more employees who were simply grateful to have a job. At present, however, employers are experiencing greater difficulty filling jobs and employees can demand more consideration. Some companies are developing family-friendly policies to attract and retain employees.

As organizations seek to become more productive, adaptable, and faster in responding to competitive pressure they need to be sensitive to the new demands they are placing on employees. Beyond being responsive to employee needs to balance work and non-work demands, employers should also ensure that employees are equitably compensated for their efforts. Profit-sharing plans are a way to ensure that employees reap the benefits and not just the costs of increased productivity. A recent *Wall Street Journal* article noted that the "one indisputable trend that puzzles economists across the political spectrum is the slow growth of wages during the past six years of solid economic growth."[46] Rewards do not seem to be keeping up with performance expectations.

In seeking to become more strategically adaptable, organizations must be fair in all aspects of employment and share in the social costs of changing career practices. Only recently has there been systematic study of issues of fairness and justice in employment relationships. As businesses seek to create more flexible organizations they need to be increasingly vigilant regarding their responsibilities in light of new career patterns. Simply shifting the burden back to employees will not be sufficient. Better organizations will seek to develop collaboratively new work practices that continue to jointly meet the needs of employees as well as of other stakeholders in the organization.

CONCLUSION AND THEOLOGICAL REFLECTION

The values guiding responses on environmental issues shown in Figure 1 can also be applied to work/family balance and family-friendly business policies. At the left hand side of the continuum we find managers and owners who are adamantly opposed to providing anything but a paycheck to employees. Pragmatic opposers point to the additional costs of family-friendly policies and, like the adamant opposers, have a very limited perception of the role of business in the larger society. The manipulators establish programs like concierge services merely to advertise themselves as family-friendly businesses and to ensure that workers have more time to devote to work. Espousers talk about the importance of not exploiting employees but do not back up this talk with action. Pragmatic believers institute work/family balance policies because it is good for business and helps them to attract and retain skilled employees. Adamant protectors sincerely believe in the need to help employees lead a balanced life. Thus it comes as no surprise that work/family balance programs are a controversial topic. Research indicates that such policies result in improved productivity, less absenteeism, and less attrition.[47]

With regard to both environmental and human resources one's position on this continuum depends in part upon where the boundary around stakeholders is drawn. If only the narrow interests of a single company and its stockholders are considered, behavior that harms the interests of employees, society, or the ecosystem is easier to rationalize. Civilization, however, has a better chance for harmonious long-term survival if we draw a larger boundary that incorporates all stakeholders and if we see ourselves as stewards of both forms of resources.

The Natural Step program is an example of a systematic approach to continual consideration of environmental impacts. A similar program does not exist with regard to human resources. A model or program similar to The Natural Step could provide needed visibility to issues such as work overload and would offer firms guidance as they move to full stewardship of their human resources. This chapter has proposed such a model with the belief that firms demonstrating a balanced approach to their resources will benefit in the long term.

The responsibility of business in the United States is circumscribed by what it measures. A narrow focus on the bottom line and accounting procedures that fail to consider the cost to the environment or to human resources limit the perceived responsibility of managers. There are few checks on business. Even though work overloads and under-utilization of employees harm all of society by impoverishing the other spheres of life, there are few voices crying out to criticize these practices. Most important, at present there is no social contract regarding the exploitation of human resources with respect to the environment. The warning contained in this chapter is that the time has come for critical reflection and action regarding the need for better stewardship of human resources.

Finally, this chapter creatively links traditional notions of steward-ship of both human and natural resources with The Natural Step pro-gram, an innovative if not radical process for redesigning the way organizations do business on this planet that is more in harmony with the economy of creation. This linkage is entirely appropriate. Etymo-logically the terms steward *(oikonomos)*, economy *(oikonomia)*, ecu-mene *(oikoumenē)*, and ecology *(oikologia)* share a common linguistic root in the Greek *oikos,* meaning house or household. The Old and New Testaments contain twenty-six explicit references to the steward or stewardship. According to Douglas John Hall "the steward is one who has been given the responsibility of the management and service of something belonging to another, and his office presupposes a particular kind of trust on the part of the owner or master."[48] In the Old Testament the term is often used in a technical fashion to denote a specific office or vocation in society. As the term evolved it became linked with Israel's king who, as ruler of the chosen people, is God's steward and conse-quently accountable to God. The royal imagery is best seen in the term dominion (Gen 1:26), but it never came to mean domination. James Limburg writes that "for a king to 'have dominion' does not mean to ex-ploit, to destroy, or to use selfishly. To 'have dominion' in the biblical sense means to care for, especially to care for the poor and weak."[49] The use of the term dominion for humankind in Gen 1:26 suggests, there-fore, the royal stewardship of Earth incorporating both natural and human resources—particularly care for the most vulnerable in our midst.

The uniqueness of this essay lies in its provocative connection be-tween stewardship of natural and human resources within a business-organizational context and the notion of sustainability, without a doubt one of the most important catchwords in human parlance, particularly as the twenty-first century unfolds. The U.S. Catholic bishops acknowledge this when they declare that "the overarching moral issue is to achieve during the twenty-first century a just and sustainable world."[50] That businesses, as national and transnational actors, must play a crucial role in achieving a sustainable world is undeniable. Business leaders and workers are asked by the bishops "to make protection of our common environment a central concern in their activities and to collaborate for the common good and the protection of the earth."[51] By using The Natural Step process this essay offers a unique paradigm within a business context that inherently links the stewardship of natural and human resources for achieving a sustainable world. The Natural Step program recognizes that sustainability is not only a scientific-biospheric matter but must involve the just and equitable distribution of economic resources to meet human needs.[52] This view that socioeconomic and ecological justice are inextricably connected is entirely compatible with current Catholic social teaching as well as the theological position of most mainline church traditions in the United States. Business and the economic enterprise are vital participants in the hope of achieving a just and sustainable world and the overall good of our common *oikos,* Earth.

NOTES: CHAPTER 9

[1] Peter Block, *Stewardship: Choosing Service over Self-Interest* (San Francisco: Berrett-Koehler, 1993) xx.

[2] This model was developed by business professors Joyce Osland, Bruce Drake, and Howard Feldman, authors of this chapter.

[3] Andrew Hoffman, *From Heresy to Dogma: An Institutional History of Corporate Environmentalism* (San Francisco: New Lexington Press, 1997).

[4] Ibid.

[5] William E. Halal, *The New Management: Democracy and Enterprise Are Transforming Organizations* (San Francisco: Berrett-Koehler, 1996) 159.

[6] See Hoffman, *From Heresy to Dogma* passim.

[7] Halal, *The New Management* 158.

[8] Ibid.

[9] Wirthlin Worldwide Report Online, "Environmentalism: No Letting Up" (McLean, Va.: Wirthlin Worldwide, August 1997) 2.

[10] Halal, *The New Management* 157.

[11] Mark Starik, "When Business Goes for the Green," *GW Magazine* 3/4 (Summer 1993) 11–16.

[12] See Hoffman, *From Heresy to Dogma* passim.

[13] Ibid. 143.

[14] Michael Porter and Claas van der Linde, "Green and Competitive," *Harvard Business Review* 73 (September 1995) 120–33.

[15] Hoffman, *From Heresy to Dogma* 149.

[16] Doug Hinrichs, "The Natural Step: An Interview with Paul Hawken," *Ecological Economics Bulletin* 1/4 (October 1996) 6–10.

[17] Ibid.

[18] *The Natural Step: From Consensus to Sustainable Development* (Sausalito, Calif.: The Natural Step, 1997).

[19] Thomas Petzinger, "The Front Lines: Business Achieves Greatest Efficiencies When at Its Greenest," *Wall Street Journal* (July 11, 1997) B1.

[20] Paul Hawken, *The Ecology of Commerce: A Declaration of Sustainability* (New York: HarperBusiness, 1993).

[21] Petzinger, "The Front Lines."

[22] For further discussion see Petzinger, "The Front Lines" (n. 19 above).

[23] For further particulars see the Collins Pine document "Kane Hardwood," 1997.

[24] Eric Hansen and John Punches, "Collins Pine: Lessons from a Pioneer. Case Study," in *The Business of Sustainable Forestry. Case Studies* (Chicago: The John D. and Catherine T. MacArthur Foundation, 1997) 4.

[25] Ibid.

[26] Tom Kenworthy, "One Tranquil Story of Timber Cutting," *The Washington Post* (October 14, 1992) A3.

[27] Param Srikantia and Diana Bilimoria, "Isomorphism in Organization and Management Theory: The Case of Research on Sustainability," *Organization & Environment* 10/4 (December 1997) 391.

[28] Sunil Babbar and David Aspelin, "The Overtime Rebellion: Symptom of a Bigger Problem?" *The Academy of Management Executive* 12/4 (February 1998) 69.

[29] Diane Crispell, "How Executives Manage Time Pressure," *American Demographics* 17/1 (January 1995) 38.

[30] Sue Shallenbarger, "More Executives Cite Need for Family Time as Reason for Quitting," *Wall Street Journal* (March 11, 1998) B1.

[31] Bureau of Labor Statistics Data 1998.

[32] Howard Abramson, "Teamsters Authorize Strike Against UPS if Talks Fail," *The Oregonian* (July 16, 1997) C1–C2.

[33] Douglas T. Hall and Philip Mirvis, eds., *The Career Is Dead—Long Live the Career: A Relational Approach to Careers* (San Francisco: Jossey-Bass, 1996).

[34] Michael B. Arthur and Denise M. Rousseau, eds., *The Boundaryless Career: A New Employment Principle for a New Organizational Era* (New York: Oxford University Press, 1996).

[35] R. J. Barnett, "The End of Jobs: Employment Is One Thing the Global Economy Is Not Creating," *Harper's* 287 (September 1993) 47–52.

[36] For further discussion of these points see Douglas T. Hall and Philip Mirvis, "The New Protean Career: Psychological Success and the Path with a Heart," in *The Career Is Dead* 15–45.

[37] Denise M. Rousseau, *Psychological Contracts in Organizations: Understanding Written and Unwritten Agreements* (Thousand Oaks, Calif.: SAGE, 1995).

[38] James Brian Quinn, *Intelligent Enterprise: A Knowledge and Service Based Paradigm for Industry* (New York: Free Press, 1992).

[39] For further discussion see Hall and Mirvis, "The New Protean Career" (n. 36 above).

[40] Hall, "Long Live the Career," in *The Career Is Dead* 5.

[41] Robert H. Rosen and Lisa Berger, *The Healthy Company: Eight Strategies to Develop People, Productivity, and Profits* (Los Angeles: Jeremy Tarcher, 1991) 4.

[42] For further discussion see Arthur and Rousseau, eds., *The Boundaryless Career,* and Hall and Mirvis, eds. *The Career Is Dead.*

[43] For further discussion see Kenneth Gergen, *The Saturated Self: Dilemmas of Identity in Contemporary Life* (New York: Basic Books, 1991), and Robert Kegan, *In Over Our Heads: The Mental Demands of Modern Life* (Cambridge, Mass.: Harvard University Press, 1994).

[44] Jeffrey Pfeffer, "Producing Sustainable Competitive Advantage Through the Effective Management of People," *Academy of Management Executive* 9/1 (February 1995) 55–72.

[45] Manuel London, "Redeployment and Continuous Learning in the 21st Century: Hard Lessons and Positive Examples from the Downsizing Era," *Academy of Management Executive* 10/4 (November 1996) 67–79.

[46] Jacob Schlesinger and Bernard Wysocki, "Score Card: 'UPS Pact Fails to Shift Balance of Power Back Toward U.S. Workers,'" *Wall Street Journal* (August 20, 1997) A1.

[47] Arlene Johnson, "The Business Case for Work-Family Programs," *Journal of Accountancy* 180 (August 1995) 53–59.

[48] Douglas John Hall, *The Steward: A Biblical Symbol Come of Age* (rev. ed. New York: Friendship Press; Grand Rapids: Eerdmans, 1990) 32.

[49] James Limburg, "The Way of an Eagle in the Sky: Reflections on the Bible and the Care of the Earth," *Catholic World* (July/August 1990) 149.

[50] "Renewing the Earth," *Origins* (December 12, 1991) 432.

[51] Ibid.

[52] For more information on The Natural Step process see the following websites: *www.naturalstep.org; www.Web.net/~tnscan/papers.html;* and *www.ifsia.com/ecosense.*

10

Development of Environmental Responsibility in Children

Listen to me, my child, and acquire knowledge,
and pay close attention to my words.
I will impart discipline precisely
and declare knowledge accurately.
When the Lord created his works from the beginning,
and, in making them, determined their boundaries,
he arranged his works in an eternal order,
and their dominion for all generations.
They neither hunger nor grow weary,
and they do not abandon their tasks.
They do not crowd one another,
and they never disobey his word.
Then the Lord looked upon the earth,
and filled it with his good things,
With all kinds of living beings he covered its surface
and into it they must return. (Sirach 16:24-30)

*I*n this short poem from the Wisdom tradition Ben Sirach urges a child, perhaps his son or one of his students, to listen to what he is about to say so that the child may acquire knowledge (vv. 24-25). What follows in vv. 26-30 is Ben Sirach's personal reflection on the wonders of creation and his sense of marvel at God who with wisdom created all that is. One can only imagine what awe the child may have felt at listening to such a marvelous story.

This passage reminds readers that children need to hear and experience the wonders and joys of creation. However, the lesson—the story and experience of creation—can no longer end with a child coming to appreciate creation. Today children need to learn how to care for their social and natural world, first because of its intrinsic goodness by virtue of its creation, and second because without the beauty of creation the child of today will have no wonder-full lessons to pass on to tomorrow's children. The restoration and renewal of the earth lies in the handful of seeds a small child clutches tightly, waiting to plant them at the first signs of spring.

> "SO . . . Catch!" calls the Once-ler. He lets something fall. "It's a Truffula Seed. It's the last one of all! You're in charge of the last of the Truffula Seeds. And Truffula Trees are what everyone needs. Plant a new Truffula. Treat it with care. Give it clean water. And feed it fresh air. Grow a forest. Protect it from axes that hack. Then the Lorax and all of his friends may come back."[1]

> Train up a child in the way he should go, and when he is old he will not depart from it.[2]

STATEMENT OF THE ISSUE

From Dr. Seuss's *The Lorax* to Shel Silverstein's *The Giving Tree*[3] and innumerable books in between children are given messages that the environment is an important part of their lives and they have a responsibility to care for it. These messages are heard and incorporated into children's lives in a variety of ways. A classroom of children "adopts" a tree, exploring its seasonal changes and learning about the life cycle of growing things; another class plants a tree in memory of a classmate who has died; a third participates in a community cleanup day, discussing the stress humans put on their environment. Activities in which children interact with their physical environment strengthen and reinforce an environmental consciousness. But what is the initial source of this consciousness? How do children develop an appreciation of nature and a sense of responsibility toward their environment?

This chapter contends that an environmental awareness is a product of the same processes by which children develop moral and ethical values. These processes create in children a sense of right and wrong, a spiritual and emotional integrity from which behaviors stem. Ultimately individuals are able to express a social consciousness in relation to other people and the world around them; they have a true a sense of self. This essay explores some of the processes that occur in children's development and learning and makes some suggestions as to how we can enhance the process of helping children become environmentally responsible.

The creation of values and beliefs in children is related to their developmental stage, and some people will argue that one cannot expect very young children to understand and practice moral behavior because they do not have the cognitive and critical thinking skills to make necessary distinctions between right and wrong. But the creation of a sense of moral integrity is a learning process, a part of a child's developing social reasoning, and even very young children, guided by their caregivers, can see, learn, internalize, and demonstrate moral behavior. It is certainly during early childhood that the foundation for later moral reasoning, judgments, and ethical social behavior is laid, and extensive research shows that family environment and early childhood experiences are most influential in developing ethical behavior.

DEVELOPMENTAL THEORIES RELATED TO MORAL BEHAVIOR

Developmental theories offer explanations of children's moral behavior. Moving beyond Freud's theories of ego development as a product of interpersonal relationships, Erik Erikson[4] contended that ego integrity, or the mature sense of self in a social context, is a result of the successful mastery of developmental tasks confronted during sequential stages of individuals' lives. Infants must establish a sense of trust, gaining confidence that their needs will be met. Toddlers engage in a conflict between autonomy, shame, and doubt. Autonomy is achieved as children gain control over physical and emotional functions, learning to walk, for example, to self-toilet, to understand the meaning of "no," or to find ways to comfort themselves. Shame and doubt predominate if children do not have the opportunity to practice newly developing skills or are consistently given the message that their performance is inadequate. Preschool children strive to achieve initiative, to use their skills to some purpose. They energetically explore an expanding environment outside the home, use their imagination, master new skills, and become more dependable. By the end of this stage children have begun to establish a sense of self that is differentiated from others. The school-age period, between six and twelve years of age, is characterized by industry versus inferiority. Success in this stage includes learning to solve problems, plan, organize, persevere, master new skills, and develop interests beyond the present and outside oneself. During adolescence children establish a sense of identity or a sense of self that has permanence. This sense of self is a contrast to role diffusion in which limits between the self and others and the specialness of the individual are blurred. Adolescents very self-consciously define their personalities and struggle with issues of self-esteem and meaning, forming loyalties to groups and significant others.

Jean Piaget's theory of cognitive development in infants, children, and adolescents[5] identifies four different stages in the developmental process: sensorimotor, preoperational, concrete operations, and formal operations. Learning is a process involving maturation, nutritional status, active physical interaction with the environment, and stimulation through language and social interaction. The sensorimotor stage, characteristic of infants and young toddlers, is one in which the world is perceived and responded to primarily through the senses of taste, sight, sound, smell, and touch. In this stage major cognitive achievements include establishing object permanence, and beginning to understand the concepts of time and the relationships between cause and effect.

The preoperational stage (ages two to seven) is the period in which children master language skills. According to Piaget, children in this stage are very egocentric, with a worldview focused on self and on the present. Their thinking often appears "illogical" to adults because it expresses animism (inanimate objects have lifelike qualities), realism (everything is real, e.g., wishes and dreams), magical omnipotence (the child can make things happen just by thinking of them), and artificialism (all things are created by humans). Children in the preoperational stage are curious, learn by imitation, ask lots of questions, and actively explore their environment. Consequences are best understood as they relate to the self rather than to abstract "others."

In the concrete operations stage (ages seven to twelve) children are able to understand concepts of relationships, ordering, reversibility, and conservation. Their approach to thinking about the world becomes more "scientific" as they develop the ability to classify objects, tell time, and read. They are less egocentric and better able to appreciate the perspectives and needs of others and, as a result, develop a sense of justice and equality.

The formal operations stage is represented by the ability to think logically, work with abstract ideas, synthesize concepts, and understand the relationship of past, present, and future. Adolescents in the formal operations stage begin to develop a philosophy of life, exploring ideas about meaning, values, and ethics.

Building on Piaget's theory, Lawrence Kohlberg[6] identifies three stages involved in the development of moral reasoning: preconventional, conventional, and postconventional. The preconventional stage has two phases: *punishment and obedient orientation* and *individual instrumental orientation*. The first phase, seen in young children, is one in which moral decisions are made in an effort to avoid punishment from the parent figure who has determined what is good or bad. In the second phase, the individual instrumental orientation, children reason that moral behavior, or acting "good," will lead to a reward. This latter phase is generally seen through elementary school years.

The conventional stage of moral development also has two phases, both of which, according to Kohlberg, last into adulthood. In the phase of *mutual interpersonal expectations* moral behavior is based on the desire to meet the expectations of others, to gain their approval. In the *respect for authority* phase conformity, loyalty, and adherence to laws, rules, obligations, and social order guide moral judgments. According to Kohlberg, most women in the U.S. never progress beyond the first of these two phases and most people in general remain in the second phase.

Kohlberg's final stage of moral development, the postconventional stage, is divided into phases of *social contract* and *universal ethical principles*. The social contract phase is based on the belief that societies have sets of norms and expectations that define which behaviors are appropriate, that not all laws are just, and that moral individuals must freely choose ethical behavior, changing the system if need be. Moral reasoning in the universal ethical principles phase is based on abstract principles, not social norms, and individuals follow their conscience, acting against the rules if they have identified a principle that they believe to be of a higher order.

Carol Gilligan and others[7] counter Kohlberg's model by asserting that moral development originates in the individual's "awareness of self in relation to others" and evolves from two distinctive relationship modes, inequality and attachment. Specifically, very young children are small, helpless, and powerless. In this state of inequality vis-à-vis others they interpret morality in terms of fairness and justice, and if treated fairly will develop a sense of self-strength and independence. As they grow, children form connections to others, wanting to be with others. In this second form of relationship, attachment, children's morality is based on love, and if love is reciprocated children will learn to care for others.

Closely paralleling Erikson's stages of the development of ego integrity are James Fowler's stages of faith development.[8] Faith development reflects the extent to which one achieves a level of spirituality or the way in which one conducts one's daily life in relation to a transcendent or immanent "sacred." For children, Fowler claims, four stages are preeminent. Stage 0, in infancy, is a state of primal or undifferentiated faith in which children establish a sense of trust with others. Stage 1 reflects intuitive-projective faith and is characterized by beliefs based on images, feelings, and symbols. The imaginative and egocentric thinking seen in early childhood, especially during the preschool years, are important processes in this stage. The third stage, mythic-literal faith, is a combination of (1) concrete beliefs, (2) a rigid system of order and activities, and (3) the initial exploration of ultimate issues in an effort to understand the world order and the meaning of life. Developmentally school-age children are most likely to reflect this stage. In the fourth stage of faith development, synthetic-conventional faith, ideas about spirituality are synthesized from peers, parents, and other significant adults. This stage, Fowler believes, begins in adolescence and moves into adulthood. Conventional values and beliefs are examined and adolescents seek to develop an identity through self-reflection, demonstrating insight, a sense of inner spiritual process, a connection to the world, and a relationship to what Fowler calls "the ultimate environment." At this stage children continue to develop more fully their understanding of ultimate questions, of the meaning of life.

The various developmental models presented above provide explanations of the dynamics that occur during the ego, cognitive, moral, and spiritual development of children. Each theory derives from the fact that children interact with their social and physical environments; without interaction growth does not occur. The theories also contend that it is in our relationships with others that we have a need for moral behavior.

RELATIONSHIP BETWEEN MORAL DEVELOPMENT AND ENVIRONMENTAL LEARNING

Current research on the question of children's moral relationship with the environment suggests that developmental theory can be used to understand children's behaviors toward the environment.[9] For example, the environment can be a laboratory used to assess the level of children's sense of moral integrity. Michael Piburn[10] contends that scenarios involving environmental "dilemmas" (such as an oil spill or famine) can be used to examine the extent to which children have achieved certain levels of moral reasoning and to challenge them to move to even higher levels.

Peter Kahn and Ann McCoy[11] reviewed two studies in which school-aged children were presented with such environmental dilemmas and concluded that children think about the environment from several moral perspectives. From one perspective children demonstrate a homocentric approach in which they perceive the natural world as an intermediary through which one's actions might harm or restrict the rights of other humans. For example, if people throw their garbage in the water supply members of the community will be harmed. A second perspective involves an "intrinsic values and rights" approach, reflecting the idea that nature has a moral standing separate from the benefit it provides humans. From this viewpoint children might express a sense that animals have a right to live "just because." A third approach, that of "relational reasoning," is one in which animals serve human psychological needs. Pets, for example, provide comfort to children. A final perspective, syllogistic reasoning about the harmony of humans with nature, reflects a more complex level of moral thinking. An example might be children who express the sentiment that the quality of their lives depends on having a healthy environment.

Much research on ecological awareness in children has focused on older children because of assumptions that one must possess the ability to reason abstractly in order to understand and manage issues of relationships between people and their environment. Stewart Cohen and Diane Horm-Wingerd[12] assessed young children's ability to "recognize and respond to ecological concerns" and found that even preschoolers were aware of ecological events and were sensitive to environmental problems "at a level commensurate with their existing knowledge and concern."[13] This finding supports the argument that ecological awareness does not magically appear with the development of abstract thinking. Its potential is present from the moment of birth and its growth is a function of children's learning, fostered or hindered by the nature of interactions among environment, caregiver, and child. Given this new assumption, the way in which children are taught to engage with their environment is critical to the future of the natural world.

Although none of the developmental models presented above explicitly discusses the development of an ecological consciousness or the need for moral behavior in relationship to the environment, the potential to do so is there. Fowler's work in particular implicitly suggests the need for a moral consciousness in relationship to the environment.[14] Fowler states that spirituality is the way one lives on a day-to-day basis with the "relationality" of the ecology of self, others, and the "ultimate environment" in mind. That is, one reflects on and one's behavior is based on the relationships among the individual, other humans, and a transcendent or ultimate environment. Spiritual maturity seeks to achieve a unified balance of this ecological system—in essence to realize the Reign of God in which all creation is restored and renewed. Implicit in this notion is that relationality is both social and physical in nature; the self relates to others but also to the physical environment. In essence the ultimate environment encompasses the natural world, the earth, and *all* its creatures.

For most children, parents provide the most influential source of interaction. In their parental role they relate to their children as one person to another and they provide children with examples and opportunities of how people can relate to the physical environment. As children become older, family systems, peer groups, and community resources (e.g., daycare centers, schools) augment the input of parents. Within the context of these social interactions children develop a sense of moral responsibility to their physical environment.

DEVELOPMENT OF AN
ENVIRONMENTAL CONSCIOUSNESS

A most striking use of this idea can be found in the work of Maria Montessori in which curricula are created that allow children to relate to and explore material things in their environment in a way that appropriately stimulates their senses and maximizes their growth. Montessori's teachings are explicitly based on the premise that children will teach themselves "so long as the environment [is] prepared, the materials utilized, and the goals or directions made clear."[15] E. M. Standing[16] identified three factors that inhibit children's development and that Montessori's approach confronts: "(1) when the child has the will to act but his movements are inhibited; (2) when the will of the adult is unnecessarily substituted for that of the child . . . [and (3)] when children are abandoned to their own devices."[17] The Montessori approach stresses the need for adults in the child's environment to articulate "goals or directions" and to provide the means to their achievement. This assumption has led to the creation of a number of environmental learning models in Montessori schools focused on developing an ecological awareness in children that will result in a non-exploitative relationship with the earth.[18]

As the Montessori method illustrates, principles of ecology and biodiversity are best learned as children interact with their physical environment. Many educators have found that teaching "facts" alone is inadequate, but providing children with "hands-on" opportunities structured to their developmental level helps them to make sense of their world, finding consistency and meaning in it.[19] Claire Freeman,[20] for example, emphasizes that since children learn through play it is essential that natural environments form a significant component of their play experience.

Raymond Chipeniuk claims that humans have a predisposition to foraging, which he defines as "gathering and putting to some purpose a natural kind of thing."[21] One could argue that children's first encounter with their environment is a beginning kind of foraging. Young infants stretch for objects beyond their reach, capture them, and explore them with fingers and mouth. Older infants manipulate and control objects more purposefully, e.g., by banging blocks and stacking rings. Preschool and school-age children, given the opportunity, will become full-fledged foragers, collecting and using natural things in their world. Foraging in childhood, according to Chipeniuk, leads to "competence in assessing landscapes for their richness in wild plant and animal resources."[22] The experience of foraging, he claims, is a requisite as children gain a sense of biodiversity.

The concern is often expressed that children in the United States, especially children in urban areas, have little exposure to living systems, so interactions with the natural environment rarely occur and are certainly not spontaneous as is the case with foraging. In addition, for urban children much of what they learn about nature comes to them through the media and may not be accurate or particularly meaningful. Although providing children with environmental interactions may present a challenge for parents, caregivers, and educators, assessment of the views and values of children from inner-city neighborhoods indicates that it can be done and that doing so results in a heightened awareness of biodiversity.[23]

One outcome of the Montessori method applied to environmental education is an increased awareness of natural biodiversity; another is the ability to apply ethical and moral principles to decisions about how to live in a biodiverse world and ultimately be able to deal with "environmental crises." John J. McDermott offers an example of a pedagogical technique to help students master such lessons. In addition to the classical materials of the Montessori classroom, he says,

> I would introduce materials that are highly desirable, but not enough of them to go around, rather just enough to be frustrating. This situation would introduce the children to a structural sense of scarcity. Other materials would be introduced but, when used, would be consumed and non-renewable. The question here is who gets to use them. Finally, I would introduce materials which not only corrode themselves but corrode the other materials as well. And here we have the experience of pollution. Unpleasant pedagogy? Yes, decidedly so, but a necessary pedagogy, nonetheless.[24]

CHALLENGES AND SUGGESTIONS FOR EDUCATORS AND CAREGIVERS

The strength of our natural environment and with it the health of the human race depend on decisions that will be made by our children. How can we, as parents, caregivers, and educators, best prepare our children to understand, value, and make choices that affirm the complexity of the natural order? The previous discussion has identified processes through which children develop a sense of self and master the skills of interaction with others. These same processes underlie the ways in which children learn to relate to their physical environment. To use Fowler's term, developing a sense of "relationality" to all creation becomes a part of children's spiritual development and a real responsibility of religious education. If we would have our children appreciate, care about, and live sensitively with their natural neighbors, we must teach them how to do so.

Several principles can guide our work in this arena. First and underlying all other principles is the notion that interactions between children and those who guide their learning occur on two levels: in the informal, unstructured exchange of daily events and in formally structured learning experiences. It is relatively easy to construct special "environmental projects," but parents and caregivers must learn to take advantage of the "teachable moments" that present themselves spontaneously in the course of day-to-day living.

Second, children need chances to interact with nature pure and simple. In order to develop an awareness of how biologically diverse their world is children must engage with that biodiversity. For many of us, living in a natural world is a bit like being a fish in water. We grew up in rural environments where birds and bugs, large animals and small, domestic and wild were all part of our daily experience. Lying in green grass and watching a ladybug make her way up our arm before she flew off to some fiery home and roaming child-bugs[25] was a summertime "taken for granted." As adults we could not survive without our trees, waterways, gardens, walks in remote wilderness areas, sun, moss, and fireflies. We are so connected to nature that it is a part of us, the water in which we swim. Although our children may not have the same intensity of exposure to nature that some of us had, they can experience it in their own context. Our children can join us, small trowel in hand, as we turn over our raised garden beds, located on our fifty-by-one-hundred-foot urban lot, and we can discuss the workings of newly discovered earthworms as they squirm in small hands. Our children can plant lettuce in a window box or flower pot in our urban apartment building and we can talk about what plants need to "eat and drink" to grow healthy. Even the most commonplace experiences offer a chance for learning. For example, seeing a dove strutting on a sidewalk can lead to questions such as "I wonder where she lives? and if she has eggs in her nest? and what is a nest anyway? and how is it built? and how do the mother and father bird decide where to build it? And. . . ." The questions, encouraged by adults, can go on forever. These everyday experiences of children are rich with potential interactions with nature.

Structured experiences also provide opportunities for children to learn about biodiversity. School-based projects are a classic example of such structured learning. Thousands of children have planted tomato seeds or beans in styrofoam cups, placed them in schoolroom windows, watered them faithfully, and drawn and colored pictures of seeds, germs, roots, stems, leaves, and fruit. Classrooms abound with terrariums and thousands of children have taken field trips to urban wetlands, parks, and farms. City parks, urban green spaces, visits to country farms can provide a wealth of learning about nature if adults take advantage of teaching opportunities. On a larger scale some school districts or states create environmental study options for students. The state of Oregon, for example, mandates that all sixth-grade students attend a week-long Outdoor School located in camps in the Coast Range or the foothills of the Cascade Mountains. At Outdoor School, Oregon children study natural ecological systems and their interactions.

A third principle of environmental education is that the interaction children have with nature must be developmentally appropriate. Infants, for example, need sensory stimulation to develop neurologically. Taking them for walks along residential streets and into parks where they can hear bird songs and running water, where they can feel the warm sun on their skin and see the mottled light filtered through leafy trees, where they can toddle on grass and feel its texture under their feet—all these experiences stimulate the infant in a healthy way.

As noted above, a primary developmental task of infants is to establish a sense of trust that their needs will be met and their demands will receive an appropriate response. When infants interact with their natural environment, care must be taken to ensure their safety and to strengthen that sense of trust. Exploring their natural environment must be a closely monitored activity in which they *feel* and *are* safe. For example, adult caregivers need to set physical limits on the activities of infants and young children and be quickly responsive to mishaps. Toddling children can enjoy splashing in shallow pools but they must be watched closely and guided safely. In many cases they should not even be allowed near water, as would be the case with deep or flowing streams. Caregivers are responsible for keeping dangerous or toxic things out of infants' mouths; a six-month-old infant is not able to distinguish between a banana and a banana slug and either could end up being chewed on. Without safe adult guidance what could have been a positive sensory experience can quickly become noxious and frightening.

For toddlers and preschoolers the primary task of developing autonomy can be facilitated as they engage with their natural environment. Digging in the dirt and playing with water give them practice with their physical skills and refine coordination, dexterity, and strength. These activities encourage young children to manipulate materials, and by doing so they develop an awareness that they, as individuals, are separate from other things and that those things have integrity and consistency. Young children come to expect this consistency, a feature that reinforces the sense of trust previously developed, and they are often surprised when change occurs. The amazement on the face of a two-year-old who wakes to a snow-covered world is truly a gift to see, and for parents it presents a wonderful teaching moment.

The preschool years are, as noted above, the time in which children master language skills. Reading, telling stories, and having discussions about experiences with nature are excellent mechanisms to help children as they work on this important business. The imagination and sense of magic in children of this age provide fertile ground for the use of new words and ideas, and children's comments can be creative, humorous, and profound. For example, four-year-old children listening to the fable of how the bear lost its tail[26] reflected for a moment, then asked: "What happened to the tails that were left in the ice?" The storyteller turned the question around and asked them what they thought happened. After a few moments of thought one little boy answered: "The little fishes at the bottom of the lake came up and nibbled them off and took them home to their houses and made neckties," an answer that illustrates his ability to use previous ideas to construct new ideas (the fish "nibbled" for a different purpose), his sense of conservation (the tails were used to a purpose), as well as his "animistic" thinking (the fish lived in houses and wore neckties).

In the school-age years children can more purposefully manipulate natural materials, connect and generate ideas, and begin to explore the ethics of decisions about the use of natural resources. Structured opportunities to perform "scientific experiments" with nature should be provided. In a classic example, hundreds of eggs have been sacrificed by school children in their search for the most shock-absorbent container that can be built of natural materials. Wrapped in cotton, surrounded by elaborate wood and paper structures, suspended by string or tape, eggs have been dropped from innumerable schoolroom windows or rooftops to help children discover the properties of physical elements. By learning what the characteristics of natural elements are, children at this age come to appreciate the constancy of nature (e.g., water will always flow downhill). By manipulating the physical elements themselves children develop a sense of the power they have over nature (e.g., water will always flow downhill unless a siphon is created). McDermott's pedagogical model in which children would physically explore the concepts of scarcity, distribution, consumption, and pollution could further expand children's thinking.[27] This would be particularly relevant in the adolescent years when children begin more clearly to apply abstract reasoning and refine their self-identity separate from and as part of the world around them. Using McDermott's model, children could move from simply knowing about nature and being aware that human actions have an impact on it to discovering the significance of the relationship between nature and humans. This awareness strengthens the balance of their moral and spiritual development.

The experiences children have interacting with the natural world and its diversity will create a sense of awareness, understanding, and appreciation for the natural world. This awareness is enhanced through use of a fourth principle essential to developing an environmental consciousness: children must receive reinforcement for behaviors that demonstrate an appreciation of and support for biodiversity. This principle often applies in those everyday spontaneous moments between children and caregivers. For example, when parents acknowledge the gift of a foraged item (e.g., a bird's feather, a small stone, a flower) from their child they reinforce the foraging behavior and convey their own positive attitudes toward nature. Conversely, children should not be deterred from interacting with nature by the parents' reactions. Too often one sees a reaction such as that of a mother whose baby found several dusty, cobweb-covered flower pots and began to explore them. The mother, screaming, grabbed the baby, slapped the dust from her hands and face, and rushed into the house to give her a bath. The baby, frightened and in tears, learned a powerful lesson about nature.

Parents reinforce children's ecological behavior by being role models for responsible interaction with the environment. Children are most likely to do as the adults around them do, not as they say, and ethical behavior is learned, often unconsciously, through daily repetition and reinforcement of that behavior. When children see an adult toss litter on the street, for example, they are given the message that the physical environment is of little value, certainly not worth keeping clean.

A fifth principle on which environmental education is based is that children must be given opportunities to practice their developing environmental consciousness. Developmental research has shown that prosocial behavior is facilitated when children are given an opportunity to *be* altruistic.[28] The same appears to be true with pro-environmental behavior: structuring a clean-up day for a group of children, carrying a plastic bag to pick up litter on every hike parents take with their children, planting and tending seeds in the classroom are all activities that allow children to apply the values they are beginning to articulate about the importance of nature and their own obligation to care for it.

A final principle is that children must be given the opportunity to reflect on what the awareness, understanding, and developing values around biodiversity mean to them as children. Developmental theorists point out that learning occurs as children explore ideas and that content and structured settings for exploration are essential for this process to succeed. "Making new connections depends on knowing enough about something in the first place to be able to think of other things to do, of other questions to ask."[29] Caregivers who have provided the materials and guidance for children to begin to learn ideas about nature must structure times for reflection and thought and must be able to listen and respond to ideas that come spontaneously during everyday interactions. A three-year-old child sits in her mother's lap and, gazing out the window, comments: "Look, Mommy, the trees are saying 'yes' and 'no'!" Such a simple yet profound observation! It illustrates her developmental sense of animism, that the trees have the ability to answer. It demonstrates her wealth of knowledge: about the meaning of "yes" and "no," that responses are connected to physical movement, that there is a category of things called "trees," that there is something, though she may not have the name for it, called communication, and so on. Having these ideas gives her the basis for developing more, and her mother's response is crucial to the process. Often, as with the Montessori method, an effective response is one that asks the child to explore the idea further: "The trees are saying 'yes' and 'no'?" can encourage the child to explain what she is seeing and thinking and can lead to more complex ideas.

Knowing about biodiversity, having a general understanding of ecological principles, and being aware of how their behavior can affect their physical environment gives children the content to examine new connections, create new ideas about relationships among all living things, and further clarify and refine their values. Structured settings for reflection, ones that allow "children to ask their own questions—at the right time,"[30] need to be built into home, educational, and community experiences so that they can begin to make sense of it all.

CONCLUSION AND THEOLOGICAL REFLECTION

In summary, when parents and caregivers teach children about biodiversity, introduce them to experiences with the natural environment, give them chances to practice what they have learned, and reflect with them on how essential is the interconnectedness between humans and nature, children will gain a sense of environmental responsibility. That sense will be further strengthened as children are given the message that their actions are critical, that they may make all the difference, that they, as part of the human community, are in charge of the last of the truffula seeds.

From a theological perspective the "development of environmental responsibility in children" highlights an essential pastoral task in the

Church's response to the environmental crisis: the necessity to educate for ecological consciousness and responsibility. This ecclesial task has not gone unnoticed by the pastoral leadership of the Church. For example, in 1989 Pope John Paul II declared that "An education in ecological responsibility is urgent: for oneself, for others and for the earth. . . . Churches and religious bodies have a precise role to play in such education."[31] Likewise the U.S. Catholic bishops "invite teachers and educators to emphasize, in their classroom and curricula, a love for God's creation, a respect for nature and a commitment to practices and behavior that brings these attitudes into the daily lives of their students and themselves."[32] Furthermore, the bishops "remind parents that they are the first . . . teachers of children" and that "it is from parents that children will learn love of the earth and delight in nature."[33] In addition to Roman Catholic support for ecological education, the creation of the Religious Partnership for the Environment in the U.S. is also encouraging. This group's production of environmentally related curriculum materials strongly indicates that many religious denominations and traditions recognize that ecological education is a religious imperative. While recognition of the need for ecological education in a religious context is significant, challenges nevertheless remain. A particular hurdle is convincing religious education leaders in congregations, parishes, and dioceses that environmental awareness and responsibility are noteworthy enterprises for religious education.

Drawing on insights from developmental psychology, this essay also offers several key implications for ecological education. The first is the claim that environmental education ought to be interactive and developmentally appropriate. This point is true for all age categories and honors the long-held axiom that sound pedagogical practice must attend and respond to the learner's experience and needs. Moreover, the interactive nature of environmental education is crucial in assisting learners to establish a sense of relatedness to the natural world, which is necessary for ecological consciousness and for understanding the biblical notion of creation.

The second and third implications for environmental education—that children ought to be given opportunities to practice and reflect on their developing environmental consciousness—are consistent with several contemporary models of Christian religious education, the most notable of which is Thomas Groome's process of "Shared Christian Praxis."[34] For Groome the concept of praxis (reflective activity) is central to his method of religious education, the overall goal of which is to promote lived Christian faith and ethical responsibility. A shared praxis approach would be an ideal way of engaging in ecological education within a Judeo-Christian context. Thus, this chapter echoes the sentiments of Groome, namely that the purpose and horizon of educational activity in a Judeo-Christian framework of faith would be "to realize the Reign of God in which all creation is restored and renewed."[35]

Principles of Developing Environmental Consciousness in Children

- Children must interact with biodiverse natural environments
- Children's interactions with nature must be developmentally appropriate
- Environmentally conscious behavior must be reinforced by adults
- Children must have opportunities to practice environmentally responsible behavior
- Children must have opportunities to reflect on the meaning of environmentally responsible behavior

---

NOTES: CHAPTER 10

[1] Dr. Seuss (Theodore Seuss Geisel), *The Lorax* (New York: Random House, 1971).

[2] Proverbs 22:6.

[3] Shel Silverstein, *The Giving Tree* (New York: Harper & Row, 1964).

[4] Erik H. Erikson, *Childhood and Society* (2d ed. New York: W. W. Norton, 1963).

[5] Jean Piaget, *The Theory of Stages in Cognitive Development* (New York: McGraw-Hill, 1969).

[6] Lawrence Kohlberg, "Stages and Sequence: The Cognitive-Development Approach to Socialization," in David A. Goslin, ed., *Handbook of Socialization Theory and Research* (Chicago: Rand McNally, 1969) 347–480.

[7] Carol Gilligan and Grant Wiggins, "The Origins of Morality in Early Childhood Relationships," in Carol Gilligan, et al., eds., *Mapping the Moral Domain: A Contribution of Women's Thinking to Psychological Theory and Education* (Cambridge, Mass.: Center for the Study of Gender, Education, and Human Development, Harvard University Graduate School of Education: Distributed by Harvard University Press, 1988).

[8] James Fowler, "Stages of Faith," *Psychology Today* 17/11 (1983) 56–62.

[9] Peter H. Kahn and Batya Friedman, "Environmental Views and Values of Children in an Inner-City Black Community," *Child Development* 66/5 (1995) 1403–17.

[10] Michael D. Piburn, *The Environment: A Human Crisis* (Rochelle Park, N.J.: Hayden Book Co., 1974).

[11] Peter H. Kahn and Ann McCoy, "Children's Moral Relationships with Nature," a paper presented at the meeting of the Jean Piaget Society (Montreal, Quebec, Canada, May 1992). One of the studies is discussed more fully in Kahn and Friedman, "Environmental Views and Values of Children in an Inner-City Black Community" (see n. 9 above).

[12] Stewart Cohen and Diane M. Horm-Wingerd, "Children and the Environment: Ecological Awareness among Preschool Children," *Environment & Behavior* 25 (January 1993) 103–120.

[13] Ibid. 116.

[14] James Fowler, *Stages of Faith: The Psychology of Human Development and the Quest for Meaning* (New York: Harper & Row, 1981).

[15] John J. McDermott, "Do Not Bequeath a Shamble. The Child in the Twenty-First Century: Innocent Hostage to Mindless Oppression or Messenger to the World?" *Namta Journal* 20/3 (Summer 1995) 93–106.

[16] E. Mortimer Standing, *Maria Montessori: Her Life and Work* (New York: New American Library, 1962).

[17] Ibid. 171.

[18] Robert Muller, "A World Core Curriculum," *Namta Journal* 18/3 (Summer 1993) 93–102. See also James P. Cummesky, "The Montessori Erdkinder: Three Abstracts," *Namta Journal* 18/1 (Winter 1993) 173–82; Peter Gebhardt-Seele, "Why Not Consider Erdkinder?" *Namta Journal* 21/3 (Spring 1996) 138–48; and Patricia Ludick, "Reflections from the Farm," *Namta Journal* (Summer 1996) 122–39.

[19] Stewart Cohen, "Promoting Ecological Awareness in Children," *Childhood Education* 68/5 (1992) 258–59. See also Alfred James, "Will It Hurt 'Shade'? Adopting a Tree," *Childhood Education* 68/5 (1992) 260–62; and Claire Freeman, "Planning and Play: Creating Greener Environments," *Children's Environments Quarterly* 12/3 (September 1995) 382–88.

[20] "Planning and Play: Creating Greener Environments" (n. 19 above).

[21] Raymond Chipeniuk, "Childhood Foraging as a Means of Acquiring Competent Human Cognition About Biodiversity," *Environment & Behavior* 27/4 (July 1995) 490–512.

[22] Ibid. 494.

[23] Kahn and Friedman, "Environmental Views and Values of Children in an Inner-City Black Community" (n. 9 above).

[24] McDermott, "Do Not Bequeath a Shamble" (n. 15 above).

[25] *The Real Mother Goose* (Chicago: Rand McNally, 1916). The poem reads: "Ladybird, ladybird, fly away home! Your house is on fire, your children all gone. All but one, and her name is Ann, and she crept under the pudding pan."

[26] The fable (from this author's childhood) is, briefly, as follows: "At the beginning of time, when the Creator made the world, bears had beautiful, long, flowing tails. They were very vain about their tails and thought they were better than the other animals because of their beauty. So the Creator decided to teach them a lesson. Now the bears' tails were useful as well as beautiful. They used them to catch the fish that they needed to live, dropping their tails down in the water and waiting for the fish to come nibbling. In the winter the bears would make a hole in the ice that covered the lake and fish every day. One winter day as the bears fished the Creator blew a hard, cold wind that quickly froze the holes in the ice and trapped the bears. They cried and they roared, but they could not get their tails free! Poor bears! The cold ice froze their tails off, and they ran crying home to their caves in the winter woods where, embarrassed and ashamed, they hid all winter long. And that is why today bears have short tails and sleep in caves all winter long."

[27] McDermott, "Do Not Bequeath a Shamble" (n. 15 above).

[28] Alice Sterling Honig, "Research in Review: Prosocial Development in Children," *Young Children* 37/5 (July 1982) 51–62.

[29] E. Duckworth, "The Having of Wonderful Ideas," *Harvard Educational Review* 42/2 (1972) 217–31.

[30] Ibid. 231.

[31] John Paul II, *The Ecological Crisis: A Common Responsibility* (Washington, D.C.: U.S. Catholic Conference, 1990) 4.

[32] "Renewing the Earth," *Origins* (December 12, 1991) 432.

[33] Ibid.

[34] For a thorough treatment of shared praxis see Thomas Groome, *Christian Religious Education* (San Francisco: Harper & Row, 1980).

[35] See above, p. 200.

11

An Ecological View of Elders and Their Families: Needs for the Twenty-First Century

"Honor your father and your mother, so that your days may be long in the land that the Lord your God is giving you." (Exod 20:12)

C entral to the Israelite social structure was the importance of family, an attitude that is reflected in one of the commands contained in the Decalogue, God's law given to Moses and the people on Mount Sinai. One's duties toward one's parents are also highlighted in Sir 3:1-16. Care for one's parents continues to be a value within the human community today. However, the population increase of the elderly and the changing character of the family now require certain paradigm shifts that the ancient biblical people did not have to experience but that are inevitable today for parents and caregivers. This chapter looks at the ecological framework for the family and the challenges confronting elders and their families.

INTRODUCTION

Ecology is about the relationship over time between human beings and their biophysical environment. Most often this relationship is thought of in a concrete way as the connection between humans and the earth. This chapter challenges the reader to expand the concept of ecology to human ecology and the environment of human relationships. Stewardship means care for both humans and the physical environment. Connection and connectedness of human beings to one another within the context of family is essential to the survival of the planet and is a sub-field of human ecology.

An ecological framework is presented in this essay to illustrate the connection of human beings and their environment by exploring relationships between elders, their families, and the environment. The first section presents an ecological framework in which to view family. The second part outlines specific challenges for elders and their families at the close of the twentieth century. The last section suggests significant changes in beliefs, ideas, and paradigms regarding the aged, their families, and the environment that are necessary for successful adaptation in the twenty-first century. The major theme throughout this chapter is on the connection between people and the environment.

AN ECOLOGICAL FRAMEWORK FOR FAMILY

The family is the principal context in which all humans develop and interact on a daily basis.[1] The family is the smallest social system and is dependent on its environment. An ecological framework for understanding human beings allows for an integration or multidimensional approach to the complexity of the family. The emphasis of ecology theories is on the reciprocal process among individuals, their families, and the environment, not on the workings of the systems.[2]

In a human ecological framework, the four interacting systems that affect the family are the microsystem, the mesosystem, the exosystem, and the macrosystem.[3] The microsystem consists of the interacting members of a self-defined family group. The microsystem is what has traditionally been thought of as "the family." The mesosystem focuses on relationships between the family and other settings or systems in which the family actively interacts. Examples of the mesosystem are social support systems of the family, e.g., school, workplace of family members, health care provider, church, and neighbors. The exosystem encompasses settings or social systems that have an indirect impact on the family, e.g., the health care system, Medicare, Medicaid, Social Security, retirement benefits, and insurance plans. The macrosystem consists of larger environments that impact the belief system of the family, e.g., policies, values, ethics, population trends, and world events.

An additional concept, the chronosystem, is critical to understanding the family from an ecological perspective. Chronosystem refers to the changes experienced by the individual family members, the family, and the environment over time. These are both expected changes or normal life transitions and unexpected changes such as illness, sudden death, homelessness, or unemployment.

In this study we emphasize the interface or relationship between the systems and the impact on the aged and their families. Using an ecological framework, the next section explores current trends that impact the elderly and their families.

CHALLENGES CONFRONTING ELDERS AND FAMILIES

1. Increase in the Number of Elderly

Global population growth is a significant ecological factor that, in combination with resource consumption, determines the overall human impact on the earth. A function of this growth is the fact that in the majority of developing and developed countries of the world the elderly population is increasing due to declining fertility rates and decreased mortality rates. In smaller countries the increase in the elderly population is further enhanced because of migration of the younger members outside their country.[4] The fastest-growing segment of the elderly in all countries is the oldest of the old, people over eighty-five years of age. In the U.S. the over-eighty-five age group has tripled as a percentage of the total population in the last forty years.[5]

From a human ecological standpoint this trend in the macrosystem has an indirect impact on the family. In this global trend people over eighty-five years of age are more likely to be frail, dependent, and have multiple health needs. In the U.S. fifteen percent of the elderly population have adult children who also are over sixty-five years of age. In essence the frail elders have old children who themselves are adapting to aging issues.[6]

2. Reduced Kin Availability

Care of the elderly by members of the informal family support system is a microsystem characteristic of all countries in the world.[7] With the declining fertility rates in a significant number of developed nations there are fewer family members available to provide or manage the care of elderly family members.[8] A macrosystem factor that impacts kin availability is that many women delay childbearing and childrearing until a later age. The effect of this trend is that families with young children also are families caring for aging family members.

Kin availability is impacted by the increase in mobility of families. Often elderly family members do not live in the same geographic area as their major informal family support system. One result of this change is that decisions for and with the elderly are managed from a distance via phone calls, letters, and electronic communication, thus increasing the complexity of the interface between the microsystem and the macrosystem.[9] The paradigm shift is that more families are managing the care of the elderly rather than providing the direct caregiving. Even though many of the issues and stressors of managing the care of an elder are different from those arising from providing the actual care the amount of stress involved in managing the care of an elder is equal to that of providing the actual care. The issue is not whether one ought to provide care for the elder or to manage it, but that both aspects have significant stress and potential role overload within the family microsystem.

3. Increased Employment of Women

Traditionally female family members have shouldered the responsibility of caring for elderly family members. This mesosystem phenomenon is true for most of the countries of the world.[10] Such reliance on females is being challenged by the increasing number of women worldwide who are entering the work force and by female role changes.[11] The potential role strain and sacrifice of personal and family time is significant for employed women who are also caring for elderly family members. Research has shown that women employed outside the home provide as much support as their non-employed counterparts.[12] Between the ages of thirty-five and forty-four one in four women will become a caregiver of an elder and one in three in the fifty-five to sixty-four age range will become a caregiver.[13] In the United States one out of every ten people, mostly women, leave the work force to care for an elderly family member.[14] The financial implications for women who leave the work force to care for an elderly family member significantly threaten their financial security. Almost all care that is provided by the informal family network, the majority of it by women, is provided voluntarily without remuneration.[15]

When this demographic macrosystem trend is coupled with the issues presented above in kin availability the potential pressures and

conflicts for women are enormous and affect all systems from an ecological perspective. The issues are the following: How and by whom will
care be provided for elder family members given that more women are
entering the work force, which affects the microsystem? What formal
and informal support networks, both the mesosystem and the exosystem, will be available in the future? On a macrosystem level policies
must be adapted to support the female caregivers. Changes in the health
care needs and increase in acuity level of the frail elders make it impossible for one person to provide required care around the clock, which
creates a significant challenge for the microsystem of the family.

4. Changing Marital Status

The effect of changing marital status on the elderly and their families is twofold. The first effect is from the discrepancy between the number of widowed elderly women and men. In many countries more than
fifty percent of all women are widows.[16] There are several reasons for
these gender differences. The most notable is that women outlive men.
This factor is compounded by the worldwide macrosystem trend for
women to marry older men. Another explanation for the gender discrepancy is the macrosystem trend that widowed men are more likely to
remarry than widowed women. In the U.S. seventy-seven percent of
men over sixty-five years of age are married, compared to forty-six percent of women.[17]

Elderly single women are more likely to be poor and live alone.
When this aspect is combined with the fact that one-third of the caregivers for the elderly are spouses who themselves are over sixty-five
years of age the question arises as to who will care for the aging single
woman.[18] The number of elderly single women will rise in the future as
more women choose to remain single and/or are part of a childless
couple.

The second effect of changing marital status on the elderly is the
exosystem trend of increase in divorce and remarriage of their children.
Intergenerational helping patterns are impacted by the rising divorce
and remarriage rates.[19] The elderly are found to receive fewer types of
care when their children are divorced and remarried.[20] The opportunities for family arguments and disagreements about care for the elderly
are compounded by the complexities of decision-making and relationships when families become blended through divorce and remarriage.
The burden of caring for several sets of elderly family members is in-

creased with the complexity of family ties. Elders may not even be sure where and by whom they will be buried.

5. Altered Living Arrangements

In the last three decades the number of elderly people living alone has risen sharply in the developed countries. The majority of the elderly population that lives alone is female.[21] In the U.S. eighty percent of the elderly women live alone compared to sixteen percent of the elderly men.[22] In Japan the single household percentage rose from five percent in 1960 to twenty-one percent in 1985.[23] Despite the sharp increase in elderly living alone, in most nations the elderly live with someone else. The main reason cited for this macrosystem trend is economic.[24] In many countries the aged are cared for by their families not necessarily because of the cultural aspects but because of unavailability of alternatives.[25] Again elderly women are more likely to experience living alone. Coupling the increase in elderly who live alone with the mobility of families clearly challenges the family mesosystem.

6. Family Caregiving

In the United States the health care trend is for people to spend less time in the hospital setting. This trend stresses the family microsystem as elders are being sent home very ill and still requiring significant assistance from family members. Often these family members are not prepared to care for the ill elder in their home. In rural areas community-based care and assistance are poorly funded, uncoordinated, and sparse.[26]

Providing care for an elderly family member in the home becomes more complex when one-third of the caregivers are spouses who themselves are over sixty-five years of age.[27] Caregiver burden has been documented around the world on a macrosystem level in relation to meeting the needs of the elderly.[28] In addition to normal stresses on families elder abuse increases in the presence of family caregiving responsibility. Elder abuse and maltreatment are problems in both developed and developing nations.[29] According to the National Alliance for Caregiving there are 22.4 million households that provide care to elders.[30] In these households sixty-four percent are cared for by family members who are working part or full time outside of the home. The possibility of role overload and stress on the microsystem is tremendous.

There are clearly defined gender caregiver roles in Western cultures. Females typically provide personal hygiene, meal preparation, and household tasks. Males are found to support family caregiving with financial management, transportation, and home repairs.[31] Again major stress can be found to be on the women's caregiver roles.

CONNECTEDNESS IS ESSENTIAL FOR HEALTH IN THE TWENTY-FIRST CENTURY

The twenty-first century requires significant changes in beliefs, ideas, and paradigms regarding the aged. This section presents paradigm shifts that allow for growth, change, and an increased sense of connectedness with the environment for elders, their families, and society. The future depends on understanding relationships and how to use them effectively with compassion.

A necessary and critical paradigm shift is in the macrosystem belief that elders are all the same and make health care decisions in isolation. The elderly are not "lone atomistic agents"; neither are they a homogeneous group. They are members of families, the basic social unit of society. Within most societies of the world the elderly have been well integrated within the family.[32] Aging clearly is a "family affair."

The traditional and historical definition of family has been crafted from a legal perspective with specific focus on relationships via blood ties, adoption, marriage, guardianship, and biologically from a genetic perspective. Most of the formal governmental regulatory agencies, religious communities, and insurance companies continue to operate under this restricted definition of family. In essence the areas that regulate many aspects of our lives have not caught up with the human behaviors of family life.

In the past the norm was two parents of different gender living with biological children: the "nuclear family." Today the most common type of family structure in the U.S. is the blended family. A blended family is one in which the current parental couple had previous marriages with children, hence the stepfamily phenomenon. There has been a decline in the number of children per family. The increase in the number of single-parent families, of children born to single mothers, of grandparents taking care of grandchildren (the skip-generation), and of childless couples significantly affects relationships within families. The number of unmarried couples (cohabitants) has risen from 520,000 in 1970 to three million in 1990.[33] In the current century there are myriad family forms that are currently not addressed in research and by family health policies. Who knows what family configurations the future may present?

What is the family? That is an important question for the twenty-first century. A suggested working definition from which to begin has been offered by Shirley M. H. Hanson and Sheryl T. Boyd: "Family refers to two or more individuals who depend on one another for emotional, physical, and/or economic support. The members of the family are self-defined."[34] The focus of this definition is on the relationships and support systems for family members. Given this definition, the systems that will be developed in the future will be based on the strengths of elders and families and not built around conflicting systems.

Many of the issues raised in the section above on kin availability have the potential to be positively affected by a more relationship-based definition and application of family. The most binding and significant relationship in an aging family is that of the elderly couple. The likelihood that the aged couple will go through old age together is slim. The surviving spouse will need to depend on other "family" relationships. Siblings are an untapped resource; they have the potential to decrease the likelihood of institutionalization and are underutilized by single widowed elders. The whole category of age-related peers and contacts with friends as family components actually exceeds all others in frequency, yet these are seldom considered viable resources. The concept of intergenerational reciprocity will be fundamental to the future.

The family is the constant in the elder's life. The caring familial relationship will be a crucial component of connectedness for elders in the future. Marjorie Fiske Lowenthal and Clayton Haven in a classic study demonstrated that families are essential buffers for "age linked social losses."[35] It is known that when older people need assistance families assume more responsibility for their care. In fact, so many families are confronted by elderly caregiving that parent care is now considered normative.[36]

Changing the microsystem metaphor of "parenting the parent" to one that recognizes the evolutionary development of new roles, new behavior expectations, and different stressors on the elders and families offers direction to the necessary social supports that compliment the reality of family caregiving for elders. Simply to characterize the whole picture of caring for elder family members as "parenting the parent" negates the normal developmental process of a human being. Human beings do not become children or childlike when they age. Elders progress through a normal process that presents new social, intrapersonal, and interpersonal challenges to living. To suggest a regression in the relationships between family members creates barriers to possibilities that may be explored when developing necessary support systems. Elders and family members are empowered when the expectation is that the relationship continues to evolve over time—the chronosystem in an ecological framework. Recognition of the stresses that accompany the chronosystem transition to a family with aging members allows for a healthy adaptation to unfolding relationships.

A whole set of macrosystem metaphors that needs immediate attention pertains to the negative attitudes about the aging process. Ageism is the term for discrimination against the elderly. The mass media has a field day when it comes to ageist marketing.[37] One excellent example is the indication that urinary incontinence is a normal aging process. Nothing could be farther from the truth. Annette Lueckenotte noted that "more than $10 billion per year are spent on direct costs related to urinary incontinence, yet less that 0.5% of this money is spent on the evaluation and treatment of this problem."[38] The economic aspect of this is staggering and even more so when it is known that the majority of urinary incontinence problems in elders can be cured or significantly improved with medical and nursing interventions.

Historically, the process of aging has been viewed as negative throughout the ages. Only within the last twenty years has this collective negative image begun to change. One reason for this change may be the news media's more positive portrayals of the aged and aging.[39] Elders are notorious for ageism and their attitudes about the elderly are far more rejecting than those of other segments of the population. Altering macrosystem attitudes that fuel ageism to one that embraces aging as a developmental process allows for integration and not separation. Some prevalent metaphors of the past twentieth century that need to be changed are "sandwich generation," "race against time," "over the hill," "stages" for everything, "family caregiving" as an expectation, "nuclear family" as the historical norm, and the "quick fix" mentality of modern medicine.[40] The twenty-first century is a grand time to be old. The almost aged baby boomers will have a positive influence as they are more knowledgeable about health and healthy lifestyles and have a more interactive understanding of ways to negotiate change in the family environment. Creating positive metaphors for the next century is limited only by carrying over ageist views of the aging process.

The microsystem reality is that families are caring for their elders. The expectation and responsibility is given to families: what does not jibe is the policy of the macrosystem in such aspects as the health care delivery system, health policy, and family policies that do not allow for family well-being. "Although all government policies affect families, in both negative and positive ways, the United States has no overall, official, explicit family policy."[41] Families will get little relief from the increasing demands that are placed on them for family caregiving until consistent parameters and clearly overt policies are defined to support family caregiving.

The managed health care delivery system prevalent in the U.S. needs to base access to health care and support on family caregiving (microsystem) instead of restricting family health care resources (mesosystem). If managed health care delivery systems focused on prevention, rehabilitation, and management of chronic diseases they would be more cost effective, family focused, and prepared for the increase in elderly populations in the next century.

The health care delivery exosystem and many employee assistance programs (also part of the exosystem) need to be designed to empower families. The expectation is that families will provide the necessary care but there is little follow through or dependability regarding family policy in the societal contract to protect and maintain family integrity during such known transitions. While the majority of part- or full-time care-givers are engaged in the work force outside the home,[42] at the same time there is a decrease in the number of employee assistance programs in corporations.[43] Numerous studies have shown that there is quality productivity and employee satisfaction when there is positive meso-system support and programs are provided for the care of families in the corporate world. Companies that are family focused and place overt value on family relationships will succeed in the next century by establishing a strong sense of connectedness between work and family.

During the twenty-first century the above suggested changes in macrosystem values and ethics must be made for successful adaptation of elders. One significant factor to recognize from the human ecological perspective is that the flow of relationships is not unidirectional. Elders have much to give to their families and society. Integration of relationships between systems is necessary for movement in a positive direction in the future.

CONCLUSION AND THEOLOGICAL REFLECTION

The focus of this essay has been on relationships between elders, their families, and the environment. This human ecological perspective allows for a holistic approach to humanity through the lens of relationships. When viewed through the human ecological lens of connection people become more than just pieces of the whole. As a matter of fact, people become integral components over time in the relationship between human beings and the environment.

Finally, this critical assessment of the family and care of the elderly is an interesting excursion into the relatively new field of inquiry known as human ecology, a sub-discipline of ecology. Ecology is often defined as the "study of living organisms and their relationship to one another and the environment."[44] Human ecology narrows the focus to human relationships and can move in one of two directions. First, human ecology can focus on the relationship between the human species and the biophysical environment. This approach studies the role or "niche" humanity occupies within the web of life and is very similar to the original science of ecology in its utilization of such scientific disciplines as biology and chemistry. The second approach of human ecology focuses on the interrelationships within the human community and studies the patterns of relations that have evolved over time. This analytical perspective has much in common with the human sciences, particularly sociology. "An Ecological View of Elders and Their Families" is consistent with this second approach in its assessment of the family as a primary social unit in caring for the elderly.

As a science, ecology investigates relationships and communities within ecosystems. Many ecologists are probably unaware that the language they commonly use, with its references to "relationship" and "community," has great theological significance especially from a biblical perspective. For example, in the worldview of ancient Israel community and relationship were primary. Creation was experienced as a relational-harmonious order, a community of being in which all creatures stood in profound relationship to each other and God. Within Israel's human community the communal bonds of loyalty and obligation took precedence over individual identity. Furthermore, this communal-relational world was governed by ethical considerations. The very basis of creation's orderliness is God's justice and righteousness. Consequently the order of creation is maintained when its relational structure is governed by the practice of justice and righteousness. From a communal-relational perspective the practice of justice and righteousness is acting in faithfulness to the demands and responsibilities of the relationship between humans, creation, and God. A failure to do so fractures the relatedness of creation and threatens its orderliness with chaos.

"A Ecological View of Elders and Their Families" argues that, given the population increase of the elderly and the shifting character of the family, the future will require "paradigm shifts" that will create a greater "sense of connectedness with the environment for elders, their families, and society."[45] Accordingly the essay declares that "The future depends on understanding relationships and how to use them effectively with compassion."[46] In other words it is calling for the creation of new structures of community that will support and augment the primary family in caring for the elderly in the future. Embedded in this vision is the recognition that current social structures are either inadequate or non-existent. The author states that "the health care delivery system, health policy, and family policies . . . do not allow for family well-being."[47] In the language of biblical theology this essay desires the emergence of new forms of community wherein the experience of relationship is primary. Ultimately it is a call for justice and righteousness, which means in this specific case acting in faithfulness to the demands and responsibilities of our relationship to the elderly.

NOTES: CHAPTER 11

[1] Uri Bronfenbrenner, *The Ecology of Human Development* (Cambridge, Mass.: Harvard University Press, 1979); see also S. D. Wright and D. A. Herrin, "Family Ecology: An Approach to the Interdisciplinary Complexity of the Study of Family Phenomena," *Family Science Review* 1 (1988) 253–82.

[2] Nancy Lackey and B. Lee Walker, "An Ecological Framework for Family Nursing Practice and Research," in Beth Vaughan-Cole, et al., eds., *Family Nursing Practice* (Philadelphia: Saunders, 1998) 38–48.

[3] For further discussion see Bronfenbrenner, *The Ecology of Human Development* 21; Wright and Herrin, "Family Ecology" (n. 1 above); and Lackey and Walker, "An Ecological Framework" (n. 2 above), 40.

[4] Kevin G. Kinsella, "Aging and the Family: Present and Future Demographic Issues," in Rosemary Blieszner and Victoria H. Bedford, eds., *Aging and the Family: Theory and Research* (Westport, Conn.: Praeger, 1996) 32–56.

[5] U.S. Bureau of the Census, *Growth of America's Oldest Old.* Profiles of America's Elderly 2 (Bethesda, Md.: U.S. Department Health and Human Services, National Institutes of Health, National Institute on Aging, 1992).

[6] For further study see Annette Lueckenotte, *Gerontologic Nursing* (St. Louis: Mosby, 1996); see also Jordan I. Kosberg, ed., *Family Care of the Elderly: Social and Cultural Changes* (Newbury Park, Calif.: SAGE, 1992).

[7] N. L. Chappel, "Aging and Social Care," in Robert H. Binstock and Linda K. George, eds., *Handbook of Aging and the Social Sciences* (San Diego: Academic Press, 1990) 438–54.

[8] C. L. Himes, "Social Demography of Contemporary Families and Aging," *Generations* 23/3 (1992) 13–16.

[9] Lueckenotte, *Gerontologic Nursing.*

[10] For a detailed study see the material from the United Nations Department of International Economic and Social Affairs (UNDIESA), *Overview of Recent Research Findings on Population Aging and the Family.* United Nations International Conference on Aging Populations in the Context of the Family (Kitakyusha, N.Y.: United Nations [IESA/P/AC.33/6, October 1990]).

[11] Mary Jo Storey Gibson, "Family Support Patterns, Policies, and Programs," in Charlotte Nusberg, ed., with Mary Jo Gibson and Sheila Peace, *Innovative Aging Programs Abroad: Implications for the United States* (Westport, Conn.: Greenwood, 1984).

[12] Lueckenotte, *Gerontologic Nursing* 136–66.

[13] Priscilla Ebersole and Patricia Hess, *Toward Healthy Aging: Human Needs and Nursing Response* (5th ed. St. Louis: Mosby, 1998).

[14] "National Survey Describes Caregivers," *Parent Care* 2/3 (1987) 1–2.

[15] See Chappel, "Aging and Social Care" (n. 7 above).

[16] For further discussion see Kinsella, "Aging and the Family" (n. 4 above), Lueckenotte, *Gerontologic Nursing,* and Carol Miller, *Nursing Care of Older Adults: Theory and Practice* (Philadelphia: Lippincott, 1995).

[17] See Lueckenotte, *Gerontologic Nursing* 136–66, and Miller, *Nursing Care of Older Adults* 5–13.

[18] R. Stone and P. Kemper, "Spouses and Children of Disabled Elders: How Large a Constituency for Long-Term Reform?" *Milbank Quarterly* 67/3–4 (1990) 485–506.

[19] C. L. Johnson, "Divorced and Reconstituted Families: Effects on the Older Generation," *Generations* 22/3 (1992) 17–20.

[20] V. G. Cicirelli, "A Comparison of Helping Behavior to Elderly Parents of Adult Children with Intact and Disrupted Marriages," *Gerontologist* 23 (1983) 619–25.

[21] See Kinsella, "Aging and the Family" (n. 4 above), 41–47; Lueckenotte, *Gerontologic Nursing* 136–66; and Miller, *Nursing Care of Older Adults* 5–13.

[22] Kinsella, "Aging and the Family."

[23] Ibid.

[24] Ibid.

[25] B. Carpenter, "Filial Obligation, Ethnicity, and Caregiving," a paper presented at the meeting of the Gerontological Society of America, Washington,

D.C., November 19, 1996. See also Roseann Giarrusso, et al., "A Cross-Cultural Comparison of the Intergenerational Stake Phenomenon over the Life Course," a paper presented at the meeting of the Gerontological Society of America, Washington, D.C., November 19, 1996.

[26] H. J. Lee, "Health Perceptions of Middle; 'New Middle' and Older Rural Adults," *Family & Community Health* 16 (1993) 19–27. See also M. C. Henderson, "Families in Transition: Caring for the Rural Elderly," *Family & Community Health* 14 (1992) 61–70.

[27] Stone and Kemper, "Spouses and Children of Disabled Elders."

[28] Jordan I. Kosberg, "Policies Encouraging and Requiring Family Care of the Aged: A Critical Assessment," a paper presented at the 12th International Congress of Gerontology, New York, 1985. See also Gibson, "Family Support Patterns, Policies, and Programs" (n. 11 above).

[29] Jordan I. Kosberg and J. L. Garcia, "Social Changes Affecting Family Care of the Elderly," *Journal of the International Institute on Aging* 1/2 (1991) 2–5.

[30] "National Family Caregiver Alliance: Selected Caregiver Statistics," *Family Caregiver Alliance Newsletter* (San Francisco, 1996).

[31] J. W. Dwyer and R. T. Coward, "A Multivariate Comparison of the Involvement of Adult Sons Versus Daughters in the Care of Impaired Parents," *Journal of Gerontology* 46 (1991) 259–69. See also R. Stone, et al., "Caregivers of the Frail Elderly: A National Profile," *Gerontologist* 27 (1987) 616–26.

[32] Ken Tout, *Ageing in Developing Countries* (New York: Oxford University Press for HelpAge International, 1989).

[33] U.S. Bureau of the Census, *Current Population Reports* Series 20, No. 218 (Washington, D.C.: U.S. Government Printing Office, 1990).

[34] Shirley M. H. Hanson and Sheryl T. Boyd, eds., *Family Health Care Nursing: Theory, Practice, and Research* (Philadelphia: F. A. Davis, 1996).

[35] See Marjorie Fiske Lowenthal and Clayton Haven, "Interaction and Adaptation: Intimacy as a Critical Variable," *American Sociological Review* 33/1 (February 1968).

[36] For further discussion see Vicki L. Schmall, *What Do You Know about Aging? Facts and Fallacies.* Pacific Northwest Extension Publication PNW 453 (Corvallis, Ore.: Oregon State University Extension Service, 1993); C. O'Neill and E. Sorenson, "Home Care of the Elderly: A Family Perspective," *Advances in Nursing Science* 13/4 (1991) 28–37; and E. M. Brody, "Parent Care as a Normative Family Stress," *Gerontologist* 25 (1985) 19–29.

[37] Ageism was a term coined by Robert Butler in the 1960s. The segment of the population most noted for discrimination against the elderly are the elderly themselves.

[38] Lueckenotte, *Gerontologic Nursing* 694.

[39] See J. Bell, "The Search for a Discourse on Aging: The Elderly on Television," *Gerontologist* 32/3 (1992) 305.

[40] T. R. Cole, "What Have We 'Made' of Aging?" *Journal of Gerontology* 50/6 (1995) 341–43.

[41] Shirley Zimmerman, *Family Policies and Family Well Being: The Role of Political Culture* (London: SAGE, 1992).

[42] See above, pp. 215–17 and n. 30.

[43] Steven H. Sandell and Howard M. Iams, "Caregiving and Future Social Security Benefits: A Reply to O'Grady-LeShane and Kingson," *Gerontologist* 36/6 (1996) 814.

[44] Daniel D. Chiras, *Environmental Science: Action for a Sustainable Future* (4th ed. Redwood City, Calif.: Benjamin/Cummings, 1994) 579.

[45] See above, p. 218.

[46] Ibid.

[47] See above, p. 221.

12

Symphonies of Nature: Creation and Re-creation

It is good to give thanks to the Lord
to sing praises to your name, O Most High
to declare your steadfast love in the morning,
and your faithfulness by night,
to the music of the lute and the harp
to the melody of the lyre.
For you, O Lord, have made me glad by your work;
at the works of your hands I sing for joy. (Ps 92:1-4)

T hroughout the centuries the magnificence of creation has inspired poets, prophets, musicians, singers, composers, and artists. Psalm 92:1-4 captures this sentiment. Here the psalmist is gladdened by God's work and cannot help but sing for joy. The first four verses of Psalm 92 set the tone for this chapter that looks at how creation has inspired later composers to give expression to their experience of the power of creation wherein lies the Spirit of the Divine.

In the creative phase of the aesthetic process the musician offers the totality of his or her being to the art object. Possibilities awaken with the first notes; a dialogue ensues between music and music maker. Each new sound suggests others. The composer explores these directions and potentialities, basing each decision—intuitively more often than not—in his or her own unique nature as a musician and person. While many prominent writers on music have addressed this interactive process, it is described most directly (and ingenuously) by jazz musician Sidney Bechet: "A musicianer (sic) . . . all sorts of things happen to him and he don't know what all it was till he gets it into the music. That's where you find out. You tell it to the music, and the music, it tells it to you."[1] Those composers, then, who have a profound awareness of, identification with, and sensitivity to the natural world are apt to write music that reflects these characteristics, and as Wilfrid Mellers writes, "perhaps this oneness in Nature is one of the few means whereby an artist may approach religious experience in a non-religious and materialistic society."[2]

The most obvious and basic evocation of nature through instrumental music is a type of imitation of the natural world's sounds. These programmatic pieces (or sections of pieces) describe—usually in spectacular fashion—specific natural places or events. At its most superficial this kind of music is merely a sort of sound effect; at its finest it is an effective, expressive, and well-crafted onomatopoeic composition, representative of some of the most popular selections in the orchestral repertoire. Even a piece such as Grofé's *Grand Canyon Suite,* however, usually is more demonstrative of the composer's acute ear and mastery of orchestration than of any particular internalization of the natural world. Another plane indeed is possible. When a composer profoundly perceives and identifies with the "sounds of creation," using and reshaping them as the raw materials of organic musical structures, then he or she literally becomes a re-creator. The nature sounds still remain identifiable as such but they transcend mere imitation or impression; they now become the basis of a new created order, the cosmos of the composition itself.

This chapter examines the music of four interrelated composers: Ludwig van Beethoven, the progenitor of symphonic re-creation; Gustav Mahler and Jean (Jan) Sibelius, who complemented each other by carrying Beethoven's symphonic innovations into the twentieth century; and Peter Maxwell Davies, who incorporates and blends the traditions of the other three into a unique, contemporary sensibility.

The wellspring for any discussion of nature music expressed through large-scale instrumental forms is Beethoven's Sixth Symphony, the "Pastoral," premiered in Vienna in 1808. While programmatic evocations of nature existed prior to this work they had largely a dramatic function (e.g., the storm scenes in so many French Baroque operas), or were imitative of human activity against a natural background (e.g.,

Vivaldi's *Four Seasons*). The formal structure for these pieces was grounded in thematic and tonal repetition and contrast; each movement expressed a single feeling, a state of "being." The classical symphony of Haydn, Mozart, and Beethoven, while still employing the basic aesthetic principles of repetition and contrast, adds to those aspects the crucial idea of development. It is not enough for themes to have contrasting characters and keys; they also must have the potential for evolution, for "becoming." Thus in his Sixth Symphony—which Beethoven specifically stated was not to be considered pictorially descriptive—the composer uses some "audible aspects of Nature"[3] as dynamic and growing thematic material. Beethoven takes these sounds and manipulates them as building blocks to generate a structure that is uniquely his. They take on a new life; he literally has used them for an act of re-creation.

Accounts of Beethoven's life invariably cite his passion for nature, his love of long walks in the Viennese woods, the musical inspiration that came to him in these surroundings. For this reason the title of the first movement of the "Pastoral," "Awakening of Joyful Feelings on Arrival in the Country," is most appropriate. This movement, along with the third ("Joyous Gathering of Country Folk") and fifth ("Shepherd's Song: Happy and Thankful Feelings after the Storm") are primarily expressive of human feelings *about* the natural world. However, the second and fourth movements ("By the Brook" and "Storm" respectively) are "in no way concerned with expressing human responses but with Nature itself. They show a landscape without figures."[4] And it is in these two movements that Beethoven explicitly employs "sounds of nature."

"By the Brook," with its Andante tempo marking, includes passages of extremely slow harmonic rhythm, a rate of chord changes that seems stretched as far as possible. It is difficult not to perceive the timelessness of the stream itself in such music. Toward the end of this movement Beethoven incorporates unequivocal sounds of nature, i.e., the readily identifiable songs of three kinds of birds, for which he often has been criticized. Do Beethoven's critics suppose him to have believed that nightingale, quail, and cuckoo would all sing together at a brookside? This is a reminder, in regular normal phrases, that themes such as we have heard in this movement have their counterparts in the only true non-human music nature possesses.[5]

It is in the "Storm" movement that Beethoven most effectively integrates nature sounds with his own compositional style. The music plainly depicts a storm, yet there is no sound that is purely imitative, that does not serve a structural purpose. Almost every passage bears a stylistic resemblance to one of Beethoven's non-programmatic, absolute works. Even the tympani, the *sine qua non* of a musical storm, are used in a way that is essentially the same as in any other of his symphonic movements. Beethoven does not imitate a tempest; he has created his own storm.

The expression of human feelings about the natural world and the portrayal of nature in and of itself are the two main facets of post-Beethoven orchestral, programmatic music dealing with Creation. By the late Romantic period two composers—Gustav Mahler and Jean Sibelius, in many ways antithetical in their approaches to and philosophies of composition—brought these aspects of the "Pastoral" Symphony to their final fruition, particularly in the symphonic form. Both were born in the 1860s, grew up against a backdrop of nature (Mahler in Bohemia, Sibelius in Finland), and were musically trained in a similar Germanic tradition. Their first significant symphonic efforts date from the late 1800s. In 1907 the two met and discussed their views of the symphony; by this time Sibelius was established as a national figure in Finland and Mahler was one of the most eminent conductors of the day (who also happened to write enormous, often puzzling symphonies). For Mahler "the symphony must be like the world—it must be all-embracing."[6] Sibelius argued, however, "that a symphony must be distinguished, rather, by its style and severity of form and by the profound logic that creates an inner connection between its various motifs."[7] Much of Mahler's music (the First and Third Symphonies in particular) addresses the Beethoven ideal of expressing human feelings about nature; and even if Sibelius had written no other nature music his final major work—*Tapiola*—is the paramount presentation of Nature alone.

The seeds of Mahler's subsequent development as a composer of the natural world are apparent in the very opening of his First Symphony (premiered in 1889). The phrase *"Wie ein Naturlaut"* (Like a sound of Nature) appears over the opening measure. The first sound is that of hushed, multi-octave A's (that most elemental of orchestral pitches), over which fragments of themes drift. Then comes the sound of the cuckoo—a cuckoo whose call consists not of the falling third of the real bird, but of a descending fourth. Yet the evocation—because of timbre, rhythm, and melodic direction—is unmistakable; it has become *Mahler's* cuckoo. This sound not only encapsulates the nature-world of this movement but also becomes the building block for much subsequent thematic material. Indeed, themes built on the falling fourth became one of Mahler's most characteristic compositional devices throughout his career. Mahler himself wrote of this movement: "That Nature embraces everything that is at once awesome, magnificent, and lovable, nobody seems to grasp. Nobody seems to think of the mighty underlying mystery . . . and just that mystery is the meaning of my phrase '*Wie ein Naturlaut.*'"[8] For Mahler "any collection of natural sounds could furnish him with a starting point. But such things never remained themselves alone. It was humanity and human reactions with which he was concerned. . . ."[9] Mahler, then, calls upon an audible natural event, re-creates it in his own manner, and uses it as a fundamental building block not only for the "sound of nature" first movement of this First Symphony but also for the dance-like second movement, the ironic funeral march of the third, and the inferno-to-paradise finale. His symphony truly is a continuation of Beethoven's musical-natural world.

Mahler, as a product of the nineteenth century, lived in a time that saw—and often fabricated—a programmatic element for virtually every piece of music, even if not intended as such by the composer. Mahler cautioned against reading programs into his music and in his later career rejected those he himself had suggested for some of his earlier pieces. He believed that each listener should discover for himself or herself what was to be experienced in a given work. "But even with that, in the end, the tense, emotional Mahler was too much the romantic to create a whole new palette of orchestral colors and then not paint pictures with them."[10] No work of Mahler's gives better evidence of this than his Third Symphony of 1896, the largest and most encompassing of all nature pieces.

Mahler, like Beethoven, was often at his happiest in natural surroundings. His favorite summer vacation spot (where he did most of his composing in a specially-built lakeside cottage) was at Steinbach-am-Attersee, about thirty miles from Salzburg. In July 1896 Mahler wrote to conductor Bruno Walter, "No use looking up there [at the mountains surrounding Steinbach-am-Attersee]. That's all been composed by me!"[11] That same month Mahler wrote to the soprano Anna Bahr-Mildenburg:

> Now, imagine a work of such scope that the whole world actually is reflected in it—one becomes, so to speak, only an instrument upon which the universe plays. . . . My Symphony will be something that the world

has never heard before! In this score, all nature speaks and tells such deep secrets as one may intuit in a dream![12]

In August 1896 Mahler sent these titles for the new symphony and its movements to Max Marschalk, a Berlin music critic:

A Summer Noon's Dream
  First Section:
      I. Introduction: The awakening of Pan; Summer marches in
         (procession of Bacchus).
  Second Section:
      II. What the flowers of the meadow tell me.
      III. What the animals in the forest tell me.
      IV. What man tells me.
      V. What the angels tell me.
      VI. What love tells me.[13]

When Mahler conducted the 1902 premiere of the symphony he had these titles printed in the program and promptly rued it. Shortly after this premiere he wrote to another conductor:

> Those titles I originally intended for non-musicians as a point of reference and a guide to the thought, or rather, mood-content of individual movements, of movement to movement and to the whole. . . . These titles . . . will certainly tell you something *after* you have become acquainted with the score. From them, you can gain some suggestion of how I imagined the constantly increasing articulation of feeling, from the brooding, elementary forces of nature, to the tender creations of the human heart, which in turn reach out beyond themselves, pointing the way to God.[14]

The Third Symphony is an enormous work, befitting its subject matter: the first movement alone is longer than Beethoven's Fifth and the finale is one of Mahler's most expansive and sublime adagios. The titles of the individual movements may or may not be helpful to the individual listener. What is most significant about the work's program is that Mahler carries Beethoven's emotions about nature to their ultimate end, the composer's explicit expression of feelings about all Creation.

Unlike Mahler, Sibelius indicated very few programmatic references for any of his symphonies, yet his music is consistently cited as evoking a sweeping Nordic atmosphere. One reason for this, as conductor Sir Simon Rattle suggests, may be that Sibelius's melodic structures reflect Finnish speech rhythms. Another possibility is the nature of his bass lines, which may be likened to the world turning on its axis: slow-moving, yet inevitable and unstoppable.

It is through his orchestral tone poems that Sibelius distinctly invokes nature; in *Tapiola* (1925) he composed what "is surely one of the most terrifying pieces of music ever written."[15] As a preface to the score Sibelius wrote this quatrain:

> Wide-spread they stand, the Northland's dusky forests,
> Ancient, mysterious, brooding, savage dreams;
> Within them dwells the Forest's mighty God,
> And wood-sprites in the gloom weave magic secrets.[16]

Tapiola may be the ultimate example of a musical expression of nature itself. Unlike Beethoven's and Mahler's incorporation of nature sounds into the essentially developmental form of the symphony, *Tapiola* is monothematic and has virtually one tonic throughout. The entire piece grows from the opening measures; any likely thematic contrast derives from this motif rather than from any truly differing material. Even more marked is the tonality of the work, which is relentlessly in B minor. *Tapiola* is not a symphony's music of "becoming," but rather music of "being." The essentially eternal, unchanging presence of nature is expressed.

> Sibelius, as he communes with Nature, goes further in self-obliteration. . . .
> The search for oneness could hardly be carried further, for here the entire
> structure is monothematic, proliferating from a single seed. *Tapiola* is the
> *ne plus ultra* of Sibelian technique; and in it the human personality seems
> to dissolve away in Nature's infinities of time and space.[17]

As with Beethoven's storm and Mahler's cuckoo the tempest music of *Tapiola*, while readily identifiable as such, is constructed of materials and techniques that are uniquely Sibelian. Whereas in Beethoven's "Pastoral" the storm grows from the dance of the peasants' merrymaking and leads clearly to a hymn of thanksgiving, Sibelius's simply *is*. It is one aspect of an eternal presence; it is the nature of Nature itself. The final chords are not the closing notes of a human paean but Nature—untouched and unpopulated by humanity—simply presenting us with another of its boundless facets.

Sibelius, a native of a largely non-industrial society, applied his mastery of musical logic to the aesthetic expression of a truly impersonal Nature. Mahler, the cosmopolitan conductor, drew on every musical resource available to him to voice the totality of human response to the natural world. Mahler died in 1911; Sibelius ceased his compositional activity in the late 1920s, even though he lived until 1957. In the present day another composer, Sir Peter Maxwell Davies (b. 1934), has continued and drawn together these two nature-music traditions. Significantly, Beethoven, Sibelius, and Mahler have often been cited as direct influences on Davies' compositional style, particularly in regard to his symphonies.

The most immediate influence of the natural world on Davies' music has been the Orkney Islands where he makes his home. The sea in particular is a ubiquitous presence in this windswept, remote place. Davies' first two symphonies especially "are permeated by the haunting landscape and seascape of Orkney."[18]

Much of Davies' early music consists of chamber pieces, often characterized by theatrical features and/or a singular use of medieval and Renaissance materials and techniques. While he continues to incorporate such elements into his music the 1976 First Symphony took him in a new direction, inaugurating a series of works in that form that is as notable as any written in this century. He has "reinvented the symphony in a way that gives it new meaning and continued relevance late in the twentieth century. His Symphony No. 1 takes on board both the Beethoven model and Sibelius' filtering of it."[19]

About his first symphony Davies writes, "The symphony . . . grew into the first extended orchestral work where the music was permeated by the presence of the sea and the landscape of this isolated place off the north coast of Scotland."[20] The slow third movement in particular "becomes another evocation of the extraordinary, almost unearthly, treeless winter land-and-seascape of the Orkney Islands where I live. But it is not merely descriptive or atmospheric. . . ."[21] As Mahler used the sound of the cuckoo in his First Symphony as a structural device, Davies also extracts the sounds of sea and landscape to build his very complex structures. A unique point of Davies' Symphony is that an unusually large percussion section consisting exclusively of tuned instruments is often called upon to generate the nature sounds.

In his Second Symphony (1980) Davies wrote what might be the definitive "sea" symphony, one in which the source of inspiration and the musical materials are inseparable. The composer writes:

> At the foot of the cliff before my window, the Atlantic and The North Sea meet, with all the complex interweaving of currents and wave shapes,

and the conflicts of weather, that such an encounter implies. Symphony No. 2 is not only a direct response to the sounds of the ocean's extreme proximity, subtly permeating all of one's existence . . . but also a more considered response to the architecture of its forms.[22]

Davies observed two particular wave types, "that where the wave-shape moves though the sea, while the water remains (basically) static . . . and that where the wave-shape is static and constant, while the water moves through it."[23] He saw musical potentialities in these two phenomena and eventually generated materials and techniques from them that pervade the work. Some phrases have wave-like contours; one of the elements of form, melody, or rhythm may remain static while the others change. Davies in his Second Symphony has gone beyond use of natural sounds; he has captured the essence of a natural event in original melodic and rhythmic figures and uses them to create a new sound-world of *Davies'* cliffs, ocean, and waves.

CONCLUSION AND THEOLOGICAL REFLECTION

The four composers discussed in this chapter provide landmarks for the symphonic response to nature: Beethoven established the patterns, Mahler and Sibelius refined and expanded them, and Davies synthesized them, revitalizing both aesthetic content and formal structure. In every case, though, the ultimate consequence of their music lies not in sound sources or structure but in the true and unfeigned sensitivity it expresses. Aesthetician Bennett Reimer writes, "Creating art, and experiencing art, do precisely and exactly for feeling what writing and reading do for reasoning."[24] Furthermore, if art exists when the perceiver finds himself or herself reflected in the art object then creating art and experiencing art *about the natural world* do precisely and exactly for feeling what writing and reading do for reasoning *about Nature*.

The implications of this idea are far-reaching and provocative. For example, as our present-day world becomes less and less like that of Beethoven is it imaginable that at some point his nature sounds will be perceived as nostalgic expressions of entities that exist no longer? If great forests dwindle or disappear will the expressive power of Sibelius's *Tapiola* be changed permanently, in fact diminished as well? If one considers only the extra-musical associations of these pieces, these developments are quite possible.

If, however, we accept the idea that in some works of composers such as Beethoven, Mahler, Sibelius, and Maxwell Davies the sounds of nature have fresh significance as they become building blocks of new created orders the aesthetic life of the music remains intact. Indeed, through the organic formation and unity of musical materials these pieces offer expressive insights into the character and power of creation itself, and at their most profound they conceivably provide a glance into the spirit of the ultimate source of all creation.

Finally, music as an artistic form of expression is in itself a unique and powerful form of communication. Aaron Copland writes, "The power of music to move us is something quite special as an artistic phenomenon."[25] Over the years aestheticians have debated the power and meaning in music as a communicative medium. Some hold that the meaning of music is in the music itself. Others argue that music is a "symbolic language." Copland states, "music is a language without a dictionary whose symbols are interpreted by the listener according to some unwritten *esperanto* of the emotions."[26] This suggests that the power of music lies in its ability to communicate to us at the level of emotion and imagination. When applied to the "Symphonies of Nature," emotion and imagination are involved in a twofold manner. First there is the composer who, inspired by the sounds of creation, is moved imaginatively to reinterpret or re-create what has been heard through symphonic composition. The composer may also use the musical score to express his or her experience and feelings about the natural world. The author of this chapter declares that "When a composer profoundly perceives and identifies with the 'sounds of creation,' using and reshaping them as raw materials of organic musical structures, then he or she literally becomes a re-creator."[27] The symphonic re-creation then becomes available to the listener's imagination, which is free to be transported into new realms of meaning and perception. Here—to use Copland's language—"the imagination must take fire," inviting the listener to experience and "distinguish subtle nuances of feeling."[28] Thus the nature symphony becomes a unique form of communication wherein creation and re-creation constitute the message and evoke the possibility of disclosing a sacramental universe.

When we consider nature symphonies there are deeper possibilities, possibilities with a theological dimension. Joseph Gelineau suggests this when he writes that "Music as art would not have such a wide range of connotations nor such a strong capacity to stimulate if it was not rooted in the totality of the cosmos and the human body, if it was not allied so closely to the mind and to the Spirit."[29] Gelineau argues that "sound —voice or music—constitutes a sacred link with the transcendent being."[30] Nature symphonies contain this possibility. A good example, according to this chapter, is the work of Gustav Mahler, especially his Third Symphony, which he speculatively entitled "A Summer Noon's Dream." The author quotes Mahler's reflection on this work: ". . . I imagined the constantly increasing articulation of feeling, from the brooding, elementary forces of nature, to the tender creations of the human heart, which in turn reach out beyond themselves, pointing the way to God."[31] Aaron Copland is also aware of the spiritual possibilities of music when he writes that "a masterwork awakens in us reactions of a spiritual order that already exists in us, only waiting to be aroused."[32]

Taken from a theological point of view the symphonies of nature can be a powerful communicative medium, a symbolic language, and even a sacramental experience through which the sacred is encountered in creation and in its artistic re-creation. It is true that humans have the capacity to encounter creation *in itself* as sacramental. But it is also true that cultural re-creations of the natural world can be sacramental. As wheat and grapes, through the cultural "work of human hands," become the sacramental sign and symbol for sacred presence, so does the composer's work of human hands and heart become a potential sacramental re-creation of Creation. In this way the symphonies of nature "offer expressive insights into the character and power of creation itself, and at their most profound they conceivably provide a glance into the spirit of the ultimate source of all creation."[33]

NOTES: CHAPTER 12

[1] Bennett Reimer, *A Philosophy of Music Education* (Englewood Cliffs, N.J.: Prentice Hall, 1989) 60.

[2] Wilfrid H. Mellers, *Romanticism and the Twentieth Century.* Man and His Music: The Story of Musical Experience in the West 4 (New York: Schocken, 1969) 130.

[3] Basil Lam, "Ludwig van Beethoven (1770–1827)," in Robert Simpson, ed., *The Symphony 1: Haydn to Dvorak* (Baltimore: Penguin, 1969) 135.

[4] Ibid. 138.

[5] Ibid. 139.

[6] Bettina Fellinger, liner notes for Jean Sibelius, *Symphonies No. 2 and No. 7,* Eugene Ormandy conducting the Philadelphia Orchestra. Sony CD SBK 53509, 1994.

[7] Ibid.

[8] Helen H. Less, liner notes for Gustav Mahler, *Symphony No. 1*, Jascha Horenstein conducting the Vienna Symphony Orchestra. Vox Legends CDX2 5508, 1992.

[9] Harold Truscott, "Gustav Mahler (1860–1911)," in Robert Simpson, ed., *The Symphony 2: Elgar to the Present Day* 2/11 (Baltimore: Penguin, 1967) 30.

[10] Grant Michael Menzies, "Composer as Lord of Creation—Mahler's Third Symphony," *Sforzando* 2/11 (November 1997) 18.

[11] Michael Kennedy, Łiner notes for Gustav Mahler, *Symphony No. 3,* Sir John Barbirolli conducting the Halle Orchestra. BBC Legends CD BBCL 4004–7, 1998.

[12] Edward Downes, *The New York Philharmonic Guide to the Symphony* (New York: Walker and Company, 1976) 535–36.

[13] Ibid. 536.

[14] Ibid.

[15] Mellers, *Romanticism* 128.

[16] Jean Sibelius, *Tapiola, Symphonic Poem for Orchestra, Op. 112* (Wiesbaden: Breitkopf and Härtel, 1985).

[17] Mellers, *Romanticism* 129.

[18] Stephen Pruslin, liner notes for Peter Maxwell Davies, *Trumpet Concerto and Symphony No. 4,* Sir Peter Maxwell Davies conducting the Scottish National Orchestra and Scottish Chamber Orchestra. Collins Classics CD 11812, 1991.

[19] Stephen Pruslin, liner notes for Peter Maxwell Davies, *Symphony No. 5, Chat Moss, Cross Lane Fair, and Five Klee Pictures,* Sir Peter Maxwell Davies conducting the Philharmonia Orchestra and BBC Philharmonic. Collins Classics CD 14602, 1995.

[20] Peter Maxwell Davies, liner notes for idem, *Symphony No. 1,* Sir Peter Maxwell Davies conducting the BBC Philharmonic. Collins Classics CD 14352, 1995.

[21] Peter Maxwell Davies, "Symphony," in *Peter Maxwell Davies: Studies from Two Decades,* selected and introduced by Stephen Pruslin (London: Boosey and Hawkes, 1979) 94.

[22] Peter Maxwell Davies, liner notes for idem, *Symphony No. 2,* Sir Peter Maxwell Davies conducting the BBC Philharmonic. Collins Classics CD 14032, 1994.

[23] Ibid.

[24] Reimer, *A Philosophy of Music Education* 33.

[25] Aaron Copland, *Music and Imagination* (Cambridge, Mass.: Harvard University Press, 1952) 9.

[26] Ibid. 12.

[27] See above, p. 228.

[28] Copland, *Music and Imagination* 14–15.

[29] Joseph Gelineau, "The Path of Music," in Mary Collins, David Power, and Mellonee Burnim, eds., *Music and the Experience of God* (Edinburgh: T & T Clark, 1989) 136.

[30] Ibid. 137.

[31] See above, p. 232.

[32] *Music and Imagination* 17.

[33] See above, p. 236.

13

A Sense of Place

"While I was on my way and approaching Damascus, about noon a great light from heaven suddenly shone around me. I fell to the ground and heard a voice saying to me, 'Saul, Saul, why are you persecuting me?' I answered, 'Who are you, Lord?' Then he said to me, 'I am Jesus of Nazareth whom you are persecuting.' Now those who were with me saw the light but did not hear the voice of the one who was speaking to me. I asked, 'What am I to do, Lord?' The Lord said to me, 'Get up and go to Damascus; there you will be told everything that has been assigned to you to do.' Since I could not see because of the brightness of the light, those who were with me took my hand and led me to Damascus." (Acts 22:6-11)

*A*s part of a defense speech to the crowd (Acts 22:1-21) Paul tells the story of the conversion experience that changed his whole life, and then he retells the story as he defends himself before King Agrippa (26:1-18). Storytelling is at the heart of the biblical tradition whether it be stories told about Jesus on the road to Emmaus or autobiographical stories like Paul's (see also 2 Cor 11:16-33). Stories have a way of connecting storyteller and listener to places, experiences, and memories. They have the potential to unite one's heart to another's. Different in focus from Chapter One, "Stories from the Heart," this chapter is both autobiographical and narrative as it recaptures places, experiences, and memories and then joins them together to create an alluring, profound, and challenging message of hope. The story begins:

In *Habits of the Heart* Robert Bellah and his co-authors speak of a wisdom-seeking community as a "community of memory," one that does not forget its past. Such a community will tell stories of achievements and stories of shared suffering, including dangerous memories of suffering inflicted, memories that call a community to alter ancient evils. Others have written about "a sense of place" and have suggested that a major sign of our times is a widely felt sense of displacement, up-rootedness, and movement at a frenetic pace.[1]

Perhaps people affected by the pace of today's globalizing economy and information highway are among those who hunger for a more intimate sense of place. At times they may intuit that a place can hold an intensity of meaning. This chapter explores how communities of memory and a sense of place emerge in narrative. As family stories of relations across generations are recounted, such narratives may begin to evoke memories of ties to the land, rivers, particular places. Contemplating particular geography may inspire, in turn, a capacity to recollect the communities that have shaped human character.

A place can unlock memories even as conscious memories deepen our sense of place. Together they form repositories of wisdom to be plumbed through stories. These stories, when honest, serve to guide participants in striving to live into justice understood in the biblical sense as a call to restore right relationship with God, each other, and all of creation. How can one possibly respond to a call to live in right relationship with *all* of creation or *every* human being? Justice is better understood not as a rigid and abstract principle, like a giant anvil dropped into the flower garden of our fragile lives, but rather as a call heard sometimes faintly and now and then poignantly as real stories are shared and collective narratives of sin and grace are encountered. Justice, in this view, is intrinsically relational and invites a turn to stories in order that we may recognize creaturely relations with particular creation—not "all of creation" in the abstract.[2]

Humans live, however, in a globalizing culture and a time heavily invested in patterns of distraction, bent on not remembering repositories of wisdom and not finding an intensity of meaning in particular places even though geography may be laden with lessons that could help restore our sense of roots. The musical mantra of the global economy seems at times hooked on "don't stop thinkin' about tomorrow, don't stop, it'll soon be here." Some of the pressures thwarting our sensitivity to communities and places of memory deserve much more attention than allowable, given the particular path chosen for the present inquiry. Many of these pressure points deal with the global economy and an overwhelming tendency to redefine too much of our lives and ecosystems by a narrow calculus of utility.[3]

If people wish to be effective in responding to the global phenomena of displacement and uprooting in these times, who can afford to neglect the potential insights drawn from particular communities and places of memory? These are personal stories, though not fully private, and many are latent with public relational wisdom to help guide the formation of an alternative calculus: practical reason, much closer to an Aristotelian understanding of the habits of character than to the utilitarian reductionism that has decimated both land and memory. What would happen if we turned to our stories not as individualistic or psychological autobiographies but rather as wellsprings of social and ecological memory vital to the development of ethical imagination and vision?[4]

My own story involves several generations and family connections to work and land. When I recall how our family moved, or visit the places we lived and see all the signs of speculative development, it is a sense of place that wells up in me. A good way to evoke the significance of a place is to enter into the very communities of memory that have shaped our character. In so doing we may discover that certain places are at the very heart of those communities, so that we come to recognize communities of memory as intrinsically ecological, geological, and even cosmological. The most intimate of places in our memory can become gateways to stories far richer than any memoir. An attenuated sense of place must have something to do with the crude rape of the land and other habits that pave over or dam up the flow of natural systems and intergenerational memories. Such pressures will not be dealt with if stories remain individualistic. This exercise in narrative social ethics is also an invitation to readers to do likewise and thereby discover the relational power of their stories when shared in real conversation.[5]

This is one story, told from a conversation-fed contemplative perspective about people and places and how our family and friends have related to each other, to work, and to the land.

Perhaps the best way to develop a sense of place is simply to practice it in a particular spot, say a garden or an orchard, and to relate to others what one experiences in communion with such a place. In a way this is what happens when one spends time genuinely trying to cultivate the "garden" of family memories and places. If one spends lots of honest time in both the physical and metaphorical garden she just might discover that her own story shares the same soil with the stories of many other human beings and other creatures. After a while she might begin to let a place or two co-narrate, in a sense. The idea here is that a place may be full of memories and voices one did not previously recognize, unaware that they were shaping her own voice and giving form to the very language of her soul. In such a story, as we see later on in this chapter, seeds one never planted may grow.

The very telling of the story invites the emergence of meanings heretofore unimagined. When places and communities of memory evoke each other it is possible to receive gifts running deep and far, like a river fed by an underground spring flowing with the story and its resident creatures. As I participate—never truly as an isolated self—in the telling of a family story of human relations across generations I remember the land, rivers, and particular places in Oregon and in the *Frommherz* (German spelling) ancestral land of Germany.[6] As I contemplate and literally revisit special places, Yachats on the Oregon Coast, Mother's grave, our berry farm near Silverton and the dairy farm south of Tillamook, my home in Mount Angel and the Shalom Center there, Corvallis (literally, "heart of the valley" on the Willamette River), and Kiger Island where my father began, and our roots in the Black Forest that has been affected by sylvan ecological degradation, these places in turn enhance my capacity to recollect the complex communities of memory that have shaped character and would call us to alter certain habits.[7] Biblical stories of uprootedness, exile, and covenantal calls to fidelity, along with so many epic struggles of whole peoples found in the human part of the grand story of the universe have much more immediacy to offer when read in light of the relational story known in the marrow of our bones. The same must be said of our unfolding efforts to shape social power and the political economy toward a culture of respect and away from economic and political models that spew topdown cover stories of collective self-deception. Scientific stories of ecological, geological, and cosmological time and space can also be glimpsed in a new and, paradoxically, intimate light. Who can know for sure where a story may lead? We can try to tell it with an ear for relational justice.[8] It is in this spirit that the following story is told.

PLACES AND COMMUNITIES OF MEMORY

The maroon AMC pacer wagon pulled up. Shalom Center, on the grounds of Queen of Angels Monastery, Mount Angel, Oregon, spring

1985, served as a sort of human sanctuary for some troubled hearts. Her new husband got out of the car. It was time to say goodbye to my very young sons, Chris and Nick, neither old enough to be in elementary school yet about to experience uprooting from their native Oregon home.

I watched as our family car headed down the road from Shalom. Her new husband drove, she sat in the front passenger seat and in the back, still in the child car seats we had purchased a few years earlier around the time Mount St. Helens erupted, were my sons I had just hugged. Chris, born in October of 1979, was five. Nick, born in June of 1981, was not yet four.

Tears swept over Shalom in a way I never could have imagined. So much seemed out of control. A figurative bulldozer had just ripped into the Mount Angel ground of our home at 250 South Cleveland. Things were not going according to plan. My reflections on a sense of place have been influenced by this drama. On one side of a chasm I stood and looked with longing. On the other side were my sons, first in Colorado and then later in upstate New York. But beneath all the turmoil there was a sense of place that somehow remained, though I was in no condition to articulate it at the time.

I was not the only person with some sense of place. My wife had asked for the divorce and she was not a native of Oregon. Colorado had been her home growing up and upstate New York was where many members of her family were living in those years and since. I thought long and hard about moving across the country to be close geographically to my sons year round. I knew that it was so important for them to have the experience of being with their mother. I could have moved to Colorado that first year after the divorce but decided that it would be unwise to cut Oregon ties. Married at twenty-three, both of us were finding our identities during those early years. To be sure, I was a difficult person to live with on many occasions because I struggled sometimes in long bouts of depression, searching for clear calling and purpose in life. Somehow I had enough sense to know that my roots in Oregon were a vital part of a developing character.

I did love being a father. We were close, which made the geographical distance looming ahead seem unthinkable to one who loved to play "high in the sky," tell them stories, or pull his sons around Mount Angel in our Red Flyer wagon whenever rainy western Oregon saw fit to relent. Our divorce arrangement and my semi-articulate sense of place meant that I would not see my sons from late August until Thanksgiving or Christmas each year, and then again not until the summer, although their mother and I did work things out because of their winter break from school so that my sons and I could spend a week together most Februaries. It seemed a good idea to sustain the roots. If I moved to Colorado and then later on to New York I would have been following my former wife to whatever places she chose. What would become of my own sense of vocation and place? Would these be eclipsed by a pattern of following another's odyssey? My mind did not yet know what my heart and place were trying to say, but the roots were beginning to find a voice and I would have to listen.

I wanted my sons always to have some sense of roots in Oregon even as I knew that they would develop their own sensitivities to places in the course of their developing stories. In their case the odyssey of movement and uprooting would offer its own unique insights, enriching the larger story along the way. They have taught their father much about tenacity and resilience. Yet it was here in this part of the country that their lives began. In Mount Angel they learned to crawl, walk, tumble, thump down the stairs with laced blankets in hand, enjoy our home-built playhouse, help plant the family garden, and eat from the two blueberry bushes we had planted side by side to symbolize them.

SHADES OF PLACED MEANING

For many of us linked to virtual reality, a sense of place may be something wished for when venturing outside after a day in the office of phones, faxes, e-mails and web "sites" only to find that we cannot remember where we parked the car. A place can be a particular portion of space, a spot set apart or used for a ritual purpose: a place of worship, for example. Place can also be understood as a position of power, a function or duty, a social rank. Words associated with the notion of place include hive, resort, moorage, paradise, portage, hideout, Erebus (a mythological place of darkness under the Earth), Elysium (place of great delight), and the no-place called utopia. There are notions such as the *locus classicus* cited to illustrate or explain a subject, or place as a repository for safekeeping, or a sanctuary to provide refuge and safety. Meanings include places of repose and bedlam, and in the language of law place may be a venue where a trial is held. So manifold are the shades of meaning that it seems we are not likely to be faced with a metaphorical cul-de-sac—yet another meaning of place, one with only one outlet. And it is not too difficult to imagine the rich variety of expressions shaped by the term, such as "between a rock and a hard place" or "your place or mine?" or "a place at the table" or *déjà vu*, the sense that we have been in this place before. Any serious reflection on a sense of place has to acknowledge an amusing paradox. To study this idea honestly demands remembering that the horizon of its potential meanings will not yield to any definitional empire one attempts to build or govern.

To want a bond with a particular place is to long for a meaning-laden place, a world charged with the grandeur of God where there still "lives the dearest freshness deep down things," as Gerard Manley Hopkins wrote, or one that gives intimate meaning to our very lives and serves as an ecological confessional where we go to seek reconciliation and penance for human habits of degradation.[9]

Human beings yearn for roots, as the young Simone Weil wrote so passionately in *The Need for Roots*.[10] We long for the lived experience of justice understood as the call to right relationship. In all of its vitality a place can lend meaning to us even as we assign it sacred meaning as a source of revelation. A place of natural beauty can be a revelation of our call to right relations with creator, creatures, creation, when like a psalmist we lie down in green pastures. A place that has suffered severe ecological degradation, often simultaneously a site of labor injustice and sometimes a battlefield, may speak poignant and disturbing revelations of our human capacity to smother a sense of relational justice. Think of the open devastation wrought in Butte, Montana, by mining, or Pennsylvania farms actually collapsing into old underground mines. Think only of war-drenched places and times: Hiroshima, Tokyo, Dresden, indigenous communities in the Americas five hundred years ago and since, Carthage, Rome, and other ancient and not so ancient places described in sacred texts and memorials across the ages.

Zones of ecological degradation are no less numerous. How is a sense of place related to the ecological notion of habitat? Over half the tidal swamp and marsh area of the Pacific Northwest's Columbia River estuary has been lost to dredging, filling, diking, and channeling since the 1880s. The tidal swamp and marsh are habitats that ought to stretch our recognition that not all lovely places are meant for human residence, yet they can be "homes" for our development of ecological memory. The estuary was long defined according to an acutely utilitarian notion of place, and it is this pattern of suffering inflicted that a genuine community of memory will acknowledge and alter.[11]

When we think of a place, do we tend to associate it with the stationary, a firm rock such as Gibraltar or some other image of rootedness and stability? Would our patterns of relating come closer to ecological wisdom if we viewed a place as simultaneously stable and fluid, a field of both Benedictine-like stability and narrative energy?[12] A natural epic, the great Columbia is a living story deeply carved into a particular region, yet fluid and moving. Stand with all your senses alert along its banks and you may come to know that this is only one placed point of view experienced in just one timed point in history. Ushered in by the river as co-narrator, a sense of place could open the imagination and any degree of scientific awareness to the many creatures—including human beings—who may have stood at different times in that one place. What meanings might they have assigned to a moving river? Next imagine with any degree of historical and geological knowledge all the other placed points of view and timed perspectives along the banks, even before there were banks at all, shaping this twelve-hundred-mile watery epic.[13] Along great rivers one is embraced by an intensity of meaning that can also arise from contemplative encounters with other more humble places, such as one's backyard in an urban setting or that as-yet-undeveloped farm field spotted along a so-called freeway taking us nowhere fast. Still, the great panoply of "assigners of meaning" that have graced the shores of the Columbia might add questions about meanings found and they may ask about those creatures who have lived in its dark depths. James Michener once tried to envision the meaning of place through the eyes of a migrating salmon.[14]

This is the sort of reflection that could stumble into humility and humus. To be low, close to the ground, not proud or arrogant, but unpretentious is to be in touch with humility. Humus is brown or black, a complex variable stemming from the partial decomposition of plant or animal matter, forming the organic portion of soil. We sometimes say someone is "down to earth." Now add humor to the mix. This word stems from a Latin root, *humere,* which means "to be moist or fluid." Normal functioning bodily semi-fluids or fluids served as the focus of early physiological meditation relating to the original meaning. Brought together the three notions could suggest a rather interesting sense of place—a fluid, down-to-earth rootedness.

To enter truly into the heart of a place and its significance in our time would seem to require a certain sense of humor understood not as the insidious mindlessness of sitcoms but instead as the capacity to bear up with fluidity under so many ludicrous and absurd signs of human disregard for Creator, creation, and creatures. In this way a sense of humor about our ways of faltering in relation to nature might help us recover a healthy humility and intellectual honesty. It is, in this regard, no doubt preposterous even to attempt to assign definitive meaning to the Columbia River by virtue of one point of view in one place and time. Woody Guthrie sang of the river: "Roll on, Columbia roll on; Roll on, Columbia roll on; Your power is turning our darkness to dawn; Roll on, Columbia roll on." And as he sang the dams went up, electricity grew cheap, and the river was never the same again. An assignment of meaning in one time and location may have implications unseen at the time, even though Guthrie's meaning celebrated an era of New Deal government investment, the Bonneville Power Administration, and many jobs and industries in the region. William Dietrich writes in *Northwest Passage: The Great Columbia River:*

> We have not just harnessed the Columbia, we have turned it into a body of water utterly different from its natural state, and in doing so have deliberately thrown the entire Northwest ecosystem out of whack. None of that got much debate when it was happening—Guthrie's enthusiasm was typical—and there is little allusion to the costs of it now.[15]

Few assignments of meaning turn out to elicit either entirely pure or fully negative consequences, a point we, the ecologically passionate, would do well to remember. A sense of humor about the very notion of assigning meaning to a place hastens in a companion sense of pathos, opening us to awareness of the communities of memory that shape our relations to a place, or in this case a river. We are called to tell the stories of suffering inflicted on the river, its inhabitants, and its watersheds. Another image enters from another time and place, Gethsemani: ludicrous-looking apostles fast asleep in the midst of an imminent passion narrative while he wept in fluids and earth, agony in the garden.

If we are to speculate about God's contemplation of the matter we ought to remember our human proclivity to let a sense of place grow dormant or become a rationalization for territorial control. It will take humility for us even to begin to recover a sacramental understanding of the global commons—air, oceans, fish, grasslands, rain forests—or to square the intimacy of a particular place with a global appreciation of common places. What does it mean to call a place *our* home? What becomes of our sense of place when we use human construction metaphors to describe natural places, albeit with religious intent as in the case of calling a stand of forest a sacred cathedral? We must allow a little sense of humor about the human tendency to assign anthropocentric meanings.

Humility is a way to remember that we could allow a more honest sense of place to emerge in our consciousness through questions and passionate narratives instead of relying on lofty and abstract pronouncements. We ourselves and our better insights may be emerging from places. In a sense we can actually try to dwell truly *within* a place, as if we were back in the womb! By contrast, what happens when land is under the control of outside owners who rarely know the place (if at all), who have forgotten from where they come, who effectively rape *in absentia* the womb upon which we all depend for life, who view both places and labor as cheap and expendable?

On the other hand, it is quite possible to bring together business activity and a deep sense of place, especially when ecology is viewed as an indispensable framework for an enlightened approach to costs and benefits. We are sometimes tempted to over-romanticize the natural character of a place and thereby fail to develop a healthy economic sense—*oikonomia*—the root of the word *economy,* meaning "household management." The problem with utility is not usefulness itself but excess, as when private property becomes an excuse to treat ownership as a license to plunder. The land trust idea provides one way to begin to recover a sense of the commons and the common good. The land is deeded to a trust that then arranges for people to make use of appropriate parts of the land for dwelling and other ecologically sustainable purposes, but always with a recognition that the land is a community trust. Such an arrangement would actually give a community the deed to their ecological and historical communities of memory and hope.[16]

Both economy and ecology ought to have prominent roles in the emergence of memory. What are the aspects of a sense of place closest to the heart of the reader? Is place all about being at home, having a sense of roots? And what of the relation between work and a sense of place? What stories stand out in our own family histories of relations to work and land? How could a profound cross-generational shared awareness of a specific region, say for example the Pacific Northwest, shape our capacity to recognize acute signs of ecological degradation and economic injustice, patterns of distraction in ways of life and habits of destruction that prey not only on the soil but also on our community memories, threatening to disfigure real places and our knowledge of the past?

Communities of amnesia have no time for such questions. What are our deepest fears related to particular places? our deepest energies and inspirations? What kind of public power and negotiating courage are to be found in telling and retelling the stories of three or more generations going back together over ties to the land, standing with parents and grandparents on the ground of ancestral roots, recognizing not only each other in a new light (old light, really) but recognizing anew the geography that has in part shaped our character? Might we discover some patterns common to the historic pressures on families and the pressures on the natural environment where we have lived? Might we then take these prophetic voices to the tables where economic power brokers make decisions that too often lack the wisdom of democratic and ecological accountability? How does one put together the psalmist's call to "be still and know that I am God" and the prophetic rage of Amos asking that "justice roll down like water . . . and righteousness like an everflowing stream"?

One excellent example of this blend of ecological story and communities of memory is the Portland Organizing Project, church-based efforts to tell the stories of work and land over time and to bring these narratives to the negotiating tables with the power elite. Much of the work has been focused on economic justice, but recently the trend of Industrial Areas Foundation affiliates such as the Portland Organizing Project has been to weave together concerns for such things as affordable housing, living-wage jobs, and ecologically sustainable economic habits in response to local uprooting brought about by the globalized economy. The classic question shaping the Organizing Project's thousands of individual meetings and house meetings in recent years has been this: "What are the pressures on the family?" Gradually many are beginning to see the links between economic and ecological displacement. They are answering the question with the emerging capacity to recover a sense of confidence and public voice, and they are deepening their sense of the common need for sustainable roots. The stories are the heart of the process.[17]

Of course it would be presumptuous to assume that long years or generations in one place will of themselves breed affinity and deep ecological care. Long histories of closeness to a parcel of land could conceivably breed contempt or possessiveness. We cannot ignore historic examples of territorialism and fortifications so often associated with a certain claim of place tied to a people's identity, i.e., nationalism. Northern Ireland, the former Yugoslavia, or the great conflict in "the Holy Land" are only three examples of many bitter struggles over land and territory.

Ponder the profound communities of memory—that capacity to remember not only suffering endured but also suffering inflicted—bound up with historic battlefields such as Gettysburg. Are we beginning to recognize the wounds of battles we have waged with nature? Are we conscious of ecological Gettysburgs today such as Washington state's Hanford plutonium legacy and its Cold War repositories that threaten to leach war into the Columbia River? Who are the Lincolns able to incarnate those communities of memory in eloquence, the Lincolns reflecting on the battlefields of wars with creation?[18]

These thoughts of Gettysburg bring to mind questions relating our sense of place to our sense of finitude. Could we kindle a thoughtful awareness of place by asking ourselves and others, such as our loved ones including parents and children and grandparents, where we want our bodies to be placed when life comes to an end and how we hope to be placed there? One remembers that image, "bury my heart at Wounded Knee."[19] Can we relate to land, rivers, oceans as if our loved ones were buried there? living there? present, right there, in that place that comes to mind? Can we achieve a sacramental view? Could we envision any given place as home to our loved ones and develop a sensitivity to it that is bound up with our love for particular human beings?

What of refugees who for fear of threats to life and limb have fled their homelands? Let us ask them about their sense of place. Are we able to think also of non-human refugees who have had to flee their homeland habitats and face the threat of extinction?

What might it mean truly to feel at home in the universe, to have what Martin Buber called *Behausung* (habitation, to feel at home)? or the obverse, *Hauslosigkeit,* a feeling of being homeless or marooned in the universe?[20] homeless on the street in American cities? How do such questions and sensitivities affect our visceral and intellectual sense of place? A sense of place could engage our passionate solidarity with those who are poor, strangers, widows, orphans, aliens in the land. Are migrant farmworkers, always on the move, closer in some ways to the earth and a deep sense of place than some who hire them and many who reap the harvest of their labor?

Do place and purpose cohere, so that a sense of place strengthens one's sense of purpose or *telos* in life? How have early childhood tales of mythical terrain affected our adult understandings of places and their meanings? Songs and symphonies, operas and dramas, poems and prose often evoke lasting consciousness of place. One thinks of "America the Beautiful" and "spacious skies with amber waves of grain, purple mountain majesties above the fruited plains," or Beethoven's Pastoral Symphony, or Steinbeck's *Grapes of Wrath,* or Cervantes and the land of

La Mancha where I once traced some of the path Don Quixote may have journeyed. All lend shades of meaning.

Think, too, of someone like Chief Joseph with his Nez Perces (a name given them by French fur trappers; they called themselves "Nimi-Pi"), people who were forced off their ancestral land. Chief Joseph never gave up the hope of returning to his homeland. How does exile shape one's sense of place? The biblical authors pondered this question as well. Is it possible to put into words some inkling, too, of the "languages" spoken by the land, rivers, mountains when they too have been forced off their ancestral home, so to speak, reshaped by strip mining or massive dams and parking lots? It is through particular stories and places that we might see creation groaning with the pain of exile and death and the labored hope for return and rebirth.[21]

What would happen if we updated the Second Vatican Council's *Pastoral Constitution on the Church in the Modern World* so that the opening lines would embrace a wider understanding of relational justice? Compare: "The joys and hopes, the griefs and anxieties of all the people of this earth, especially those who are poor or in any way afflicted, these too are the joys and hopes, the griefs and anxieties of the followers of Christ. Indeed, nothing genuinely human fails to raise an echo in their hearts"[22] with a suggested update for the new millennium that permits us to imagine a rather fascinating Third Vatican Council of creatures: "The joys and hopes, the griefs and anxieties of this earth, especially all creatures who are poor or in anyway afflicted, these too are the joys and hopes, the griefs and anxieties of the followers of Christ. Indeed, nothing genuinely created fails to raise an echo in their hearts."

Place and pilgrimage may actually belong together. A deeper sense of place sometimes goes hand in hand with a sense of adventure and journey. Place invites paradox, as mystics say when they speak of "the cloud of unknowing" or "the palace of nowhere." Contemplatives have noted that human intelligence can only find rest in paradox, echoing Augustine's insight that our hearts would remain "restless until they rest in Thee." A certain restless quality, oddly enough, may be an essential feature of a growing consciousness of place. This restlessness would not be like the frenetic treadmill of a market culture. The *via negativa* of mystical unknowing and *kenosis* or self-emptying could be the threshold to a sense of place unknown to those who have not yet experienced even some moments of contemplative awareness.[23] A sense of the presence and absence of the divine and of place may be at the heart of a contemplative wisdom.

Failure to practice contemplation is the outcome of highly invested paradigms and habits of distraction that fuel certain economies of vast scale and consumption. The habits of consumption are not identical to the patterns of contemplative hospitality. What is the relationship between a sense of place and the practice of hospitality? What does it mean to be an inhabitant, a denizen? A denizen can be an alien who is admitted to the rights of citizenship by a hospitable people. This raises questions about the meaning of citizenship in ecological terms, in global terms. What does it mean for people across national borders to share a deep and abiding sense of place? Birds and other creatures that do not stop at border crossings might serve as mentors.

Perhaps this litany of questions pointing to the complexity of our subject matter can be mercifully concluded (for the moment) by simply saying that any specific sense of place at best reveals a glimpse into a great range of meanings. A drop of rain on a peach-colored rose petal in my backyard in the late afternoon shade of Mount Tabor in southeast Portland, Oregon, is a particular spot and moment within a specific dwelling place abundant with meaning, even as the range of places expands out to Vivaldi's rendering of the seasons, planet Earth viewed from Apollo 8, our solar system seen from the Hubble space telescope, or the planets of just one solar system of the great cosmos orchestrated in a splendid symphony by Gustav Holst.

Most, though clearly not all of these shades of meaning are brushed aside when a home is defined merely as a piece of real estate. This is why the stories that recollect our honest memories of communities and places remain crucial. Stories lead us on paths where we can recover repositories of wisdom. Stories, however, can also become cover stories of self-deception displacing our real stories. This happens, for example, when some too easily borrow language from remnant forests in western Oregon and call the hi-tech economy a "Silicon Forest" (now booming in Washington County west of Portland). Such language is an illusory attempt to retain some semblance of a sense of place through words and virtual language even as fewer groves of Douglas fir stand here and there, remnant ecological communities of memory. Pace itself threatens to leave behind both place and purpose. Globe-hurdling CEOs who have "home" addresses in gated "communities" come to mind. Often they have the best high-rise office view money can buy, yet one imagines they might feel rather "homeless" at times. Language affects our sense of place ever so profoundly, as do technology and the tendency to equate information access with wisdom, the equivalent of equating silicon chips with ancient forests.[24]

It is ill-advised to romanticize narratives as if somehow their likability and "down-home" feel will preclude falsehood and keep us on the path of truth-seeking. But when stories involve efforts of communities striving to become communities of memory, they can indeed bring profound awareness of our historic and current relations to Creator, creatures, and creation. A place, any place, has the potential to remind us of finitude and yet points to the infinite. In this regard we probably best understand who we are when we know where we are, as the Kentucky farmer and poet Wendell Berry has argued. "My subject is my place in the world, and I live in my place."[25] Yet, in the paradox illustrated by all these questions that only begin to suggest thousands more, our best understanding of who we are probably includes a strong sense of the limits of that very knowledge, just as our best grasp of where we are likely includes a recognition that we never really fully know where we have been, are, or will be. The fragility and limited nature of stories, when consciously recognized, shed valuable light on our placed and displaced communities of memory, offering wisdom for the journey and thick loamy soil for the toes.

PLACES AND COMMUNITIES OF DEEPER MEMORY

Yachats, a small town on the Oregon coast, serves as threshold to my memories of my mother and as powerful bond with my sons. She died bleeding internally while giving birth to my brother Louis when we were living on a small berry farm near Silverton, Oregon. She was only thirty-six, so Dad found himself with eight kids to raise alone, at least for several years before he remarried. A place such as Yachats would hold an intensity of meaning for me through all those years and would be a place I wanted my sons to know in their bones as well.

My mother's folks had a little home on ground just south of the Yachats River, probably better described as a large stream, at least at low tide. Their place perched next to a quiet road. Just beyond were rugged volcanic basalt rock formations, open books of geological time that once spilled into a waiting Pacific. The great ocean came right up over some of these rock formations and sometimes sent foamy signs of cavernous turbulence into the air and onto the ground of my grandparents' place. The Heceta Head lighthouse a few miles south blends into a memory I have of standing in front of their house and looking across to the north at high tide late one evening, seeing the lights of the town off in the distance on the other side of the beach that was now all covered with waves. Gramps and I watched the waves go by. It is always a grace to watch a wave from solid ground and see its mighty back as well as its countenance. When it is coming toward you only the face shows.

At low tide when I was a two- and three-year-old I would join my brother and sisters as we built the city of Portland in the sand, learning some hard lessons about the ephemeral nature of human construction. On one occasion I was digging sand alongside the banks of the Yachats when the bank gave way and the outgoing tide began to take me out to the mouth of the river and into the dubious mercy of a great Leviathan. Dad was there and paying attention.

Not far from the house of Gramps and Grandmother was what we kids knew rather simply as "the spout." At high tide, especially if a storm was brewing, it could become a liquid creature surging up into the sky and a reliable accomplice willing to be partially obstructed by one's very young body, pants soaked in the process. At low tide we kids often hiked down on the sand to enter the cave beneath and look up through the small hole in the rocks. As far back as I can remember we did this, and I gave the same experience years later to my young sons.

That spout holds an intensity of meaning and bonding for my sons and me, for it is a place shared by several generations of our family. The Pacific at Yachats could rise up with mighty power, waves rushing headlong among those caves and engulfing most of the basalt formations, a great natural force overwhelming those very places we had hiked during low tide and would hike again after the storms. Such proximity to the power and beauty of nature gave us kids, and my sons later, a sense of fragility. The place, Yachats, also brought us "over the river and through the woods, to grandmother's house we go . . . ," words we sang on every family trip as kids to a place on the edge of the firm and the fluid.[26]

The spout sang too, displaying energy, fleeting and returning beauty, evanescent loss and faithful renewal. Perhaps it had a sense of humor because it behaved like a very small finger of a mighty and dangerous ocean, reaching out to comfort and soak us. The Pacific was immense, transcending our grasp, but this particular place concentrated the imagination. One could look out over the great Pacific and watch the sun set, but often we simply looked down into the slight opening in the rocks and listened for the imminent surge swelling up from the cave below. We tried to keep eyes alert so we could pull back in time, leap across the rocks over the spot when the water danced, and so be baptized again and again. We needed the ritual. Only of late have I begun to wonder what we might have been doing to the rock surface in the midst of all our innocent glee. I do remember some encounters with rock shrimp and mussels that probably felt worse under our feet than our feet did when we made contact. The next sacrament that now comes to mind after baptism, appropriately enough, is ecological penance. At the time I thought it was all communions!

When they were not even old enough to be out of diapers and long before I had developed much ecological sensitivity I wanted my sons to know such places that carried so much history and adventure in the life of our family. We frequently visited Yachats. My grandparents had both died many years earlier and their place had been sold. The people who owned the place in those years, the early 1980s, let us pitch our little tent on the edge of the property. I showed my sons the wild strawberry plants and thick blades of cut grass I remembered from the 1950s. We propped pillows up near the tent entrance and watched, with care for our eyes, as a magnificent ball of light dropped into the ocean, each vying "I can still see it, I can still see it," again and again until two of us mercifully conceded and one could lay imperial claim to the final view before the dot disappeared into the night sea. A minuscule speck of light winked, turning the mind's eye to other lights painting the heavens above.

I can still see it. At the very same time that we were nurturing a bond with a place and community of memory my little family was being torn apart and both parents bore responsibility for a dissolution. So Yachats was becoming a place that could speak as few others could. It evoked images of resilience and continuity. It suggested the intensity of meanings we start to appreciate when a place itself becomes a participant in a community of memory and hope.

It was in the 1950s that Yachats provided a home for my mother's parents. This place bonded me with my grandparents and my mother. Gramps was an artist. Aloysius DeRyke loved the coast and often painted its beauty. He took me down to the caves, among the volcanic rocks, showed us children cut agates he would polish or green glass floats he collected. He often wore a fedora and not infrequently a cigar. His energy personified the great marine creature, the sea itself. Grandmother's gifts were especially in music. She had given this love to her four daughters. In the early years our home in Salem was filled with melodies and images of the "Waltz of the Flowers," "Galway Bay," and

"Ave Maria," as Mother shared with us the love her mother had given to her.

I returned to Yachats not long ago to spend a few hours there thinking about this chapter on a sense of place. A realtor had staked a For Sale sign on the property in a spot not far from where my sons and I once pitched that tent: a piece of real estate on the Oregon coast, with a great view and a small rectangular one story structure, priced at $180,000. The place, by market value, was worth no more than a few thousand dollars when my grandparents lived there. When it sells the new owners will almost certainly tear down the humble dwelling and replace it with a spacious investment. The pressures of speculative development and amnesia are bearing down on far too much of the Oregon edge of the sea.[27]

Why return to Yachats? I cannot afford to buy the place, although the thought has crossed my mind that it would be a wonderful candidate for a land trust by the Fromherz-DeRyke families. If only our DeRyke relations had not been largely scattered after Mother's death. I am troubled with the thought that the new owners will probably have paltry knowledge of the intense meaning this place holds for some. It is true, to be sure, that new residents could develop into participants in real communities of memory and place. I wonder whether my own family has yet arrived at that point of understanding. I find myself wondering about people and other creatures who form communities of memory that far transcend my family story.

The place of my earliest memories includes communities and stories about which I knew nothing as a child and have only begun to know as a middle-aged adult. A few years ago Joanne and Norman Kittel bought some headland acreage south of Yachats. From their place on a clear day they can see the curvature of the earth out across the ocean. They can also see the place I have been recollecting. Working with the Oregon State Park and Recreation Service, the Kittels have transformed part of their private property into a public path for the Oregon Coast Trail. This section of the trail running through their twenty-seven acres is linked up with a special geography of memory called "Amanda's Trail," which climbs up Cape Perpetua to its summit. Joanne wrote in a letter to me about their discoveries: "The name, Amanda, is in memory of a blind Coos woman, who was forced to march around the Cape barefoot, leaving a trail of blood."[28]

Newcomers to Oregon who have only recently made their home in Yachats, the Kittels wanted to deepen their understanding of the region and especially the history of how indigenous communities were treated by more recent immigrants. So Joanne and others looked at one particular time frame for initial insights, the period of the Alsea Sub-Agency (1859–1875), essentially a reservation that became a prison camp. Tribes in the larger coastal area included, among others, the Coos. It was on one of the occasions when soldiers and agents set out to recapture and bring back Indians to the reservation that Amanda was subjected to indignity marked for memory on the path. In the conclusion of "Early Yachats History: The Yachats Indians, Origins of the Yachats Name, and the Reservation Years," Kittel and Curtis write:

> The way Indian people related to the land was very different from whites. . . . Alsea Sub-Agency, like most reservations, was a brutal prison camp meant to destroy indigenous cultures as dictated under guidelines from the Bureau of Indian Affairs. A few of the agents were sympathetic. However, with no money, few and inferior supplies, and being denied their traditional ways of gathering food, the Indian people were forced to survive as agriculturalists on the ocean shores. Between the sandy soil and the salty air, crop failures were inevitable. Despite extremely harsh conditions, these people began to subsist and make a new home for themselves. After the Coos, Umpqua, Alsea and Siuslaw people made this area habitable for homesteaders, they were forced out again.[29]

This one period from nineteenth-century Yachats history adds a dimension to the story and invites humility about just what we know when we think we have developed a sense of place. Yachats is where I made the first custom-shaped pancakes for my very young sons, fashioned to their imaginations into spouts and whales and such, with eyes made from salal berries picked near our camp spot. Only a few months ago did I learn that those same salal might have been picked by Amanda and a people I never knew.

The "trail of tears" inflicted by the Alsea Sub-Agency evokes the image of blood and soil mixing as Amanda was forced to return to a reservation of amnesia. In the next stream of consciousness I find my mother, hemorrhaging, and then I am met with an umbilical cord of memory and hope. My mother's womb—as a place—holds an intensity of meaning. Could this be so for each of us as we remember the womb our mother once offered as home? Mother Earth in Native traditions comes to mind to help us ponder the ecological trail of blood upon and within a planet earth we call home. Suffering inflicted and suffering endured, earth as place and community of memory. The story I know best, a narrative that has shaped my passion for relational justice and communities of memory giving birth to communities of hope, is one of new life coming forth even in the very midst of great tragedy. My mother loved the piano. Her son Louis, born that day in August 1961 at the Silverton Hospital, plays piano today with natural abandon. And Amanda's Trail gives the Kittels and all of us opportunities to walk places intense with public meaning and memories that might call us to alter cultural patterns of disrespect. It is in the stories, honestly developed in real conversation and enriched with new complexity over time, that we can attune our moral imaginations to the ecology and history of the places that have hosted those narratives. A sense of place may be indispensable to a sense of eloquence now, given the ecological crisis we all face, although it has always been an ingredient of genuine "down-to-earth" utterance. Platitudes are inherently lofty and off the ground. Real stories and honest language demand some debt to milieu.[30]

My mother's grave is very close to Silverton, a farming community in the Willamette Valley of western Oregon. A few miles away is the small farm where we lived in the early 1960s. We children were in the midst of the annual evergreen blackberry harvest when she died. In those years after her death we would run behind Dad and the old Oliver 60 tractor, clinging to the wooden drag behind the disk, letting our toes sink into the fresh soil. These memories of our close contact with the earth bring to mind the role music plays in a storied ecology of place.

Mother was actually one-fourth Irish, but one delightful narrative tradition has it that when she and her sisters first heard about their Emerald Isle heritage she proclaimed that all four quarters were hers! Maybe a bit possessive, she sounded like a true native of that land when she sang:

> If you ever go across the sea to Ireland
> Then maybe at the closing of your day
> You will sit and watch the moon rise over Claddagh
> And see the sun go down on Galway Bay.[31]

Music and poetry have much to offer to our sense of place, as Mother understood. More recently my sons and I have come to know good friends in Cuernavaca, Mexico. Cristóbal and Delfina Acosta have taught us about another evocation of the indelible hold a place can have, "México Lindo y Querido," beautifully rendered by Jorge Negrete:

México lindo y querido
Si muero lejos de ti
Que digan que estoy dormido
Y que me traigan aquí.
(Mexico beautiful and beloved
If I should die far from you
May they say that I am asleep
and may they bring me here.)[32]

Sometimes lyrics and haunting melodies conjure feelings of acute uprootedness, as in the African-American lyrics, "Sometimes I Feel like a Motherless Child," or in "Go down, Moses, 'Way down in Egypt land, Tell ole Pharaoh, Let my people go." One of the earliest musical memories I have is of my father singing "Ol' Man River."[33] He had always been close to rivers. He began his life in 1918 on Kiger Island in the middle of the Willamette River. His father had come over from the southwestern-most part of Germany, just a good Black Forest shout away from where the Rhine turns north. I took my sons over to Germany a few years ago to see the lands that their great-grandfather left when he came to the States just before the turn of the century. Some of our relatives still live there, and we stayed with my father's second cousin and family for a short while. It was good to see and touch the soil. We talked with Herr Leo about what it was like to be a farmer there when the Nazis came to power. He fought in the war as a member of the German Army. He talked about how it is possible for a whole people to become blind to an evil in its midst. Since then have I begun to consider what might be a new and more subtle manifestation of the quest for *Lebensraum* ("living space") under the banner of aggressive forces seeking markets for the global economy. Are they plundering cultures and places in the process?[34]

It was, however, in a day trip to Kiger Island a year or two later that my sons and I were introduced to the place of my father's earliest memories. My dad wrote about this later in a letter to his brothers and sisters:

Frank, with boys, Nick and Chris, went with Dad to Kiger Island near Corvallis, where he was born 77 years ago. We looked over the old farm-land and took a canoe ride up the smaller stream on the West side, where the boys had a good swim. We also visited the Rock Hill School near Peterson's Butte, Lebanon where many of us attended the one-room school with Perry Ginther as teacher, walking about 1 mile to and fro.

A pipefitter most of his adult life, Dad got his start in the Portland ship-yards during the war, a place I can view from the Bluff where I now teach. My dad wanted to be a farmer close to the soil as he had been growing up, so we were raised on the land, first on an acre at the corner of Cherry and Pine in Salem, on the berry farm near Silverton during my elementary school years, and then on a dairy farm south of Tilla-mook during high school.

The dairy farm did not work out, partly because the banks were un-willing to make a loan essential to upgrade our milking system to meet new regulations. We were forced to sell the place that was bordered by the Big Nestucca River. Dad returned to pipefitting. Developers bought the property and began to build. They had less trouble obtaining fi-nancing.

Rivers have a role in the stories: the Rhine, Willamette, Yachats, Scism Creek that ran through our berry farm and became a flood every winter, the Big Nestucca, and the mighty Columbia.

The particular character of a family story can find rapport with words that arise in distant minds and places. Small wonder that images of water run so deep in the biblical narratives. The poet Langston Hughes wrote "The Negro Speaks of Rivers" early in the twentieth cen-tury. He had just graduated from high school and was on a train to Mexico to visit his father. As the locomotive crossed the Mississippi River just outside St. Louis at sunset he thought about what the river might have meant to others in the past. He knew that during slavery many had been sent down the river to hard labor in the rice fields of the Delta region. He knew too that Abe Lincoln as a young man had visited New Orleans and had seen human beings sold on the auction block. A whole people and their memory converge in his marvelous poetic sense of place:

> I've known rivers:
> I've known rivers ancient as the world and older than the flow of human
>   blood in human veins.
> My soul has grown deep like the rivers.
> I bathed in the Euphrates when dawns were young.
> I built my hut near the Congo and it lulled me to sleep.
> I looked upon the Nile and raised the pyramids above it.
> I heard the singing of the Mississippi when Abe Lincoln went down to
>   New Orleans, and I've seen its muddy bosom turn all golden in the
>   sunset.
> I've known rivers:

Ancient, dusky rivers.
My soul has grown deep like the rivers.[35]

Such eloquence calls each human being to ponder one's place in these "rivers of memory and hope." We cannot long inhabit a place without the habits of our hearts and the character of the place becoming a story waiting to be remembered.

CONCLUSION AND THEOLOGICAL REFLECTION

Wallace Stegner once said: "No place is a place until things that happened in it are remembered in history, ballads, yarns, legends, or monuments."[36] In similar fashion Walter Brueggemann has written that "place is space with historical meanings, where some things have happened which are now remembered and which provides continuity and identity across generations."[37] These definitions of place accurately describe the intent of this poignant chapter, "A Sense of Place." Using a narrative style, an example of what Brueggemann has called "storied place,"[38] the author artfully composes an eco-theological reflection weaving together the notion of "communities of memory" and "a sense of place" with the overall aim of igniting our moral imagination. The chapter is profoundly ecological. The understanding of community, memory, and place offered herein is all-inclusive, embracing all the components and inhabitants of the land in any given place. It is also profoundly theological. In the confluence of autobiographical memories with particular places the author generates an "intensity of meaning" that is sacramental, holding the capacity for revelatory and sacred experience. From this view the narrative remembrance of place reflects no ordinary place, but sacred place where God, human, and earth intersect in one small point of this immense creation. Finally, this chapter is profoundly ethical. Through the remembrance of suffering endured and inflicted the author calls us to remember our relationship to place and the obligation and duty to do justice—"to restore right relationship with God, each other, and all of creation."[39]

According to Brueggemann "a fresh look at the Bible suggests that a sense of place is a primary category of faith."[40] But in the biblical world the notion of place is not a vacuous reality; it is rather an overarching reference to the land. The land, therefore, is the nexus where communities of memory and a sense of place coalesce. On one hand the land, from our contemporary perspective, has significant ecological overtones. It reminds one of Aldo Leopold's "land ethic" wherein the land comes to mean the entire biotic and abiotic community including "soils, waters, plants and animals" to which humans belong as "plain member and citizen."[41] On the other hand from a biblical view the land is laden with theological import. The land is after all God's land where the people of Israel encounter YHWH. "It is," in Brueggemann's words, "land that provides the central assurance to Israel of its historicality, that it will be and always must be concerned with actual rootage in a place which is a repository for commitment and identity."[42]

When linked with "A Sense of Place," Brueggemann's analysis of the land in the biblical narrative raises two issues for consideration. First, the land is a gift; it is grace, even salvation. Moreover, it is covenanted land that "binds Israel in new ways to the giver."[43] The land, in other words, is a place of relationship where love of God and neighbor is grounded in the earth. In a commodity culture such as the U.S., where a sense of place frequently refers to conquering the land, absolute ownership, and property rights, it is imperative to remember that we—as communities of memory bound both to this land and the biblical heritage—are only "tenants" on the land. The recognition that the land is gift challenges us to relinquish our idolatrous possessiveness of place and enlarge our capacity for respect and gratitude. With this comes the humility to acknowledge Brueggemann's second point: "the land as task."[44] By this he means that the gift of land requires moral responsibility to the land itself and those who inhabit it. The land, like its inhabitants, requires sabbath; it requires rest and honor. But this consciousness of gift and responsibility only occurs after we have cultivated a sense of place with the land, when amnesia gives way to remembrance and ownership gives way to belonging. Then we will be able to recognize—as Wallace Stegner has—that "only in the act of submission is the sense of place realized and a sustainable relationship between people and the earth established."[45]

NOTES: CHAPTER 13

[1] For this notion of "communities of memory" see Robert Bellah, et al., *Habits of the Heart: Individualism and Commitment in American Life* (Berkeley: University of California Press, updated ed. 1996) 153. See also Johann Baptist Metz, *Faith in History and Society: Toward a Practical Fundamental Theology* (New York: Seabury, 1980). Among authors who have influenced the present writer's thoughts on "a sense of place" are Wallace Stegner, *Where the Bluebird*

Sings to the Lemonade Springs: Living and Writing in the West (New York: Penguin, 1992); Wendell Berry, *Another Turn of the Crank* (Washington, D.C.: Counterpoint, 1995); T. C. McLuhan, *The Way of the Earth: Encounters with Nature in Ancient and Contemporary Thought* (New York: Simon & Schuster, 1994); Leroy S. Rouner, ed., *The Longing for Home* (Notre Dame: University of Notre Dame Press, 1996); Anne Buttimer, *Geography and the Human Spirit* (Baltimore: Johns Hopkins University Press, 1993); Joshua Meyrowitz, *No Sense of Place: The Impact of Electronic Media on Social Behavior* (New York: Oxford University Press, 1985); Derrick Jensen, *Listening to the Land: Conversations About Nature, Culture and Eros* (San Francisco: Sierra Club, 1995); Frederick W. Turner, *Spirit of Place: The Making of an American Literary Landscape* (San Francisco: Sierra Club, 1989); Alan Gussow, *A Sense of Place: The Artist and the American Land* (New York: Seabury, 1971; San Francisco: Friends of the Earth, 1972–73); and two excellent essays in the Summer 1997 (vol. 16, no. 2) issue of *Portland* (the University of Portland magazine): Barry Lopez, "A Literature of Place," 22–25 and John Daniel, "Holy Waters," 28–31.

[2] For the notion of biblical justice understood as relational see John R. Donahue, "Biblical Perspectives on Justice," in John C. Haughey, ed., *The Faith that Does Justice* (New York: Paulist: 1977) 68–112.

[3] The musical reference is to words from a popular hit by Fleetwood Mac used as something of a theme celebrating President Clinton's election to the U.S. presidency. For a trenchant analysis of the global economy and utilitarian habits see William Greider, *One World, Ready or Not: The Manic Logic of Global Capitalism* (New York: Simon & Schuster, 1977).

[4] Alasdair MacIntyre, *After Virtue: A Study in Moral Theory* (Notre Dame: University of Notre Dame Press, 1984) 154. For an excellent example of this notion of habit formation and ethics see ch. 1 of Wayne Meeks, *The Origins of Christian Morality: The First Two Centuries* (New Haven: Yale University Press, 1993).

[5] I am indebted to Richard Harmon, director of the Portland Organizing Project, for helping me to *practice* narrative social ethics. Many authors, often influenced by Paul Ricouer, have written about the theories of narrative ethics, but the actual practice has proven most significant for my understanding of the potential relational power of our stories. For one textual reference see Paul Nelson, *Narrative and Morality: A Theological Inquiry* (University Park, Pa.: Pennsylvania State University Press, 1987). Two other excellent examples of narrative social ethics are Roger G. Betsworth, *Social Ethics: An Examination of American Moral Traditions* (Louisville: Westminster/John Knox, 1990) and Philip P. Hallie, *Lest Innocent Blood Be Shed: The Story of the Village of Le Chambon, and How Goodness Happened There* (New York: Harper & Row, 1979). Hallie writes eloquently about the difference between abstract ethics and narrative social ethics: "I am a student and teacher of good and evil, but for

me ethics, like the rest of philosophy, is not a scientific, impersonal matter. It is by and about persons, much as it was for Socrates. Being personal, it must not be ashamed to express personal passions, the way a strict scientist might be ashamed to express them in a laboratory report. My own passion was a yearning for realistic hope. I wanted to believe that the examined life was more precious than this Hell I had dug for myself in studying evil" (pp. 7–8). I would only add that ecological ethics is about persons and their actual relation to places and other creatures. Hence, to update Socrates, could we suggest that the unexamined place will not be remembered and restored?

[6] *Frommherz,* with the extra *m,* is still used by our relatives in Germany. The name means pious or dedicated heart, an ideal to try to remember though I have long since let go of any illusions of actually having such a heart by any of my *own* doing!

[7] For a marvelous study of place and community see Simon Schama, *Landscape and Memory* (New York: Vintage, 1996); he writes of *Waldsterben* (forest-death) on p. 120.

[8] David S. Toolan, "Praying in a Post-Einsteinian Universe," *Cross Currents* 46/4 (Winter 1996/1997) 437–70.

[9] Gerard Manley Hopkins, "God's Grandeur," in the splendid anthology edited by Jaroslav Pelikan, *The World Treasury of Modern Religious Thought* (Boston: Little, Brown, 1990) 175–77.

[10] Simone Weil, *The Need for Roots. Prelude to a Declaration of Duties Toward Mankind,* translated by Arthur Wills (Boston: Beacon, 1952). Her discussion of uprootedness is both eloquent and prescient.

[11] Oregon Department of Environmental Quality, Lower Columbia River Bi-State Water Quality Program, *Report* (June 1996).

[12] Hugh Feiss, "Watch the Crows: Environmental Responsibility and the Benedictine Tradition." See this reflection on Benedictine stability and sense of place in Drew Christiansen and Walter Grazer, eds., *"And God Saw That It Was Good." Catholic Theology and the Environment* (Washington, D.C.: U.S. Catholic Conference, 1996) 147–64.

[13] William Dietrich, *Northwest Passage: The Great Columbia River* (New York: Simon & Schuster, 1995).

[14] James Michener, *Alaska* (New York: Random House, 1988) 525–29.

[15] Dietrich, *Northwest Passage* 308–309.

[16] The development of land trusts throughout the Pacific Northwest is a sign of hope.

[17] The Portland Organizing Project (P.O.P.) is a broad-based/church-based nonprofit involving more than eighteen congregations in a process of small faith-community development. For example, P.O.P. sponsors leadership

institutes where people share real stories of pressures on families. They also conduct public negotiations to alleviate such pressures. This is one of over fifty affiliates of the Industrial Areas Foundation (IAF) located throughout the United States.

[18] For an outstanding study of President Lincoln's rhetoric see Garry Wills, *Lincoln at Gettysburg: The Words that Remade America* (New York: Simon & Schuster, 1992).

[19] From Stephen Vincent Benet's poem, "American Names." See Dee Brown, *Bury My Heart at Wounded Knee: An Indian History of the American West* (New York: Holt, Rinehart & Winston, 1970).

[20] As discussed by Walter Brueggemann in *The Land: Place as Gift, Promise and Challenge in Biblical Faith* (Philadelphia: Fortress, 1977) 14.

[21] Bill and Jan Moeller, *Chief Joseph and the Nez Perce: A Photographic History* (Missoula, Mont.: Mountain Press, 1995) 72.

[22] *Gaudium et Spes (Pastoral Constitution on the Church in the Modern World)*, in David J. O'Brien and Thomas A. Shannon, eds., *Catholic Social Thought: The Documentary Heritage* (Maryknoll, N.Y.: Orbis, 1992) 166.

[23] Bernard McGinn, *The Foundations of Mysticism: Origins to the Fifth Century* (New York: Crossroad, 1994), "Precisely because of the incommensurability between finite and Infinite Subject, Christian mystics over the centuries have never been able to convey their message solely through the positive language of presence. The paradoxical necessity of both presence and absence is one of the most important of all the verbal strategies by means of which mystical transformation has been symbolized" (p. xviii). See McGinn's references to Augustine and to *The Cloud of Unknowing* in the General Introduction, pp. xi–xx. The reference to "the palace of nowhere" is from James Finley, *Merton's Palace of Nowhere: A Search for God through Awareness of the True Self* (Notre Dame: Ave Maria, 1983) 8.

[24] The term "Silicon Forest" has been used frequently in recent years in news coverage of the economic transformation of the Oregon economy from a natural resource base to a hi-tech boom. By no means is this solely a story of degradation. It echoes, nonetheless, the equally disturbing California language of the "Silicon Valley."

[25] Wendell Berry, *What Are People For?* (San Francisco: North Point Press, 1990) 6. See also the outstanding essay on "The Sense of Place" and "A Letter to Wendell Berry" by Stegner, *Where the Bluebird Sings* 199–213.

[26] I am indebted to the insights on the firm and the fluid so eloquently rendered by the marine biologist Rachel Carson. Carson expresses a remarkable scientific *and* poetic awareness of life at the place where land and ocean meet. See her essay "The Marginal World" in Karen Knowles, ed., *Celebrating the Land: Women's Nature Writings,1850–1991* (Flagstaff, Ariz.: Northland Press, 1992) 47–51.

[27] Forty-six percent of the Oregon coastline is in private ownership, much of it zoned for development. People have mistakenly assumed that Oregon's land-use laws will protect the land from speculative development. See Foster Church and Peter D. Sleeth, "Sanctuary Under Siege," *The Sunday Oregonian* (July 6, 1997) A11.

[28] The letter from Joanne Kittel was sent to me on October 3, 1997. The Kittels have given thoughtful consideration to the relationship between the concept of "private property" and the notions of "public history" and "public future."

[29] Joanne Kittel and Suzanne Curtis, "Early Yachats History: The Yachats Indians, Origins of the Yachats Name, and the Reservation Years," (Typescript © Confederated Tribes of the Coos, Lower Umpqua, and Siuslaw Indians, and the Confederated Tribes of the Siletz Indians of Oregon, 1996) 12.

[30] I have found the work of Leslie Marmon Silko to be an outstanding guide in my efforts to begin to understand the profound sense of place characteristic of particular Native American tribal traditions. See her essay "Landscape, History, and the Pueblo Imagination," in *Celebrating the Land* (n. 26 above) 107–17. Another remarkably insightful essay is by Emily Cousins, "Mountains Made Alive: Native American Relationships with Sacred Land," *Cross Currents* (Winter 1996/1997) 497–509.

[31] The song is entitled "Galway Bay." Other verses contrast awareness and ignorance of place, such as the political lines: "And the women in the uplands diggin' praties speak a language that the strangers do not know, for the strangers came and tried to teach us their way. . . ."

[32] Cristóbal and Delfina Acosta have bequeathed much of their family heritage of land near Cuernavaca for people who were without homes. We visited these families one day, and later listened to the great Mexican vocalist Jorge Negrete in "México Lindo y Querido." The translation to English is my own.

[33] See James J. Fuld, *The Book of World-Famous Music: Classical, Popular and Folk* (New York: Crown, 1971). Unlike the other two songs cited, which are authentic African-American spirituality, "Ol' Man River" was created for a musical, *Showboat* (1927). Some of the words in "Ol' Man River" point to the challenge of building genuine communities of memory, i.e., those in which we remember human as well as non-human ecological and economic relations: for example, "He don't plant taters, he don't plant cotton, and d'em d'at plants em, is soon forgotten." Fuld notes: "The words of Ol' Man River have subsequently been modified to eliminate certain references deemed by some to be offensive" (p. 412).

[34] The final chapter "Oikonomia," in William Greider's *One World, Ready or Not* (n. 3 above) develops a somber yet hopeful analysis of ecological awareness and global capitalism. "The economic luxury hidden in the capitalist process is

space—capitalism's ability to move and re-create itself, abandoning the old for the new, creating and destroying production, while trailing a broad flume of ruined natural assets in its wake. Because globalization has narrowed distances, the luxury has diminished visibly. It is now possible for people to glimpse what was always true: the wasteful nature of their own prosperity. So long as the consequences could be kept afar from the beneficiaries, no one had much incentive—neither producers nor consumers—to face the collective implications" (pp. 446–47).

[35] *Selected Poems of Langston Hughes* (New York: Vintage, 1990) 4.

[36] Stegner, "The Sense of Place," *Where the Bluebird Sings to the Lemonade Springs* 202.

[37] Brueggemann, *The Land* (n. 20 above) 5.

[38] Ibid. 185.

[39] See above, p. 241.

[40] Brueggemann, *The Land* 4.

[41] Aldo Leopold, "The Land Ethic," A *Sand County Almanac and Sketches Here and There* (New York: Oxford University Press, 1949) 202.

[42] Brueggemann, *The Land* 5–6.

[43] Ibid. 47.

[44] Ibid. 59.

[45] Stenger, *Where the Bluebird Sings to the Lemonade Springs* 206.

14

Hope Amidst Crisis: A Prophetic Vision of Cosmic Redemption

"The earth dries up and withers,
    the world languishes and withers;
    the heavens languish together with the earth.
The earth lies polluted
    under its inhabitants;
for they have transgressed laws,
    violated the statutes,
    broken the everlasting covenant." (Isa 24:4-5)

INTRODUCTION

*T*he ancient Israelite prophets present a picture of the unjust suffering of creation because of human sin. Their proclamations show us how ecological devastation is the result of war and people's sinfulness.[1] But the issues of eco-injustice that we face today were not their issues. The violence within the contemporary world now surpasses the violence of the ancient world. Despite all human growth and development, technological advancement, and the move to become a "global community," members of our human community continue to destroy not only many of our family members on the Blue Planet but also creation itself, the natural world that is our first home and home to all other creatures who share life with us on our planet.

We are slowly coming to grips with the reality that life is now gasping in the ever-tightening clutches of both social and ecological injustice. Daily many of us are becoming more acutely aware of the web of violence that is ensnaring the human family, causing us to turn on one another—adults on adults, parents on children, children on parents, and children on children. Daily many of us are becoming more acutely aware of the suffering of our natural world due to human violence, greed, abuse, and the lack of reverence for all that has breath. We are the ones who are directly and indirectly responsible for deforestation, pollution, soil erosion, global warming, toxic waste dumping, overcultivation, overfishing, etc. Even the domestic animals—the cows, lambs, pigs, chickens—who have been friends to us for a long, long time and who have helped to sustain our lives are now being looked upon as sources of profit. Some of us fatten them up and pump them up so that they can be "heartier" and more "productive."

As a people, many of us have broken covenant with God, with each other, and with the natural world. Hence human sin not only causes human suffering but is now inflicting suffering on all creation. The magnificent, wonder-full Blue Planet is in crisis; creation is groaning. All of us must now face a new disorder: ecological destruction, or more bluntly, sin against creation. As we teeter totter between life and death, survival and extinction, the ethical issue for the human community is clear: all people have to stop abusing and destroying creation. We have no choice but to confront and deal with two counteractive and counterproductive forces at work on our planet, namely human power, domination, and control on the one hand and human malaise on the other. We wonder to ourselves, if we can still wonder, "Is there really any hope amidst such disorder and ecological crisis?" And then come the words of Isaiah: "I am about to create new heavens and a new earth . . ." (Isa 65:17).

TOWARD AN ALTERNATIVE VIEW: DIVINE PROMISE AND PROPHETIC VISION

Not only do the Israelite prophets show us that there is a systemic connection between human sinfulness and ecological destruction, but they also show us through their proclamations that there is an inherent link between creation and redemption, specifically that the redemption of humankind is connected to the restoration of the natural world through divine promise.[2] This redemption and restoration leads to a vision of a new creation characterized by a return to harmonious relationships between God, ourselves, and the natural world. It is the prophets' eschatological vision that can provide us with a basis for hope and a paradigm for faithful living. But the next question is: "Is hope something we receive as grace, or is it something we do as an ethical practice to bring about the prophetic promises and visions that are already unfolding in our midst?"

In an attempt to respond to these two questions this chapter examines selected prophetic texts that link creation and redemption with divine promise and speak of an eschatological vision of a new creation and harmonious relationships.[3] The chapter also suggests how we can hasten the prophets' eschatological vision as we struggle to choose life and not death, hope and not despair.

While the essay makes some reference to the historical situations behind selected texts, its primary focus is on the received text in its setting among the believing community today, living in a time of ecological crisis caused by eco-injustice. It is written from the perspective of a believer and is addressed to the human community: to anyone else who has "ears to hear."

Divine Promise: Redemption and Restoration

The Major Prophets

The major prophets link redemption to creation by way of divine promise. In Isaiah 30, God, speaking through the prophet, upbraids the rebellious Israelites for senselessly placing their trust in the protection and power of Pharaoh and the Egyptian people (vv. 1-7), for their lack of faithfulness and their refusal to be instructed by God (vv. 8-14), and for their bold self-assurance and lack of confidence in God (vv. 15-17). Therefore God assures them that their actions will have consequences. They will suffer at the hands of an enemy nation, Assyria (see vv. 27-33), whose invasion, as we know from history, was inevitable.

Following the series of divine judgment statements and the foreshadowing of the coming of the Assyrians is a statement of confidence about God (v. 18), a divine promise (vv. 19-26), and a statement of judgment on the Assyrians (vv. 27-33) which for the Assyrians is an oracle of doom but for the Israelites an oracle of hope. God will act on behalf of the Israelites. What is important in Isaiah 30 is the divine promise (vv. 19-26) nestled between the judgment statements.

In vv. 19-26 the prophet heartens the Israelites by proclaiming that God, a God of justice and mercy (v. 18), will be gracious to them, will hear and respond to their cry (v. 19) even though they may be chastised for a while (v. 20), and will instruct them in the way they should walk

(v. 21). The prophet then tells the Israelites that as a result of God's actions they will abolish their lifeless gods (v. 22) and become the recipients of God's promise. In vv. 23-26 one sees that the divine promise has implications not only for human beings but also for the rest of creation. First, God will indeed give rain to water the seeds that the Israelites have sown, and the grain that will sprout will be rich and plenteous (v. 23). Both the seed and the people will receive God's blessing. Second, livestock will enjoy broad grazing pastures and eat good fodder (vv. 23-24). Third, mountains and hills will stream with water (v. 25), and fourth, the light from the moon and the sun will be more effulgent than their natural radiance (v. 26) "on the day that God binds up the injury of his people and heals the wound of his blow" (v. 26). In other words, after the people have experienced the consequences of their faithlessness and lack of trust and when they turn to God and reform their ways then they, their natural world, and creation will be the recipients of the divine promise that entails redemption and healing for humanity and results in a fuller, richer life for all creation.[4]

In Isa 41:17-20 humankind's redemption also has a bearing on the natural world. God, again speaking through the prophet, promises that when "the poor and the needy" seek water and there is none, and their tongue is parched, God will answer them and provide for them, thus relieving their thirst and redeeming them from their oppressed state (v. 17).

How will God work to achieve this goal? By creating new things that transform the natural world. Rivers will be opened in bare places; fountains will be in the midst of the valleys; the desert will become a pool of water and the dry land springs of water (v. 18); trees will be planted in the desert (v. 19). Redemption on behalf of humanity goes hand in hand with new acts of creation that help to enliven and transform the natural world, and as it is cultivated and transformed so is humanity restored to health through the relief of basic needs. The divine promise in vv. 17-20 suggests, then, that the redemption of humankind is achieved through the development of the natural world whereby nature is enriched instead of raped.

Similar in theme and thought to Isa 41:17-20 is Isa 44:1-5. God, speaking through the prophet, offers reassurance to the sinful, suffering Israelites (vv. 1-2) and then discloses the divine plan of redemptive action on their behalf (vv. 3-5).[5] The redemptive action that is intended to renew the Israelites is to happen in conjunction with the cultivation of the natural world. God promises first to pour water on the thirsty ground and streams on the dry land (v. 3), and then to pour out divine spirit and blessing on the Israelites' descendants who will, in turn, sprout up "like grass" and "like poplars by streams of water" (v. 4). Peter D. Miscall notes that "similar to the vision of transformation in 32.14-20, water and spirit are in parallel; both are poured out and lead to fertility and growth (42.9; 43.19)."[6] God's redemptive actions not only underscore the relationship that exists between humanity and creation but also pave the way for humanity to enter into relationship with God who is the creative, sustaining, and redeeming spirit within all of life (v. 5).[7]

In Isa 51:1-8, another divine promise of redemption, v. 3 is significant because God's promise to comfort Zion is mentioned in conjunction with the restoration of nature:

> For God comforts Zion;
> > he comforts all her desolation
> when he makes her wilderness like Eden,
> > and her steps like God's garden.[8]

The comparisons "like Eden" and "like God's garden" recall the Genesis creation account (see specifically Gen 2:8, 15). One can deduce, then, that God's comfort is associated with the beauty of the primeval natural world insofar as God's actions do not facilitate a return to that world but rather a transformation of life's present condition so that the present world is restored to its original beauty. Hence redemption of humanity (vv. 1-2) is linked to the transformation and restoration of the natural world (v. 3a-b) that will result in joy and gladness (v. 3cα), thanksgiving and song (v. 3cβ).

Like Isaiah, Jeremiah also speaks of restoration in relation to the natural world. In Jeremiah 3, God promises to build Israel (v. 4), and the people in turn will plant vineyards and enjoy the fruit (v. 5). When God redeems Jacob, namely the Israelites (v. 11),

> They shall come and sing aloud on the height of Zion,
> > and they shall be radiant over the goodness of YHWH,
> over the grain, the wine, and the oil,
> > and over the young of the flock and the herd;
> their life shall become like a watered garden,
> > and they shall never languish again (v. 12).

With the redemption of humanity comes celebration and fertility. As in Isa 44:4 nature provides the basis for comparison. Those redeemed will be like watered gardens. The image here is one of perpetual beauty and vitality for both humanity and the natural world.

In Jeremiah 33 the promise of redemption, healing, and restoration of humanity (vv. 1-11) is linked to the promise of land restoration:

> In this place that is a waste, without human beings or animals,
> and in all its towns there shall again be pasture
> for shepherds resting their flocks (v. 12).

In the writings of Ezekiel, another of the major prophets, one discovers that the natural world provides imagery and symbols for the prophet's proclamations of what God's intentions are with respect to people and creation. In Ezek 34:11 sheep symbolize God's people, whom God will rescue from bondage (vv. 12-13) and later release into the midst of a lush natural environment where they will graze and eat heartily (vv. 13-15). After rescuing and nurturing this flock God will provide a shepherd for them (vv. 23-24) and then establish "a covenant of peace" with them and banish wild animals from the land so that the flock can live securely (v. 25). Both the flock and the land will then be the recipients of God's blessing, making the earth a fruitful and peaceful place for life (vv. 26-31).[9] Thus the picture that Ezekiel paints in ch. 34 is idyllic but it does attest to a link between the redemption of humanity and the natural world, both of which will be graced into new and fuller life and deep peace when God's promised blessing comes to pass.

In Ezek 36:33-35 the prophet proclaims that God will cleanse the people from their iniquities and then transform their desolate land so that it resembles the Garden of Eden. Again humankind's redemption and the restoration of the natural world are interwoven. A similar divine promise, along with the promise of peace and security, is found in Ezek 39:25-29.

The Minor Prophets

The minor prophets, specifically Hosea, Joel, and Amos, continue the theme of redemption and restoration. In Hos 2:16-18 God redeems Israel, God's people, from idolatry (vv. 16-17) and then creates a covenant for them that will establish a relationship between them and all of creation and life, symbolized by the wild animals, the birds of the air, and the creeping things of the ground, and by the abolition of the bow, the sword, and war from the land (vv. 18-19). Finally the covenant will be extended farther to include God renewing and reestablishing relationship with the people and the people with their God, with creation responding accordingly (vv. 19-23). Once again, along with the redemption of people the natural world is also redeemed.[10]

As in other past prophetic proclamations the natural world in Hosea 14 plays a central role in the divine plan for humanity's redemption (cf. Ezekiel 34). Verses 4-7 contain another divine promise in which God pledges to heal and thus restore the Israelites. In v. 5a nature becomes the central simile that describes God's redemptive and restorative act. God will be "like dew to Israel." In turn Israel will "blossom like a lily" (v. 5b) and "strike root like the forests of Lebanon" (v. 5c). Israel's "shoots shall spread out" (v. 6a); Israel will be as beautiful as an olive tree, and fragrant too (vv. 6c, 7cβ). The Israelites "will flourish like a garden" (v. 7b) and "blossom like the vine" (v. 7cα).

One can see from this passage that God's redemptive act on behalf of humanity is linked to the forces and beauty of the natural world. When healed, humanity is meant to reflect that beauty. But in order for this reflection to occur, both humanity and the natural world need to be cared for. Furthermore, the reference to God becoming like "dew" in order to heal humanity suggests that within creation there are natural gifts that have restorative potential for humankind, especially since, according to the Genesis creation account, humanity and the things of nature share a common origin (see Genesis 1–2).

In Joel 2:18-27 God promises to redeem the people from mockery and oppression (vv. 18-20). In vv. 21-22 God speaks directly to creation:

> Do not fear, O land;
>> be glad and rejoice,
>> for God is doing great things.
> Do not fear, beasts of the field,
>> for the pastures of the wilderness are green,
> for the tree bears its fruit,
>> and the fig tree and vine give their yield.

In vv. 23-24 God addresses the people directly. Here rain from the natural world plays a major role in the people's vindication (v. 24). J. E. and D. R. Kirk observe that in vv. 21-24

> Joel is giving God's response to a plea for mercy. If the people truly repent, God promises restoration, rest, and protection, as well as benefits to the natural world. God through Joel addresses the land and the beasts,

talks of the yield of the fig tree and vine, and the coming rains. The renewed rain is another outward symbol of an inward reality, the restored fellowship with God. The arrival of the rain demonstrates God's blessing on the heart with the promise that God's people will experience the abiding presence of God himself, dwelling in their midst.[11]

Thus vv. 21-24 are hopeful words that speak of redemption and restoration, with humanity and the natural world in relationship with each other and God in relationship with both.

In Amos 9:11-15 the prophet proclaims a message of divine promise that speaks of restoration for God's people and their civilization as well as new creation for the natural world. The verses also highlight the unity that exists between God, humanity, and the natural world. God's gracious acts on behalf of humanity become the spark for humanity's cultivation of the earth that will, in turn, bless the people with its fruitfulness (vv. 13-14). The imagery in v. 15 suggests a new relationship that the people will have with the natural world. Not only will they share in its fruitfulness but they will also be an intricate part of it, for they will be planted in their land, a land that is not their human right but their divine gift.

In summary, the prophets' proclamations of the divine promises pave the way for a contemporary reader and listener to come to the following realizations: (1) that the redemption of humankind is linked to the natural world, and the natural world's experience of transformation and new creation often happens in the process of humanity's being redeemed from its sinfulness, liberated from its oppressive situations, and healed of the sufferings it undergoes on account of its sinfulness; (2) that the natural world can provide delightful and invigorating images, metaphors, and similes that allow people to envision how beautiful and liberating life can be when there is a sense of balance, order, reverence for, and relationship with all of creation; and (3) that God's plan for salvation is one of cosmic redemption secured by promises that are divine and eschatological.

Prophetic Vision: New Creation and Harmonious Relationship

While the Israelite prophets' proclamations of divine promise do offer hope it is their prophetic, eschatological visions that capture our imaginations, kindle our spirits, and warm our hearts. It is their visions that can fill us with amazement and make us stop and wonder, if we can recover our wonder, that yes, perhaps there is hope amidst such disorder and ecological distress, and yes, the Blue Planet and all that lives and breathes in it can become, once again, a safe home for everyone and everything, with flourishing gardens, land reforested with new baby pines for nestlings and fledglings, smog-free skies, sea lions swimming with steel heads in clean waters, wild life roaming and grazing freely without fear of the hunter's bullet. Perhaps the Blue Planet can once again be a home with unlocked doors and unbarred windows where human beings of all ages and kinds cultivate their patch of earth and sit peacefully under a tree, in simple reverence for other human beings and all of creation, without forgetting that life is a gift, more precious than a right, and that what needs to be at the heart of all is "lovingkindness," "compassion," because lovingkindness and compassion are at the heart of God, the creator of all life that is good and wholesome and holy. It is a vision similar to this that the prophet Isaiah sees, and one that begs a response.

Isaiah 11, one of several prophetic, eschatological visions, is "a poem, and one of extraordinary generative power."[12] In the poem the prophet presents a magnificent vision of a new creation. Using metaphorical language characteristic of the natural world combined with historical and religious references the prophet in vv. 1-5 describes a future leader, one who is in relationship with a righteous and faithful God (v. 5), whose governance embraces and exhibits the qualities of "righteousness," and whose decisions will be carried out powerfully but nonviolently.[13]

In vv. 6-9 the prophet describes a beautiful pastoral picture of domestic animals: "the lamb" (v. 6), "the kid" (v. 6), "the calf" (v. 6), "the fatling" (v. 6), "the cow" (v. 7), and "the ox" (v. 7), and the wild animals: "the wolf" (v. 6), "the leopard" (v. 6), "the lion" (v. 6), "the bear" (v. 6), and human beings symbolized by "a little child" (v. 6), "a nursling child" (v. 8), and "the weaned child" (v. 8), all living together peacefully without harm or destruction on God's "holy mountain" (v. 9).[14]

The combination of the domestic and wild animals dwelling together and a nursling child playing over the asp's hole (v. 8a) as a weaned child puts his/her hand on the adder's den (v. 8b) adds a sense of simplicity, innocence, and playfulness to the picture. And why will life be peaceful? Because all will be filled with the knowledge of God "as waters cover the sea" (v. 9b). Once again nature provides a metaphor to vivify the picture of how life can be lived (see also v. 1).

In summary, what Isaiah sees in his vision is a new creation, one that is characterized by "righteousness," "faithfulness," and a state of "peace."

Isaiah's vision presents a picture of harmonious relationships between God, humanity, and the animals. Such a way of life is one that models the fullness of covenant that is part of the prophet Hosea's message (see Hos 2:16-23).

In Isa 32:16-20 the prophet presents a vision similar to the one in Isa 11:1-9. Following a picture of devastation and disaster (vv. 9-14) the prophet proclaims a new life characterized by peace and prosperity. The natural world will flourish (v. 15), animals will roam freely (v. 20), people will live peacefully and securely (v. 18), all because of the restorative presence of "justice" (v. 16) and "righteousness" (v. 16) that brings "peace" (v. 17a), "quietness" (v. 17b), and "security" (v. 17b) forever.[15]

A magnificent vision that speaks of creation and redemption simultaneously is Isaiah 35. Following yet another picture of disaster (Isaiah 34), Isaiah in ch. 35 very strikingly describes the beauty of the natural world.

In vv. 1-2 Isaiah uses personification and a simile to describe the new life in the wilderness and desert, and in vv. 3-7 the prophet speaks of God coming to redeem God's people. This redemptive act will affect in a positive way not only humanity but also the natural world (vv. 5-7). The simile in v. 6 where the prophet states that "the lame shall leap like a deer" indicates an implicit relationship between two diverse earth creatures and also ascribes the nimbleness and freedom of a beautiful animal to a human being. Life in this transformed desert and wilderness will have a freshness about it along with a sense of divine guidance and purpose (v. 8). There will be no violence (v. 9), sorrow, or sighing (v. 10), only everlasting joy and gladness (v. 10). Richard J. Clifford notes that "Isaiah 35 is another text that parallels the healing of the desert and the healing of the restored humanity."[16] Thus this vision not only reinforces the link between the redemption of humanity and the restoration of the natural world but also speaks of a harmonious relationship that exists between God, people, and the natural world when human beings and nature are restored to their intended beauty through God's graciousness (vv. 2, 4; cf. Amos 9:11-15). And new creation begins.

Perhaps the most extraordinary visions of a new creation are in Isa 43:16-21 and Isa 65:17-25. In the first of these the prophet confesses God's strength (vv. 16-17) and then delivers God's message that speaks of new creation within the natural world coupled with refreshment for humanity (vv. 19-21). The phrase "my chosen people" (v. 20) is the language of covenant. J. Alec Motyer adds: "Here we see the acts of God bringing the whole world into harmony, a feature which will be perfected in the Messianic day (11:6-9). Here, the journeying people are met by a transformed world (19cd) into which the animal creation gladly enters with benefit."[17] Thus Isa 43:16-21 is a hopeful vision of a new world sustained by harmonious relationships.

The vision of a new creation continues and climaxes in Isa 65:17-25. Unlike the former vision (Isa 43:16-21), this one has more of a cosmic ring to it. God will create a new heaven and a new earth. Everyone and everything will be made new; cities, people, civilization, and the natural world will all flourish. The vision celebrates the fullness of life, and like the vision in Isa 11:1-9; 32:16-20; 35; and 43:16-21, Isa 65:17-25 speaks of a creation full of joy (vv. 18-19), blessing (vv. 21-23), and nonviolence (v. 25). The vision also celebrates a "oneness" between God and all of creation, God and humanity, humanity and God, humanity and the natural world, and the animals with one another. And yet the vision of a transformed creation is still incomplete: the serpent, the image from the Genesis creation account (see Genesis 3) still eats dust (v. 25) and thus has to continue to bear the brunt of humanity's free will and poor choice.

In summary, Isaiah's five prophetic, eschatological visions are powerful and poignant pictures of what God's intention is for the cosmos and all of life. The visions highlight justice and righteousness as key virtues essential to a new way of life that is marked by harmonious relationships. Such relationships attest to the presence of the holy within all of life.

CONCLUSION AND THEOLOGICAL REFLECTION

The Israelite prophets show us through their writings the following points: (1) that there is indeed an inherent link between redemption and creation, specifically that the redemption of humankind is connected with the restoration of creation either through cause or effect; (2) that the redemption of humanity and the restoration of creation are divinely promised; (3) that the divine promise of redemption and restoration leads to a vision of a new creation embraced by justice, righteousness, and peacefulness and ordered by harmonious relationships; (4) that the divine intention for creation is not universal annihilation but rather cosmic redemption; and (5) that even in the midst of what seem to be ash heaps and ruins, chaos and crisis, God is at work, acting according to the divine nature of creativity and compassion to hasten life's redemption and liberation.

In a time of ecological crisis, human brokenness, and spiritual con-fusion and self-absorption the divine promises and prophetic, eschato-logical visions that the Israelite prophets herald fill us with hope as they did our ancestors when they struggled with different yet related prob-lems. However, these promises and visions are not yet fulfilled because even though they are part of a particular historical time frame and re-late to contemporary situations they *are* eschatological. Therefore how we understand hope in relation to these promises and visions is impor-tant.

The question posed earlier now comes into play again: "Is hope something we receive as grace or is it something we do as an ethical practice to bring about the prophetic promises and vision that are al-ready unfolding in our midst?" In other words, do we sit back and wait for God to do the work, as the biblical text sometimes seems to suggest, or do we roll up our sleeves and get to work? Hope is something we re-ceive as a grace and something we must do as an ethical practice to bring about the prophetic promises and visions. As a human commu-nity struggling and journeying together with all of creation we need to continue to embrace an ethical attitude toward life that challenges us to reform our ways and calls us to be rooted in prophetic action:

> [God] has told you, O mortal, what is good
>   and what God requires of you:
> to do justice, to love kindness,
>   and to walk humbly with your God (Mic 6:8).

This prophetic action can no longer be interpreted anthropocentrically. Jeffrey G. Sobosan argues that

> What is needed is an expansion of our ethical concerns and commit-ments. While we recognize, for example, that maliciously damaging an-other human being is wrong, we must extend this principle (even when at first we think it will be honored more in the breach than the keeping) to all living things. So too with such generally acknowledged norms as sheltering the homeless, feeding the hungry, caring for the sick. This task is not easy, but it is possible, and we must muffle in our spirits the sweet temptation to give up. With the Buddhist saint we must strive toward that point where we can say, "All that is alive is a part of me, and I am nothing save for them." This is sanctity at a high pitch, beyond the con-cerns of formal religion, recognizing that non-human life includes not just the animals but God as well. For God too survives in our lives only when we protect and nourish our feelings for the divine.[18]

Hence prophetic action means being in an active relationship with God (Isa 55:6-13) who desires us to be in relationship with one another (Isa 58:6-14) and with all of creation (Hos 2:16-23). Only then will we break the chain of violence and become prophetic people of hope, deeply rooted in the Judeo-Christian values of covenant and compassion.

The words of Ephrem of Syria seem most fitting as this chapter draws to a close:

> An elder was once asked, "What is a compassionate heart?" He replied: "It is a heart on fire for the whole of creation, for humanity, for the birds, for the animals, for demons and for all that exists. At the recollection and at the sight of them such a person's eyes overflow with tears owing to the vehemence of the compassion which grips his [or her] heart; as a result of his [or her] deep mercy his [or her] heart shrinks and cannot bear to hear or look on any injury or the slightest suffering of anything in creation."[19]

Finally, over thirty years ago in his now infamous article "The Historical Roots of Our Ecologic Crisis" Lynn White, Jr., made the audacious and inflammatory claim that the Judeo-Christian tradition was the primary cause of our environmental crisis. Drawing on biblical sources, particularly the Genesis creation narratives, White claimed that "no item in the physical creation had any purpose save to serve man's purposes" leading him to conclude that Western Christianity "is the most anthropocentric religion the world has seen."[20] White's conclusions stirred a fury of response especially from biblical scholars who argued that his interpretation of the biblical text was erroneous. Nevertheless, in spite of the errors and oversimplifications of White's historiography his essay raised two very important issues—anthropocentrism and biblical hermeneutics—for biblical-theological reflection. Perhaps, as White's essay suggested, Christians have read and interpreted the biblical text as if only humans mattered. After thirty years of retrospective reflection—after which we find ourselves still in the midst of environmental destruction—White's essay ought to be perceived as a catalyst that has ignited a new hermeneutical approach to the biblical tradition. Faced with continuing deterioration of the earth's biosphere, many contemporary biblical scholars are returning to the roots of the Judeo-Christian tradition in search of sources of hope and empowerment. This chapter is a prime example of this endeavor.

"Hope Amidst Crisis: The Israelite Prophets' Vision of Cosmic Redemption" is a significant contribution to the ongoing task of reinterpreting the biblical message through an ecological set of lenses. The main thesis of this chapter—"that redemption of humankind is connected to the restoration of the natural world through divine promise"—serves as a necessary corrective to the commonly held belief that only humans are the beneficiaries of God's redemptive action.[21] Drawing on the writings of the Old Testament prophets this chapter makes clear that the eschatological hope of humanity's redemption is intrinsically linked to the restoration of all creation. This prophetic vision of salvation will be characterized by a renewal of "harmonious relationships" between God, human, and earth. This eschatological vision is offered here as a foundation for hope as humanity, searching for solutions to its self-induced environmental mess, welcomes the twenty-first century.

The biblical promise of future redemption, however, requires response. The prophetic vision of new creation is a false and empty hope unless it empowers us to embrace new ways of living on this planet that anticipate the future. Indeed, this will require grace, but it will not be cheap. Hope will arise from the eschatological horizon of faith and the day-to-day commitment to do justice and righteousness to all creation. The task of working for a just and sustainable world will appear to some as unattainable; consequently, the praxis of hope will be a key ingredient. The U.S. Catholic bishops are aware of this when they write:

> Without justice, a sustainable economy will be beyond reach. Without an ecologically responsible world economy, justice will be unachievable. To accomplish either is an enormous task; together they seem overwhelming. However, "all things are possible" to those who hope in God. Hope is the virtue at the heart of a Christian environmental ethic. Hope gives us the courage, direction and energy required for this arduous common endeavor.[22]

The ethical response required to accomplish the "arduous common endeavor" of creating a just and sustainable world will lead us in new directions. It will require, in other words, a wholesale paradigmatic shift in the way humans live on the earth. This will require hope and faith in the alluring biblical vision of God's promise of cosmic redemption.

NOTES: CHAPTER 14

[1] See, e.g., Isa 13:1-5; 24:4-5; 33:7-9, etc.

[2] The term "redemption" is being used here as synonymous with "liberation" and "restoration."

[3] In a book chapter of this brief length it is impossible to examine adequately all the prophetic texts that link creation and redemption. Nor is it possible to go into great detail with those passages that have been selected for study. However, salient comments on selected passages should lay the foundation for further study and give support to the previously stated argument that there is, in fact, a connection between creation and redemption.

[4] In his comments on vv. 23-26 John N. Oswalt (*The Book of Isaiah: Chapters 1–39.* NICOT [Grand Rapids: Eerdmans, 1986] 562) states that ". . . the language here speaks of the effects in nature that redemption will bring, but it speaks of more than that, as the supernaturally heightened figures indicate. Springs do not break out on mountaintops, nor could any living thing endure a sun seven times brighter than at present. Thus Isaiah makes it plain he is speaking of something more than mere physical blessing. He is speaking of a time when all that is good about human life will be made incredibly better, and that includes love, integrity, faithfulness, justice, righteousness, etc."

[5] For a description of Israel's sinfulness and the suffering that resulted from it see, e.g., Isa 42:21-25; 43:22-24.

[6] For further discussion, see Peter D. Miscall, *Isaiah* (Sheffield: JSOT Press, 1993) 108–109.

[7] For further discussion on the idea of creation in relation to redemption see Ronald A. Simkins, *Creator & Creation: Nature in the Worldview of Ancient Israel* (Peabody, Mass.: Hendrickson, 1994) 105–106.

[8] The verbs here are understood as present tense. When used in prophetic oracles the qatal Hebrew verb form can be interpreted as both a prophetic perfect (Paul Joüon, *A Grammar of Biblical Hebrew,* translated by Takamitsu Muraoka. Subsidia Biblica 14/II [Rome: Pontifical Biblical Institute, 1991] §112h) and a *perfectum confidentiae* (Emil F. Kautzsch and Arthur E. Cowley, eds., *Gesenius' Hebrew Grammar* [2d ed. Oxford: Clarendon Press, 1910] §106n).

[9] On this point Simkins (*Creator & Creation* 235) states further that "because the people have already experienced God's judgment through war and exile, the prophets of the exile herald the dawn of God's new creation—the redemption of Israel and the natural world. With the catastrophe past, God is about to redeem God's people through a new creation."

[10] For further discussion of Hos 2:16-23 and the interrelatedness of redemption and creation see Simkins, *Creator & Creation* 219–20.

[11] J. E. and D. R. Kirk, *Cherish the Earth* (Scottsdale, Ariz.: Herald Press, 1993) 91.

[12] Robert Murray, *The Cosmic Covenant: Biblical Themes of Justice, Peace, and the Integrity of Creation* (London: A Heythrop Monograph published by Sheed & Ward; Westminster, Md.: Christian Classics, 1992) 108.

[13] The phrase "and he shall strike the earth with the rod of his mouth" in v. 4b is to be understood metaphorically. The reference indicates the worldwide power and influence of the leader and not the actual cursing of the land. For further discussion see George Buchanan Gray, *A Critical and Exegetical Commentary on the Book of Isaiah I–XXXIX.* ICC (Edinburgh: T & T Clark, 1912) 218.

[14] Simkins (*Creator & Creation* 226) notes that "the domestic animals serve as the key for understanding Isaiah's oracle. This oracle is not envisioning the cessation of violence among wild animals but between the animal world and the human world. In the new creation the ingroup/outgroup enmity between humans and the wild animals will be reconciled."

[15] Isaiah 32:19, a subject of much scholarly debate, seems out of place in this particular vision (Isa 32:16-20) that speaks of creation and life, and not destruction. While the verse may be understood in several ways scholars in general consider it either an interpolation or a fragment from the preceding oracle (Isa 32:9-15) that should be placed directly after v. 14. At any rate vv. 16-18, 20 create a unified picture that is similar in thought and theme to Isaiah's other eschatological visions (see, e.g., Isa 11:1-9). For further discussion of v. 19 see Oswalt, *Isaiah* 589 and Joseph Jensen, *Isaiah 1–39.* OTM 8 (Wilmington, Del.: Michael Glazier, 1984) 253.

[16] Richard J. Clifford, "The Bible and the Environment," in Kevin W. Irwin and Edmund D. Pellegrino, eds., *Preserving the Creation: Environmental Theology and Ethics* (Washington, D.C.: Georgetown University Press, 1994) 14.

[17] J. Alec Motyer, *The Prophecy of Isaiah* (Downers Grove, Ill.: InterVarsity, 1993) 337.

[18] Jeffrey G. Sobosan, *Bless the Beasts: A Spirituality of Animal Care* (New York: Crossroad, 1991) 23.

[19] *Des heiligen Ephraem des Syrers Hymnen de paradiso und contra Julianum,* edited and translated by Edmund Beck. CSCO 174–175 (Louvain: Secrétariat du CorpusSCO, 1957); English translation (with Commentary on Genesis, section 2): *Hymns on Paradise,* by Sebastian P. Brock (Crestwood, N.Y.: St. Vladimir's Seminary Press, 1990).

[20] Lynn White, Jr., "The Historical Roots of Our Ecologic Crisis," in Ian G. Barbour, ed., *Western Man and Environmental Ethics* (Reading, Mass.: Addison-Wesley, 1973) 25.

[21] See above, p. 270.

[22] "Renewing the Earth," *Origins* (December 12, 1991) 432.

Epilogue

$\mathcal{A}$ wise sage once wrote, "For everything there is a season, and a time for every matter under heaven:

> a time to be born, and a time to die;
> a time to plant, and a time to pluck up what has been planted;
> a time to break down, and a time to build up." (Eccl 3:1-2, 3b)

As dusk gently succumbs to the first rays of dawn, creation—indeed, the entire earth itself—now stands at a crossroads between peril and promise, depravity and grace, despair and hope. Now is the season and now is the time for every matter under heaven as the twenty-first century greets the dawn of the third millennium. God has poured out the Spirit upon all creation as it groans in pain, longing to be freed from bondage while laboring to give birth to new dreams and new visions. This book, *All Creation Is Groaning: An Interdisciplinary Vision for Life in a Sacred Universe,* offers a glimpse at creation's pain and pregnant possibilities as it beckons its readers to become bearers of new paradigms.

One of the new paradigms that must be born is a multi-disciplinary approach to the current environmental crisis. This text demonstrates that this approach needs to be taken and, in fact, it can be done when people from all walks of life, academic disciplines, and faith traditions come together to talk, to dream, to study, to envision, to educate, to create, to be educated, and to give birth to concrete ways that can turn the prophet Isaiah's words about a new heaven and a new earth from vision into reality. As the sage proclaims, "For everything there is a season. . . ." Now is the season; all creation is groaning.

Another new paradigm that must be born is the existence of a community of scholars within the field of education, especially within higher education. The past trend of the compartmentalization of knowledge must be relinquished. It is time for unhealthy competition and turf battles to die so that the academic community can embrace its ethical responsibility to communicate knowledge to the larger world community and not be engaged merely in debate and argumentation among themselves. It is also time for the academic community to listen to the wisdom of non-academicians gained through myriad life experiences. It is also time for conversations among scientists and theologians, philosophers and poets, economists and health care professionals, political scientists and engineers, storytellers and musicians to be born. Not only do such conversations spark creativity and clarify values and ethics, but they also free and stimulate the imagination to generate fresh ideas, to gain new insights, and to envision and search for new ways of living faithfully upon the earth. This text exemplifies that such conversations are indeed possible. Out of diverse conversations comes a golden thread that can unravel many life problems while weaving together, in a holistic way, life's many complexities. As the sage proclaims, "For everything there is a season. . . ." Now is the season; all creation is groaning.

For years biblical scholars and theologians have, in some cases, worked independently of one another as well as independently of their faith communities. Also, biblical scholars and theologians have worked independently of other disciplines. An additional paradigm that must come to life is collaboration among Scripture and theology, and Scripture, theology, and other academic disciplines. For example, theologians must be in conversation with scientists, philosophers, poets, and theologians. The human community can no longer expect biblical scholars and/or theologians to give explicit answers to many of the pressing questions and concerns of today. Furthermore, it is the common hermeneutical task of both biblical scholars and theologians to interpret the biblical and theological traditions in the face of a common enterprise or concern. Again, this text provides a model that speaks of the openness of biblical scholars and theologians to engage in conversations among themselves and among those scholars in other disciplines. As the sage proclaims, "for everything there is a season. . . ." Now is the season; all creation is groaning.

No longer can one speak only of "social justice." What is needed today is justice for all creation. The older model of justice grounded in anthropocentric attitudes is insufficient. The new paradigm that must be born is one that speaks of cosmic redemption for all creation. As this text has made clear in various chapters, the redemption of humankind is inextricably linked to the restoration of the natural world. This linkage points to the ethical demands that all intellectual disciplines bear in the face of environmental crisis. None of us can prescind from the urgent need to embrace ethical praxis that seeks to renew and restore the planet earth. This ethical mandate is not a theory. Unless scholars, within their multi-disciplinary contexts, move their students to envision new ways of living ethically we will not achieve the vision proposed in this volume. For this redemption and restoration, all creation groans. ". . . I have set before you life and death, blessings and curses. Choose life so that you and your descendants may live . . ." (Deut 30:19)—so that you and *all* creation may live.

Finally, a new series such as this Connections Series, of which this book is a part, is a new paradigm for scholarship that needs to emerge more widely among publishing houses and journals alike. We, the weavers of and contributors to this text, are especially indebted to Linda Maloney and The Liturgical Press for their vision that has allowed new seeds to germinate on dry but fertile soil. These seeds have brought new life and vision to one community of scholars "on the bluff" in Oregon. We hope that our work will be a sign of hope and grace for all life in our sacred universe.

Bibliography

Abramson, Howard. "Teamsters Authorize Strike Against UPS if Talks Fail," *The Oregonian,* July 16, 1997, C1–C2.

Al-Daffa, Ali, and John Stroyls. *Studies in the Exact Sciences in Medieval Islam.* New York: John Wiley, 1984.

Alexander, David. "Feeding the Hungry and Protecting the Environment," infra, 77–98.

Al-Hassan, Ahmad Y., and Donald R. Hill. *Islamic Technology.* Cambridge: Cambridge University Press, 1986.

Andersen, Francis I., and David. N. Freedman. *Hosea.* AB 24. New York: Doubleday, 1980.

Anderson, Bernhard W. *From Creation to New Creation.* Overtures to Biblical Theology. Minneapolis: Fortress, 1994.

_____, ed. *Creation in the Old Testament.* Philadelphia: Fortress, 1984.

Arberry, A. J., ed. *The Legacy of Persia.* Oxford: Clarendon Press, 1953.

Arthur, Michael B., and Denise M. Rousseau, eds. *The Boundaryless Career: A New Employment Principle for a New Organizational Era.* New York: Oxford University Press, 1996.

Auld, A. G. *Amos.* Sheffield: JSOT Press, 1986.

Avery, Dennis. "The Myth of Global Hunger," in *The World and I* (January 1997), reprinted in Theodore D. Goldfarb, ed., *Taking Sides. Clashing Views on Controversial Environmental Issues.* 8th ed. Guilford, Conn.: Dushkin Publishing Group, 1998, 359–63.

Baasten, Matthew. "Christian Values, Technology, and the Environmental Crisis," infra, 58–76.

_____. *Pride According to Gregory the Great.* Lewiston, N.Y.: Edwin Mellen, 1986.

Babbar, Sunil, and David Aspelin. "The Overtime Rebellion: Symptom of a Bigger Problem?" *The Academy of Management Executive* 12/4 (February 1998) 68–76.

Barfield, Owen. *Saving the Appearances: A Study in Idolatry.* New York: Harcourt Brace & World, [1965?].

Barnett, R. J. "The End of Jobs: Employment Is One Thing the Global Economy Is Not Creating," *Harper's* 287 (September 1993) 47– 52.

Barry, Vincent. *Moral Issues in Business.* 3d ed. Belmont, Calif.: Wadsworth, 1986.

Bell, John "The Search for a Discourse on Aging: The Elderly on Television," *Gerontologist* 32/3 (1992) 305.

Bellah, Robert, et al. *Habits of the Heart: Individualism and Commitment in American Life.* Updated Edition. Berkeley: University of California Press, 1996.

Berman, Morris. *The Reenchantment of the World.* Ithaca: Cornell University Press, 1981.

Berry, Wendell. *Another Turn of the Crank.* Washington, D.C.: Counterpoint, 1995.

_____. *The Gift of Good Land: Further Essays Cultural and Agricultural.* San Francisco: North Point Press, 1981.

_____. *Home Economics.* San Francisco: North Point Press, 1987.

_____. *What Are People For?* San Francisco: North Point Press, 1990.

Betsworth, Roger G. *Social Ethics: An Examination of American Moral Traditions.* Louisville: Westminster/John Knox, 1990.

Bhatia, S., and J. P. Neglia. "Epidemiology of Childhood Acute Myelogenous Leukemia," *Journal of Pediatric Hematology and Oncology* 17/2 (1995) 94–100.

Birch, Bruce C., and Larry L. Rasmussen. *Bible and Ethics in the Christian Life.* Minneapolis: Augsburg, 1976.

_____. *The Predicament of the Prosperous.* Philadelphia: Westminster, 1978.

Blackstone, William. "Ethics and Ecology," in W. Michael Hoffman and Jennifer Mills Moore, eds., *Business Ethics: Readings and Cases in Corporate Morality.* New York: McGraw-Hill, 1984, 356–62.

Blieszner Rosemary, and Victoria H. Bedford, eds. *Aging and the Family: Theory and Research.* Westport, Conn.: Praeger, 1996.

Block, Peter. *Stewardship: Choosing Service Over Self-Interest.* San Francisco: Berrett-Koehler, 1993.

Boadt, Lawrence. *Jeremiah 26–52, Habakkuk, Zephaniah, Nahum.* OTM 10. Wilmington, Del.: Michael Glazier, 1982.

Bordo, Susan. *The Flight to Objectivity: Essays on Cartesianism and Culture.* Albany: SUNY Press, 1987.

Botkin, Daniel, and Edward Keller. *Environmental Science. Earth as a Living Planet.* 2d ed. New York: John Wiley, 1998.

Boyle, Nicholas. *Who Are We Now? Christian Humanism and the Global Market from Hegel to Heaney.* Notre Dame, Ind.: University of Notre Dame Press, 1998.

Brady, Nyle C., and Ray R.Weil. *The Nature and Properties of Soils.* 11th ed. Upper Saddle River, N.J.: Prentice Hall, 1996.

Bredahl, Carl. *New Ground: Western American Narrative and the Literary Canon.* Chapel Hill, N.C.: University of North Carolina Press, 1989.

Brody, E. M. "Parent Care as a Normative Family Stress," *Gerontologist* 25 (1985) 19–29.

Bronfenbrenner, Uri. "Ecological Systems Theory," *Annals of Child Development* 6 (1989) 187–249.

_____. "Ecology of the Family as a Context for Human Development: Research Perspectives," *Developmental Psychology* 22 (1986) 723–42.

_____. *The Ecology of Human Development.* Cambridge, Mass.: Harvard University Press, 1979.

Brooks, Paul. *Speaking for Nature: How Literary Naturalists from Henry Thoreau to Rachel Carson Have Shaped America.* San Francisco: Sierra Club, 1980.

Brown, Dee. *Bury My Heart at Wounded Knee: An Indian History of the American West.* New York: Holt, Rinehart & Winston, 1970.

Brown, Lester Russell. "Analyzing the Demographic Trap," in idem, project director, *State of the World 1987: A Worldwatch Institute Report on Progress Toward a Sustainable Society.* New York: W. W. Norton, 1987, 20–37.

_____, et al. *Vital Signs 1994: The Trends that Are Shaping Our Future.* Washington, D.C.: Worldwatch Institute, 1994.

Brown, Seyom. *International Relations in a Changing Global System.* New York: St. Martin's Press, 1997.

Browne, Malcolm W. "Scientists Deplore the Flight from Reason," *New York Times,* June 6, 1995.

Brueggemann, Walter. *Genesis.* Atlanta: John Knox, 1982.

_____. *The Land: Place as Gift, Promise and Challenge in Biblical Faith.* Philadelphia: Fortress, 1977.

Buell, Lawrence. *The Environmental Imagination: Thoreau, Nature Writing, and the Formation of American Culture.* Cambridge, Mass.: Harvard University Press, 1995.

Burton, Linda. *Families and Aging.* Amityville, N.Y.: Baywood, 1993.

Bush, Mark B. *Ecology of a Changing Planet.* Upper Saddle River, N.J.: Prentice Hall, 1997.

Butkus, Russell A. "Sustainability: An Eco-Theological Analysis," infra, 144–167.

Buttimer, Anne. *Geography and the Human Spirit.* Baltimore: Johns Hopkins University Press, 1993.

Carley, Keith W. *Ezekiel.* Cambridge: Cambridge University Press, 1974.

Carpenter, B. "Filial Obligation, Ethnicity, and Caregiving." Paper presented at the meeting of the Gerontological Society of America, Washington D.C., November 19, 1996.

Carson, Rachel. "The Marginal World," in Karen Knowles, ed., *Celebrating the Land: Women's Nature Writings, 1850–1991.* Flagstaff, Ariz.: Northland Press, 1992, 47–51.

_____. *Silent Spring.* Boston: Houghton Mifflin, 1962.

Chappel, N. L. "Aging and Social Care," in Robert H. Binstock and Linda K. George, eds., *Handbook of Aging and the Social Sciences.* San Diego: Academic Press, 1990, 438–54.

Chipeniuk, Raymond. "Childhood Foraging as a Means of Acquiring Competent Human Cognition About Biodiversity," *Environment & Behavior* 24 (July 1995) 490–512.

Chiras, Daniel D. *Environmental Science: Action for a Sustainable Future.* 4th ed. Redwood City, Calif.: Benjamin/Cummings, 1994.

_____. *Environmental Science: A Systems Approach to Sustainable Development.* 5th ed. Belmont, Calif.: Wadsworth, 1998.

Church, Foster, and Peter D. Sleeth. "Sanctuary Under Siege," *The Sunday Oregonian,* July 6, 1997, A11.

Cicirelli, V. G. "A Comparison of Helping Behavior to Elderly Parents of Adult Children with Intact and Disrupted Marriages," *Gerontologist* 23 (1990) 619–25.

Clapp, Rodney. "Why the Devil Takes Visa," *Christianity Today* 40 (October 7, 1996) 18–33.

Clements, Ronald E. *Isaiah 1–39.* NCBC. Grand Rapids: Eerdmans, 1980.

Clifford, Richard J. "The Bible and the Environment," in Kevin W. Irwin and Edmund D. Pellegrino, eds., *Preserving the Creation: Environmental Theology and Ethics.* Washington, D.C.: Georgetown University Press, 1994, 1–26.

Cody, Aelred. *Ezekiel, with an Excursus on Old Testament Priesthood.* OTM 11. Wilmington, Del.: Michael Glazier, 1984.

Cohen, Joel E. "Population Growth and Earth's Carrying Capacity," *Science* 269 (1995) 341–46.

Cohen, Michael. *The Pathless Way: John Muir and American Wilderness.* Madison: University of Wisconsin Press, 1984.

Cohen, Stewart. "Promoting Ecological Awareness in Children," *Childhood Education* 68 (1992) 258–59.

Cohen, Stewart, and Diane M. Horm-Wingerd. "Children and the Environment: Ecological Awareness Among Preschool Children," *Environment & Behavior* 25 (January 1993) 103–120.

Cole, T. R. "What Have We 'Made' of Aging?" *Journal of Gerontology* 50/6 (1995) 341–43.

Collins Pine Document. "Kane Hardwood," 1997.

Commoner, Barry. *The Closing Circle: Nature, Man, and Technology.* New York: Bantam Books, 1972.

_____. *Making Peace with the Planet.* New York: Pantheon, 1990.

Conrad, Edgar W. *Reading Isaiah.* Overtures to Biblical Theology. Minneapolis: Fortress, 1991.

Cooke, George A. *A Critical and Exegetical Commentary on the Book of Ezekiel.* ICC. Edinburgh: T & T Clark, 1985.

Cooper, Lamar E., Sr. *Ezekiel.* NAC 17. Nashville: Broadman & Holman, 1994.

Copland, Aaron. *Music and Imagination.* Cambridge, Mass.: Harvard University Press, 1952.

Cousins, Emily. "Mountains Made Alive: Native American Relationships with Sacred Land," *Cross Currents* 46/4 (Winter 1996/1997) 497–509.

Crispell, Diane. "How Executives Manage Time Pressure," *American Demographics* 17/1 (January 1995) 38(2).

Crossette, Barbara. "How to Fix a Crowded World: Add People," *New York Times* Week in Review (November 2, 1997) 1.

Cummesky, James P. "The Montessori Erdkinder: Three Abstracts," *Namta Journal* 18 (Winter 1993) 173–82.

Cunningham, William P., and Barbara Woodworth Saigo. *Environmental Science: A Global Concern.* 4th ed. Dubuque, Iowa: William C. Brown, 1997.

Curran, Charles, et al. *Feminist Ethics and the Catholic Moral Tradition.* New York: Paulist, 1996.

Dallmeyer, Dorinda G., and Albert F. Ike, eds. *Environmental Ethics and the Global Marketplace.* Athens Ga.: University of Georgia Press, 1998.

Daniel, John. "Holy Waters," *Portland* 16/2 (Summer 1997) 28–31.

Davies, Sir Peter Maxwell. "Symphony," in *Peter Maxwell Davies: Studies from Two Decades*. Selected and Introduced by Stephen Pruslin. London: Boosey & Hawkes, 1979, 94–97.

_____. Liner notes for idem, *Symphony No. 2*. Sir Peter Maxwell Davies conducting the BBC Philharmonic. Collins Classics CD 14032, 1994.

_____. Liner notes for idem, *Symphony No. 1*. Sir Peter Maxwell Davies conducting the BBC Philharmonic. Collins Classics CD 14352, 1995.

"Declaration on the Relation of the Church to Non-Christian Religions," in Austin Flannery, o.p., ed., *Vatican Council II: The Basic Sixteen Documents*. Northport, N.Y.: Costello, 1996, 738–42.

Dempsey, Carol J. "Hope Amidst Crisis: A Prophetic Vision of Cosmic Redemption," infra, 269–84.

Descartes, René. *Philosophical Works*. Vols. I and II, edited by Elizabeth Haldane and G.R.T. Ross. Cambridge: Cambridge University Press, 1969.

_____. *Selected Philosophical Writings*. Translated by John Cottingham, Robert Stoothoff, and Dugald Murdoch. Cambridge: Cambridge University Press, 1988.

Devall, Bill, and George Sessions. *Deep Ecology: Living as if Nature Mattered*. Salt Lake City: G. M. Smith, 1985.

Devlin, Keith. "Rather than Scientific Literacy, Colleges Should Teach Scientific Awareness," *Chronicle of Higher Education,* January 23, 1998.

DeWitt, Calvin B. *The Environment and the Christian: What Does the New Testament Say about the Environment?* Grand Rapids: Baker Book House, 1991.

Diamond, Irene, and Gloria Feman Orenstein, eds. *Reweaving the World: The Emergence of Ecofeminism*. San Francisco: Sierra Club, 1990.

Dietrich, William. *Northwest Passage: The Great Columbia River*. New York: Simon & Schuster, 1995.

Donahue, John R. "Biblical Perspectives on Justice," in John C. Haughey, ed., *The Faith That Does Justice*. New York: Paulist, 1977, 68–112.

Downes, Edward. *The New York Philharmonic Guide to the Symphony*. New York: Walker and Company, 1976.

Dreman, Solly, ed. *The Family on the Threshold of the 21st Century: Trends and Implications*. Mahwah, N.J.: Lawrence Erlbaum Associates, 1997.

Duckworth, Eleanor. "The Having of Wonderful Ideas." *Harvard Educational Review* 42 (1972) 217–31.

Dunn, Ardys. "Development of Environmental Responsibility in Children," infra 193–211.

Durning, Alan B. "Ending Poverty," in Lester R. Brown, project director, *State of the World 1990: A Worldwatch Institute Report on Progress Toward a Sustainable Society.* New York and London: W. W. Norton, 1990, 135.

Dwyer, J. W., and R. T. Coward. "A Multivariate Comparison of the Involvement of Adult Sons Versus Daughters in the Care of Impaired Parents," *Journal of Gerontology* 46 (1991) 259–69.

Ebersole, Priscilla, and Patricia Hess. *Toward Healthy Aging: Human Needs and Nursing Response.* 5th ed. St. Louis: Mosby, 1998.

The Economist (London), December 13, 1997, 13.

Eichrodt, Walther. *Ezekiel.* OTL. Philadelphia: Westminster, 1970.

Elder, John C., ed. *American Nature Writers.* New York: Scribner's, 1996.

_____. *Imagining the Earth: Poetry and the Vision of Nature.* Urbana: University of Illinois Press, 1985.

Ellul, Jacques. *The Technological Society.* New York: Knopf, 1964.

Emmerson, Grace I. *Isaiah 56–66.* Old Testament Guides. Sheffield: JSOT Press, 1992.

Ephrem of Syria, Saint. *Des heiligen Ephraem des Syrers Hymnen de paradiso und contra Julianum.* Edited and translated by Edmund Beck. CSCO 174–175. Louvain: Secrétariat du CorpusSCO, 1957. English: *Hymns on Paradise.* Translated by Sebastian P. Brock. Crestwood, N.Y.: St. Vladimir's Seminary Press, 1990.

Erikson, Erik H. *Childhood and Society.* 2d ed. New York: W. W. Norton, 1963.

Estes, Clarissa Pinkola. *Women Who Run with the Wolves: Myths and Stories of the Wild Woman Archetype.* New York: Ballantine Books, 1992.

Feenstra, Gail, et al. University of California Sustainable Agriculture Research and Education Program. http://www.sarep.ucdavis.edu/concept.htm. University of California, Davis, 1997.

Feiss, Hugh. "Watch the Crows: Environmental Responsibility and the Benedictine Tradition," in Drew Christiansen and Walter Grazer, eds., *"And God Saw That It Was Good." Catholic Theology and the Environment.* Washington, D.C.: U.S. Catholic Conference, 1996, 147–64.

Fellers, Pat. "Practice the Skills You Want to Achieve," *Catholic Sentinel* 125/20 (May 20, 1994) 16.

Fellinger, Bettina. Liner notes for Jean Sibelius, *Symphonies No. 2 and No. 7*. Eugene Ormandy conducting the Philadelphia Orchestra. Sony CD SBK 53509, 1994.

Finley, James. *Merton's Palace of Nowhere: A Search for God through Awareness of the True Self*. Notre Dame, Ind.: Ave Maria, 1983.

Fowler, James. "Stages of Faith," *Psychology Today* 17 (1983) 56–62.

_____. *Stages of Faith: The Psychology of Human Development and the Quest for Meaning*. New York: Harper & Row, 1981.

Frank, André G. "World System in Crisis," in William R. Thompson, ed., *Contending Approaches to World System Analysis*. Beverly Hills: SAGE, 1983, 27–42.

Freeman, Claire. "Planning and Play: Creating Greener Environments." *Children's Environments Quarterly* 12 (September 1995) 381– 88.

Fromherz, Frank. "A Sense of Place," infra, 240–68.

Fuld, James J. *The Book of World-Famous Music: Classical, Popular and Folk*. New York: Crown, 1971.

Gaiman, Neil, and Terry Pratchett. *Good Omens*. New York: The Berkley Publishing Group, 1990.

Gebhardt-Seele, Peter. "Why Not Consider Erdkinder?" *Namta Journal* 21 (Spring 1996) 138–48.

Gelineau, Joseph. "The Path of Music," in Mary Collins, David Power, and Mellonee Burnim, eds., *Music and the Experience of God*. Edinburgh: T & T Clark, 1989.

Gephart, Roy, and Regina Lundgren. *Hanford Tank Clean Up: A Guide to Understanding the Technical Issues*. PNL-10773. Richland, Wash.: Pacific Northwest National Laboratory, 1997.

Gergen, Kenneth. *The Saturated Self: Dilemmas of Identity in Contemporary Life*. New York: Basic Books, 1991.

Giarrusso, Roseann, et al. "A Cross-cultural Comparison of the Intergenerational Stake Phenomenon over the Life Course." Paper presented at the Meeting of the Gerontological Society of America, Washington D.C., November 19, 1996.

Gibson, Mary Jo Storey. "Family Support Patterns, Policies, and Programs," in Charlotte Nusberg, ed., with Mary Jo Gibson and Sheila Peace. *Innovative Aging Programs Abroad: Implications for the United States*. Westport, Conn.: Greenwood, 1984.

Gilligan, Carol, and Grant Wiggins. "The Origins of Morality in Early Childhood Relationships," in Carol Gilligan, et al., eds., *Mapping the Moral Domain: A Contribution of Women's Thinking to Psychological Theory and Education*. Cambridge, Mass.: Center for the Study of

Gender, Education, and Human Development, Harvard University Graduate School of Education: Distributed by Harvard University Press, 1988, 111–38.

Global Database on Child Growth. Geneva: World Health Organization, 1995.

Global Prevalence of Iodine Deficiency Disorders. Micronutrient Deficiency Information System Working Paper Number 1. Geneva: World Health Organization/United Nations Children's Fund/ International Council for Control of Iodine Deficiency Disorders, 1993.

Global Prevalence of Vitamin-A Deficiency. Micronutrient Deficiency Information System Working Paper Number 2. Geneva: World Health Organization/United Nations Children's Fund, 1995.

Glotfelty, Cheryll, and Harold Fromm, eds. *The Ecocriticism Reader: Landmarks in Literary Ecology*. Athens, Ga.: University of Georgia Press, 1996.

_____. "Introduction: Literary Studies in an Age of Environmental Crisis," in Glotfelty and Fromm, eds., *The Ecocriticism Reader: Landmarks in Literary Ecology*. Athens, Ga.: University of Georgia Press, 1996.

Goldfarb, Theodore D., ed. *Taking Sides. Clashing Views on Controversial Environmental Issues*. 6th ed. Guilford, Conn.: Dushkin Publishing Group, 1995.

Gordon, Anita, and David Suzuki. *It's a Matter of Survival*. Cambridge, Mass.: Harvard University Press, 1990.

Gore, Albert. *Earth in the Balance*. New York: Plume, 1993.

Grant, George P. "Thinking about Technology," in idem, *Technology and Justice*. Notre Dame, Ind.: University of Notre Dame Press; Toronto: Anansi, 1986, 11–34.

Gray, Elizabeth Dodson. "Come Inside the Circle of Creation: An Ethic of Attunement," in Frederick Ferré and Peter Hartel, eds., *Ethics and Environmental Policy*. Athens: Ga.: University of Georgia Press, 1994, 21–41.

Gray, George Buchanan. *A Critical and Exegetical Commentary on the Book of Isaiah, I–XXXIX*. (Contains I–XXVII only.) ICC. Edinburgh: T & T Clark, 1912.

Greenblatt, Stephen, and Giles Gunn. *Redrawing the Boundaries: The Transformation of English and American Literary Studies*. New York: Modern Language Association of America, 1992.

Greider, William. *One World, Ready or Not: The Manic Logic of Global Capitalism.* New York: Simon & Schuster, 1997.

Groome, Thomas. *Christian Religious Education.* San Francisco: Harper & Row, 1980.

Gussow, Alan. *A Sense of Place: The Artist and the American Land.* 2 vols. New York: Seabury, 1971; San Francisco: Friends of the Earth, 1972–1973.

Halal, William E. *The New Management: Democracy and Enterprise Are Transforming Organizations.* San Francisco: Berrett-Koehler, 1996.

Hall, Douglas John. *Imaging God.* Grand Rapids: Eerdmans, 1986.

_____. *The Steward: A Biblical Symbol Come of Age.* Library of Christian Stewardship 7. New York: Friendship Press, 1982; rev. ed. New York: Friendship Press; Grand Rapids: Eerdmans, 1990.

Hall, Douglas T. "Long Live the Career," in idem, ed., *The Career Is Dead—Long Live the Career: A Relational Approach to Careers.* San Francisco: Jossey-Bass, 1996, 1–12.

_____, and Philip Mirvis. "The New Protean Career: Psychological Success and the Path with a Heart," in Hall, ed., *The Career Is Dead—Long Live the Career: A Relational Approach to Careers,* 15–45.

Hallie, Philip P. *Lest Innocent Blood Be Shed: The Story of the Village of Le Chambon, and How Goodness Happened There.* New York: Harper & Row, 1979.

Hansen, Eric, and John Punches. "Collins Pine: Lessons from a Pioneer. Case Study." *The Business of Sustainable Forestry. Case Studies.* Chicago: The John D. and Catherine T. MacArthur Foundation, 1997.

Hanson, Paul D. *Isaiah 40–66.* Interpretation. Louisville: John Knox, 1995.

Hanson, Shirley M. H., and Sheryl T. Boyd, eds. *Family Health Care Nursing: Theory, Practice, and Research.* Philadelphia: F. A. Davis, 1996.

Hardin, Garrett. "The Tragedy of the Commons," *Science* 162 (1968) 12–43.

_____. *Exploring New Ethics for Survival: The Voyage of the Spaceship Beagle.* New York: Viking, 1972.

_____, and John Baden, eds. *Managing the Commons.* San Francisco: W. H. Freeman, 1977.

Harding, Sandra. "Rethinking Standpoint Epistemology: 'What Is Strong Objectivity?'" in Linda Alcoff and Elizabeth Potter, eds., *Feminist Epistemologies.* New York: Routledge, 1993, 49–82.

Hardison, O. B., Jr. *Disappearing through the Skylight: Culture and Technology in the Twentieth Century.* New York: Viking Penguin, 1989.

Harman, Willis. "Business as a Component of the Global Ecology," *Noetic Sciences Review* 19 (Autumn 1991) 18–23.

Hartley, Robert. *Business Ethics: Violations of the Public Trust.* New York: Wiley & Sons, 1993.

Hawken, Paul. *The Ecology of Commerce: A Declaration of Sustainability.* New York: HarperBusiness, 1993.

Hayes, John R., ed. *The Genius of Arab Civilization: Source of Renaissance.* 1st M.I.T. paperback of the English ed. Cambridge, Mass.: M.I.T. Press, 1978.

Henderson, M. C. "Families in Transition: Caring for the Rural Elderly," *Family Community Health* 14 (1992) 61–70.

Herbert, Arthur Sumner. *The Book of the Prophet Isaiah, Chapters 1–39.* Cambridge: Cambridge University Press, 1973.

_____. *The Book of the Prophet Isaiah, Chapters 40–66.* Cambridge: Cambridge University Press, 1975.

Herrin, D. A., and D. S. Wright. "Precursors to a Family Ecology: Interrelated Threads of Ecological Thought," *Family Science Review* 1 (1988) 163–83.

Hileman, Bette. "Energy Department Has Made Progress Cleaning Up Nuclear Weapons Plants," *Chemical and Engineering News* 74 (July 22, 1996) 14–20.

Himes, C. L. "Social Demography of Contemporary Families and Aging," *Generations* 23/3 (1992) 13–16.

Hinrichs, Doug J. "The Natural Step: An Interview with Paul Hawken," *Ecological Economics Bulletin* 1/4 (October 1996) 6–10.

Hoffman, Andrew. *From Heresy to Dogma: An Institutional History of Corporate Environmentalism.* San Francisco: New Lexington Press, 1997.

Hoffman, W. Michael, and Jennifer Mills Moore, eds., *Business Ethics: Readings and Cases in Corporate Morality.* New York: McGraw-Hill, 1984.

Holladay, William L. *Jeremiah 2.* Edited by Paul D. Hanson. Hermeneia. Minneapolis: Fortress, 1989.

Honig, Alice Sterling. "Research in Review: Prosocial Development in Children," *Young Children* 37 (July 1982) 51–62.

Hook, N. C., and Beatrice Paolucci. "The Family as an Ecosystem," *Journal of Home Economics* 62 (1970) 315–18.

Hope for a Global Future: Toward a Just and Sustainable Human Development. Louisville: The Office of the General Assembly, Presbyterian Church, U.S.A., 1996.

Hopkins, Gerard Manley. "God's Grandeur," in Jaroslav Pelikan, ed., *The World Treasury of Modern Religious Thought*. Boston: Little, Brown, 1990, 175–77.

Hopper, David. *Technology, Theology, and the Idea of Progress*. Louisville: Westminster/John Knox, 1991.

Hughes, Barry B. *Continuity and Change in World Politics. The Clash of Perspectives*. 2d ed. New York: Prentice Hall, 1994.

Hughes, Langston. *Selected Poems of Langston Hughes*. New York: Vintage, 1990.

Husaini, S. Waqar Ahmed. *Islamic Environmental Systems Engineering. A Systems Study of Environmental Engineering and the Law, Politics, Education, Economics, and Sociology of Science and Culture of Islam*. London: Macmillan; Indianapolis: American Trust Publications, 1980.

Ihre, Don. "The Experience of Technology: Human-Machine Relations," *Cultural Hermeneutics* 2 (1974).

International Conference on Nutrition. *Proceedings*. Rome, December 1992.

International Institute on Aging. *Preliminary Findings of Survey on Training Needs in Developing Countries*. Report presented at the Expert Group Meeting on Short-Term Training in Social Gerontology, Valletta, Malta, February 1989.

Irwin, Kevin W., and Edmund D. Pellegrino, eds. *Preserving Creation: Environmental Theology and Ethics*. Washington, D.C.: Georgetown University Press, 1994.

Izzi Deen, Mawil Y., J. Ronald Engel, and Joan Gibb Engel, eds., *Ethics of Environment and Development: Global Challenge, International Response*. Tucson, Ariz.: University of Arizona Press; London: Bellhaven, 1990.

Jackson, John Brinckerhoff. *Discovering the Vernacular Landscape*. New Haven: Yale University Press, 1984.

James, Alfred. "Will It Hurt 'Shade'? Adopting a Tree," *Childhood Education* 68 (1992) 260–62.

Jensen, Derrick. *Listening to the Land: Conversations About Nature, Culture and Eros*. San Francisco: Sierra Club, 1995.

Jensen, Joseph. *Isaiah 1–39*. OTM 8. Wilmington, Del.: Michael Glazier, 1984.

John Paul II. *The Ecological Crisis: A Common Responsibility*. Washington, D.C.: U.S. Catholic Conference, 1990.

Johnson, Arlene. "The Business Case for Work-Family Programs," *Journal of Accountancy* 180/2 (August 1995) 53–59.

Johnson, C. L. "Divorced and Reconstituted Families: Effects on the Older Generation," *Generations* 22/3 (1992) 17–20.

Joüon, Paul. *A Grammar of Biblical Hebrew*. 2 vols. Translated by Takamitsu Muraoka. Subsidia Biblica 14. Rome: Pontifical Biblical Institute, 1991.

Kaakinen, Joanna. "An Ecological View of Elders and Their Families: Needs for the Twenty-First Century," infra, 212–26.

Kahn, Peter H., and Ann McCoy. "Children's Moral Relationships with Nature." Paper presented at the meeting of the Jean Piaget Society, Montreal, Quebec, Canada, May 1992.

_____, and Batya Friedman. "Environmental Views and Values of Children in an Inner-City Black Community," *Child Development* 66 (1995) 1403–17.

Kaiser, Otto. *Isaiah 1–12: A Commentary*. Translated by John Bowden. OTL. 2d ed. Philadelphia: Westminster, 1983.

_____. *Isaiah 13–39: A Commentary*. Translated by R. A. Wilson. OTL. Philadelphia: Westminster, 1974.

Kardong, Terrence G., O.S.B. "Ecological Resources in the Benedictine Rule," in Albert J. LaChance and John E. Carroll, eds., *Embracing Earth: Catholic Approaches to Ecology*. Maryknoll, N.Y.: Orbis, 1994, 163–73.

Kaufman, Donald, and Cecilia Franz. *Biosphere 2000: Protecting Our Global Environment*. 2d ed. Dubuque, Ia.: Kendall/Hunt, 1996.

Kautzsch, Emil F., and Arthur E. Cowley, eds. *Gesenius' Hebrew Grammar*. 2d ed. Oxford: Clarendon Press, 1910.

Kegan, Robert. *In Over Our Heads: The Mental Demands of Modern Life*. Cambridge, Mass.: Harvard University Press, 1994.

Keitzar, Renthy. "Creation and Restoration," in David G. Hallman, ed., *Ecotheology: Voices from South and North*. Geneva: WCC Publications; Maryknoll, N.Y.: Orbis, 1994.

Keller, Evelyn Fox. *A Feeling for the Organism: The Life and Work of Barbara McClintock*. New York: W. H. Freeman, 1983.

_____. *Reflections on Gender and Science*. New Haven: Yale University Press, 1985.

Kelman, Steven. "Cost-Benefit Analysis: An Ethical Critique," in W. Michael Hoffman and Jennifer Mills Moore, eds., *Business Ethics*. New York: McGraw-Hill, 1984, 74–82.

Kennan, George F. *At a Century's Ending. Reflections 1982–1995*. New York: W. W. Norton, 1996.

Kennedy, Michael. Liner notes for Gustav Mahler, *Symphony No. 3*. Sir John Barbirolli conducting the Hall Orechestra. BBC legends CD BBCL 4004–7, 1998.

Kenworthy, Tom. "One Tranquil Story of Timber Cutting," *The Washington Post* (October 14, 1992) A3.

Khan, Khalid H. "Contributions of Asians and Asian Americans to Science." Asian Base Line Essay on Science, submitted to Portland Public Schools System 1996.

_____. "An Islamic Perspective on the Environment," infra, 46–57.

Kinsella, Kevin G. "Aging and the Family: Present and Future Demographic Issues," in Rosemary Blieszner and Victoria H. Bedford, eds., *Aging and the Family: Theory and Research*. Westport, Conn.: Praeger, 1996, 32–56.

Kirk, J. E., and D. R. Kirk. *Cherish the Earth*. Scottsdale, Ariz.: Herald Press, 1993.

Kittel, Joanne, and Susan Curtis, "Early Yachats History: The Yachats Indians, Origins of the Yachats Name, and the Reservation Years." Confederated Tribes of the Coos, Lower Umpqua, and Siuslaw Indians, and the Confederated Tribes of the Siletz Indians of Oregon, 1996.

Kleszynski, Kenneth. "Symphonies of Nature: Creation and Re-creation," infra, pp. 227–39.

Knierim, Rolf. "Cosmos and History in Israel's Theology," *Horizons in Biblical Theology* 3 (1981) 59–122.

Koestler, Arthur. *The Sleepwalkers*. New York: Grosset & Dunlap, 1959.

Kohlberg, Lawrence. "Stages and Sequence: The Cognitive-Development Approach to Socialization," in David A. Goslin, ed., *Handbook of Socialization Theory and Research*. Chicago: Rand McNally, 1969, 347–480.

Kolodny, Annette. *The Lay of the Land: Metaphor as Experience and History in American Life and Letters*. Chapel Hill: University of North Carolina Press, 1979.

Kolmes, Steven. "Mental Cartography in a Time of Environmental Crisis," infra, 99–125.

Kosberg Jordan I., ed. *Family Care of the Elderly: Social and Cultural Changes*. Newbury Park, Calif.: SAGE, 1992.

_____. "Policies Encouraging and Requiring Family Care of the Aged: A Critical Assessment." Presented at the 12th International Congress of Gerontology, New York, 1985.

Kosberg, Jordan I., and J. L. Garcia. "Social Changes Affecting Family Care of the Elderly," *Journal of the International Institute on Aging* 1/2 (1991) 2–5.

Krimsky, Sheldon, and Roger Wrubel. *Agricultural Biotechnology and the Environment.* Chicago: University of Illinois Press, 1996.

Kroeber, Karl. *Ecological Literary Criticism: Romantic Imagining and the Biology of Mind.* New York: Columbia University Press, 1994.

LaChance, Albert J., and John E. Carroll, eds., *Embracing Earth: Catholic Approaches to Ecology.* Maryknoll, N.Y.: Orbis, 1994.

Lackey, Nancy, and B. Lee Walker. "An Ecological Framework for Nursing Practice and Research," in Beth Vaughan-Cole, et al., eds., *Family Nursing Practice.* Philadelphia: Saunders, 1998, 38–48.

Lam, Basil. "Ludwig van Beethoven (1770–1827)," in Robert Simpson, ed., *The Symphony 1: Haydn to Dvorak.* Baltimore: Penguin, 1969.

Landes, David S. *The Wealth and Poverty of Nations.* New York: W. W. Norton, 1998.

Lane, Belden C. *Landscapes of the Sacred: Geography and Narrative in American Spirituality.* New York: Paulist, 1988.

Lee, Helen J. "Health Perceptions of Middle, 'New Middle,' and Older Rural Adults," *Family & Community Health* 16 (1993) 19–27.

Leopold, Aldo. *A Sand County Almanac and Sketches Here and There.* New York: Oxford University Press, 1949.

_____. *A Sand County Almanac: 1949.* New York: Ballantine, 1966.

_____. *Round River.* Edited by Luna B. Leopold. London: Oxford University Press, 1953.

Less, Helen H. Liner notes for Gustav Mahler, *Symphony No. 1.* Jascha Horenstein conducting the Vienna Symphony Orchestra. Vox Legends CD CDX2 5508, 1992.

Limburg, James. "The Way of an Eagle in the Sky: Reflections on the Bible and the Care of the Earth," *Catholic World* 233 (July/August 1990) 148–52.

Lloyd, Genevieve. *The Man of Reason.* Minneapolis: University of Minnesota Press, 1984.

London, Manuel. "Redeployment and Continuous Learning in the 21st Century: Hard Lessons and Positive Examples from the Downsizing Era," *Academy of Management Executive* 10/4 (November 1996) 67–79.

Lopez, Barry. "Natural History: An Annotated Booklist," *Antaeus* 57 (Autumn 1986) 97.

_____. "A Literature of Place," *Portland* 16/2 (Summer 1997) 22–25.

Love, Glen A. "Revaluing Nature: Toward an Ecological Criticism," in Glotfelty and Fromm, eds., *The Ecocriticism Reader: Landmarks in Literary Ecology.*

Lowengart, R. A., et al. "Childhood Leukemia and Parents' Occupational and Home Exposures," *Journal of the National Cancer Institute* 79/1 (1987) 39–46.

Lowenthal, Marjorie Fiske, and Clayton Haven. "Interaction and Adaptation: Intimacy as a Critical Variable," *American Sociological Review* 33/1 (February 1968) 20–30.

Ludick, Patricia. "Reflections from the Farm," *Namta Journal* 21 (Summer 1996) 122–39.

Lueckenotte, Annette. *Gerontologic Nursing.* St. Louis: Mosby, 1996.

Lyon, Thomas J., ed. *This Incomperable Land: A Book of American Nature Writing.* Boston: Houghton Mifflin, 1989.

MacIntyre, Alasdair. *After Virtue: A Study in Moral Theory.* Notre Dame, Ind.: University of Notre Dame Press, 1984.

Malthus, Thomas. *An Essay on the Principle of Population as It Affects the Future Improvement of Society.* London: J. Johnson, 1798.

Mander, Jerry. *In the Absence of the Sacred: The Failure of Technology and the Survival of the Indian Nations.* San Francisco: Sierra Club, 1991.

Martin, Norah. "New Ways of Knowing and Being Known," infra, pp. 21–45.

Mathews, Jessica Tuchman. "Redefining Security," *Foreign Affairs* 68/2 (Spring 1989) 167–77.

McDaniel, Jay B. *With Roots and Wings.* Maryknoll, N.Y.: Orbis, 1995.

McDermott, John J. "Do Not Bequeath a Shamble. The Child in the Twenty-First Century: Innocent Hostage to Mindless Oppression or Messenger to the World?" *Namta Journal* 20 (Summer 1995) 93–106.

McGinn, Bernard. *The Foundations of Mysticism: Origins to the Fifth Century.* New York: Crossroad, 1994.

McHarg, Ian. *Design with Nature.* Garden City, N.Y.: Published for the American Museum of Natural History by the Natural History Press, 1969.

McKeating, Henry. *Amos, Hosea, Micah.* Cambridge Bible Commentary. Cambridge: Cambridge University Press, 1971.

McKenzie, John L. *Second Isaiah.* AB 20. Garden City, N.Y.: Doubleday, 1968.

McKinney, Michael, and Robert Schoch. *Environmental Science, Systems and Solutions.* Web Enhanced Edition. Sudbury, Mass.: Jones and Bartlett, 1998.

McLuhan, T. C. *The Way of the Earth: Encounters with Nature in Ancient and Contemporary Thought.* New York: Simon & Schuster, 1994.

McNeely, Jeffrey A., et al. *Conserving the World's Biological Diversity.* Prepared and published by the International Union for Conservation of Nature and Natural Resources, World Resources Institute, Conservation International, World Wildlife Fund-US, and the World Bank. Gland, Switzerland: IUCN; Washington, D.C.: WRI, CI, WWF-US, World Bank, 1990.

Meeker, Joseph W. *The Comedy of Survival: Studies in Literary Ecology.* New York: Scribner's, 1972.

Meeks, Wayne. *The Origins of Christian Morality: The First Two Centuries.* New Haven: Yale University Press, 1993.

Mellers, Wilfrid H. *Romanticism and the Twentieth Century.* Man and His Music: The Story of Musical Experience in the West 4. New York: Schocken, 1969.

Menzies, Grant Michael. "Composer as Lord of Creation," *Sforzando* 2/11 (November 1997) 18–19.

Merchant, Carolyn. *The Death of Nature: Women, Ecology and the Scientific Revolution.* San Francisco: HarperCollins, 1980.

Metcalf, Robert. "An Abbreviated History of Insecticide Toxicology," in Jean Adams, ed., *Insect Potpourri: Adventures in Entomology.* Gainesville, Fla.: Sandhill Crane Press, 1992.

Metz, Johann Baptist. *Faith in History and Society: Toward a Practical Fundamental Theology.* New York: Seabury, 1980.

Meyrowitz, Joshua. *No Sense of Place: The Impact of Electronic Media on Social Behavior.* New York: Oxford University Press, 1985.

Michener, James. *Alaska.* New York: Random House, 1988.

Miller, Carol. *Nursing Care of Older Adults: Theory and Practice.* Philadelphia: Lippincott, 1995.

Miscall, Peter D. *Isaiah.* Sheffield: JSOT Press, 1993.

Moeller, Bill, and Jan Moeller. *Chief Joseph and the Nez Perce: A Photographic History.* Missoula, Mont.: Mountain Press, 1995.

Moltke, Konrad von. "Institutional Interactions: The Structure of Regimes for Trade and the Environment," in Oran R. Young, ed., *Global Governance: Drawing Insights from the Environmental Experience.* Cambridge, Mass.: M.I.T. Press, 1998, 247–72.

Moltmann, Jürgen. *God in Creation*. San Francisco: Harper & Row, 1985.

_____. *The Coming of God*. Minneapolis: Fortress, 1996.

Morgenthau, Hans J. *Politics among Nations*. 3d ed. New York: Knopf, 1956.

[Mother Goose]. *The Real Mother Goose*. Illustrated by Blanche Fisher Wright. Chicago: Rand McNally, 1916.

Motyer, J. Alec. *The Prophecy of Isaiah*. Downers Grove, Ill.: InterVarsity, 1993.

Muir, John. *On National Parks*. Boston: Houghton Mifflin, 1901.

Muller, Robert. "A World Core Curriculum," *Namta Journal* 18 (Summer 1993) 93–102.

Murphy, Patrick D. *Literature, Nature, and Other: Ecofeminist Critiques*. Albany: SUNY Press, 1995.

Murray, Robert. *The Cosmic Covenant: Biblical Themes of Justice, Peace, and the Integrity of Creation*. London: A Heythrop Monograph published by Sheed & Ward; Westminster, Md.: Christian Classics, 1992.

Myerson, Emile. *Identity and Reality*. Authorized translation by Kate Loewenberg. New York: Dover Publications, 1962.

Nash, James A. *Loving Nature: Ecological Integrity and Christian Responsibility*. Nashville: Abingdon, 1991.

Nash, Roderick. *The Rights of Nature*. Madison: University of Wisconsin Press, 1989.

Nasr, Seyyed Hossein. *Islamic Science: An Illustrated Study*. Several locations: World of Islam Festival Publishing Company, 1976.

"National Family Caregiver Alliance: Selected Caregiver Statistics," *Family Caregiver Alliance Newsletter* (San Francisco, 1996).

"National Survey Describes Caregivers," *Parent Care* 2/3 (1987) 1–2.

The Natural Step: From Consensus to Sustainable Development. Pamphlet published by The Natural Step, Sausalito, Calif., 1997.

Nebel, Bernard J., and Richard T. Wright. *Environmental Science*. Upper Saddle River, N.J.: Prentice Hall, 1996.

Neihardt, John G. *Black Elk Speaks*. Lincoln: University of Nebraska Press, 1961.

Nelson, Paul. *Narrative and Morality: A Theological Inquiry*. University Park, Pa.: Pennsylvania State University Press, 1987.

O'Brien, David J., and Thomas A. Shannon, eds. "Gaudium et Spes: Pastoral Constitution on the Church in the Modern World," *Catholic Social Thought: The Documentary Heritage*. Maryknoll, N.Y.: Orbis, 1992.

O'Neill, C., and E. Sorenson. "Home Care of the Elderly: A Family Perspective," *Advances in Nursing Science* 13/4 (1991) 28–37.

Onís, M. de, et al. "The Worldwide Magnitude of Protein-Energy Malnutrition: An Overview from the WHO Global Database on Child Growth," *WHO Bulletin* 71 (1993) 703–12.

Oregon Department of Environmental Quality, et al. *Lower Columbia River Bi-State Water Quality Program. Report* (June 1996).

Osland, Joyce, Bruce Drake, and Howard Feldman. "The Stewardship of Natural and Human Resources," infra, pp. 168–92.

Oswalt, John N. *The Book of Isaiah: Chapters 1–39.* NICOT. Grand Rapids: Eerdmans, 1986.

Paul VI. "Message of Paul VI for the World Day of Environment," in Vincent P. Mainelli, ed., *Official Catholic Teachings: Social Justice.* Wilmington, N.C.: Consortium Books, 1978.

Pearce, David. "Auditing the Earth: The Value of the World's Ecosystem and Natural Capital," *Environment* 40/2 (March) 1998, 23–28.

Pelikan, Jaroslav, ed. *The World Treasury of Modern Religious Thought.* Boston: Little, Brown, 1990.

Perdue, Leo G. *Wisdom & Creation: The Theology of Wisdom Literature.* Nashville: Abingdon, 1994.

Peterson, M. J. "International Organizations and the Implementation of Environmental Regimes," in Oran R. Young, ed., *Global Governance,* 115–51.

Petzinger, Thomas. "The Front Lines: Business Achieves Greatest Efficiencies When at Its Greenest," *Wall Street Journal* (July 11, 1997) B1.

Pfeffer, Jeffrey. "Producing Sustainable Competitive Advantage Through the Effective Management of People," *Academy of Management Executive* 9/1 (February 1995) 55–72.

Piaget, Jean. *The Theory of Stages in Cognitive Development.* New York: McGraw-Hill, 1969.

Piburn, Michael D. *The Environment: A Human Crisis.* Rochelle Park, N.J.: Hayden Book Company, 1974.

Pomerleau, Claude. "Toward an Understanding of International Geopolitics and the Environment," infra, pp. 126–43.

Popiden, John. "The Problem of Technology and Morality." Unpublished paper. Loyola Marymount University.

Porteous, J. Douglas. *Landscapes of the Mind: Worlds of Sense and Metaphor.* Toronto: University of Toronto Press, 1990.

Porter, Gareth, and Janet Welsh Brown. *Global Environmental Politics.* 2d ed. Boulder, Colo.: Westview, 1996.

Porter, Michael, and Claas van der Linde. "Green and Competitive," *Harvard Business Review* 73 (September 1995) 120–33.

President's Council on Sustainable Development. *Sustainable America: A New Consensus*. Washington, D.C.: U.S. Government Printing Office, 1996.

Pruslin, Stephen. Liner notes for Peter Maxwell Davies, *Trumpet Concerto and Symphony No. 4*. Sir Peter Maxwell Davies conducting the Scottish National Orchestra and Scottish Chamber Orchestra. Collins Classics CD 11812, 1991.

_____. Liner notes for Peter Maxwell Davies, *Symphony No. 5, Chat Moss, Cross Lane Fair, and Five Klee Pictures*. Sir Peter Maxwell Davies conducting the Philharmonia Orchestra and BBC Philharmonic. Collins Classics CD 14602, 1995.

Pyle, Robert Michael. *Wintergreen: Listening to the Land's Heart*. Boston: Houghton Mifflin, 1996.

Qadir, Chaudhry Abdul. *Philosophy and Science in the Islamic World*. London and New York: Croom Helm, 1988.

Quinn, James Brian. *Intelligent Enterprise: A Knowledge and Service Based Paradigm for Industry*. New York: Free Press, 1992.

Rasmussen, Larry L. *Earth Community, Earth Ethics*. Maryknoll, N.Y.: Orbis, 1996.

Reed, David. "The Environmental Legacy of Bretton Woods: The World Bank," in Oran R. Young, ed., *Global Governance*, 227–45.

Rees, William R. Unbroadcast Portion of an Interview for the Canadian Broadcasting Corporation Radio Series "It's a Matter of Survival." Quoted by Anita Gordon and David Suzuki, *It's a Matter of Survival*. Cambridge, Mass.: Harvard University Press, 1990.

_____, and Mathis Wackernagel. "Ecological Footprints and Appropriate Carrying Capacity: Measuring the Natural Capital Requirements of the Human Economy," in AnnMari Jansson, et al., eds., *Investing in Natural Capital: The Ecological Economics Approach to Sustainability* (Washington, D.C.: Island Press, 1994) 362–90.

Reimer, Bennett. *A Philosophy of Music Education*. Englewood Cliffs, N.J.: Prentice Hall, 1989.

Rescher, Nicholas. *Studies in Arabic Philosophy*. Pittsburgh: University of Pittsburgh Press, 1967.

Richards, Beverly. "Gerontological Family Nursing," in Shirley M. H. Hanson and Sheryl T. Boyd, eds., *Family Health Care Nursing: Theory, Practice, and Research*. Philadelphia: F. A. Davis, 1996, 329–50.

Ricklefs, Robert E. *The Economy of Nature: A Textbook in Basic Ecology.* 3d ed. New York: W. H. Freeman, 1997.

Roberts, C. S., and S. L. Feetham. "Assessing Famly Functioning Across Three Areas of Relationships," *Nursing Research* 21 (1982) 231–35.

Rockefeller, Steven C., and John C. Elder, eds., *Spirit and Nature: Why the Environment Is a Religious Issue.* Boston: Beacon, 1992.

Rogers, Pattiann. *Firekeeper: New and Selected Poems.* Minneapolis: Milkweed Editions, 1994.

_____. "Surprised by the Sacred," *U.S. Catholic* 63/3 (March 1998) 25–27.

Rorty, Richard. *Philosophy and the Mirror of Nature.* Princeton: Princeton University Press, 1979.

Rosen, Robert H., and Lisa Berger. *The Healthy Company: Eight Strategies to Develop People, Productivity, and Profits.* Los Angeles: Jeremy Tarcher, 1991.

Rouner, Leroy S., ed. *The Longing for Home.* Notre Dame, Ind.: University of Notre Dame Press, 1996.

Rousseau, Denise M. *Psychological Contracts in Organizations: Understanding Written and Unwritten Agreements.* Thousand Oaks, Calif.: SAGE, 1995.

Rueckert, William. "Literature and Ecology: An Experiment in Ecocriticism," in Glotfelty and Fromm, eds., *The Ecocriticism Reader: Landmarks in Literary Ecology.* Athens, Ga.: University of Georgia Press, 1996, 105–23.

Russett, Bruce, and Harvey Starr. *World Politics. The Menu for Choice.* 4th ed. New York: W. H. Freeman, 1992.

Sandell, Steven H., and Howard M. Iams. "Caregiving and Future Social Security Benefits: A Reply to O'Grady-LeShane and Kingson," *Gerontologist* 36/6 (1996) 814.

Santmire, H. Paul. *The Travail of Nature.* Minneapolis: Fortress, 1985.

Sardar, Ziauddin. *Explorations in Islamic Science.* London and New York: Mansell, 1989.

Schama, Simon. *Landscape and Memory.* New York: Vintage, 1996.

Schlesinger, Jacob, and Bernard Wysocki. "Score Card: UPS Pact Fails to Shift Balance of Power Back Toward US Workers," *Wall Street Journal* (August 20, 1997) A1.

Schmall, Vicki L. *What Do You Know About Aging? Facts and Fallacies.* Pacific Northwest Extension Publication PNW 453. Corvallis, Ore.: Oregon State University Extension Service, 1993.

Schmid, H. H. "Creation, Righteousness, and Salvation," in Bernhard W. Anderson, ed., *Creation in the Old Testament,* 102–17.

"Science: The Islamic Legacy," *Aramco World Magazine*, 1986.

Seitz, Christopher R. *Isaiah 1–39*. Interpretation. Louisville: John Knox, 1993.

Seuss, Dr. [Theodore Seuss Geisel]. *The Lorax*. New York: Random House, 1971.

Shallenbarger, Sue. "More Executives Cite Need for Family Time as Reason for Quitting," *Wall Street Journal* (March 11, 1998) B1.

Sibelius, Jean. *Tapiola, Symphonic Poem for Orchestra, Op. 112*. Wiesbaden: Breitkopf and Härtel, 1985.

Silko, Leslie Marmon. "Landscape, History, and the Pueblo Imagination," in Karen Knowles, ed., *Celebrating the Land: Women's Nature Writings, 1850–1991*, 107–17.

Silverstein, Shel. *The Giving Tree*. New York: Harper & Row, 1964.

Simkins, Ronald A. *Creator & Creation: Nature in the Worldview of Ancient Israel*. Peabody, Mass.: Hendrickson, 1994.

Simon, Julian L. "More People, Greater Wealth, More Resources, Healthier Environment," a version from *Economic Affairs* (April 1994), reprinted in Theodore D. Goldfarb, ed., *Taking Sides. Clashing Views on Controversial Environmental Issues*. 7th ed. Guilford, Conn.: Dushkin/McGraw Hill, 1997, 187–96.

Slovic, Scott. *Seeking Awareness in American Nature Writing: Henry Thoreau, Annie Dillard, Edward Abbey, Wendell Berry, Barry Lopez*. Salt Lake City: University of Utah Press, 1992.

Smith, Huston. *The World's Religions*. San Francisco: HarperCollins, 1991.

Snyder, Gary. *The Practice of the Wild*. San Francisco: North Point Press, 1990.

Sobosan, Jeffrey G. *Bless the Beasts: A Spirituality of Animal Care*. New York: Crossroad, 1991.

Srikantia, Param, and Diana Bilimoria. "Isomorphism in Organization and Management Theory: The Case of Research on Sustainability," *Organization & Environment* 10/4 (December 1997) 384–406.

Standing, E. Mortimer. *Maria Montessori: Her Life and Work*. New York: New American Library, 1962.

Starik, Mark. "When Business Goes for the Green," *GW Magazine* 3/4 (Summer 1993) 11–16.

Stegner, Wallace. *Where the Bluebird Sings to the Lemonade Springs: Living and Writing in the West*. New York: Penguin, 1993.

Stone, R., and P. Kemper. "Spouses and Children of Disabled Elders: How Large a Constituency for Long-term Reform?" *Milbank Quarterly* 67/3–4 (1990) 485–506.

Stone, R., et al. "Caregivers of the Frail Elderly: A National Profile," *Gerontologist* 27 (1987) 616–26.

Sweeney, Marvin A. *Isaiah 1–39*. FOTL XVI. Grand Rapids: Eerdmans, 1996.

Thomas, Lewis. "Are We Fit to Fit In?" *Sierra* 67/2 (March/April 1982) 49–52.

Toolan, David S. "Praying in a Post-Einsteinian Universe," *Cross Currents* 46/4 (Winter 1996/1997) 437–70.

Tout, Ken. *Ageing in Developing Countries*. New York: Oxford University Press for HelpAge International, 1989.

Trible, Phyllis. *God and the Rhetoric of Sexuality*. Philadelphia: Fortress, 1978.

Trimble, Stephen. *Words from the Land: Encounters with Natural History Writing*. Salt Lake City: Peregrine Smith, 1989.

Trimble, Stephen, and Terry Tempest Williams, comps. *Testimony: Writers of the West Speak on Behalf of Utah Wilderness*. Minneapolis: Milkweed Editions, 1996.

Truscott, Harold. "Gustav Mahler (1860–1911)," in Robert Simpson, ed., *The Symphony 2: Elgar to the Present Day*. Baltimore: Penguin, 1967.

Turner, Frederick W. *Spirit of Place: The Making of an American Literary Landscape*. San Francisco: Sierra Club, 1989.

United Nations Department of International Economic and Social Affairs (UNDIESA). *Overview of Recent Research Findings on Population Aging and the Family*. United Nations International Conference on Aging Populations in the Context of the Family. Kitakyusha, N.Y.: United Nations (IESA/P/AC.33/6), October 1990.

_____. "Economic and Social Implications of Population Aging" (ST/ESA/SER.R.85), New York, 1988.

United Nations Food and Agriculture Organization. *World Food Summit Report*. Rome, 1996.

_____. *Sixth World Food Survey*. Rome, 1996.

United Nations World Commission on Environment and Development. *Our Common Future*. Oxford and New York: Oxford University Press, 1987.

U.S. Bureau of the Census. *Current Population Reports*, Series 20, No. 218. Washington, D.C.: U.S. Government Printing Office, 1990.

U.S. Bureau of the Census. *Growth of America's Oldest Old Population.* Profiles of America's Elderly 2. Bethesda, Md.: U.S. Department of Health and Human Services, National Institutes of Health, National Institute on Aging, 1992.

U.S. Bureau of Labor Statistics. "National Employment, Hours, and Earnings." Reference: cesinfo@bls.gov (June 5, 1998).

U.S. Catholic Bishops Conference. "Renewing the Earth." *Origins* 21/27 (December 12, 1991) 425–32.

Vaughan-Cole, Beth, et al., eds. *Family Nursing Practice.* Philadelphia: Saunders, 1998.

Vaught-Alexander, Karen. "Stories from the Heart," infra, pp. 1–20.

Velasquez, Manuel. *Business Ethics.* 2d ed. Englewood Cliffs, N.J.: Prentice Hall, 1988.

Waage, Fredrick O. *Teaching Environmental Literature: Materials, Methods, Resources.* New York: Modern Language Association, 1985.

Wallerstein, Immanuel, ed. *World Inequality: Origins and Perspectives on the World System.* Montreal: Black Rose, 1975.

Watts, James D. W. *Isaiah 1–33.* WBC 24. Waco: Word, 1985.

_____. *Isaiah 34–66.* WBC 25. Waco: Word, 1987.

Weil, Simone. *The Need for Roots. Prelude to a Declaration of Duties Toward Mankind.* Translated by Arthur Wills, with a preface by T. S. Eliot. Boston: Beacon, 1952.

Westermann, Claus. *Isaiah 40–66.* Translated by D.M.G. Stalker. OTL. Philadelphia: Westminster, 1969.

White, Lynn, Jr. "The Historical Roots of Our Ecologic Crisis," in Ian G. Barbour, ed., *Western Man and Environmental Ethics.* Reading, Mass.: Addison-Wesley, 1973, 18–30.

Whitney, Eleanor, and May Hamilton. *Understanding Nutrition.* St. Paul: West, 1977.

Williams, Oliver, and John Houck. *Full Value: Cases in Christian Business Ethics.* San Francisco: Harper & Row, 1978.

Williams, Terry Tempest. *Refuge: An Unnatural History of Family and Place.* New York: Vintage, 1992.

Wills, Garry. *Lincoln at Gettysburg: The Words That Remade America.* New York: Simon & Schuster, 1992.

Wilson, Edward O. *The Diversity of Life.* Cambridge, Mass.: Harvard University Press, 1992.

_____., and William H. Bossert. *A Primer of Population Biology*. Sunderland, Mass.: Sinauer and Associates, Inc., 1977.

Wirth, Louis. "Human Ecology," in G. A. Theodorson, ed., *Studies in Human Ecology*. New York: Harper & Row, 1961, 71–76.

Wirthlin Worldwide Report Online. "Environmentalism: No Letting Up." McLean, Va.: Wirthlin Worldwide (August 1997).

Worster, Donald. *The Wealth of Nature: Environmental History and the Ecological Imagination*. New York: Oxford University Press, 1993.

Wright, S. D., and D. A. Herrin. "Family Ecology: An Approach to the Interdisciplinary Complexity of the Study of Family Phenomena," *Family Science Review* 1 (1988) 253–82.

Yoder, John Howard. *The Priestly Kingdom*. Notre Dame, Ind.: University of Notre Dame Press, 1984.

Young, Oran R. *Global Governance*. Cambridge, Mass.: The MIT Press, 1997.

Zimmerli, Walther. *Ezekiel 1*. Translated by Ronald E. Clements. Hermeneia. Philadelphia: Fortress, 1979.

_____. *Ezekiel 2*. Translated by James D. Martin. Hermeneia. Philadelphia: Fortress, 1983.

Zimmerman, Shirley. *Family Policies and Family Well Being: The Role of Political Culture*. London: SAGE, 1992.

Zorpette, Glenn. "Hanford's Nuclear Wasteland," *Scientific American* (May 1996) 88–97.